Campaigns and Elections
American Style

TRANSFORMING AMERICAN POLITICS

Lawrence C. Dodd, Series Editor

Dramatic changes in political institutions and behavior over the past three decades have underscored the dynamic nature of American politics, confronting political scientists with a new and pressing intellectual agenda. The pioneering work of early postwar scholars, while laying a firm empirical foundation for contemporary scholarship, failed to consider how American politics might change or recognize the forces that would make fundamental change inevitable. In reassessing the static interpretations fostered by these classic studies, political scientists are now examining the underlying dynamics that generate transformational change.

Transforming American Politics is a series that brings together texts addressing four closely related aspects of change. A first concern is documenting and explaining recent changes in American politics—in institutions, processes, behavior, and policymaking. A second is reinterpreting classic studies and theories to provide a more accurate perspective on postwar politics. The series looks at historical change to identify recurring patterns of political transformation within and across the distinctive eras of American politics. Last and perhaps most important, the series presents new theories and interpretations that explain the dynamic processes at work and thus clarify the direction of contemporary politics. All of the books focus on the central theme of transformation—transformation in both the conduct of American politics and in the way we study and understand its many aspects.

BOOKS IN THIS SERIES

Campaigns and Elections American Style

FOURTH EDITION

Edited by James A. Thurber
and Candice J. Nelson
American University

WESTVIEW
PRESS

A MEMBER OF THE PERSEUS BOOKS GROUP

Westview Press was founded in 1975 in Boulder, Colorado, by notable publisher and intellectual Fred Praeger. Westview Press continues to publish scholarly titles and high-quality undergraduate- and graduate-level textbooks in core social science disciplines. With books developed, written, and edited with the needs of serious nonfiction readers, professors, and students in mind, Westview Press honors its long history of publishing books that matter.

Every effort has been made to secure required permissions for all text, images, maps, and other art reprinted in this volume.

Westview Press books are available at special discounts for bulk purchases in the United States by corporations, institutions, and other organizations. For more information, please contact the Special Markets Department at the Perseus Books Group, 2300 Chestnut Street, Suite 200, Philadelphia, PA 19103, or call (800) 810-4145, ext. 5000, or e-mail special.markets @perseusbooks.com.

Library of Congress Cataloging-in-Publication Data
  Campaigns and elections American style / edited by James A. Thurber and Candice J. Nelson, American University.—Fourth edition.
    pages cm
  Includes bibliographical references and index.
ISBN 978-0-8133-4835-3 (paperback)—ISBN 978-0-8133-4836-0 (e-book) 1. Political campaigns—United States. 2. Campaign management—United States. I. Thurber, James A., 1943–
  JK2281.C353 2013
  324.70973—dc23
                                                    2013005321

10 9 8 7 6 5 4 3 2 1

Contents

Acknowledgments

The rich lessons and knowledge from American University's Campaign Management Institute (CMI) was the genesis of the first edition of this book. CMI was started in 1983 by campaign professionals and academics to bring together academic and practical knowledge of campaigning. It is offered twice a year at the Center for Congressional and Presidential Studies (www.american .edu/spa/ccps) at American University. It is an intense two-week hands-on learning experience focused on actual election campaigns. Students receive professional guidance and evaluation from academics and campaign professionals, including pollsters, media specialists, campaign strategists, and managers.

We thank the thousands of students who have attended CMI and the many dozens of campaign professionals who have lectured at CMI for their insights and inspiration to write this book. We appreciate those CMI speakers for sharing their invaluable practical knowledge and the strategy and tactics of winning campaigns in America. They have also been wonderful mentors to our students and our alumni who are working in the campaign management field. We also thank the many readers of previous editions for their comments and suggestions that have helped us improve this edition. Thanks to our colleagues at the Center for Congressional and Presidential Studies, Aaron Ray, Lindsey Mears, and Rebecca Prosky, who provided invaluable research assistance at various stages of the project. We have special thanks for the support of the Center and this project by the School of Public Affairs at American University.

We thank our friends at Perseus Books and Westview Press. Ada Fung, Stephen Pinto, Anthony Wahl, Cathleen Tetro, Annie Lenth, Kelsey Mitchell, and Beth Cavaliere deserve special appreciation for their encouragement and help in producing this edition.

Clearly this is a collective effort. We thank all the contributors for their chapters. We take full responsibility for any omissions or errors of fact and interpretation.

—James A. Thurber
—Candice J. Nelson

1

Understanding the Dynamics and the Transformation of American Government

JAMES A. THURBER

This book, a study of campaign management and elections, marries academic wisdom and the practical knowledge of professional political consultants, although the two worlds rarely overlap. Academics use explicit hypotheses and scientific methods for making systematic observations about campaigns and elections, whereas professionals draw generalizations based on direct experience. Campaign consultants "test hypotheses" by winning and losing elections. Both use theoretical perspectives about campaigns and voters, although one is academic and one practical. The common dimension to both worlds is the major changes that have occurred in the way campaigns are waged and elections won or lost in the past twenty years, as especially shown in the 2012 election campaign of President Barack Obama and his opponent, former governor Mitt Romney. This book analyzes the impact of the changes in the 2012 presidential election cycle from a variety of perspectives. The authors show the evolution and innovation in campaign strategy, the use of survey research, the changes in fundraising strategies, the role of communications and media, the use of digital and social media, the advancements in microtargeting and fieldwork, as well as the stability and changes in election law and turnout in 2012.

Academics use large data sets and systematically test hypotheses to make careful statements about voters and elections. They attempt to explain individual and collective political behavior and try to answer questions about who votes and why. When political scientists write about campaigns and how candidates get elected, their approach is based on scholarly analysis rather than experience (Polsby et al. 2012; Kenski et al. 2010; Nelson 2011; Dulio and Nelson 2005; Thurber and Nelson 2000; Thurber 1998). Other political scientists forecast election outcomes, not by the strategies and tactics of the candidates, but by using basic variables in their models that are known before the election and cannot easily be changed in a campaign, such as measures of the state of the economy or the popularity of the incumbent president or party (*PS* Symposium 2012). Because the state of the economy and the popularity of the president were very poor in this election, many predicted a Romney victory, but strategies, tactics, messages, and innovations in the Obama and Romney campaigns made a difference in the outcome of the election. In short, campaigns matter—a basic conclusion of this book.

Campaign professionals focus on who votes and why, but to develop a winning strategy to attract voters to their candidate, knowing full well that factors such as the state of the economy and the popularity of the candidates make a difference, they try to change voter perceptions in order to win over those barriers, as shown in 2012. When campaign consultants write about campaigns, it is to explain why their candidates have won and to give general advice in how-to-win "manuals," or to offer anecdotal "insider" accounts of campaigns (Jamieson 2009; Napolitan 1972; Shea 1996). They are hired activists who develop strategies and tactics to influence voters and election results (Dulio and Nelson 2005; Thurber 2001; Thurber and Nelson 2000). They focus solely on how to win. While political scientists try to understand voters, candidates, elections, and the consequences of electoral battles for purposes of governing and developing public policy, campaign professionals use the vast knowledge gained from their previous campaigns. They know what works through their experience of winning or losing elections and are seasoned by their involvement with campaigning (Thurber and Nelson 2000). The strategies and tactics of campaigns are constantly evolving through innovating and testing what works and what does not work in each election cycle. Campaign consultants learn from each other and bring change to each election cycle. In this book we describe and analyze those changes, looking at the 2012 election from a variety of perspectives from both political scientists and campaign professionals.

Campaign consultants often assert that the academic literature on campaigns and elections is either obvious or wrong (Thurber and Nelson 2000), while also admitting that they lack time to read the latest political science research findings. Academics often argue that campaign professionals promote the latest folk wisdom about campaign tactics and do not know what works and what does not until it is too late. The winners possess the "truth," creating new "geniuses" of campaign management each election cycle, and the wisdom gained by the losers is often even more important. All successful consultants try to learn from their mistakes and from the mistakes of others. Winning consultants pick up more clients and business, while the losers often leave the campaign business and move into issue campaigns and advocacy or public relations.

Academics study campaigns and elections but rarely talk with campaign professionals about what they believe regarding their electoral track record. Academics often may not be aware of the latest developments in campaign strategies, tactics, and tools until an election is over (recent exceptions to this are the studies of Dulio and Nelson 2005; Nelson, Dulio, and Medvic 2002; Johnson 2007; Thurber 2001; Thurber and Nelson 2000). Political scientists study campaign professionals but rarely enter the world of political campaigning. When they do, they bring important contributions to the literature (Johnson 2007).

Mutual distrust often characterizes relations between campaign professionals and academics. Many professionals feel that academic research is not applicable to the real world of election campaigns. On the other hand, academics consider professionals' practical how-to knowledge unscientific and their general narratives of campaigns simply descriptive histories. They are critical of claims not based on the systematic collection of data and the testing of hypotheses that are part of a broader theory of campaigns and elections. And when commentary from political pundits, journalists, and retired political leaders is added to the mix, it becomes difficult to distinguish reality from myth, marketing, and self-centered political spin.

When the worlds of academics and professionals do converge, however, insights result, as shown in this book. Whether explaining or managing campaigns, whether treating campaign management as a science or an art, academics, professionals, and pundits all agree that American election campaigns have been especially transformed in the last twenty years. Every campaign cycle reveals new strategies and tactics, as shown so clearly in the 2012 election.

In these pages, campaign professionals and political scientists confront each other's perspectives. They examine changes in the organization and operation of campaigns and the impact of campaign strategies and tactics at the local, state, and national levels that have had a significant impact on American elections in the last three decades. Political consultants are using recent technological advances in microtargeting, the social media, and the Internet to make campaigns operate smarter and faster and often more cheaply.

Chapters by campaign professionals and political scientists cover the major elements of campaign advancements and provide different perspectives on the same campaign topic. Our contributors do not always agree. Dialogue between campaign consultants and political scientists offers a new, more complete view of election campaigns that is essential to an understanding of twenty-first-century American campaigns and elections.

Election Campaigns Are Wars: The Battle of 2012

The 2012 campaign was a war between the Democrats and the Republicans. It was a battle for the hearts and minds—and the votes—of the American people. The word "campaign" comes from military usage: a connected series of military operations forming a distinct phase of a war or a connected series of operations designed to bring about a particular result. An election is like a war, complete with "war rooms" and campaign managers. Candidates and campaign organizations are fighting to capture government control and to advance their policies. Campaigns are battles to define public problems and develop policy solutions and, of course, to persuade voters to support those ideas.

For candidates and professionals, campaigns are zero-sum games, or even minus-sum games: there are always winners and losers, and more campaigners are disappointed by the election outcome than pleased by it. For academics, on the other hand, campaigns are objects of analysis; they do not represent a personal gamble, a deeply felt ambition, or a commitment to the objective of winning. Campaigns are not political causes but rather a focus of intellectual interest. Academics are interested in why people vote (e.g., explanations of turnout); professionals are interested in how to get them to vote for a particular candidate (e.g., field and microtargeting tactics). Academics study who contributes money to campaigns and why; professionals persuade people to give funds to their candidates. Both need to know the legal framework of campaign finance law. This book joins these two worlds and shows how both the academic and campaign professional perspectives are needed in order to understand election campaigns.

Those who manage election campaigns, be they presidential, congressional, or down-ballot races (local and state candidates), evaluate the existing political environment, develop strategies and plans within that political environment, pursue a strategic theme and message for a candidate, establish an organization, solicit and use campaign money, buy advertising and attempt to use free (news) media, schedule candidates, organize and use a field organization, use opposition research, and conduct survey research and focus group analysis, among a variety of other activities. In the last three decades the basic elements of campaigning have changed dramatically due to the power of the media (especially television and social media), technological advancements, and the professionalization of campaigns. What has not changed is that successful campaigns need to develop an explicit strategy, theme, and message, linked to appropriate tactics.

Campaign Strategy and Message, Funding, and Organization

Campaigns do not happen in a vacuum and they are not predetermined by economic and political circumstances. Prevailing economic and political conditions influence a campaign, and candidates and campaigns in turn can have an impact on those conditions, as was the case with the 2012 election of President Barack Obama.

There are three fundamental elements of campaigning: strategy and message, organization, and funding. On the strength of these three elements, Barack Obama ran a second nearly perfect campaign in 2012. His strategy and message were focused. This contrasted with Mitt Romney's lack of discipline and wavering message during the primaries and the general election, which depicted him as uncaring about the middle class in America. President Obama's campaign cultivated a positive image of a president caring about the middle class and the unemployed, and it projected an unfavorable perception of Governor Romney as uncaring and out of touch with the American people.

Some analysts suggested that the widespread disapproval of President Obama during his first term predetermined a loss for him in the 2012 election (*PS Symposium 2012*). But these analysts and Romney's campaign consultants underestimated the effects of a candidate's campaign strategy, tactics, and message on the outcome. A winning campaign pays close attention to campaign fundamentals (Dulio and Nelson 2005; Thurber and Nelson 2000; Medvic 2001, 2006). The most important elements of a campaign are strategy, theme, and message. Raising money, setting the candidate's schedule, doing opposition research, linking resources to campaign tactics, preparing for debates, advertising on television and radio, and mobilizing supporters to vote all follow from the campaign's strategy, theme, and message. In a well-run campaign, the message is expressed in communications with voters: television and radio ads, social media, and the direct mail campaign.

Campaign Strategy and Message

Obama's strategy encompassed a commitment to the fundamentals of campaigning (Thurber and Nelson 2000)—a clear strategy, theme, and message linked to appropriate tactics. Obama's campaign rarely wavered from its central theme and message. When the Obama campaign faced challenges, such as his poor first debate performance, he returned to the central theme and message of the campaign.

Running a campaign involves a variety of functions, such as scheduling and advance work, press arrangements, issue research and debate preparation, speech writing, polling and focus group analysis, voter targeting and mobilization, print and electronic media advertising and placement, campaign budgeting, legal analysis, and party and interest group action. These demands require a highly disciplined campaign organization (Thurber and Nelson 2004). A campaign manager must know how many votes are needed to win and where these votes will come from. This is not as simple as it may sound. Many pundits thought Obama would not win in 2012 because of the poor economy, but the Obama campaign's early focus on building a national campaign finance operation with "ground" and "air" operations in the battleground states paid off. By methodically focusing on the battleground states through advertising, social media, microtargeting, get-out-the-vote mobilization, campaign visits, and other tactics, the Obama campaign was able to overtake the early advantage that Mitt Romney had because of the economy and the low rating of the president.

Obama also ran a nearly perfect campaign in terms of message discipline and quick response to criticism or attack. The campaign never let a news cycle go by without responding, often within hours or even minutes. The campaign strategy and message were driven by defining Romney as insensitive to the middle class and out of touch with the needs of the American people. David Axelrod, Obama's chief strategist, and David Plouffe, the campaign manager, had an obsessive focus on the message of contrasting the president to a negative image of Romney. Romney was not able to finesse the perpetual problem of Republican presidential politics: needing one message to win over a party's ardent supporters in the primaries and another when trying to capture women, moderates, independents, Hispanics, and the few up-for-grab voters who helped decide the 2012 general election.

The Strategic Raising and Use of Campaign Funds

How a campaign spends money is just as important as how much money is raised. Much has been written about the fundraising prowess of the Obama campaign in 2008 and 2012. In many ways, Obama has changed the way that money is raised in presidential elections. Any serious campaign for federal office requires a sophisticated online fundraising component. Obama and Romney both raised a record of over a billion dollars (which includes money raised during both the primary and general election).

Campaign Organization

President Obama's organization dominated the media "air war" early, with overwhelming investment in the 2012 battleground states through television, cable, radio, direct mail, social media, and even advertising in video games. He also dominated in the "ground war," including the organization of field staff and offices. Obama had more staff and offices in more states than Romney in 2012, repeating what he did in 2008 against McCain.

Obama's staff (paid and volunteer) advantage allowed him to get his message out to more people and to organize more supporters than the Romney campaign did. Campaign staff members worked in local offices that served as gathering places for local volunteers and supporters. Some campaign offices operated phone banks, some served as the gathering point for volunteer door-to-door canvasses, and many served as storefronts where locals could get campaign literature, buttons, and stickers. The campaign's field staff (which typically makes up the bulk of a campaign's in-state operation) identified and contacted potential voters, persuaded them to become supporters, and then got them to vote, especially in the target states.

The Obama campaign organization at the national level was made up of experienced, disciplined people who had gone through the 2008 campaign battle. The discipline of their internal organization and message was directly linked to the candidate and a group of well-tested professionals. This was often not the case for Romney.

The Obama campaign's online organizing tools that had been honed in 2008 were improved, tested, and changed in 2012. The campaign advanced the use of technology and used new social media forums to communicate the message and to recruit volunteers. Obama's website served as a recruiting tool for volunteers and donors, and the campaign was constantly reaching out to supporters through its e-mail list, social networking sites such as Facebook and Twitter, and other innovative methods of reaching volunteers and voters. These techniques helped turn out volunteers and also crowds at his rallies. Campaign staff and volunteers positioned themselves at these events to get names of supporters and to recruit them to volunteer.

The Obama campaign outperformed the Romney campaign in voter contact. Studies of voter contact efforts indicate that mobilization works.

Randomized field experiments have shown that door-to-door canvassing increases the likelihood that individuals will turn out to vote by 8 to 10 percent (Gerber and Green 2000). Professional phone banks have been shown to be less effective than canvassing, but personal phone contacts among peers can be as effective as canvassing. The technical skill and efficiency of the Obama campaign allowed it to expand on traditional voter contact techniques.

Measuring the Organizers' Performance: Voter Turnout Numbers

Successful campaigns must concentrate their resources on identifying potential voters and ensuring that their supporters in the electorate show up at the polls. Campaigns refer to these efforts as the field campaign, the "ground war," or Get Out the Vote (GOTV). Obama's 2012 organization put paid field staff and extensive volunteer networks in every battleground state early (in fall 2011), which helped him turn out voters in November 2012. The extended battle for the Republican nomination did not give Romney the opportunity to organize in traditional battleground states, as had been the case for the Democrats and Obama in 2008. Romney's long Republican primary battle allowed Obama to quietly organize the "ground war" in more battleground states than the Romney campaign.

Campaigns are dynamic and combative, as seen in the 2012 election. They do not happen in a vacuum, and they are not predetermined by economic or political circumstances. Successful campaigns develop a clear message that focuses on groups of voters that will help the candidate win—party loyalists (the base) and swing voters (often moderate and ideologically in the middle). Candidate Obama understood this. He had the organization, strategy, and money to run a robust ground campaign. Although the political environment and economic conditions had seemed to benefit the Romney campaign in the late spring of 2012, with the president's popularity falling and a continued poor economy, Obama overcame these difficulties with his unwavering message discipline and his outstanding organization, using technological advancements to target and mobilize voters on the ground and to inspire voters and volunteers through the televised and new media air war.

The 2012 campaign cycle shows clearly that candidates and their campaign managers must evaluate environmental conditions (such as the economy) early and develop campaign strategies and plans that take advantage of them, but must revise their plans when events (like a poor debate performance) call for it. Some think that a campaign plan must be adhered to with almost military discipline and precision. Campaign strategy charts a path to winning the election, but it recognizes that campaigns are dynamic and must be flexible enough to react to events and opponents. Campaigns are frequently underfunded, disorganized, and understaffed, and their personnel often lack enough information to make rational decisions. In order to start with a strategy and plan, it is essential to develop a campaign theme and message, making the best use of campaign resources, reducing liabilities, and establishing a set of objectives whose achievement will maximize the probability of winning an election or attaining a plurality—50 percent plus one of the total votes cast. The campaign plan to achieve this is a program of specific activities designed to accomplish the objectives and eventually to win the election within a given political and economic environment. Campaign strategies and plans must take into account a vast number of factors, such as the candidate, the constituency, the level of office being sought, the nature of the electoral system, the party organization (or lack of it), the economic situation, the financial and political resources available, and the nature of the voters.

Until the mid-1960s, campaign strategy and tactics were solely the realm of political parties. Today they are the domain of professionals: campaign managers, media consultants, campaign finance specialists, pollsters, field (GOTV) specialists, television producers, schedulers, and many others (Dulio and Nelson 2005; Dulio 2004; Johnson 2007; Thurber 2001; Thurber and Nelson 2000; Sabato 1981). In the past three decades campaigns have evolved into complex organizations featuring distinct divisions of labor and elaborate teams of (usually) outside professionals who coordinate with party organizations (Thurber, Magleby, and Patterson 2002). However, recent studies that examine the impact of political party organizing and funding on campaigning suggest that local parties may be playing important roles in campaigns (Thurber, Prevost, and Bohne 2008).

An Overview of This Book

The authors in this book analyze the 2012 presidential election and discuss the major elements of successful campaigns. All campaigns analyze the political environment, choose tactics or tools to implement the campaign strategy, and establish the campaign budget (the allocation of money, time, and personnel to each element of the campaign plan). Campaign tactics are the specific activities designed to achieve the strategic objective: victory in the election. Campaign tactics, managing the message to target groups of voters, are at the operational level of the campaign.

Campaign Strategy and Financing

The critical elements of campaign strategy and planning have evolved with each election cycle, amid dramatically changing methods and tactics for achieving strategic goals, as shown in the 2012 presidential campaign. David Winston, a Republican Party campaign professional with more than thirty years of experience in the field, describes how to develop a successful campaign plan in Chapter 2, "Creating a Winning Campaign Strategy." In it he argues that a campaign without a plan is a journey without a map. Campaign strategy is about achieving a desired outcome using a structured approach based on understanding existing and potential environmental elements as well as your opponent's potential strategies.

Strategy requires good instincts, an understanding of politics, historical context, and careful quantifiable and qualitative research. A campaign must be organized into a plan (often written) to present a message to voters about a candidate, but that plan is always subject to change and debate, a dynamic and endless series of dialogues within the campaign to sharpen the focus of the message. It is the compass that points toward victory. According to Winston, good campaign strategies should include five key steps: define a desired outcome; develop situational awareness; identify your opponent's potential strategies; define a winning coalition; and create a strategic communication plan. Campaign strategy answers the questions of who will vote for the candidate and why. The principles of sound campaign strategy are the same whether the candidate is running for a seat on a school board or for the presidency of the United States. Without a strategy, a campaign becomes a series of unplanned reactions to unanticipated events.

Winston also elucidates four major dimensions of campaign strategy: (1) dividing the electorate into three groups in any given contest (supporters, opponents, and the vast majority of voters who are generally uninterested in the candidate and the campaign); (2) using political research to identify the voters who fall into each of the three groups; (3) selecting a large enough subset of undecided voters to target to effect the outcome of the election; and (4) allocating resources to targeted voters or identifying how to win the necessary numbers of voters by directing campaign resources (money, time, effort, message) to those key voters. Resource allocation is defined by campaign strategy.

Public opinion polling is central to shaping campaigns. Polling directs the development and refinement of strategy, message, and tactics in campaigns. Polls are the best tool available at this time for shaping the strategy and content of a campaign, as described by pollster Glen Bolger in Chapter 3, "The

Use of Survey Research in Campaigns." Bolger describes how surveys are used in election campaigns. He offers a concise history of polling in campaigns, and he explains why polling is done, the methodology of polling, and how to understand polls. He argues that survey research (public opinion polling) is most important to a campaign as a planning tool. Campaigns use polling to make a whole host of decisions throughout the race, such as targeting voters, modifying the message, and reallocating resources of time and money. Polling helps a campaign team put together a road map to win. Polling helps provide message discipline and voter targeting. Campaigns use polls in a variety of ways: to measure the mood of the electorate, to confirm issues and measure intensity, to measure name identification and images, to test potential theses and messages, to determine the impact and intensity of vulnerabilities, to chart movement during the race overall and among subgroups, to determine the impact of a major hit on either (or both) candidates, and to establish credibility. Bolger concludes that polling is the central tool that drives political strategy and focuses the campaign message.

"Money is the mother's milk of politics," as the late speaker of the California Assembly, Jesse Unruh, said in the mid-1960s. Money has become even more important in twenty-first-century politics, as shown by the precedent-setting six-billion-dollar 2012 election cycle. There was an unrelenting and some-times unseemly chase for campaign dollars, spurring candidates to innovate and use any way legal and available to try to raise money.

Sam Garrett, author of Chapter 4, and Anthony Corrado, author of Chapter 5, are two political scientists who study campaign finance. They offer com-plementary perspectives on the importance of the money chase in 2012 and in campaigns generally. Both scholars describe how the two campaigns orga-nized their finance efforts, focusing on changes in campaign finance law and on where the campaign money came from, how it was collected, and how it was spent. The methods of raising money and the amount of money collected and used in a campaign can raise ethical questions that may become an issue in a campaign, something Obama avoided again in 2012. Skillful use of money is central to a campaign strategy.

Sam Garrett's chapter, "Money, Politics, and Policy: Campaign Finance Before and After *Citizens United*," describes the complex rules of campaign finance and shows how contribution limits and reporting requirements apply to various people and groups. He details substantial changes in permissible campaign spending for the 2012 campaigns. His analysis of history serves as an important reminder that the Supreme Court's *Citizens United* decision was the culmination of decades of debate about what should be permitted in campaign finance. Garrett's history of campaign finance law shows that it has remained more or less constant for more than forty years. He discusses three factors that have shaped federal campaign finance law: (1) Congressional limits on contributions in an effort to reduce the potential for corruption motivated by political money; (2) Occasional congressional attempts to limit spending—distinct from contributions—although the Supreme Court has generally declared spending restrictions unconstitutional; and (3) Congressional requirements to disclose information about which people and groups contribute to campaigns or independently spend funds to influence elections.

In Chapter 5, "Fundraising Strategies in the 2012 Presidential Campaign," Corrado analyzes the new cycle of strategies and tactics of campaign fundraising in the post–*Citizens United* world of 2012. The fundraising activity in 2012 was built upon practices that had been used in recent elections, but it evolved because of more permissive rules on campaign funding established well in advance of the election. He highlights the major change that has taken place in the ways candidates, parties, and nonparty organizations raise money. Corrado shows that the 2012 election offered a new strategy to presidential fundraising, one in which multi-million-dollar donors and Super PACs (political action committees) played a major role. He concludes that with an open race for the White House in 2016, it is likely that Super PACs and nonparty organizations will once again be active participants in campaign finance and may prove to be an even more important source of campaign funding. If so, the 2012 election may come to be viewed as the start of a new stage in the evolution of campaign finance: the era of the megadonor.

Campaign Advertising and the Media

Paid advertising and earned media are cardinal elements in a modern election campaign. Most Americans rely heavily on the news media—television, radio, print media, and social media on the Internet—for information about candidates and issues in a campaign. Candidates who have enough money to buy significant amounts of advertising and who attract positive free news coverage (earned media) benefit by becoming better known, which in turn positions them to frame issues and influence voters to support them. The media projects to the public the theme and message of the campaign and is critical to success.

In any electoral system, political communication has several basic functions. The first, name identification, is critical because few voters will vote for a name they do not recognize. The second function, candidate image, may be defined as the answer to the question, what kind of person is this candidate? Competent media consultants do not force their clients into a predetermined mold but instead seek ways to present the real person in a positive light. The third function, issues, forms the basis for discussions of the differences between the candidates. If name identification is carried in signage and headlines, and image identification through pictures, then issues are the body copy. The two tests of legitimacy for the fourth function, attacks on the opponent, are truth and relevance, with the voters as the ultimate judges. The fifth function, defense, often employs the same medium used in the attack and at the same level. Defense tactics include denial, explanation, apology, and counterattack.

Political advertising simplifies complex issues and takes them out of context. Political ads are simply another product of our mass culture, no better or worse than the rest of the media. We must be cautious about condemning ads when they merely reflect our larger media culture. More importantly, we need to understand the role of ads in politics and give Americans the tools to decode them and avoid being manipulated by them. Both positive ads and attack ads prey on people's emotions—attack ads on fear, positive ads on hope.

Campaign ads must conform to the rules that govern the rest of the mass media culture and accommodate themselves to the conventions of television. In devising ads, candidates and their strategists understand that most undecided and swing voters make up their minds based on televised impressions, symbols, and cues. Political advertising in the television age is more about projecting a likable persona than communicating ideas about governance. Campaigns must find ways to differentiate their candidate from rivals, and they do this by highlighting the one quality that seems to matter most with voters—character.

Political campaigns sometimes shape a candidate's personal dreams and sometimes a nation's myths. Conveying a narrative the public relates to and understands is a primary goal of political ads. For example, narratives linking the candidate to the middle-class American Dream, narratives drawn from our distrust of accumulated power, narratives of the candidate as common man, and leadership narratives were all used in the 2012 presidential campaigns.

In Chapter 6, "Difference of Degree: Issue Agendas in a Polarized Media Environment," Danny Hayes analyzes the setting of issue agendas in the 2012 campaign. Hayes argues that issue agenda setting is an important element of a campaign because salient issues are more likely to influence voting behavior than those that are not on the public's radar. Candidates spend a lot of time trying to control a campaign's issue agenda because they want voters to be thinking about things that give them an advantage and to ignore issues that put them at a disadvantage. Campaign issue agendas in a "transformed media age" or the "post–broadcast media environment" exist in an information environment that is less homogenous than it used to be. News outlets have an incentive to cover the issues that they believe are most interesting and are at the center of political debate—lest viewers and readers turn elsewhere for information. The Romney campaign focused on high unemployment, a failing economy, budget deficits, to a lesser degree welfare, and a failed Obama national security policy exemplified by the attack and deaths at the US consulate in Benghazi. President Obama focused on falling unemployment, an image of Romney as "out of touch with average Americans," and controversial Medicare budget cuts that were championed by vice-presidential candidate Paul Ryan.

The economy was the number one issue for every news outlet. However, the substance and thrust of economic news was rather different in the partisan media, according to Hayes. That so many people on opposites sides of the political divide agreed about the election's central issue owes much to media coverage of the presidential campaign. News outlets devoted similar amounts of attention to other issues that were being emphasized by one campaign or the other. The substance of coverage in the partisan media was very different and similarity in the issue agendas of highly partisan news outlets is striking. Partisan media seeks to promote their favored candidate's fortunes, but do not ignore issues that appear to be disadvantageous to his campaign.

Communication specialist Dotty Lynch, with decades of experience assisting campaigns and covering campaigns for the news media, analyzes the roles of campaign advertising and of media in campaigns in Chapter 7, "How the Media Covered the 2012 Election: The Role of Earned Media." Lynch defines "earned media" as "positive coverage of an event, issue, or person by the news media which has been initiated by a campaign." One of the most efficient and cost-effective ways to reach a large audience is through earned media. Earned media is positive news coverage that campaign staff actively work to get. By creating newsworthy stories or events and by offering the stories to local news outlets, campaigns can generate effective media coverage that targets specific audiences with a specific message.

Lynch describes three basic components to earned media: the messenger, the message, and the conveyor of the message through the news media to the public. Lynch analyzes the history of earned media and its evolution in political communications theory. She describes the news environment of 2012 and examines how the attempts to earn positive media, control the message, and set the news agenda were executed. For example, the Obama campaign and their Super PAC, Priorities USA Action, spent millions of dollars "defining" Mitt Romney as a wealthy businessman who cared only about the bottom line. The Romney campaign was busy trying to portray Obama as a well-meaning but failed president and jumped on any opportunity to reinforce that message. She shows that debates, and conventions, and even leaked videos leave a deeper impression than any single story or even set of media stories. She concludes that while the words were negative, pictures of Obama were positive, which gave him an edge. Finally she evaluates how successful the 2012 campaigns were in generating earned media and what lessons candidates and political professionals can learn for the future. Looking ahead to 2016, Lynch argues that it is clear that the Internet will be dominant, although TV is holding its own. Data mining and microtargeting are likely to be even more sophisticated, and campaigns at all levels will be devising strategies for niche audiences. Reporters will be using more technology as well, and YouTube (or the next generation of YouTube) is likely to grow into an even bigger political influence.

Field Organization, Grassroots Campaigning, and the Digital Campaigns

Election campaigns rely on thousands of volunteers and party activists to get out the vote during the critical last few hours that the polls are open. The functions of these field organizations—voter registration, targeting, literature distribution, and GOTV drives—have been integral elements of campaigns and elections since the 1990s. As Karl Rove and President Bush reminded campaign professionals in the 2000 election, and President Obama in 2008, there is no substitute for a well-organized, focused field operation. A strong field operation works the phone banks and streets to identify supporters, reinforce the candidate's message, persuade voters to support the candidate, and get them to actually vote for the candidate. Field operations need to be linked to the campaign strategy and plan. These operations were formerly performed primarily by the party organization. The party organization is still the most important building block for a campaign, but modern campaigns often obtain the assistance of a field operations specialist.

The purpose and activities of a successful field organization focus on voter contact, which is the heart of the field operation. The structure, duties, and size of a campaign field operation depend on the strategy and plan of the overall campaign. Few successful campaigns have no field operation. Some campaigns that have a field operation still cannot overcome the odds against a particular candidate.

Alan Rosenblatt, social media expert at the Center for American Progress, describes the latest developments in the use of the Internet and digital networks in modern campaigns in Chapter 8, "Dimensions of Campaigns in the Age of Digital Networks." Although the vast majority of the electorate spends little time going to political sites on the Internet, key constituents do. Several lessons emerge from the study of its use in 2012. First, campaigns must include the Internet in their tactics, maintaining websites, blogs, and meet-ups, and developing innovative ways of contacting voters through the Internet. Second, innovative use of the web in campaigns can provide the volunteers and finances to play a critical part of a candidate's strategy, as shown with John McCain in 2000 and Obama in 2008. Third, Rosenblatt argues the Internet has revolutionized campaigns and has become an essential part of all successful campaigns. The diversity and range of digital networking tools and the strategies for using them in political campaigns will continue to make a big impact on electoral politics, as they did again in the 2012 presidential campaign. Rosenblatt concludes that these tools are in the hands of voters as well as campaigns. This creates a more chaotic environment for spreading campaign messages than there was in the past. Digital tools provide new solutions for getting the message out and organizing voters and volunteers. He argues that election campaigns must now develop strategies that take into consideration all of the strategic dimensions created by these new technologies. Rosenblatt shows that while strategy, message, and organization remain most important in a campaign, digitally networked technology has altered the playing field, not just in scope and scale but also in more fundamental ways. Network technologies are distinct from other media tools in that they are ubiquitous, unfiltered, powerful, and social. Regardless of technology, campaigns come down to message and organization. With the new media there are three important dimensions: broadcasting a one-way campaign message, building transactional or two-way relationships with voters, and unleashing social masses in support of a candidate. All of these were used in the 2012 campaigns. Rosenblatt argues that the big political change in 2008 and 2012 was the ability of voters to take campaigns into their own hands, to talk to each other, to produce and share their own media content, and to create counter campaigns, which increased the voters' impact on candidates and the political process.

Alicia Prevost, political scientist and campaign professional, describes the goals of fieldwork—to identify, communicate with, and mobilize campaign

supporters—in Chapter 9, "The Ground Game: Fieldwork in Political Campaigns." Although the techniques have changed dramatically over the last fifty
years, especially in the 2008 and 2012 Obama campaigns, these goals have
not. One of the first activities conducted by a campaign organization is voter
research: determining which groups of voters are inclined to support them,
support their opponent, or be undecided. After classifying voters into relevant groupings, campaign strategists determine the intensity of each group's
support. In addition to group loyalties, campaigners also consider group size
and turnout level when designing their targeting strategies. Once the target
audiences are determined, demographic, geographic, and polling information
is used to create a campaign plan that determines where voter mobilization
activities will be conducted, the content of the candidate's message, and where
and how that message will be communicated to voters.

Getting the message out is central because a campaign that is unable to define itself risks being defined by its opponents. The basic goals and strategies
of campaign communications are to introduce the candidate to voters, give
them a reason to support that candidate, discourage them from supporting
the opponent, excite supporters enough to get them to vote, and demoralize
opponents' supporters so they will be less inclined to vote. Personal contact
with voters in the form of candidate-citizen interactions in the field allows
for spontaneous learning and expressions of concern. Field activities are also
used to generate free media coverage and usually play a big role in campaigns
for state and local offices.

Prevost argues that although isolating the effects of fieldwork is difficult,
it has been found to affect election outcomes. She concludes that campaign
fieldwork is good for democracy because it helps increase political participation, efficacy, and support for government by encouraging people to get involved in politics, which was shown by the Obama campaign and presidency.

Campaign consultant Robert Blaemire, author of Chapter 10, "The Evolution of Microtargeting," analyzes the evolution and the strategic use of microtargeting in the 2012 campaign cycle. The primary goal of a campaign is to
win more votes than the opposition. Blaemire traces the history of targeting
back to the founding of the country, when candidates met with voters in town
squares and even saloons. His history of voter targeting from the eighteenth
century to 2012 concludes with an explanation of how modeling is used to extrapolate about larger communities' predicted voting behavior, a key element
of targeting. Models allow campaigns to more precisely select voters based on
predictive behavior and to communicate with them on issues they care about.
Broad-based early targeting (shotgun approach) and microtargeting (rifle

shot approach) give campaigns greater confidence that they are not wasting money. He argues that peer-to-peer contact on the Internet is best, but is still a limited form of targeting. It means the campaign has less control of the message, the method of communication, and determining the targets. The evolution of targeting has brought a trend of more precision and improved ability to focus on the right people with the right message. New technology will continue to speed up this trend in future elections, with a greater level of personalization both in messaging and in the method of contact.

In Chapter 11, "Voter Turnout in the 2012 Election," Pamela Bachilla, Jan Leighley, and Jonathan Nagler analyze voter turnout historically with a focus on stability and change between the 2008 and 2012 elections. The national turnout among all voters declined between 2008 and 2012, reversing a pattern of increasing aggregate turnout in presidential elections that had persisted since 2000. The authors explore the reasons why, including a lower enthusiasm for President Obama. They also discuss the impact of vastly increased campaign spending stemming from the Supreme Court's 2010 decision in *Citizens United v. Federal Election Commission,* and new voter identification laws that increased the burden for voters. The weather was also a factor in lower turnout in 2012, as election officials scrambled to maintain polling places in states affected by Hurricane Sandy.

Bachilla, Leighley, and Nagler also analyze state and demographic factors influencing voter turnout. In many ways, 2008 was a landmark election. Barack Obama rode to victory as the first African American president, and more women than ever were serious contenders throughout the primary and general races. The authors show that the demographics of the electorate in 2012 were similar to those of 2008. Efforts by campaigns to mobilize turnout through targeting specific voters and choosing strategic campaign messages did affect the final national vote count. Exactly how the efforts of the Obama and Romney campaigns, as well as the many other factors that made 2012 unique, contributed to a decline in national aggregate turnout is a question that will be taken up as better data becomes available in the years following the election.

In Chapter 12, "Election Law Is the New Rock 'n' Roll," Chris Sautter, election law and recount expert, describes how election laws have an impact on campaigns. Election rules matter for all levels of elected office, well beyond the presidential nomination process. Sautter analyzes how the regulations and laws governing elections affect how votes are counted, with a special focus on the many changes in election law in 2012.

David Dulio and John Klemanski in Chapter 13, "Republican Strategies and Tactics in the 2012 Primary and General Elections," offer a history of the 2012 primaries and an analysis of Romney's general election campaign. The brutal primary battles hurt Romney. Nearly all of Romney's long list of primary opponents had been atop the polls at one time. The number of debates was high, with at least twenty held between May 2011 and March 2012, making it difficult for the Romney campaign to focus on strategy, message, organization, and fundraising for the general election.

Dulio and Klemanski conclude that campaigns matter. They argue that the primaries weakened Romney, and that while his strategy was sound, the implementation of his strategy was not. The Romney campaign failed tactically when its high-tech voter identification and turnout effort fell short on Election Day. Voter turnout was down in 2012 compared to 2008, and Democrats had a six-point turnout advantage. If the Romney campaign had done a better job presenting a clear message and getting their voters to the polls, the result may have been different.

Conclusion

Candice J. Nelson concludes the book with Chapter 14, "Campaigns Matter," which summarizes and analyzes the impact of the many changes in the 2012 election cycle. New election administration rules, changes in campaign finance, the evolution in the use of social media, innovations in microtargeting, and other technological developments all had a transforming influence on the 2012 election. Nelson also evaluates the economic and political predictors used by political scientists and the campaign strategies used by candidates to explain what mattered in the 2012 presidential and congressional elections.

The principles and process of campaign management described in this book contributed mightily to the outcomes of American elections in the last three decades and to the 2012 campaigns of President Barack Obama and Governor Mitt Romney. The basic thesis of this book is that election campaigns influence voter behavior—that campaigns matter. Few changes have transformed American elections more in the past three decades than the professionalization of campaign management and the evolution of new strategies and tactics. What began in the 1960s as the waning of political parties evolved into the increased importance of campaign professionals, which has become a major industry, involving at least six billion dollars raised and spent in the 2012 election cycle (Nelson 2011; Dulio and Nelson 2005; Thurber and Nelson 2000; Dulio 2004). We describe what political scientists know about campaigns and what professionals know. The rivalry and collaboration between political scientists with their scientific knowledge and professionals with their campaign experience are central themes of our book. Campaign professionals are a staple of contemporary elections. This book describes and evaluates this crucial development—the professionalization and continued transformation of American political campaigns in 2012.

References

Ambramowitz, Alan I. 2009. "Time-for-Change Model Again Right on the Money in 2008." *PS: Political Science & Politics* 42 (1): 22.

Barrett, Devlin. 2008. "Video Games Feature Ads for Obama's Campaign." Associated Press, October 14. www.azcentral.com/news/election/election08/articles/2008 /10/14/20081014obama1014vg.html.

Campbell, James E. 2009. "The 2008 Campaign and the Forecasts Derailed." *PS: Political Science & Politics* 42 (1): 19–20.

Dulio, David A. 2004. *For Better or Worse: How Political Consultants Are Changing Elections in the United States.* Albany: State University of New York Press.

Dulio, David A., and Candice J. Nelson. 2005. *Vital Signs: Perspectives on the Health of American Campaigning.* Washington, DC: Brookings Institution Press.

Exley, Zack. 2007. "Obama Field Organizers Plot a Miracle." Huffington Post, August 27. www.huffingtonpost.com/zack-exley/obama-field-organizers-pl_b_61918.html.

Gerber, Donald, and Alan Green. 2000. "The Effects of Canvassing, Telephone Calls, and Direct Mail on Voter Turnout: A Field Experiment." *American Political Science Review* 94 (3): 653–663.

Jamieson, Kathleen Hall, ed. 2009. *Electing the President 2008: The Insider's View.* Philadelphia: University of Pennsylvania Press.

Johnson, Dennis W. 2007. *No Place for Amateurs: How Political Consultants Are Reshaping American Democracy.* New York: Routledge.

Kenski, Kate, Bruce W. Hardy, and Kathleen Hall Jamieson. 2010. *The Obama Victory: How Media, Money, and Message Shaped the 2008 Election.* Oxford, UK: Oxford University Press.

Lewis-Beck, Michael S. 2009. "Race Blunts the Economic Effects? The 2008 Obama Forecast." *PS: Political Science & Politics* 42 (1): 22.

Lizza, Ryan. 2008. "Battle Plans: How Obama Won." *New Yorker,* November 17, 46–55.

Luo, Michael. 2008. "Obama Hauls in Record $750 Million for Campaign." *New York Times,* December 5.

Malbin, Michael J. 2009. "Small Donors, Large Donors, and the Internet: The Case for Public Finance After Obama." Washington, DC: Campaign Finance Institute.

McDonald, Michael. 2013. "United States Elections Project: Election Turnout." George Mason University. http://elections.gmu.edu/Turnout_2012G.html.

Medvic, Stephen K. 2001. *Political Consultants in U.S. Congressional Elections*. Columbus: Ohio State University Press.

———. 2006. "Understanding Campaign Strategy: 'Deliberate Priming' and the Role of Professional Political Consultants." *Journal of Political Marketing* 5: 11–32.

Napolitan, Joseph. 1972. *The Election Game and How to Win It*. New York: Doubleday.

Nelson, Candice J. 2011. *Grant Park: The Democratization of Presidential Elections, 1968–2008*. Washington, DC: Brookings Institution Press.

Nelson, Candice J., David A. Dulio, and Stephen K. Medvic. 2002. *Shades of Gray: Perspectives on Campaign Ethics*. Washington, DC: Brookings Institution Press.

Polsby, Nelson W., Aaron Wildavsky, Steven E. Schier, and David A. Hopkins. 2012. *Presidential Elections: Strategies and Structures of American Politics*. Lanham, MD: Rowman & Littlefield.

Popkin, Samuel. 1991. *The Reasoning Voter: Communication and Persuasion in Presidential Campaigns*. Chicago: University of Chicago Press.

PS Symposium. 2012. "Forecasting the 2012 American National Elections." *PS: Political Science & Politics* 45 (4): 614–674.

Rove, Karl. 2008. "Obama's Money Advantage." *Polling News and Notes*, December 11.

Sabato, Larry J. 1981. *The Rise of Political Consultants: New Ways of Winning Elections*. New York: Basic Books.

Schaffner, Brian F. 2008. "Obama's Ground Game Advantage in Key States." Pollster .com, December 8. www.pollster.com/blogs/obamas_ground_game_advantage _i.php.

Schaper, David. 2007. "'Camp Obama' Trains Campaign Volunteers." National Public Radio, June 12. www.npr.org/templates/story/story.php?storyId=11012254.

Scherer, Michael. 2008. "A Campaign Postmortem at Harvard." *Time,* December 12. www.time.com/time/politics/article/0,8599,1866093,00.html.

Shea, Daniel M. 1996. *Campaign Craft: The Strategies, Tactics, and Art of Political Campaign Management*. Westport, CT: Praeger.

Thurber, James. 1998. "The Study of Campaign Consultants: A Subfield in Search of a Theory." *PS: Political Science & Politics* 32 (2): 145–149.

———. 2001. *The Battle for Congress: Consultants, Candidates, and Voters*. Washington, DC: Brookings Institution Press.

Thurber, James A., David B. Magleby, and Kelly D. Patterson. 2002. "Campaign Consultants and Responsible Party Government." In *Responsible Partisanship? The Evolution of American Political Parties Since 1950,* edited by John C. Green and Paul S. Herrnson, 101–120. Lawrence: University of Kansas Press.

Thurber, James, and Candice J. Nelson. 2000. *Campaign Warriors: Political Consultants in Elections*. Washington, DC: Brookings Institution Press.

Thurber, James, and Candice J. Nelson, eds. 2004. *Campaigns and Elections American Style.* Boulder: Westview.

Thurber, James, Candice J. Nelson, and David A. Dulio, eds. 2000. *Crowded Airwaves: Campaign Advertising in Elections.* Washington, DC: Brookings Institution Press.

Thurber, James A., Alicia Kelor Prevost, and Maik Bohne. 2008. "Campaign Consultants and Political Parties Today." In *The Routledge Handbook of Political Management.* New York: Routledge.

2

Creating a Winning Campaign Strategy

DAVID WINSTON

Introduction

More than twenty years ago, I was sitting at my desk at the National Republican Congressional Committee watching a show on C-SPAN. It was a lecture on targeting by Democrat Mark Gersh at American University's Campaign Management Institute. Later I would discover he was the Democratic Party's leading expert on redistricting and targeting. For the next two hours, I sat fascinated by what Mark had to say; by the time he finished, I had learned the fundamentals of targeting through the prism of the opposition party. This turned out to be a valuable perspective indeed. For the past five national elections, Mark and I have been the Democratic and Republican analysts for CBS, calling races on election night. We've become friends and colleagues, and I laugh about the origins of my targeting education. He doesn't find it quite as funny.

My point is that strategy, like targeting and other elements of campaign management, is partisan in terms of implementation but not definition. The principles of good strategy apply equally to Republicans and Democrats. The harder question to answer is, "What is strategy?" A lot has been written and said about this sometimes confusing but central component of a winning campaign, whether the strategy is designed for the beaches of Normandy or for a congressional district in Long Beach.

My favorite maxim about strategy was written by Sun Tzu, the fifth-century BC author of the *Art of War*. He said, "Strategy without tactics is the slowest route to victory. Tactics without strategy is the noise before defeat." Two thousand years later, when it comes to strategy, not much has changed.

There are as many definitions of strategy as there are strategists, but here is mine:

> Strategy is achieving a desired outcome using a structured approach based on understanding existing and potential environmental elements and your opponent's potential strategies.

This chapter focuses on the foundation of a winning campaign: strategy. Crafting a successful strategy takes good instincts, an understanding of politics, historical context, and detailed quantifiable and qualitative research. Driving the process are five key steps that the campaign manager must undertake with support from the candidate, the campaign's consultants, and other key players.

- Define a desired outcome.
- Develop situational awareness.
- Identify your opponent's potential strategies.
- Define a winning coalition.
- Create a strategic communications plan.

After taking these steps, this same group must agree on the final strategy and get behind it to achieve success.

"Think New"

Before leaping into the process of putting together a winning strategy, every campaign manager must avoid the natural tendency to think as they have always thought. Remember the early critics who scoffed at the 2008 Obama campaign's decision to change the dynamics of the presidential race by expanding the pool of participants? That was a strategic decision that took some new thinking.

History backs up this idea. In the 1930s, the French General Staff hoped to discourage a German invasion by building the Maginot Line. The French embraced a "static defense" that was based on what they had learned in World War I. The Germans, focusing on the future, out-thought them by developing a strategic doctrine based on mobility, which completely overwhelmed the French strategy.

Now, fast-forward to the 2008 election. While the McCain campaign was busy running a base strategy, as George W. Bush had done successfully in

2004. Barack Obama understood that the political environment had changed dramatically over the past four years and crafted a strategy that would leave the GOP scratching its collective head, wondering what happened. In both examples, the losers clung to the past while the successful strategists beat their opponents by "thinking new."

Break the Rules

One of the ways to think new is to break the rules. Here's what I mean. See if you can solve the following puzzle, but be warned. Solving it takes some new thinking. The task is to connect the nine dots with three lines, but do it without lifting your pen or pencil from the paper.

Here's the answer.

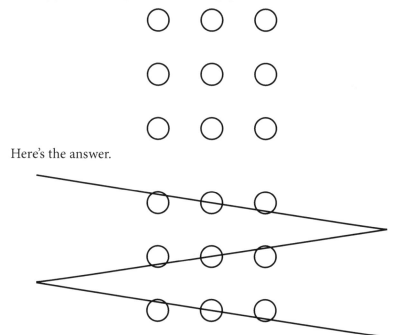

This is tritely but accurately called the "outside the box" solution. Most people fail to find the answer because they instinctively view the nine dots as a box and internally create a rule that says, "stay in the box." An important structural element is at work here. To solve the puzzle, you have to consciously decide to break rules and do things differently. Breaking rules is one of the critical elements of being creative.

For example, when Steve Jobs conjured up the iPhone, the design process got off to a rocky start. Jobs tossed the first design because the case clashed with the display, the element of the iPhone that was paramount in Jobs's eyes. It meant delay of the launch and redesign of much of the phone's interior hardware, but Jobs insisted that the look meet his design standard, and in doing so he also set a new creative standard. He broke the rules.

Competitors scoffed at the $500 price tag. Steve Ballmer, president of Microsoft, told CNBC that the phone "doesn't appeal to business customers because it doesn't have a keyboard." Ballmer was fighting the last battle in the cell phone wars, thinking like the French General Staff. Ninety million iPhones later, Apple has become one of the world's richest companies.

Change Perspective

Another way to think new is by changing your perspective. Here's another puzzle to try. Remove three sticks and leave four.

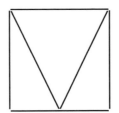

If you look at this puzzle as a group of objects, you won't solve it, but if you can transition your thought process to view it as a graphic, you can find the answer. Here it is.

Thinking new is often the crucial component in winning strategies. The 2010 congressional election for the House is a good example. Unlike the McCain presidential campaign's dated perspective, which was especially ineffective against an opposing campaign that embraced all things new, John Boehner and House Republicans learned the lessons of the 2006 and 2008 elections, changed their perspective, and thought new.

In 2006, the Republican majority coalition fell apart. The GOP lost a number of key constituencies—married women with children, middle-income voters, independents, and Catholics. The impact of these demographic losses in important states was obvious. For example, Republicans lost Catholics by eleven points nationally.

The results in 2006 should have set off alarm bells. Instead, the McCain people decided to run a tactical, base campaign. The strategy was to get out the base in large numbers everywhere, appeal to certain targeted constituencies in key electoral states, like Catholics in Ohio and Pennsylvania, and cobble together an Electoral College victory much as Bush had done.

The campaign failed to understand that voters in what I call the Big Middle had abandoned the GOP in 2006 and nothing had happened in the interim to bring them back. A nationalized campaign to reach and attract those voters was their only hope of victory. The McCain campaign should have changed perspective, looked beyond the base, and found a strategy to rebuild the Republican coalition.

For the 2010 election, President Obama, like McCain in 2008, devised a strategy based on the past. His strategy was to simply increase the Democratic base turnout of the 2006 congressional election. What he failed to realize was the level of dissatisfaction with his performance. Base voter groups had a higher level of participation in 2010 than in the 2006 election, when Democrats had won by eight points and had taken both the House and the Senate. Liberal Democrats, women, African Americans, and urban voters increased their participation in 2010, while younger voters and Hispanics matched their 2006 level of turnout.

But on election night, despite a better base turnout than in 2006, Democrats lost to Republicans by a seven-point margin. How could a slightly better turnout composition for Democrats end up generating such a dramatically different outcome? The president had assumed that the Democratic coalition of 2006 was still intact and supportive. But he failed to understand the level of dissatisfaction with his policy priorities and the lack of economic progress during his first two years.

In contrast to President Obama's base strategy, John Boehner's strategy was to try to build a majority coalition based on the idea of "winning the issues." His belief was that in a center-right country, the center-right party should win if they focused on issues, specifically jobs and the economy in the current environment.

President Obama blamed Republicans, and specifically George Bush, for the country's economic problems, claiming they had put the economic "car" in the ditch and he had spent two years trying to get it out. He argued that now wasn't the time to give the keys back to "the folks who got us in the ditch in the first place." This partisan message appealed to the Democratic base but alienated independent voters who saw the president as focused on health care when millions were out of work.

John Boehner's Republican narrative, derived from the "winning the issues" strategy, rested on one basic question—"Where are the jobs?"—reflecting the central question on voters' minds. Republicans were generally successful in defining a new issue direction with the help of the Republican "Pledge to America," which voters were broadly aware of even if they were not familiar with the specifics. Boehner's emphasis on voters' top issue—jobs—was also in direct contrast to President Obama's agenda of the previous two years, which focused on issues designed to satisfy his political base (e.g., health care, green energy, and even the stimulus package).

As a result, the closing arguments of these two strategies resulted in a decisive outcome favoring Republicans as they made significant progress with a number of important swing voter groups. But the key was their extraordinary success with the political center-independents. In 1994 Republicans gained the majority, winning independents by a fourteen-point margin. In 2006 Democrats gained the majority, winning independents by eighteen points. In the 2010 election, Republicans won independents by nineteen points. Embracing the "winning the issues" strategy wasn't an easy sell to the House GOP conference. It forced both the leadership and members to think differently and change perspective, but on election night 2010, Republicans were back in the majority and tasked with governing based on issues.

When developing their strategy, too many campaigns today fight the last election. Don't be afraid to change perspective as you develop your plan.

Step 1: Define a Desired Outcome

Now that you have your head in the right place and are ready to think new and act differently, the first step on the journey to a winning strategy is settling on a desired outcome: your goal. In the business world, it could be increasing sales by 10 percent. In college, it might be getting a 4.0 grade point average. In political races, it usually means winning the election by a 50-percent-plus-one margin. Political outcomes are a little easier to determine than most. Your goal could be a number higher than 50 percent, but in most political contests, the desired outcome is no more complicated than setting a winning percentage.

Seeking a mandate to govern rather than simply winning an election is one exception to the norm. David Cameron, leader of the Conservative Party in Great Britain, said the purpose of a political party is not to win elections but to prove it is ready to govern. To govern successfully often requires a mandate and that usually means setting a goal several points higher than 50 percent plus one.

But whatever the strategy—in politics, business, the nonprofit sector, or even war—the first step to defining a successful outcome is to ask the right questions in order to define your goal clearly and develop a strategic plan to achieve it. In politics, the goal may seem obvious, but sometimes we ask the wrong questions, sometimes literally.

In 2010, Barack Obama asked the wrong question: What do I need to do to increase turnout in the same Democratic coalition that won in 2006? Passing health care and blaming Republicans wasn't the answer voters wanted in 2010. Boehner and House Republicans asked the right question—Where are the jobs?—and supported their argument with the "Pledge" that outlined how they would govern. Obama focused on turnout while Republicans focused on winning the issues.

Another example of asking the right question occurred in 1994, when Newt Gingrich decided to ask why the GOP should continue to run campaigns based on the notion that "all politics is local." After all, it was Democratic Speaker Tip O'Neill who coined the phrase. Gingrich answered his question by deciding to nationalize the 1994 congressional elections. He violated all kinds of Republican doctrine based on the belief that candidates win locally, one race at a time. He picked up over fifty seats in one election.

In 2006 DCCC chair Rahm Emanuel looked at the playing field and said, in essence, "If there are only thirty competitive seats, we can't win." Democrats won that election because Emanuel asked the right question: "How can we turn forty more seats into competitive contests?" He tasked Mark Gersh with finding them. Ultimately, expanding the field, coupled with a favorable political environment, allowed Democrats to win back Congress. Other factors were important—fundraising and candidate recruitment—but Emanuel changed the dynamics of the election cycle when he asked the key question.

Step 2: Develop Situational Awareness

For most nonpresidential races, the bottom line is pretty simple: get the strategy right by developing a winning coalition. This takes us back to the second part of my definition of strategy: using a structured approach based on an understanding of the existing and potential environmental elements.

To do that, campaigns must engage in something called "situational awareness." The US Navy defines this as "the degree of accuracy by which one's perception of his current environment mirrors reality." In politics, your ability to assess the environment will determine, in large part, whether your campaign succeeds or fails. To understand situational awareness, a campaign manager must begin with an analysis of the *existing* elements that impact the political environment.

A word of warning before you begin: It's important to understand that every manager embarks on a campaign with personal biases. That's not necessarily good or bad. It's just a fact. We all grow up in different places and in different families with different views and values, go to different schools, and have a variety of friends and influencers. The key is to recognize your biases and incorporate them in a way that expands your options but does not limit your decisions. For example, I was once a senior fellow for statistical analysis at the Heritage Foundation, so I view issues through the prism of conservative economics. That perspective would be in total sync with most Republican candidates I might work for. But if I were a campaign manager for a Republican running on the Upper West Side of Manhattan, I would have to factor that bias out of my decision making because most people in that area probably wouldn't agree with me. It's important to remember that the campaign manager is not the candidate. The manager's job is to help get the candidate elected.

So, let's take on situation awareness.

Assessing the Existing Elements

Party Registration and Identification

First and foremost, you must know the party registration and identification numbers for your race by heart. This is an absolute necessity. The numbers tell you the size of your voter pool—how many Republicans, Democrats, and independents—and where to find them. Without these basic numbers at the core of your strategy, you cannot win. The wider the gap in party registration numbers, the less chance a party has to compete. Maryland and Massachusetts are good examples of states in which Democratic party registration can overwhelm even good Republican candidates statewide.

There can be rare exceptions. The 2010 Massachusetts special election held to fill the Senate seat of the late Ted Kennedy is one example. Under normal circumstances, Scott Brown, a Republican state legislator, wouldn't have been given a chance against Democrat Martha Coakley, the better known attorney general. But Coakley's persistent political missteps coupled with Brown's focus on his independence turned what should have been a cakewalk for Coakley in this overwhelmingly Democratic state into a major upset.

Every election sees a few unexpected wins and losses in races heavily favoring one party or the other, but in races with a narrow registration gap, party registration or identification numbers become all-important.

Previous Political Behavior

Both parties focus on reaching and turning out their base, as they should. But nationally and in most states, neither party has a sufficient electoral majority to win without looking at the Big Middle. One way to do that is to analyze previous political behavior.

Voters' past political behavior provides a gold mine of information to help develop strategic targeting. This data can answer questions like, "What was the historical turnout in past elections? How has that turnout differed in presidential and nonpresidential election years, and how has one party benefited from these patterns? What kinds of candidates have generally won in this area? Is this a ticket-splitting area?"

Answering this last question is particularly important because certain areas in the country have a history of ticket splitting. Ticket splitters, who may be registered Republicans, Democrats, or independents, vote for candidates in both parties. They make up the Big Middle and should never be taken for granted. Virginia has a large number of ticket splitters. Over the past few years, voters in Virginia, which had been reliably Republican, have elected Democrats as governor and more recently to both Senate seats. Anyone looking at previous political behavior wouldn't have been surprised to see Virginia or Indiana become a battleground state in the 2008 presidential contest. In 2006 Indiana voters gave three Republican-held congressional seats to the Democrats. Obviously something was happening with Indiana voters, and it paid off in 2008 when Obama became the first Democrat to win the state since 1964. But in 2010, Indiana swung back to the GOP as Republicans won six of the state's nine House seats.

When looking at past political behavior, remember that any targeting strategy should reflect ticket splitters. Years of election data and exit poll results have shown that most Republicans get at least 10 percent of the Democratic vote and most Democrats get at least 10 percent of the Republican vote. When you include independents, ticket splitters at the national level are somewhere in the neighborhood of 25 to 30 percent of the electorate. Precinct data can show where these swing voters are found. But that's only half the analysis. The next step is to discover who the voters in your election are and what they care about.

Demographics

A demographic analysis of an election district provides "up close and personal" information on voters by such factors as race (e.g., African American, white, Asian, Latino), income level, sex, age, and religion. The importance of demographics varies according to the nature of the election district, the candidates, and current key issues.

In Florida districts, for example, age is a significant demographic. In urban districts and, more recently, in southwestern and western areas, race is also a key demographic. The demographic makeup is critical because these groups tend to share common experiences, values, and issue positions. For example, Latinos are concerned about education, jobs, and immigration policy. Women may be concerned with security, the economy, education, and health care. Analyzing demographics helps you identify issues that concern target voter groups and connect your candidate with these key voters.

There are two main sources for demographic information. The Census Bureau can give you information on everything from the number of women fifty-five and older in your area to the number of low-income voters. It can provide data on race, age, sex, income, and union participation, to name a few variables. It does not have information on religious affiliation.

The other source for good demographic information is your state's voter files, as well as files made available by the two parties at both the national and state level. The latter is particularly important as the parties enhance their voter files with critical demographic and behavioral data.

These sources will become your references of choice as you put real numbers behind your target groups.

Issues Currently in Play

The 2008 presidential contest was overwhelmingly about one issue: the economy. The McCain campaign, however, argued that the contest was about experience rather than issues, and in so doing he forgot one of the cardinal rules of campaigns and elections: issues matter. In the 2008 election, voters wanted a president who understood their concerns and offered solutions to address them. The McCain campaign thought the election was about defining Obama. The Obama campaign thought it was about the economy. Is it any surprise, then, who won?

The 2010 election was the mirror opposite. The economy still remained the top issue by far, but the president and congressional Democrats moved to the left and focused on Democratic base issues rather than focusing on the economy and jobs. By Election Day, when the president's policies failed to produce jobs, voters were disillusioned and unhappy.

For most voters, the issue of the economy in contrast with other issues was a little like a house with a fire on the roof. While windows may be broken, electrical work needs to be done, and the foundation is cracked, fixing them, important as they are, doesn't matter until the fire is put out. That was the context of jobs and the economy in the 2010 election; and from voters' perspective, President Obama spent too much time on issues like health care rather than the fire on the roof—jobs and the economy. Despite President Obama's argument that the American people should not hand the keys back to the Republicans, voters did. But, the keys weren't to a car, they were for a fire truck, and the message was clear: Put out the fire on the roof.

In 2010, any political leader not discussing the economy and jobs was simply on the wrong topic and seemed out of touch with the concerns of the American voter. Among those who voted in 2010, according to a national postelection New Models survey conducted by The Winston Group, the economy and jobs dwarfed every other issue, including health care, the deficit and spending. This is not to say that other issues were not important but rather that the concern for jobs was overwhelming. The Republican narrative that asked "Where are the jobs?" addressed that concern.

The decision of Boehner and House GOP leaders to adopt a "winning the issues" strategy gave Republican House members an umbrella narrative that allowed them to individualize their economic message and connect with voters on their number one issue. Meanwhile, President Obama and Democrats fixated on their base by attacking Republicans and passing one partisan bill after another that failed to change the economic landscape for the better. That left independents open to hearing economic arguments from Republicans.

According to the exit poll, among all voters who said their top issue was the economy, Republicans won by an eleven-point margin; and among independents who said the economy was their top issue, Republicans won by a slightly larger margin—fifteen points. Seventy-seven percent of midterm voters agreed that "Where are the jobs?" was the central question in the election, according to the New Models postelection study. Issues won the day in 2010.

In developing a winning strategy, campaigns and candidates must address the issues people care about or risk irrelevancy. A party that is overly focused on its base, especially in races other than presidential campaigns, often only emphasizes issues that don't reflect what the majority of voters worry about on a day-to-day basis. That doesn't mean base issues aren't important, but to put together a majority coalition requires an issue matrix that focuses on broader issues that matter to both the base and the Big Middle. This is where survey research can provide crucial issue information by political areas, by demographic categories, and by geography to help you reach your winning coalition of targeted voters.

Strengths and Weaknesses: Your Candidate and Your Opponent

Every candidate has strengths and weaknesses that must be identified and agreed upon before a campaign strategy is crafted. This takes both courage by campaign managers and an accurate sense of reality. Look at the 2012 presidential race. An honest assessment of President Obama would have found his speaking ability and personal affability still a great strength but his economic record a distinct weakness. A similar critique of Romney would have shown his business experience as both his main strength and a potential weakness. Putting together a candid assessment of the candidate's and the opponent's strengths and weaknesses is the final but critical last step in understanding the *existing* political environment and its likely impact on the campaign. If you don't know that, you don't know how to win.

Assessing the Potential Elements

Once you have analyzed the existing elements impacting the political environment, it is time to assess the *potential* elements that may affect the political environment. This critical exercise in making knowledge-based assumptions begins by asking the right questions. Start with these.

What are future issues likely to be?

In assessing the current political environment, survey research provides the most reliable and current analysis of voter concerns. The issue mix, however, can change over time. Who would have guessed a few years ago that by the fall of 2008 the war in Iraq would rank behind a housing crisis, high gas prices, and a collapse on Wall Street? As you write your campaign strategy, you should focus on two or three major issues. But it's also important to make assumptions about whether that current issue mix is likely to stay the same or change and to explain why.

As with current issues, survey research can give you some sense of where the electorate could move. All of us have gut feelings about major issues. We can also get a sense from news coverage and listening to the opposition about potential issues. Early in the campaign cycle, it's wise to think about other potential issues, have a "plan B" in the desk drawer, and be ready to pivot if a new issue arises.

What in the environment is likely to change or is an unknown, and what will remain the same?

Crystal balls don't work, but we can make some educated assumptions about the political environment. For example, in the spring of 2008, assuming that George Bush's high negative job approval ratings would remain a significant factor in the fall election was a pretty good bet. The McCain campaign should have accounted for this likely situation by making a painful but necessary strategic decision to separate the candidate from an unpopular president.

In the same race, the African American turnout and the youth vote were unknowns. Both groups were important to an Obama victory. It was safe to assume they would go to the polls in higher numbers. But how high was the key question. Republicans failed to understand the importance of the youth vote, once again relying on television to reach voters. Had they assumed a higher youth vote, their communications strategy would have included the kind of new technologies that are the conduits for conversations with this voter group.

What weaknesses and strengths in both candidates are likely to be important?

By this point, you have put together what is likely to be a long list of strengths and weaknesses for your candidate and your opponent. The manager must pare down the list to the strengths and weaknesses that are likely to matter in the election.

In 1992, Bill Clinton's admission that he smoked marijuana was a weakness. So was his inexperience, but only the inexperience became a serious issue. The strength of his opponent, President George H. W. Bush, was his foreign policy experience, but it gained him little in the election because voters were focused on the economy.

Your campaign must hone in on the two or three strengths and weaknesses of each candidate that will be most important to voters, given the political context of the election. This is crucial to a winning strategy.

What is the impact of the national brands of both parties and other political races?

A bad national party brand or a tsunami of a campaign like Barack Obama's 2008 effort can have a major impact on other campaigns. In 1980, Jimmy Carter's disastrous economic record gave Ronald Reagan a huge win, and that wave helped Republicans win the Senate and pick up thirty-four seats in the House. In 1994, Democratic congressional scandals and Bill Clinton's policy mistakes in his first year as president combined to form the perfect political storm, and Republicans gained control of the House for the first time in forty years. The negative national Democratic brand simply overwhelmed many of their candidates that year.

In 2006, it was the Republicans' turn. Hurricane Katrina, the faltering war in Iraq, cost of living issues, and Republicans' inability to develop a legislative focus downgraded the GOP brand to a point where Democrats were able to regain both the House and the Senate. Winning in a difficult environment is possible, but a realistic assessment of the impact of these outside factors must be part of the situational awareness process.

Step 3: Identify Your Opponent's Potential Strategies

Campaigns are often compared to the game of chess, and it's not a bad analogy. Like campaigns, chess is a game of strategic options—yours and your opponent's. You don't make your moves in a vacuum; nor does your opponent. How well you understand your opponent and the potential strategies he or she can employ will determine the outcome of the match. Like chess, winning campaigns consider the various strategic options available to their opponent before settling on their own campaign strategy—before making their first move. The best way to begin is by making a list of those strategic options along with their pluses and minuses. Be realistic in assessing the likely effectiveness and impact of each strategy that might be employed.

Learn everything you can about the opponent's past campaign behavior to give you important clues as to his or her likely strategic choices. Campaigns have a habit of talking to the media about their plans, so put a researcher to work digging up process stories that can give you an idea of the direction the opposing campaign will likely head. Then put yourself in his or her shoes. Think like your opponent. Trying to determine what your opponent is likely to do is a critical element in developing your own campaign strategy.

This exercise works at every level of campaigning, from county council to the presidency. In the 2012 presidential election, both the Republican and Democratic campaigns had a number of strategic options available to them. President Obama could have chosen a positive approach, running on his record and arguing that he needed a second term to finish the job of repairing the economy. He could have made this a referendum on past Republican policies claiming that voting for Romney was a vote for the policies that got us here in the first place. He could have chosen a base strategy focused on class warfare and personal attacks, or he could have stayed the course with hope and change. Or he could choose a mix of strategies based on what he thought the Romney campaign might do.

Governor Romney could have chosen a base-oriented strategy, making this election a referendum on Obama's record, or he could have opted for a more positive "choice" strategy focusing on his ideas for the future and reaching out to the Big Middle. Or he could have defined his version of a choice between the two candidates and emphasized economic policy differences. These and other strategic options were available. In the early stages of both campaigns, the two teams should have put themselves in the other's shoes and made an educated assumption on which strategy the other side would likely use, and what their best response should be for the best payoff.

Here's what happened. At the beginning of the campaign, Governor Romney and his strategists opted to make this a referendum on President Obama's record. In contrast, the Obama campaign made the election a choice between the two candidates and their plans for the future. President Obama had the more effective strategy, as shown by the New Models postelection survey, in which voters said they ultimately saw the election as a choice rather than a referendum, by 77 to 22 percent.

President Obama defined Romney in terms that would create a favorable contrast for himself, particularly on economic policies. Given the poor state of the economy, it should have been an uphill climb; but in the end, he effectively defined the choice as either moving forward with the economic polices of the present (Obama's) or going back to the failed economic policies of the past (Romney's and Bush's). Because Governor Romney focused on Obama's negative record at the expense of defining himself, the Romney campaign never successfully engaged in the kind of economic debate that would have given voters a clear understanding of his economic vision for the country, why it would work, and how it differed from those of both Obama and Bush. Because the Romney campaign's strategy failed to make a persuasive economic argument, President Obama was able to neutralize the biggest threat to his reelection and voters' top issue—the economy—and go on to win.

Before writing your campaign strategy, you need to know what you're up against, and that includes the opponent's strategy. As Frederick the Great once wrote, "It is pardonable to be defeated, but never to be surprised."

Step 4: Defining a Winning Coalition

Once you have a comprehensive picture of the political environment, including your opponent's likely strategy, it's time to move to the next step: defining a winning coalition.

Start by precisely defining your coalition. This means more than simply coming up with vote totals. A precise definition requires knowing how many voters it will take to win, but you must also know who those voters are and where they are found. How many married women with children? How many Hispanics? How many Catholics? You must put both percentages and hard numbers behind the target groups.

Next, determine which groups are reliably in your column and how you will hold them. Past political behavior and survey research are critical here. For Republicans, conservatives fall into this category, which remains a larger group than self-identified liberals, according to the 2008 exit polls. Evangelical

Christians also remain reliably Republican. For Democrats, liberals and African Americans make up their most reliable voters.

Then, determine which groups are key swing groups and how to attract them. If you don't know who these groups are, find out. Survey research can tell you which groups offer your campaign the best opportunity and which the biggest challenge. It can also tell you what issues are of greatest concern to these voters and what messages will have the most resonance. Appealing to your base and attracting swing voters are not mutually exclusive. But that is one of the most difficult challenges campaigns face in trying to reach a winning coalition.

Finally, predict what your opponent's coalition will look like, and identify the friction points between the two campaigns. The single most important factor that will impact your strategy is your opponents' strategy. So, figuring out how they might win and how you think you can win will give you the overlay—the playing field where the contest will take place.

For example, in 2006 Republicans lost the women's vote by twelve points. In 2008, Obama won them by thirteen points. Two years later, President Obama's majority coalition had fallen apart and Republicans won women outright by one point, something they had not done during their previous congressional majority. Democrats had counted on women as a key voter group in their winning coalition, and they never expected Republicans to make the kind of inroads with women voters that we saw in 2010. It was a miscalculation that cost them the House.

You must put your plan to build a winning coalition on paper. Your chart or spreadsheet should list the target groups, numerical and percentage vote goals, and the issues and messages that will bring those voters into the fold. For a Republican congressional race, an abbreviated hypothetical coalition might look something like this:

Target Group	Goal	Issue/Message	Vote Total
Registered Republicans	92%	Economy/national security	121,400
Independents	52%	Economy	58,240
Women 55+	50%	Health care	44,000
$50–75K Income	55%	Economy	48,400

For Democrats, those boxes might include registered Democrats, African Americans, single women, union workers, or a host of other possible targets. Geography (i.e., selected counties or precincts) can be a target group if a particular area behaves in a unique fashion. But remember that other demographics may have more impact on voters' political behavior than where they live. For example, eighteen- to twenty-nine-year-olds in Tampa probably have more in common with eighteen- to twenty-nine-year-olds at Ohio State than with the eighty-year-old couple across the street. Given the current communications environment, in which political discourse has become nationalized thanks to cable and the Internet, geography is becoming a lesser factor in targeting. When putting together a coalition, remember that there will be overlap. Many voters will be found in more than one group. Many independents will be in the $50,000 to $75,000 group as well. Don't overcount.

The Weakness of a Base Strategy

Thanks to redistricting, a significant number of congressional districts—both Republican and Democratic—are relatively safe seats. In those races in which the base is large enough to provide the numbers needed to win, a base strategy may work. But for many races—local, congressional, statewide, and presidential—neither party's base is large enough to win outright. The voters who will push a campaign into the win column will be found in the middle. Don't make the mistake of assuming that the base alone can win the race.

Step 5: Create a Strategic Communications Plan

Strategy Versus Tactics

Once the campaign has identified the groups that make up a winning coalition, the next step is to develop an effective message. But don't mistake tactics for strategy. Strategy includes elements like defining the political environment, understanding the opponent's strategy, and developing messages to reach your audience. Tactics are methods for delivering the message and reaching voters, like direct mail, phone banks, social networks, scheduling, advertising, and the Internet. Strategy is like an architectural plan that reflects the wants and needs of the buyer and the environment in which the house will be built. Tactics are the tools to build the house. Strategy creates context for tactical decisions. Don't buy an ad because you think you should buy an ad. Do it for a reason.

Survey Research: Reaching Voters with an Effective Message

During your situational awareness phase, survey research can be a major source of crucial information about voter concerns. You may also be able to gather information from public polls and other resources. But as you put together strategic messaging, internal survey research is critical because it helps you listen to voters, learn what they're thinking, develop policy positions to address their concerns, and then develop a message for the candidate so he or she can lead. All candidates have a series of issue positions. Surveys should not be used to decide a candidate's position on issues but to assess the strength of a particular issue with a particular group. If one of your target groups is married women with children, survey research can identify their number one issue and the components of that issue. For example, it could be jobs or the cost of health care. It could be worries about how to pay for college, care for an aging parent, or deal with the national debt. Survey research can tell you which issues to emphasize with each of your target groups and gives you the ability to test the effectiveness of your candidate's issue messages and those of your opponent.

Strategic Communications

David Ogilvy, a giant of modern advertising, said, "The results of your campaign depend less on how we write your advertising than on how your product is positioned." Ultimately, it is a candidate's positions—not money, not consultants, and not campaign managers—that will make or break a campaign. Does anyone think that Barack Obama would have won the Democratic nomination in 2008 if he had supported the war in Iraq? Positioning matters.

When developing a strategy, it's important to do an analysis comparing the strategic messaging for your campaign and your opponent's. It's called a communications matrix, and it's an exercise to help you predict what the campaign narrative will look like in the months ahead. The matrix looks like this:

	Us (About our candidate)	Them (About our opponent)
Us (What we say)		
Them (What they say)		

The upper left quadrant is what are you are going to say about your candidate—what you are going to emphasize about his or her issue positions—in communications with the key groups identified in your winning coalition. The upper right quadrant reflects what you are going to say about the opponent. The lower left quadrant is what the opponent will say about your candidate, and the lower right is what the opponent will say about himself or herself.

This tool gives you a starting point for a campaign discussion based on the issues you want to talk about. Once the communications matrix is completed, you take the potential messages from each quadrant and test them using survey research to determine who wins the battle of strategic messaging. If candidate A says, for example, "The economy is on the verge of catastrophe. We need another stimulus bill to get the country moving," and candidate B says, "The country is facing tough economic times, but tax cuts for small business to create jobs is the answer, not spending billions for pet projects," how do voters react? Strategic communications is the single most important element of your strategy because winning campaigns are all about delivering a well-constructed argument as to why voters should choose their candidate.

Voter's Memory Process

Political strategic communications is impacted by what is called the voter's memory process. Average people respond to three triggers that determine whether something is remembered or not. First are issues that interest voters. Recently, the issue of the economy has swamped all other issues, and voters remember what candidates have to say or not say when it comes to their economic plans for the country.

The second type of memory trigger is what I call a sudden dramatic change. 9/11 is a good example of a searing memory that results from a highly emotional, vivid experience. Politically, we saw soccer moms suddenly become "security moms" as they watched people die in real time on television. Polls at the time showed the national security and defense issue, which had been at 4 or 5 percent, jump to 25 percent. The terrorist attack on a school in Breslan, Russia, just a few weeks before the 2004 election is another example of a dramatic moment that voters, especially women with children, remembered as they cast their vote for president that fall.

The third memory trigger is, in reality, no trigger at all. The fact is that the vast majority of voters simply aren't interested in politics. Too many politicians run ads based on what interests them rather than what connects with voters—which explains the failure of so much political advertising and messaging on both sides. People don't remember what doesn't interest them.

For example, I am not interested in quilting. You could create the most compelling ad about quilting ever made and I wouldn't remember the message. A lot of political messages are the advertising equivalent of a quilting ad. When the ads don't work, campaigns sometimes make the mistake of simply cranking up the buy or pumping up the volume with a harsher tone. Too much of what passes for strategic campaign communications today is based on this methodology. Moreover, too many campaigns don't understand why they're not getting through to voters and as a result spend even more money to fund ineffective messages.

If the challenge of every campaign is to develop a communications strategy and message that engages voters, then it must reflect the most important element of strategic communications—getting the issue mix right. Here is an example of a Republican strategic communications effort that worked because it addressed high gas prices, a key concern of voters in the summer of 2008.

With the ban on offshore drilling scheduled to be lifted at the end of the fiscal year, the question facing the House was whether to extend the ban or let it expire. The Democrats' liberal leadership had a record of inflexibility when it came to drilling and maintained its antidrilling views even with gas prices going through the roof. Democrats had the votes to extend the ban, but they didn't count on a concerted strategic communications effort by House Republicans who had long opposed the ban as a roadblock to energy independence, lower prices, and national security. Republican leaders argued for an "all of the above" energy policy that included drilling along with more funding for other energy sources like wind, solar, and biofuels. They drove home the point with assistance from vocal advocates for the policy like Newt Gingrich, and within weeks polling data showed that a large majority of Americans favored offshore drilling.

The Democrats got the message. Despite their antidrilling views and the fact that they had the votes in Congress to extend the ban, they decided to quietly let the ban expire. They didn't even take a vote. While 2008 wasn't a good year for Republicans, exit polls showed that Republicans did win voters for whom energy was the top issue. The Republican victory on the energy issue didn't result from an attack campaign against the Democratic leadership, but from a strategic campaign to offer voters a positive policy alternative on an issue that interested them. If you've got the right issue, the right position, and the right message, it is possible to win even as the minority. That lesson was learned by House Republicans and became the impetus for their "winning the issues" strategy after the election.

Means-End Theory of Communications: Laddering

Engaging the voter is the name of the game in strategic communication. But how do you make a personal connection with a voter who may be interested in the campaign but more likely is not? One method is called *laddering*. It is a process of seeing issues in a way that connects your campaign and candidate with voters and their values through language. On paper it looks like this:

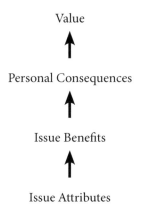

Value

↑

Personal Consequences

↑

Issue Benefits

↑

Issue Attributes

- Issue attributes are various policy components of the issue.
- Issue benefits are the results of the policy—the outcome.
- Personal consequences are the ways in which the outcome affects voters personally.
- Values are the ways in which the consequences mesh with voters' life goals.

In practice, here's how laddering works with a real issue: a 5 percent tax cut. To reach a more conservative voter, the language laddering might go like this:

Issue	**Favor a 5 percent tax cut.**
Issue benefit	"You will have more money in your pocket."
Personal consequences	"You can afford your child's education."
Value	"You are a good parent."

For a more liberal voter on the same issue, the laddering might go like this:

Issue	**Oppose a 5 percent tax cut.**
Issue benefit	"The government gets to keep more resources it needs in order to help people."
Personal consequences	"More low-income elderly can get better health care."
Value	"You are a good citizen."

Both of these examples show how to approach issues in a way that goes far beyond a policy discussion to create a personal connection between an issue and a voter's values—something that is important to him or her.

Allocating Resources

Reaching voters is not inexpensive. Whether it's through TV ads, paid television media, earned media, or new technologies, making that personal connection to voters through shared values is likely going to be the most costly part of any campaign budget. As you do your targeting and put together a potentially winning coalition, put a dollar figure on the cost of reaching each target group. You must know not only who you are going to reach and what you are going to say to them, but how you're going to reach them, how much it will cost, and whether you can raise the necessary funds. If not, go back to the drawing board.

Managing Strategy

Once a strategy is defined, too many campaigns assume that is how it's all going to play out. Winston Churchill said of strategy, "However beautiful the strategy, you should occasionally look at the results."

The military has a useful management tool that can help you manage your strategy. It's called an OODA loop:

- **Observe**
- **Orient**
- **Decide**
- **Act**

After you've begun to implement your strategy, the next step is to observe how your strategy is performing. This often begins by doing survey research, which provides a statistically based analysis of the campaign's impact and progress.

From those observations, you move on to the next stage: orienting, which is determining what has worked and what needs changing. Orienting is the process of learning from your observations and then developing options that move your strategy forward.

From those options, you decide which actions to take and then you execute them. Then you return to observation to see the impact of your actions and repeat the process. The faster a campaign can employ an OODA-loop self-assessment, the greater chance the campaign has to stay a step ahead of its opponents

Campaigns that lack an effective strategy based on the elements I have described in this chapter are unlikely to be successful. In 2006, Republican leaders operated on the assumption that it would not be a national election and so they believed success depended on turning out the base. Strategically, they couldn't have been more wrong. It was obvious months before the election that it was going to be nationalized and that a base turnout would not be sufficient to win. It didn't matter if the GOP turnout operation was better. It didn't matter if the television ads were better. The strategic assumptions were wrong, and Republicans lost badly. In 2010, Democrats made an equally devastating strategic miscalculation. Strategy matters.

Once again, "Strategy without tactics is the slowest route to victory. Tactics without strategy is the noise before defeat." Without a viable strategy based on a winning coalition, a campaign can make a lot of noise but is unlikely to make the kind of progress needed to win.

3

The Use of Survey
Research in Campaigns

GLEN BOLGER

Introduction

The controversies over polling during the 2012 election are significant, but they also divert focus from the point of survey research in campaigns. The most important use of polling for a campaign is as a planning tool, not as a predictor. The predictive value of polling understandably gets the most attention from the press and public, but campaign operatives use polling to make a whole host of decisions throughout the race. Tweaking targeting, modifying message, and reallocating resources are all key decisions made with the input of polling.

Many congressional campaigns stop polling ten to fourteen days in advance of an election, and a lot can change during that final course of the campaign. For instance, an election-night survey done by my firm, Public Opinion Strategies, found that voters who decided in November 2012 how they were voting (that is, late deciders) broke to the Democratic congressional candidates by fifteen points, which helps explain why Democrats won most of the close congressional campaigns.

Another key to the 2012 election is that Democratic voters who flirted with voting for down-ticket Republican candidates before the election ended up mostly voting a straight ticket. For instance, there were very few Democratic voters who voted for Barack Obama and then switched and voted GOP for Congress or governor.

This is not to slight the importance of the predictive capabilities of polling. In the 2012 general election, the most important part of accurate polling was determining the partisan, racial, and generational mix of the electorate. When pollsters got the mix of the electorate correct, they were generally accurate. Democratic pollsters were generally more on the mark than Republican pollsters, because Democrats had a model that looked like the 2008 electorate, while Republican pollsters looked at a partisan blend of 2008 and 2010. However, even then most of the polling done on the Republican side was on the mark.

In addition, most of the presidential primary polling was extremely accurate. The few instances in which it was not spot-on involved primaries in which the race was too close to call, or in which an event changed the situation. For example, few polls caught Newt Gingrich's rapid rise to win South Carolina, but most of the polls shut down before he had several debate lines that galvanized an uncommitted primary electorate.

The most important shift in aiding the representativeness of polling during the 2012 election cycle was the widespread acceptance by campaigns of cell phone interviewing. Contrary to conventional wisdom, campaigns are often resistant to doing things differently than they did before—particularly if it is an incumbent campaign. The thinking goes something like this: We won before by doing a, b, and c in our campaign; we should do that again, and not risk time and money on doing x, y, or z. Presidential campaigns tend to be the exceptions to this rule. They have the deep pockets to innovate and try new technologies.

Cell phone interviewing on the statewide and congressional district level, despite being a more expensive method of interviewing, was widely accepted by campaigns, as candidates and managers alike recognize that landline only interviewing is not fully representative anymore. When cell phones first came into widespread use as a replacement for landlines among younger voters, I theorized that as younger people (more specifically, younger voters) bought homes (instead of renting), got married, and had kids, they would shift to cell phones plus landlines, but I must admit my theory has proven wrong, as the move away from landlines has continued.[1] In the future, the number of interviews conducted with cell phone respondents will have to increase, and it could be 50 percent or higher by 2016.

This digression into the predictive nature of polling is not to pat the industry on the back. There are times when polling fails to pick up late movement in a campaign or incorrectly models turnout of different partisan, age, or ethnic groups. Instead, the tangent is to ensure that the topic of accuracy is not skipped over. After all, pollsters who work for campaigns have a huge economic incentive to be right. Partisan pollsters who are consistently inaccurate will soon run out of clients as word of their inaccuracy spreads. Unlike weathermen and football prognosticators, pollsters who work for campaigns need to be consistently right or they will soon be starving pollsters.

Political writers and columnists like to admonish their readers to take partisan polls with a grain of salt. As a partisan pollster, I am amused by their comments; a partisan pollster who is wrong becomes a pariah in their own party. They certainly have a lot more pressure than media pollsters to be right. When a media pollster is consistently wrong, they just chalk it up to changes in the campaign. When a campaign pollster is wrong, the candidate, the media consultant, the direct mail consultant, and the campaign manager do not work with that pollster again. That's worth more than a grain of salt.

A Brief History . . . And a Look Ahead

A brief history of political polling underscores that the industry is still scarred by a pair of seminal events early in its history. The first—the *Literary Digest* fiasco of 1936, which predicted the election of Alf Landon over Franklin D. Roosevelt based on a postcard survey of its readers—happened around the same time George Gallup was honing the techniques of random polling that used a demographically representative sample. So, at the same time that a huge "sampling" was wrong because it was not representative, a much smaller but statistically based sampling was on the mark.

The second infamous event was the prediction that Thomas Dewey would defeat Harry Truman. The prediction was based on a survey done by Gallup three weeks prior to the 1948 election and is still cited by critics as an example of the inaccuracy of polling (although it is primarily cited by candidates on the brink of defeat, nearly all of whom go on to lose). Indeed, polling can be inaccurate. However, the 1948 debacle taught pollsters and campaign operatives that campaigns matter, that undecided voters are crucial, and the campaign is not over until the last ballot has been cast.

There is little doubt that Truman was behind for most of the 1948 election season, but he garnered momentum by hitting on a compelling focused message just about the time swing voters were really focusing on the choice. The Gallup poll may well have been right at the time it was taken, but events during the campaign caused opinions to shift. Of course, the "Dewey Defeats

Truman" photo is one of the most famous touchstones in American political history, giving hope to underdog candidates and snarky political columnists alike.

At the same time as George Gallup was developing his methods and reputation, Elmo Roper was also improving polling techniques. Political polling was boosted by Lou Harris, who became the first truly national political pollster by working for John F. Kennedy's presidential campaign in 1960. This was the first time ever that a presidential campaign had hired a pollster. Up until that point, campaigns had followed the polls in the press. Harris worked mostly for Democrats, but he also polled for a few Republican candidates.

Harris eventually veered away from polling for campaigns and focused on polling for nonpolitical clients and for the press. The next step in campaign polling took a few more years, when Republican pollsters such as the late Richard Wirthlin and the late Bob Teeter, as well as Democratic pollsters such as Peter Hart and Pat Caddell, became crucial members of campaign strategy teams. These were the fathers of the modern political polling firm. They also did nonpolitical work, but their reputation came from their roles as polling gurus for their respective partisan clients, be it Wirthlin for Ronald Reagan or Caddell for Jimmy Carter.

They also were major innovators. For example, Wirthlin created the modern nightly tracking poll, and Teeter created dial testing of ads and debates. Many of the polling firms in the political business today can trace their roots back to those earlier firms, as entrepreneurial people got experience at those firms before leaving to start their own companies. In the interest of full disclosure, I got my own start in polling working for Dr. Wirthlin, and it was the best opportunity to learn the industry that I could imagine. The idea of integrating survey research into campaigns blossomed during the 1970s and was standard operating procedure by the 1980s.

Nowadays, forty-one firms are listed as being in the business of polling in the *Political Pages,* a reference guide for campaigns published by *Politics* magazine (again, in the interest of full disclosure, my firm, Public Opinion Strategies, has one of those listings).

Political pollsters face a myriad of challenges as we move forward. The first four decades of widespread polling for campaigns was relatively easy: everyone had landlines. The key was to ensure that you had the right geography and turnout models. Now, turnout models remain important, but the geography is easier because of the proliferation of computers and software. These days, declining cooperation rates are driving up the costs of campaign polling, which worries budget-conscious campaign managers. As noted earlier, voters who have only cell phones are a growing percentage of the electorate. Internet surveys are not representative—the samples are too young (which is the ironic opposite of many landline phone polls), too white, and too well educated. So, while the Internet appears to be ubiquitous in American life, it has not quite reached the penetration levels of television or of the good old landlines back in the day.

Another challenge is the rise of public polling in specific campaigns. While polls in campaigns have been around a long time, the sheer number has sky-rocketed. There used to be perhaps one or even two public polls during a campaign. Now it seems they are done on a weekly basis. The challenge is that while the campaign may have a plan to come from behind, the added pressure from public polls creates a "get in the lead now" mentality that makes it more difficult for challengers to build the momentum and fundraising they need to win at the end.

Four years ago, I wrote with concern about the direction of political polling. It is still something the industry must figure out, but the use of a blended methodology of cells and landlines has been tremendously helpful in moving forward. In 1936, 1948, and 1960, political polling stood at a crossroads. The same is true in 2012, but campaign polling has become such a staple of modern campaigns that political survey research will adapt to changing times.

The Four Elements of a Winning Campaign

There are four key elements to a winning campaign.

Candidate Quality

In a swing state or a congressional district where both political parties have a roughly equal chance of winning, the better candidate generally wins the election. That's not necessarily true in a district that tilts more heavily toward one party over the other, but in the bundle of toss-up races—for example, partisan control of the US House of Representatives is decided—the better candidate wins. The tricky part in a campaign is how voters decide who is the better candidate.

Some years, such as 1994, 2006, 2008, and 2010, the decision was heavily weighted toward the candidate belonging to the party perceived to be not "totally screwing up" Washington. In other years, such as 2000, 2002, and 2004, the result was based primarily on voter judgment as to who was the better person and more in tune with their values and issues. The most recent election,

2012, was relatively unique in recent American politics. Voters decided that they thought the direction the president was taking the country was generally the right one, so it was a relatively status quo election—Democrats retained control of the White House and the Senate. However, there is also support for a check and balance in which one party does not control all levers of the federal government, so Republicans retained control of the House and expanded their control to thirty governors' offices.

Sometimes, the contrast in candidate quality is easy to spot. In 2012, failed Missouri Republican Senate candidate Todd Akin was never taken seriously again after his incredibly stupid (and wrong) comments on rape. The voters in the Show Me state were shown all they needed to see about him. In other cases candidate quality differences are harder to spot.

Strong candidates also have the ability to overcome national tides and turn swing districts into safe districts. In 2006, Peter Roskam ran in an open-seat race in Illinois. Despite running in a Democratic wave year against a Democratic candidate who had a compelling story and was strongly backed by national Democrats like Rahm Emanuel, Roskam won a narrow (fewer than four hundred votes!) victory. Two years later, Roskam further demonstrated how a strong candidate can overcome national trends. In another very good year for Democrats, Roskam easily overcame Barack Obama's presence on the top of the ticket and cruised to a double-digit victory, outperforming John McCain by fifteen points. As a result of Roskam's resounding win in a year in which it seemed like all the stars were aligned for a Democrat to beat him, he faced only nominal Democrat opposition in the two following elections.

A variety of factors go into the sizing up of candidates by the electorate. It's clearly not the same standard of measure from race to race. Some members of Congress are handsome. Many are not. Some members of Congress are articulate. Many are not. Some members of Congress are smart. Some members are less smart. But somehow, either through working harder, hitting the right issue notes, or having a focused message that resonates, they convinced enough voters that they were the better choice.

A Focused Message

Few campaign components matter more than focused messaging. Unfocused campaigns rarely win competitive races. In 1996, popular Nebraska governor Ben Nelson started out as a heavy favorite over Republican Chuck Hagel in the US Senate race. However, Hagel and his campaign team had a disciplined message focused on fighting for lower taxes and Nebraska values. Nelson never had a message other than "You like me as governor, so send me to Washington." Hagel's focused message allowed him to slingshot past Nelson. The Democrat's campaign began to flail, putting up a new ad with a new message seemingly every other day. To be fair, sometimes a campaign flails around for a message because nothing is working. Its opponent has run over it like a freight train, and nothing can fix that.

Candidates get off message for different reasons. They may feel they need to talk about every issue to show how smart they are, or they take advice on their message from too many people and keep switching it up. It's okay early in the campaign to tinker with the message, but by Labor Day the campaign needs to exercise message discipline for the home stretch.

In one 2012 campaign that I polled for, Republican Chris Collins challenged freshman Democrat Kathy Hochul. In the final weeks of the campaign, Hochul attacked Collins for owning companies that sent jobs overseas. The Collins campaign had similar research on Hochul, specifically that she had profited from companies that sent jobs to China, and it was tempting to launch a counterattack on that issue. However, our message from the start of the campaign had been that Hochul was not a good fit for the district due to her consistent Democratic voting record. Rather than getting dragged down into a fight over outsourcing, the Collins campaign decided to stay consistent with messaging. This decision paid off, and Collins was one of the few Republican challengers to knock off an incumbent Democrat.

The need for a focused message is simple: campaigns never know when voters are going to pay attention to the race. Thus, when swing voters tune in, it is best if they hear your strong, consistent message. Do not use presidential races as a model for other campaigns. No campaign for any other office comes close to getting the amount of attention that a presidential campaign receives. Do not assume voters know why you should be elected just because you have told them. Tell them again and again. A focused message matters.

Enough Money

As stated in the Book of Ecclesiastes, the race goes not always to the fastest nor the battle to the strongest. Famed writer Damon Runyon noted that while this may be true, the safe bet is usually for the fastest and the strongest. In politics, the campaign with the most money usually wins, but not always. It is a rare challenger who wins by outspending the incumbent. When that happens, it is often the sign of a lazy or corrupt incumbent—lazy because incumbents should never raise less money than their challenger, or corrupt and unable to raise funds from anyone worried about being associated with such a problem person. But challengers do win occasionally. The same is true of open seats: generally the campaign that spends more wins, but not always.

The debate over raised funds in the 2012 campaign centers around Super PACs, and this will continue in upcoming years. In the interest of full disclosure, I did a significant amount of work for a number of Super PACs, including Restore Our Future (which was instrumental in helping Mitt Romney win the Republican nomination), American Crossroads, and Americans for Prosperity.

A Strong Grassroots Operation

The volunteer component of a campaign often gets overlooked by political professionals, but a grassroots operation that combines the latest technology and targeting tools with old-fashioned voter contact is crucial in a close race.

The Democratic advantage on grassroots campaigning in 2012 was striking, and it helped to significantly increase Obama's margin of victory, while also pulling countless weaker Democratic campaigns over the finish line. The Obama campaign effectively utilized an approach that blended "high tech and high touch" in a savvy neighbor-to-neighbor campaign that blunted the GOP's advantage by turning out voters who had been part of Obama's 2008 victory but had shown no interest in the 2010 election. Getting younger voters and minorities to turn out at levels equal to or higher than those of 2008 was an impressive feat of grassroots politics.

Summary of the Four Elements

Good polling helps shape the first two of the four elements of a winning campaign—candidate quality and having a focused message. Before antipolling conspiracy theorists shout "Aha, I always knew polling is evil because it helps candidates be chameleons and hide their true nature," let me clarify. Good polling helps shape candidate quality by better understanding what aspects of a candidate's background and issue priorities resonate most with voters. It is very difficult to change a candidate's basic personality and charisma. Voters tend to see through phonies. However, given that nearly all campaigns have a limited ability to communicate with voters, it is always best to highlight aspects of a candidate's background that matter most. Why spend money (a finite, very precious resource in most campaigns) highlighting something that doesn't matter to the electorate?

So, while disappointing to conspiracy theorists, polling helps a campaign improve the presentation of candidate quality to the voters. Polling cannot give a candidate charisma, intelligence, or that innate ability to connect with people. But it *can* help keep the candidate and the message focused instead of veering off into a message no-man's land.

Why Do Campaigns Poll?

Good polling helps a campaign spend its resources more intelligently. A campaign faces many decisions, but it boils down to a simple formula: delivering the right message to the right target groups. Nearly every decision in a campaign revolves around one or both of these questions:

- WHAT is our message? Polling is done to develop the communications strategy. What does the campaign say to voters to attract the desired percentage (often 50 percent plus one, unless there are multiple candidates) of the electorate?
- WHO are our target groups? Polling is done to define the campaign's target audience. Who does the campaign need to speak to in order to get the targeted percentage of the vote?

Rather than just guessing at target groups or hoping they've picked the right message, campaigns use polling to help refine those decisions. Just as the business adage says, "You've got to spend money to make money." A campaign must spend money on polling to better allocate the rest of its money. Why would a campaign want to spend money pushing a message that does not work, or targeting groups that it either can't win over or already has locked down? Polling helps avoid those mistakes.

There is a perception that politicians use polling excessively, leading them to make decisions they might not otherwise make. There is also a concern that politicians use polls to manipulate public opinion. Some of that may occur. However, it is far more limited than many fear. In the twenty-eight years I've been a pollster, there have only been a handful of times that a member of Congress has ever called me to talk through an issue before voting on it in the House or Senate. And even then, it was not to make the decision, but to gather more information to factor into a decision. One could make a case that, in a democracy, politicians ought to have more information about the standing of public opinion. Candidates use polling to help them make decisions about the campaign. Early polling is used to identify target groups, test themes and messages, and measure accomplishments.

How Campaigns Use Polls

There are eight good uses of polling in a campaign. Not all of them apply all of the time to every campaign, but these are the most common ways in which campaigns can benefit from polling.

Measure the Mood of the Electorate

As 2006, 2008, and 2010 showed, sometimes the political environment is a far more powerful factor than anything else in the campaign. However, just because those three elections were driven primarily by the political environment does not mean that future elections will be. After all, from 1996 to 2004 House and Senate races were primarily determined by the four elements of a winning campaign, because the political environment was mixed to neutral. The 2012 campaign proved to be a triumph of grassroots and candidate skill over the political environment (although the political environment was improving).

The key questions are: What is the political environment, and how does it impact the campaign? Is there a mood for change? Is the electorate angry, and if so, is it aimed at one party, or both? What is the partisan split in the electorate? What impact are the other races on the ticket having on your campaign? For example, in 2012 there was little to no ticket-splitting. Democrats who looked ready to vote Obama on the top of the ticket and Republican down-ticket ended up staying loyal to their party. Senator Dean Heller in Nevada was the only Republican to win a Senate or Gubernatorial race in a state carried by Obama.

Polling questions that measure the political environment include:

Would you say that things in the country are going in the right direction, or have they pretty seriously gotten off on the wrong track?

If the election for US Congress were being held today, for whom would you vote [ROTATE] . . . the Republican candidate . . . or . . . the Democratic candidate?

Do you approve or disapprove of the job Barack Obama is doing as president?

Do you approve or disapprove of the job the US Congress is doing?

Confirm Issues and Measure Intensity

It is rare that a survey will discover a "magic issue" that has not been part of the public debate thus far. Instead, issue questions are good for measuring:

- Overall attitudes
- Intensity
- Wording nuances
- Key target groups for those issues

Overall attitudes are important. If your candidate is on the right side of a 70 percent issue and your opponent is on the wrong side of the issue, usually it is a good one to drive. Highly polarized, fifty-fifty issues aren't nearly as good, unless the intensity and the independents are on your side.

Sometimes with issue questions, it is good to split-sample (ask half the respondents one wording, and the other half a slightly different version) to see which language about an issue resonates more.

Key target groups are important, because analyzing the cross-tabs tells campaigns which issues allow the campaign to be fought on their strength issues, and which issues benefit the opponent.

Examples of Issue Questions

The sample questions in this chapter are from campaigns on which I have worked, and they are reworded as needed to fit different issues and campaigns.

Which *one* of the following issues is currently *most* important to you in deciding how to vote for US Congress?
[RANDOMIZE]
1. The economy
2. Social Security and Medicare
3. Education
4. Health care
5. Moral values
6. Terrorism and homeland security
7. Taxes and spending
8. Energy and gas prices
9. Illegal immigration
10. Jobs
11. None of the above [DO NOT READ]

12. Don't know [DO NOT READ]
13. Refused [DO NOT READ]

Based on everything you have seen, read, or heard, do you approve or disapprove of the Obama health care law?

[IF APPROVE OR DISAPPROVE, ASK:] And would you say you *strongly* [approve or disapprove] or just *somewhat* [approve or disapprove]?
1. Strongly approve
2. Somewhat approve
3. Somewhat disapprove
4. Strongly disapprove
5. Don't know [DO NOT READ]
6. Refused [DO NOT READ]

Thinking now about the House Republicans' Medicare plan, I would like to read you two statements about what Democrats and Republicans are saying about the plan. After I read each statement, please tell me which one comes closest to your own opinion.
[ROTATE STATEMENTS]
1. Republicans say that Medicare is going bankrupt and this new bipartisan plan is optional, will give seniors choices in their health care, and will preserve Medicare for future generations.
2. Democrats say that the Republican plan ends Medicare as you know it and that it privatizes Medicare through a voucher system and gives insurance companies too much control over your health care.
3. Don't know [DO NOT READ]
4. Refused [DO NOT READ]

The first survey question above is an example of measuring voter priorities—what issues do they care most about? Generally, in 2012 the top issues were the economy, spending and the national debt, and jobs. Certainly campaigns could talk about other issues (Medicare, for example), and did, but the voters wanted those three issues to be a major part of the conversation.

The second question is an example of measuring attitudes on a specific issue (Obama's health care law) that was a huge part of the policy debate. It may not have been at the top of the priority list, but many voters had intense feelings about the issue. One of the challenges that the Democrats faced in 2012 was that independents did not like Obamacare, and thus there were very few swing districts or states where it was a positive. However, while it had proved to be a voting issue in 2010, it was not as salient in 2012 to voters.

The third question above is an example of combat message testing. In drafting the question in this style, the pollster is matching up as succinctly as possible the arguments that both parties are making on an issue, and seeing which side wins. It does a pollster no good to be dishonest and weaken the other side's argument—that does not accurately measure the coming battle. Democratic pollster Stan Greenberg's Democracy Corps is a good example of a pollster that uses combat message testing very well. In an ad-testing survey during the 2012 presidential election, Democracy Corps tested each candidate's strongest message on the economy:

> Obama Message: Every president inherits challenges. Few have faced so many. Four years later our enemies have been brought to justice. Our heroes are coming home. Assembly lines are humming again. There are still challenges to meet—children to educate, a middle class to rebuild—but the last thing we should do is turn back now.
>
> Romney Message: Let me tell you how I'll create twelve million jobs when President Obama couldn't. First, my energy independence policy means more than three million new jobs, many of them in manufacturing. My tax reform plan to lower rates for the middle class and for small business creates seven million more. And expanding trade, cracking down on China, and improving job training takes us to over twelve million new jobs.[2]

Another great example of combat message testing in 2012 was on the issue of Medicare. When the Democratic attack on Republicans was tested as just an attack with no GOP response given, it clearly hurt GOP candidates. However, when the push-back on the messaging was also tested, the Republican message worked quite well—and most postelection analyses show that the two parties essentially tied on the issue. GOP campaigns were aggressive in their messaging, not ceding the issue to Democrats. Conversely, Republicans could not find ways to neutralize the Democratic attacks on making the rich pay "their fair share." So while Mitt Romney won middle-income voters ($50,000 to $100,000) by six points, Barack Obama's margin among voters earning less than $50,000 gave him the election.

Measure Name Identification and Images

Many decisions about campaign strategy and tactics revolve around the name identification and images of the two candidates, as well as the images of the other key players in the race.

The opening strategy in a race usually depends on whether the candidate is unknown, well known, well liked, known but not well defined, or polarizing. It's helpful to ask open-ended questions about candidates who are well known because it provides the campaign with the building blocks of a message. It is always easier to reinforce a perception voters already believe than to create a new perception.

First Example

I would like to read you a list of names of different people active in politics here in South Carolina. For each one, please tell me first whether you've heard of the person; then, if so, please tell me whether you have a favorable or unfavorable impression of that person. If I name someone you don't know too much about, just tell me and we'll go on to the next one. The first name is Jim DeMint. The next name is Inez Tenenbaum. The next name is David Beasley.

Thinking now just about Jim DeMint, what are the first two or three things that come to mind about Jim DeMint, that is, what is it you like *most* and what is it you like *least* about him? [PROBE] What else can you tell me about that? Is there anything else? Is that all?

Second Example

Now, I would like to read you some names of different people active in politics here in South Dakota. For each one, please tell me first whether you've heard of the person; then, if so, please tell me whether you have a favorable or unfavorable impression of that person. If I name someone you don't know too much about, just tell me and we'll go on to the next one. The first name is John Thune. The next name is Tom Daschle. The next name is Stephanie Herseth.

Third Example

Thinking now about John Thune, what are the first two or three things that come to mind about John Thune, that is, what is it you like *most* about him and what is it you like *least* about him? What else can you tell me about that? Anything else?

This word cloud shows voter responses to a name identification and image question.

Among 51% Favorable to DeMint

Test Potential Themes and Messages

Given the importance of having a focused message, surveys should test the themes that the campaign is considering. There are a variety of ways to do this, but the surveys can test everything from broader messages to specific slogans to see what resonates best.

First Example

Thinking some more about Jim McCrery, I am going to read you a few statements, and after I read each one, please tell me if you think it describes Jim McCrery *very* well, *somewhat* well, *not very* well or *not at all* well.

Is ethical and honest

Cares about people like you

Is out of touch with most people

Second Example

Now I would like to read you some of Chuck Hagel's accomplishments in the Senate, and for each one, using a ten-point scale, with ten being *very important* and one being *not important at all,* please tell me how important each is to you personally. Of course, you can choose any number between one and ten.

1. Increasing local control of education and providing greater opportunities for our young people

2. Increasing agricultural exports, reducing regulatory burdens on farmers, and providing assistance to farmers and ranchers to better manage their operations

3. Providing for a strong national defense and improving our military, especially the quality of life for the men and women of the Armed Forces and their families

Determine the Impact and Intensity of Vulnerabilities

Determining vulnerabilities includes the testing of both self-research and opposition research. Generally there are a lot of opposition research points to test; the survey can help discover which issues move voters. The cross-tabs will show which hits sway undecided voters (and other key groups), and which issues shore up support among weaker groups.

Testing self-research allows the campaign an advance peek at likely opposition messaging and strategy; we learn which hits we have to absolutely push back on, and which attacks we can ignore. Recognize that the candidate often does not want to test self-research, or he or she will want to water down the likely attacks. It is important to remind them that your foe will not water down the attack language; generally, they will make it tougher.

First Example

Now, I am going to read you some statements you might hear about Jerry Weller. And after I read each statement, please tell me if the statement makes you *more* likely or *less* likely to vote for Jerry Weller, or if it would make no difference to your vote.

1. Jerry Weller wrote the legislation that redeveloped the Joliet Arsenal. That legislation has revitalized and attracted jobs and businesses to the area. In fact, Walmart recently announced they will build a large warehouse facility there that will create another one thousand jobs.

2. Jerry Weller has authored alternative fuel legislation that will help move America away from dependence on foreign oil by replacing some of those imports with domestically produced ethanol made from corn and other renewable sources.

Second Example

For whom would you vote if you learned that: [ROTATE]

1. Republican Jerry Weller supports making recent tax cuts permanent, including repealing the death tax, ending the marriage penalty, cutting tax rates, and keeping the per child tax credit.

2. Democrat John Pavich opposes making the recent tax cuts permanent because he says the country is running a huge deficit and the tax cuts help only the rich, not the middle class.

Chart Movement During the Race: Overall and Among Subgroups

As the great boxer Joe Louis once said, "Everyone has a plan until they get hit in the face." When the battle is joined, it is imperative to track the race (whether it is monthly, weekly, or nightly depends on the race and the budget). It's important to know how much movement there is, which direction the movement is going, and among what target groups the campaign is gaining or losing ground, so that assessments can be made about how to allocate remaining message and dollar resources.

In a 2008 US Senate incumbent campaign in a conservative state where we had a comfortable lead, we polled almost weekly in September, and then weekly in October. Our opponent was making gains with his positive TV ads, positioning himself as a conservative change agent. The movement by his campaign led us to switch gears and tell voters about the very liberal parts of his record that he was wisely choosing not to talk about. Once he was fully exposed, his unfavorables skyrocketed and his support dropped back down. We also shifted from weekly tracks to more frequent tracks, just to ensure that the overall movement and key groups were where we needed them to be to ensure an easy victory.

Seen, Read, or Heard Question

Thinking some more about the upcoming election for the US Senate, has what you've seen, read, or heard recently regarding Pete Domenici or his campaign for the US Senate given you a more favorable or less favorable impression of him? And what was the source of this information?

Image Trend: Pete Domenici			
Date	*Name ID*	*Fav*	*Unfav*
10/07	99%	80%	13%
08/29	98%	76%	16%
06/13	98%	81%	13%
05/16	97%	77%	14%
02/06	98%	81%	12%

Ballot Trend: 2002 Election							
03/01	02/06	05/16	06/13	08/29	10/07	10/28	
68%	71%	67%	71%	66%	67%	67%	TOTAL DOMENICI
18%	21%	25%	24%	25%	25%	27%	TOTAL TRISTANI

Determine the Impact of a Major Hit on Candidates

Is an attack by your opponent hurting your campaign, or can you ignore it and keep the pressure on? What subgroups no longer support the campaign? When a heavy blow hits the campaign, it is vital to get into the field quickly to decide how to handle the situation. Whether to respond or ignore, to shift to defense, or to stay on offense are the key questions that face campaigns when a major punch has been thrown. Perhaps aside from the introduction of the candidate to the voters, the decisions on how to handle negatives are the most important ones of the campaign. There is no single right or wrong approach. Each circumstance is dictated by a variety of factors. Get it right and win. Get it wrong and lose.

In a 2002 congressional race in a truly toss-up open seat district in Nevada, county commissioner Dario Herrera was "the anointed one" for the Democrats. A young, aggressive Hispanic who was a good fundraiser, Herrera was saluted by the pundits as all but a shoo-in. The district was new, as Nevada was expanding from two seats to three (it gained another one in the 2011 reapportionment), and the seat was a toss-up product of a compromise between the Republicans who controlled the state Senate and the Democrats who controlled the General Assembly.

In the spring, Herrera was hit hard by corruption scandals in the press. Las Vegas is a difficult market to burn a message through in earned media, so we polled to see the impact of his scandals. Herrera's image had plummeted from 28 percent favorable and 11 percent unfavorable in a January survey to 23 percent favorable and 21 percent unfavorable in March. We released the survey, and his campaign tried to minimize it, saying that a bad newspaper story wasn't going to affect a November election. That may be true, but our October ads featuring those newspaper stories did affect the election, as Herrera only got 37 percent of the vote.

First Example

As you may know, last year, while he was a county commissioner and candidate for US Congress, Dario Herrera received a no-bid $42,000 consulting fee from a political supporter who is the executive director of the Las Vegas Housing Authority. The housing authority's board members were not told about the contract and said that Herrera did little to earn the money. Board members also said the money should have been spent to help house the needy, not on a public relations contract for a politician. Does this information make you *more* likely or *less* likely to vote for Dario Herrera, or does it make no difference to your vote?

Second Example

As you may know, Christine Jennings filed an unsuccessful lawsuit and also petitioned Congress to overturn the results of the 2006 election. Does Christine Jennings' lawsuit to overturn the results of the past election make you *more* likely or *less* likely to vote for her in the 2008 congressional elections, or does it make no difference to your vote?

Establish Credibility

The campaign team often has to establish credibility with several key players in the race. First and foremost is the candidate. The team should use the survey as the template for the campaign plan, providing the candidate with confidence that there is a reason for the strategy, message, and target groups on which the campaign is focusing.

Second, polling is often used in establishing credibility with donors. Some donors contribute because they are friends with the candidate, while others will write a check out of loyalty or passion because they believe in the cause or the movement. Some donors view their check as worth writing only if the candidate can win, so they need evidence of that viability first. A poll showing a competitive race will open checkbooks, both locally and with the party.

Third, polling can be used to establish credibility with the media. Campaigns should not always release their polls. That would be like the coach of the New York Giants releasing his playbook in advance of the Super Bowl (although that might be the only way for the New England Patriots to win). However, just as there are times that a coach says, "We are going to establish the run," there are times when a campaign can release a poll to show strength or momentum.

In the 2004 South Carolina Republican primary for the US Senate, a poll was released to convince both potential donors and the press that the campaign was more competitive than conventional wisdom had it. Former governor David Beasley led in the polls, but had an underwhelming level of support for a candidate with universal name ID. Given that Beasley was only getting 37 percent on the ballot, there was no way he would survive the runoff as nominee. So, in my role as pollster for the Jim DeMint campaign, I put together a memorandum for release. The release was controversial, and the other campaigns pushed back against it, but the race played out exactly as expected.

PUBLIC OPINION
STRATEGIES

MEMORANDUM
TO: CONGRESSMAN JIM DeMINT
THE DeMINT FOR SENATE CAMPAIGN TEAM
FROM: GLEN BOLGER
RE: KEY FINDINGS—BENCHMARK SURVEY
DATE: FEBRUARY 5, 2004

The Bottom Line

Both candidates who have previously held statewide office have underwhelming numbers in the primary. Both David Beasley and Charlie Condon have higher than expected negatives, and analysis shows they will collapse like a house of cards. Jim DeMint is well positioned to be in a run-off with Beasley, and the anti-Beasley sentiment is significant and will likely propel DeMint to victory.

Key Findings

1. Charlie Condon is barely ahead of Jim DeMint—despite having significantly higher name ID.

While David Beasley leads on the ballot (37%), he is far below 50%. Just so there is no confusion—a former governor who is below 50% on the primary ballot test is in significant trouble. He won't be able to add votes—everyone knows him and 63% prefer not to back him. Underscoring his softness is that only 18% are definitely voting for Beasley—a vote of no confidence in a former governor.

Charlie Condon is in second place, with 19%, while Jim DeMint is just three points behind with 16%. Condon's problem is similar to Beasley—everyone knows Condon, and yet he's only getting support from one in five voters. Conversely, DeMint has half the hard name ID that Condon has, and yet is just three points behind. As DeMint's ID increases, he will easily pass Condon. Thomas Ravenel—who has higher name ID than DeMint—polls just 10%, while Mark McBride is down at 2%.

2. DeMint's ability to win is highlighted by a telling cross-tabs.

Among the voters who are paying closest attention to the race—the 34% of voters who have an opinion of both Beasley and DeMint, Jim leads 42%-30%-10%. Thus, given Jim's substantial cash on hand advantage over Beasley and Condon, once the DeMint campaign gets on the air, he will make significant gains with voters who don't yet know him.

Methodology

The survey was conducted January 12–13, 2004 among 500 likely Republican primary voters statewide and has a margin of error of ±4.38% in 95 out of 100 cases.

Facts and Myths About Push Polling

Besides questions of dealing with a harder-to-reach electorate, the most controversial topic in polling over the last several years is the topic of "push polling." It's controversial because there are a significant number of myths and misperceptions about it—just ask the attorney general and legislators in New Hampshire, who are oblivious to the differences between survey research and push polling and are legally persecuting legitimate survey firms on both sides of the partisan aisle. Hopefully, they will read this portion of this chapter and learn.

Simply put, push polling is not polling. Instead, it is the use of negative advocacy phone calls done under the guise of polling. It takes its name from "push questions," a polling term in vogue during the 1990s that refers to testing factual information about a candidate or candidates to see if that information has any impact on voters.

There are dramatic differences between push polling and survey research:

- Survey research seeks to collect or gather information, not to inform or change it during the process. Push polling is specifically intended to spread information (sometimes true, sometimes false).
- Every survey research firm provides its name or the name of the telephone research center conducting the interviews. Most push polls do not name a sponsoring organization.
- Survey research firms interview a limited sample of people that is designed to mirror the entire population being studied, as low as three

hundred interviews in a congressional district to a high of eight hundred or a thousand interviews in a major statewide study.

- Push polls contact thousands of people per hour with an objective of reaching tens of thousands (or more) of households to "push" their information.
- Survey research firms conduct interviews of between five to over twenty minutes for a major benchmark study.
- Push polls are generally designed to be thirty seconds to two minutes long.
- Most important, push polls are usually done in the last few days of a campaign to thousands (or tens of thousands) of voters, with a three-question script. Push polling is part of the realm of phone banks that typically do GOTV (Get Out The Vote) calls, persuasion, and ID phone calls. Push polling is a type of persuasion call that masquerades as a poll. Actual polling firms do not do push polling because the firms train their interviewers to follow certain interviewer methodologies that push polling does not follow, and because it is outside of the realm of polling.

Survey research firms use different questionnaire design techniques to assess how voters will respond to new information about candidates and their opponents. The intent of this process is not to persuade or change the view of the electorate, but to replicate information that could conceivably be available to the voter during the campaign. Push polls are designed solely as a persuasion vehicle.

One reason for the controversy around the practice of push polls is that sometimes in the past the negative advocacy hit calls pushed messages that were simply not factual. While people will disagree about whether a particular interpretation of a vote is "factual," knowingly using false information has no place in a campaign, and operatives who knowingly use made-up attacks deserve to have their candidates lose.

Do negative advocacy calls under the guise of polling work? Evidence is coming down more and more that the answer is no. It seems to have fallen out of favor in campaigns, as I've heard fewer and fewer instances of it being done late in a race. Instead, phones are being used for GOTV or to drive a straight negative message (instead of disguising the negative information as poll questions).

However, survey message testing is often mistaken for push polling in a campaign. Typically, a campaign tests opposition research messages in a benchmark survey, which tests the political environment, the state of the race, perceptions of the candidates and other key players, and important issues and themes, as well as opposition and self-research messages. Let's say it is a state with an early June primary. After winning the primary, the campaign immediately prepares to go into the field with the general election benchmark survey.

While candidates are often reluctant to test self-research messages, they are a crucial part of campaign polling. First, testing self-research makes it more difficult for your opponent to level the charge of push polling at your campaign. Second, your opponent is almost assuredly going to come after your candidate at some point, and it is better to know how harmful those attacks might be (and with which groups).

By the way, campaigns that level charges of push polling at their opponents are like the kid in that old fable, The Boy Who Cried Wolf But Is Actually a Wolf Too! Most campaigns that do polling also test opposition research, so to test it and then to whine when your opponent does the same thing is both disingenuous and tiresome. Fortunately, it appears that this is a diminishing trend, as fewer campaigns seem to be playing the "push poll" card with the media.

Some have argued that there is no difference between advocacy calls and legitimate polls that test oppo messages. Even with all those counterpoint arguments listed above, another commonsense point is that using survey research to drive negative messages would be the least efficient use of campaign dollars possible.

A statewide campaign may spend $40,000 on a twenty-minute benchmark in June, testing the impact of messages among six hundred likely voters. *If spreading a negative message is the goal of the survey*, that means the campaign spent $67 per respondent ($40,000 divided by N=600) to drive five to seven minutes worth of negative messages that 595 of those participants are going to forget by the next day (believe me, when I get on the phone with a campaign's supporter who took our opponent's survey, they can hardly remember the questions that were asked, and these are the voters who actually are interested in June!). That's not much bang for your campaign buck. Instead, opposition research (and also self-research) should be tested by the campaign to help determine what works and what does *not* work. If an opposition research point is received with a collective yawn, why would the campaign ever spend money on it?

To recap—and like Westley in the Princess Bride, I will use small words so the leadership in New Hampshire can understand—push polling is done with thousands of voters just a few days or weeks before an election. Legitimate survey research is done with a limited random sample, and tests both factual opposition and self-research.

For more resources on push polling, see the website of the National Council on Public Polls at www.ncpp.org/?q=node/41.

Questionnaire Design

Questionnaire design is part science, part art. There are certain components in questionnaire design, including question order. The art component of questionnaire design comes in the wording of message testing questions.

The most important aspect of questionnaire order on a political poll is to ensure that message testing comes after the collection of information about the current state of the race.

There is a saying that surveys should be unbiased. That's true, to a point. Surveys that test messages are conducted to see how voters react to information they will hear during the campaign. The inclusion of this information will unquestionably bias the respondent. Not every survey tests messages, but many do.

An important key to good survey design is to ensure that the information (such as the political environment, name ID and images, ballot tests, and issue priorities) is unbiased and is tested upfront, ahead of the messages. Putting messages prior to those questions is simply pollster malpractice (yes, I've actually seen it done). It is as fundamental an error in polling as leaving LeBron James uncovered in basketball. Think of a poll as a funnel with the widest point at the beginning; the questionnaire starts to narrow and focuses more and more on specifics.

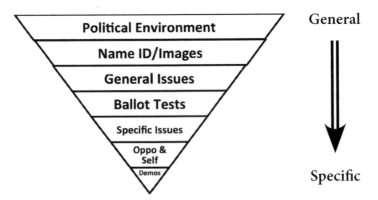

Questionnaires that ask the ballot first have very high numbers of undecideds and refusals. The interviewer needs to earn the respondents' trust or they will become skeptical and refuse to answer the key questions.

The art of wording message questions is crucial. Some firms (on both sides of the aisle, as well as some public polls) skew the question wording to put the best face forward for their client. Candidates and campaigns are ill served by such work. Instead, they are much better off with "combat message development"—taking the messages we want to use in the campaign and testing them against what our opponent is going to say. A careful reading of the opponent's website, as well as articles on the race featuring the opponent, generally provides a clear picture of what the other side believes are its strongest messages.

Combat message development allows the team to play out the campaign in advance, testing your best messages against the other side's best messages. Like a Civil War general, your job is to find the most favorable terrain for your side of the battle and fight on that ground. If your messages are stronger and more relevant, not even Pickett's charge can dislodge them. As you develop the wording of the questions, it is important to be extremely fair to your opponent and their likely message. This makes many clients uncomfortable, but they have to understand that if we don't replicate the opposition message in advance, we're not getting a realistic picture of the fight to come.

Questionnaire development is a crucial phase of the survey process for the entire campaign team. Typically, the campaign team has a conference call with the pollster and throws out images, issues, messages, and oppo- and self-research to test. The pollster should have the backup documents, especially for the oppo-research. The pollster then sends the first draft to the campaign team. That's followed by either e-mails with edit recommendations or a conference call to edit or change the draft. Sometimes the candidate is included in the process from the start, while other times the candidate doesn't care to be involved until nearly the end of the questionnaire development process. The campaign should *always* have final sign-off on the survey; as the saying goes, it's important to "get the fingerprints on the murder weapon." Even when the last edit is a minor change, it is best that the campaign give at least an e-mail sign-off.

The campaign should *never* test opposition research that has not been fully verified. Testing rumors or half-verified research can come back to bite the campaign hard in the derriere.

Early in my career, I received a call from a talented operative who passed along a fortuitous piece of opposition research that had just occurred. I added it to the survey fielding that night. However, neither he nor I tracked down the specific details of the juicier parts of oppo, so we tested a half-truth. And the part that was half-false was truly wrong. The Democratic candidate made a fuss (and rightfully so) about us spreading lies and falsehoods, and the newspaper gave it more life. Fortunately, the GOP candidate won (albeit barely) despite the grievous mistake. It was a valuable lesson: make sure the opposition research information is factual before testing.

Targeting Demographic Subgroups

Targeting is another crucial aspect of polling. There are three types of targeting in a campaign: precinct targeting, microtargeting, and demographic targeting.

Precinct targeting is using previous election results to analyze turnout, the base vote, and the swing vote precinct by precinct in order to be able to prioritize persuasion and GOTV efforts. Precinct targeting should be done by every campaign on every level to allow for better use of the candidate's time, the campaign's focus, and the campaign's volunteer and financial resources. Precinct targeting allows a campaign to prioritize by region, but it has little to do with polling.

Microtargeting allows campaigns to strictly define groups. It uses analysis of large individual and consumer databases of lifestyle information, voter information, social media usage, demographic information, consumer behavior, census data, and geographic data. These data are combined to create distinct groups of voters who can be reached with specific micromessages that will resonate with them. The 2012 Obama campaign used microtargeting at a level never before seen, disseminating their information to volunteers for maximum personalization of contact. Most campaigns do not have the financial wherewithal to maximize their microtargeting like the Obama campaign did, but there are lessons to be learned from their brilliant efforts.

Microtargeting is expensive, but it allows campaigns to reach clusters of specific types of individual voters in a more resonant fashion than other forms of media. While it has survey-like elements to it, microtargeting is not the same as polling. It allows a campaign to prioritize by individuals.

Survey research targeting focuses on demographic subgroups as well as larger geographic regions. A campaign needs to decide what subgroups and regions to focus on. The easiest ways to target in a campaign are the simplest:

1. Geography
2. Party
3. Gender
4. Age

There are certainly other ways to target—race or ethnicity, ideology, church attendance, union membership, or income, to name a few—but the four listed are generally the first four ways to approach a campaign. In areas with high minority populations, particularly Voting Rights Act states in which voter lists have ethnicity on them, race expands the above list of four to five. Use other demographic questions only if the campaign can target those voters. "Nice to know" is not a reason to spend limited survey dollars on a poll question.

The difference between precinct targeting and geographic targeting from surveys is important. The two are complementary and overlapping, not at cross-purposes. Survey targeting by geography tends to be in larger increments. For example, in the Mississippi Senate race of 2008 between Republican Roger Wicker and Democrat Ronnie Musgrove, we looked at geography on two levels in the polling. We analyzed and tracked the race by media market (DMA) and also by geopolitical region, which divided the state into areas of commonality. During the tracking, for instance, we made decisions about where to put increased media dollars, and what the mix of positive and negative ads should be in each media market. We found that certain ads worked well in certain markets, while some worked better in others. Thus, while we had an overall media message and media buy strategy for the campaign, we tweaked it on the fly based on the trends in the daily tracking.

We used geopolitical region data from the daily tracking to decide where to put volunteers and how to focus the candidate's time. We put a lot of volunteer time and effort into the coastal region based on the tracking. And, because of Wicker's strength up north, the campaign also worked to maximize turnout in northern Mississippi.

Demographic targeting from polling is used to make all sorts of decisions for campaigns. I used to say that if Republican candidates have a tie with two of the following three groups—women, seniors, and independents—they'll win. In 2012, like in 2008, only a draw among women guaranteed a Republican win, because the Democrats had a striking advantage on party ID. Romney became the first presidential candidate in exit poll history to outright win independents (by five points) and lose the election. And, of course, Romney won seniors (actually, voters age forty and older) and lost the election because of eighteen- to thirty-nine-year olds!

Regarding gender, a pollster doesn't just analyze men and women, but also younger men, older men, younger women, and older women. In the 2012 election, it seemed there were fifty shades of grey among women—white women and married women voted for Mitt Romney, but he got crushed among single women (divorced, widowed, and never married) and minority women, including African American women, Latina women, and Asian women.

It's also important to look at gender by education. Republicans get absolutely killed among white women with college degrees, while doing well among white women with some college. While it is difficult to target gender by education, media buyers can skew their buys toward those different groups based on the shows they like.

When it comes to partisanship, it is important to analyze five groups, not just three. Instead of just the typical Republican, independent, Democrat cross-tabs, I look at self-identified *base* Republicans, *soft* Republicans, independents, *soft* Democrats, and *base* Democrats. There tend to be significant attitudinal differences between base and soft partisans—at least in elections where there are swings. Base partisans are hard-core supporters who tend to unite immediately behind their party's candidate. Soft partisans are more open to persuasion. A Democratic officeholder who wins a traditionally Republican seat likely won independents by a healthy margin, while at the same time making inroads of 20 to 30 percent into the soft GOP vote. The reverse holds true for Republicans who win traditionally Democratic seats.

Base voters are important, but they rarely determine the outcome of elections. There are exceptions to that rule, with both 2004 (for Republicans) and 2012 (for Democrats) being recent examples. In 2012, most of the Senate candidates who won independents also won the race, although that was not true in Connecticut, Massachusetts, New Mexico, Ohio, Pennsylvania, and Virginia (and possibly others—exit polls were not done in all fifty states).

In most states, campaign partisan targeting should be run from the middle outward, focusing on (in the case of a Republican campaign) messaging to soft Republicans and independents. Given the partisan advantage among Democrats, Republicans also need to pick off some soft Democrats. Anytime you can force your opponent to play defense on their own side of the field, events are usually going your way in the campaign.

Targeting by gender and age allows campaigns to further refine their message. This applies to all campaign messaging, not just direct mail. Targeting ads to women (or men), skewing the buy toward a certain age group, or reaching senior citizens through recorded voice messages are all examples of using cross-tab data to make decisions about which groups need to be moved.

Understanding How to Read Polls

Learning to read and interpret polls takes a long time. Here are a few good rules of thumb that are helpful in an initial reading of the data:

- More than a prediction of the future, polls are a snapshot of the electorate at a specific point in time during a campaign. The purpose of running a campaign is either to change the numbers (if behind) or solidify the numbers (if ahead). Events can also significantly move the numbers. There are times when an experienced pollster can look at the state of the race, know the status of the two campaigns, and suggest what is likely to happen. So polls do sometimes predict the outcome, but it is usually based on knowing the direction the arc of the race is headed.

- The generic ballot is similar to the point spread in a football game. It reflects the degree of difficulty of a race, but the generic ballot does not indicate factors like the quality of the candidates or the strength of their messages.
- A candidate's image (favorable or unfavorable) generally needs to be at a two-to-one (or better) ratio, but candidates at one-to-one do win occasionally (if their opponent has a worse image!). Evaluate images in comparison to each other, not in a vacuum.
- Intensity drives voters. Pay attention to the "definite" vote support, "strong" approval scores, "strongly favor" or "strongly oppose" numbers on issues, and "much more likely" or "much less likely" on message testing sequences.
- Undecided voters generally break heavily *against* well-known and well-defined incumbents. A 48- to 35-percent lead for an incumbent with 90-percent name ID over a challenger with 50-percent name ID is not safe. If undecideds know the incumbent and are not voting for him or her, they will vote for the challenger unless that candidate then becomes negatively defined—which is why you often see incumbents attacking challengers. If your campaign has hit a wall, it is imperative to define your opponent. Remember, there are two kinds of name ID—the good kind and the bad kind. Do not hesitate to give your opponent the bad kind.
- "Informed" ballot tests are nothing more than head-to-head ballot scores after voters have heard (usually negative) information about one or both candidates. Campaigns should not release those informed ballots, and the media should not print them, unless the entire survey is released.
- Media takes time to have an impact, so don't expect to see poll numbers move the moment your candidate starts advertising. Usually it takes about 1,000 to 1,500 gross rating points (GRPs) for an ad to start resonating with the electorate. (Note: One of the worst things a campaign can do is pull down ads before they've accumulated enough GRPs. Unless the ad is over the top or has a factual error, it is best to leave it up for at least 1,000 GRPs so voters start to get the message.)

- Don't discount a poll's result just because the other side released it. More likely than not, the poll was timed to be done after a media buy, so it is very possible the race has moved from your initial reading. The other side's poll may also give you clues as to their next steps in the campaign.
- Don't just look at the overall results; look at the state of the race, the issues, and the message among the key subgroups, especially swing voters. The voter groups who will determine the difference between winning and losing provide a lot of clarity about what is important when analyzing the poll.

The Bottom Line: Campaign Polling

Polling helps a campaign team put together a road map for winning the race. It helps the campaign make decisions about allocating the rest of the campaign's resources. It helps provide focus to the message and direction to the subgroup targeting. Remember, the point of running a campaign is to move numbers; early in the campaign, the ballot test can be among the least important questions.

It is imperative to use early polling to test messages in a way that accurately reflects your potential messages, as well as your opponent's likeliest messages. Early polling also helps provide a firm foundation for the assumptions that the team is making about the campaign. Late polling is important for fine-tuning (or radically shifting) the campaign and the advertising. In a campaign, the goal of polling is to help drive your political strategy, focus your message, and set your target groups.

Notes

1. Stephen J. Blumberg and Julian V. Luke, "Wireless Substitution: Early Release of Estimates from the National Health Interview Survey, January–June 2012," Division of Health Interview Statistics, National Center for Health Statistics.

2. Data from a Democracy Corps and Greenberg Quinlan Rosner memo, "Obama Closing on Progress or Future," released October 19, 2012.

4

Money, Politics, and Policy

Campaign Finance Before and After Citizens United

R. SAM GARRETT

Introduction

Money in politics has captivated the media for decades, but rarely has the topic been as culturally prominent as it became in 2010 and 2012.* Just a few examples from these election cycles illustrate the prominence of fundraising and spending in congressional and presidential campaigns. At the presidential level, campaigns ventured into uncharted territory, as no major candidate chose to participate in the long-standing public financing system. The Obama and Romney presidential campaigns alone raised more than $1.3 billion, without even counting independent but related sums from party committees and other groups.[1] In House and Senate races, some candidates and political parties feared they would lose control of their campaign environments—if they had not already—in light of newly permissible corporate and union funds used to influence elections. New entities known as Super PACs spent some of that money, as did tax-exempt 501(c) organizations. The connections between

---

* This chapter represents the views of the author. It does not necessarily represent the views of the Congressional Research Service, Library of Congress, or any other institution with which the author is affiliated. For additional policy-oriented discussion, see Garrett (2012a; 2012b; 2012c). Anthony Corrado (2005) and Robert Mutch (1988) both offer excellent historical overviews featuring various legislative and regulatory issues. See also Hohenstein (2007) and La Raja (2008).

these entities and traditional actors like parties and candidates appeared to be lost on most voters, even though the groups' activities had to be legally separated from campaigns. Even comedian Stephen Colbert got into the action, using his popular television show to highlight his Super PAC, Americans for a Better Tomorrow, Tomorrow, to poke fun at the state of campaign finance regulation (Garrett 2012a). Some of these developments stemmed from the US Supreme Court's 2010 decision in *Citizens United v. Federal Election Commission*—arguably the most substantial campaign finance ruling in a generation—while others might have been more prominent than in the past but were nonetheless established practices.

Amid these and related developments, popular culture and media reports often portray campaigns as the Wild West, benefitting from—or perhaps fostering—a culture in which winning is everything (Burton and Shea 2003; Nelson, Medvic, and Dulio 2002). Much about daily campaign life is, indeed, more art than science. Political professionals who run campaigns emphasize gut instinct over inflexible plans and norms, although they typically reject the idea that their world lacks ethical boundaries (Garrett 2010; Garrett, Herrnson, and Thurber 2006).

Obviously, practical politics play a tremendous role in the campaign management this book emphasizes. Much of the scholarly literature emphasizes theory, but the study of "applied" politics, as the campaigns-and-elections subfield of political science is sometimes known, includes an ongoing scholarly and professional debate about whether informal "rules" can be applied to campaigns (Burton and Shea 2003; Garrett 2010). These different perspectives notwithstanding, there is one area in which professional rules—and more importantly, federal law and regulation—affect campaign operations. Federal election law—especially campaign finance law—establishes strict requirements that political campaigns, party committees, and virtually every other player in campaigns must follow.

This chapter provides an overview of those rules before and after 2010. As we will see, major changes occurred that year—most notably from the *Citizens United* ruling—that fundamentally altered decades of prohibitions about who can spend money in federal elections and how they may do so. The chapter necessarily discusses law, but it is not a legal analysis.

Instead, this chapter examines selected elements of law, policy, and politics to provide a broad overview of how and why major provisions of the federal campaign finance system arose and, in particular, what changed about that system beginning in 2010. This chapter approaches the topic from two major perspectives. First, it emphasizes the public policy surrounding federal campaign finance. That is, it explores not only the law (which this chapter refers to as statutes enacted by Congress and considered by courts), but also the regulations and other guidance from the Federal Election Commission (FEC), the federal agency responsible for administering most campaign finance law. Second, and in many ways more important for this volume, the chapter considers how major policy changes shaped the environment that candidates for Congress and the presidency face. Readers interested in the latter topic should also consult Anthony Corrado's analysis of fundraising and spending data (Chapter 5).

For those unfamiliar with campaign finance, the topics discussed here might seem esoteric or confusing. Some attention to detail is, indeed, important. Why is it important to understand these requirements? Does the average citizen—or even the average political science student—really need to know that a donor's identity would be disclosed with a contribution of $201 but not with one of $199, that being a "political committee" largely determines whether an entity files campaign finance reports, or that contributions and expenditures are treated differently? Why pay this much attention to seemingly technical details that are, in some cases, now decades old?

The "rules" of campaign finance are important for more than their own sake; they determine who can participate in elections and how. These "details" shed light on why seemingly simple matters can easily be resolved around the dinner table or in a class debate but are harder to address within a constitutional framework or to explain in a way that captures the activities of a diverse set of people and groups that might have only a tenuous connection to election law. Even if one doesn't follow every detail, knowing the basics— such as that some contributors are identified and some are not, that only some entities report their campaign activities, and that contributions are limited but expenditures generally are not—means having more knowledge about campaign finance law than the vast majority of the population, and, in some cases, members of the media.

Understanding why recent developments are so monumental also requires understanding where we have been. To understand the pressing issues of campaign finance policy and practice today—whether one believes they are "loopholes" or opportunities—a basic command of information discussed here is vital.

Major Provisions of Campaign Finance Law Before 2010

To understand why developments since 2010 have been so important, we must first understand how the campaign finance world looked before 2010. Despite some changes ushered in with *Citizens United,* most elements of federal campaign finance law have remained more or less constant for more than forty years. Some provisions go back even farther, to the beginning of the twentieth century. Whether during the past century or the past decade, three factors have shaped federal campaign finance law. First, Congress has set limits on contributions in an effort to limit potential corruption motivated by political money. Table 4.1 provides an overview of contribution limits for the 2012 election cycle.

Second, Congress has occasionally attempted to limit spending—distinct from contributions—although the Supreme Court has generally held spending restrictions unconstitutional. Third, Congress has required disclosure of information about which people and groups contribute to campaigns or independently spend funds to influence elections. On a related note, Congress has restricted the kinds of groups that can contribute to campaigns or spend funds to influence elections. Taken together, this framework of limiting the amount of donations flowing to campaigns (and parties) and tracking the flow of money going to campaigns and being spent to influence them is designed to limit quid pro quo corruption and increase transparency.

Congress first passed a major campaign finance statute in 1907. At President Theodore Roosevelt's urging, arguably in an effort to combat criticism surrounding large contributions to his 1904 reelection campaign, Congress enacted the Tillman Act.[2] The act prohibited contributions from nationally chartered banks and corporations. Other restrictions and reporting requirements followed in the 1910s and 1920s, but the measures were largely viewed as ineffective. Congress banned contributions from labor unions in the 1940s, most notably via the Taft-Hartley Act.[3]

The 1970s: Setting the Boundaries of Modern Campaign Finance Policy

Modern campaign finance law did not emerge until the 1970s, when Congress enacted the Federal Election Campaign Act (FECA) and related statutes.[4] First enacted in 1971 and substantially amended in 1974, 1976, and 1979, FECA remains the nation's primary campaign finance statute.[5] Among other points, FECA and its major amendments required disclosure (public reporting of information) about campaign receipts and expenditures. The act also limits contributions and initially limited spending—although the Supreme Court has generally invalidated spending limits on First Amendment grounds (discussed below). Three kinds of entities, known as "political committees," are principally governed by FECA and related FEC regulations. Political committees include candidate campaign committees (e.g., Johnson

TABLE 4.1 Federal Contribution Limits, 2012 Election Cycle

	To Candidate Committees	To National Party Committees	To Traditional PACs	Aggregate Limit for Entire Cycle
From Individuals	$2,500 per candidate, per election[a]	$30,800 per calendar year	$5,000 per calendar year	$117,000 ($46,200 to all candidates; $70,800 to parties and PACs)
From National Party Committees	$5,000[b] per candidate, per election	Unlimited	$5,000 per calendar year	Unlimited[d]
From Traditional PACs[c]	$5,000 per candidate, per election	$15,000 per calendar year	$5,000 per calendar year	Unlimited

Source: Adapted by the author from Federal Election Commission, "Contribution Limits for 2011–2012," accessed November 24, 2012, http://www.fec.gov/ans/answers_general .shtml#How_much_can_I_contribute.

[a] Individuals may give $2,500 to any one candidate committee during the primary and during the general (and run-off, if applicable) campaigns.

[b] This amount refers to direct contributions, not coordinated party expenditures. Coordinated party expenditures are purchases parties may make on behalf of, and in concert with, candidate campaigns.

[c] This chapter uses the term "traditional PAC" to refer to those PACs permitted to make contributions to federal candidates (i.e., non–Super PACs and not PACs operating under the *Carey v. FEC* exception that permits unlimited independent expenditures from a segregated bank account). This entry in the table also refers to "multicandidate" PACs, which are the most common type of PAC. Multicandidate PAC status is triggered when these committees make certain aggregate contributions to multiple candidates.

[d] This excludes a special $43,100 limit for contributions by party committees to Senate campaigns (shared between the party campaign committees and the national committee [e.g., the National Republican Senatorial Committee and the Republican National Committee]).

for Senate), party committees (e.g., the Democratic or Republican national committees), and political action committees (PACs). All political committees must regularly report their financial activities to the FEC (or, in the case of Senate political committees, to the secretary of the Senate, who transmits them to the FEC).[6] In some cases, individuals and other entities (e.g., interest groups) that engage in political advertising known as "independent expenditures" and "electioneering communications" (discussed below) must also report those activities to the FEC. Finally, the 1974 FECA amendments established the FEC; the 1976 amendments reconstituted the agency after the *Buckley* decision.

Buckley v. Valeo (1976) was perhaps the most consequential campaign finance decision the US Supreme Court has ever issued.[7] In brief, the case considered several challenges to the 1974 FECA amendments. The Court upheld most of the amendments' major provisions but also found some aspects unconstitutional. In one of the most important holdings, the Court distinguished between permissible limits on contributions versus expenditures. Even though contribution limits constrained the donor's political speech, the Court held, doing so was a reasonable effort to limit potential corruption. The decision struck down limits on independent expenditures (e.g., funds spent to advocate the election or defeat of a candidate without coordinating with that candidate).[8] As election scholar Michael Ortiz explains, different potential for corruption influenced the Court's distinction between contributions and spending. According to Ortiz (2005, 92–93), "Simply put, the Court believed that a candidate could become beholden to a contributor but not to someone who merely expended monies on his or her behalf. If expenditures could not indebt a candidate to a voter, they could never give rise to even the appearance of corruption."

Buckley was significant largely because it established a long-standing set of boundaries for which contribution, spending, and disclosure mechanisms were constitutionally valid. From a policy perspective, *Buckley* continues to influence which options realistically can be pursued—namely, that although contributions can be limited and reasonable disclosure can be required, spending generally cannot be limited. The distinction between "express advocacy," which explicitly calls for election or defeat of a candidate (especially in political advertising), and "issue advocacy," which at least ostensibly concerns policy issues rather than electoral outcomes, also took root in *Buckley*. All these topics would become major issues of debate for the next forty years, ultimately building to the 2010 *Citizens United* decision.

Outside Money and Outside Advertising as Emerging Policy Concerns

After *Buckley,* Congress occasionally made narrow amendments to FECA, but the law remained largely untouched for almost thirty years. It would be a mistake, however, to believe that nothing happened in campaign finance law and policy between 1976 and 2002 (when the Bipartisan Campaign Reform Act was enacted) or 2010 (when *Citizens United* was decided). In fact, it could be argued that the major developments that took place in 2010 were not relatively sudden developments, but instead had been building for years. Throughout the 1980s and 1990s, two related issues—the role of "outside" groups (especially PACs) and issue ads sponsored by those groups—demonstrated the intersection of politics and policy.

Starting in the 1980s, thanks in part to the rise of the political consulting industry and the growth of media consulting as a dedicated profession (see, for example, Thurber and Nelson 2000; Dulio 2004; Medvic 2001; Garrett 2010), television ads became a staple in enough House and Senate contests that the issue took on public policy significance even after Election Day. As political advertising became more ingrained in all kinds of campaigns, the public, editorial boards, and legislators lamented the negative tone of "attack" ads, which critics contended distracted from substantive campaigning.[9]

Typically the most important component of a campaign budget, estimates suggest that about 75 percent of all campaign spending goes to political advertising, with two-thirds of that amount dedicated specifically to broadcast television.[10] Although all campaigns rely on advertising, they are also typically wary of it, especially when opponents, parties, and groups running against those candidates take to the air themselves. Developments before and after *Citizens United* affected political advertising and, perhaps ironically, the opposition advertising with which political campaigns are often most concerned. PACs and other groups were central to emerging concerns about the role of outside advertising.

PACs emerged primarily during the 1970s as a result of an FEC advisory opinion (AO), in which, essentially, the Sun Oil Corporation asked the newly created commission whether FECA permitted it to establish a separate fund to make expenditures and contributions despite the law's ban on the corporation itself engaging in such activity.[11] Generating much controversy, the FEC answered affirmatively, thereby blessing the PAC concept and opening the door to the use of a corporate and labor presence in federal elections notwithstanding the FECA ban on corporate and union treasury funds for expenditures or contributions. Congress endorsed the move when it amended FECA in 1976 and 1979.

Importantly, although corporations and unions could (and still can) use treasury funds for limited administrative support of their PACs, they may not use the PAC to funnel treasury funds for use in otherwise prohibited campaign contributions or expenditures. Funds for those purposes must be raised from voluntary contributions, such as from corporate employees or union members, with restrictions on when and how solicitations can occur. Whether these safeguards sufficiently establish a barrier between corporate and labor activity in elections or whether they enable a thinly veiled avenue for corporate and labor influence occupied much of the debate over federal campaign finance policy in the 1980s (see, for example, Biersack, Herrnson, and Wilcox 1994). PACs nonetheless became accepted as a political and policy reality over time, and new policy dilemmas—such as the role of unlimited "soft money"—became more pressing.[12]

Eventually, PACs invested heavily in various activities affecting campaigns. Their role in political advertising—especially ads that were derided as attacks from arguably less accountable "outside" groups (e.g., in contrast to a clearly recognizable opposing candidate)—became a major issue by the late 1980s and early 1990s. Some corporations, unions, and outside groups also began spending directly on commercials known as "issue advertising." Issue ads managed to avoid FECA's ban on corporate and labor treasury funds because the commercials did not trigger *Buckley*'s "magic words" standard, which referred to a specific set of terms understood to be synonymous with calls for election or defeat.[13] By encouraging voters merely to contact members of Congress rather than explicitly encouraging a vote for or against the candidate, issue ads were ostensibly about public policy issues instead of determining electoral outcomes. Issue ads were widely believed to influence elections, even though they were not formally regulated by campaign finance law or FEC rules. This combination of "outside" money and advertising encouraged (among other factors) the next major amendment to campaign finance law—a legislative effort that began in the 1990s and culminated in enactment of the Bipartisan Campaign Reform Act (BCRA) in 2002.

Building BCRA

BCRA represented the first major amendments to FECA since the 1970s.[14] Perhaps most consequentially, BCRA—also known as McCain-Feingold for its principal Senate sponsors, Senators John McCain (R-AZ) and Russ

Feingold (D-WI)—banned soft money in federal elections. In practice, this meant that millions of dollars that political parties previously raised from otherwise prohibited sources (e.g., corporations) for generic "party-building" activities were now off limits. Congress also included in BCRA a provision designed to combat the combination of outside money and advertising that had been on the rise in the 1980s and 1990s. BCRA also contained several other provisions, including adjusting contribution limits (except for PACs) for inflation.

Congress relied on an extensive legislative-history record (including some prominent political science research) to examine whether issue ads were really mostly about public policy rather than influencing elections. BCRA supporters in the House and Senate determined that most issue ads were, in fact, what came to be derided as "sham" issue ads—meaning the communications were widely understood to be aimed at deciding elections even if they conspicuously avoided *Buckley*'s "magic words." *Buckley* precluded Congress from banning the ads outright. Nonetheless, through BCRA, Congress created a new category of political advertising—electioneering communications—that essentially are treated as campaign ads even if they do not meet the traditional standards of campaign advertising (e.g., express advocacy).

Electioneering communications include only broadcast, cable, or satellite ads, refer to a clearly identified federal candidate, and must be targeted to the relevant electorate. The ads also are aired within sixty days of a general election or within thirty days of a primary—the period when the legislative record suggested was most important for influencing elections. Effectively, enactment of the electioneering communication provision meant that although corporations, unions, or other groups could have used their treasuries to fund ads supporting or disparaging candidates before BCRA, they could not do so during preelection periods after BCRA (assuming the ads met the electioneering communication standard). As a result, the ads either had to be avoided altogether or had to be funded in limited amounts from permissible sources and disclosed under FECA.

BCRA was immediately controversial. Many observers expected at least parts of the act—particularly the electioneering communication provision—to be invalidated on First Amendment grounds. Senator Mitch McConnell (R-KY), one of Congress's leading critics of campaign finance regulation, filed suit to prevent the FEC from enforcing the act. In *McConnell v. FEC* (2003) the Supreme Court held, in a five-to-four decision, that virtually all of BCRA was constitutional—including the soft money ban and electioneering communication provision. The majority ruled that even though parts of the act burdened political speech, Congress had established a reasonable risk of corruption to warrant the restrictions.

Despite initial success in the courts, BCRA remained intact for only two election cycles (2004 and 2006). Critics continued to bring challenges, both in court and at the FEC, which was writing rules to implement the law and various court decisions. By 2007, the Supreme Court again considered the electioneering communication provision—in this instance, not as an inherent or "facial" challenge, as *McConnell* had been, but in an "as applied" challenge that evaluated how the provision affected a specific organization. In *Wisconsin Right to Life* (*WRTL II* 2007), the Court determined that the electioneering communication provision did unconstitutionally burden political speech in some circumstances. In brief, the majority sided with a tax-exempt corporation's (Wisconsin Right to Life) appeal to use its treasury funds—rather than having to form a PAC and adhere to other FECA requirements—to air electioneering communications that urged speedy votes on judicial nominees. The details of *WRTL II* are not essential for this chapter, but it is important to note that, as a policy matter, the case was significant because it marked the beginning of the end for key aspects of the electioneering communication provision. Essentially, it again opened the door to corporate treasury funds in elections, albeit in limited circumstances—and set the stage for far greater changes in 2010.

Citizens United: A Major Change in Campaign Finance Law for the 2010 Election Cycle

Immediately following the 2008 elections, when Barack Obama was elected president and Democratic majorities won House and Senate contests, the next election cycle began. Although the 2010 congressional elections were expected to be competitive, observers did not anticipate that, in the midst of those elections, a major change would occur in campaign finance law. These developments were substantial not only for the policy boundaries they created, but also because they directly affected which groups could advocate for or against candidates.

Citizens United is notable for a variety of legal, policy, and practical political reasons. Like *Buckley* before it, *Citizens United* also is important for reasons that extend far beyond the case itself. Indeed, especially as it was first presented, *Citizens United* addressed a relatively narrow question about applicability of the electioneering communication provision. The implications of the case, however, were far broader. By the time the Supreme Court issued its five-to-four decision on January 21, 2010, advocates had come before the justices not the standard single time, but twice, and the Court had expanded the issues in play. Essentially, the attorneys were asked to address the questions they had initially presented and whether those questions also had implications for other Supreme Court precedents which, in turn, had major implications for the nation's campaign finance law—and, thereby, policy questions for Congress and federal agencies.

This section presents an overview of those developments and why they are important for understanding *Citizens United* and its aftermath. Before proceeding, it is important to note that discussion here is intended to be a general academic and policy-oriented overview. Some important constitutional and legal issues are mentioned in passing, but those interested in a detailed legal discussion should also consult other sources.[15]

In *Citizens United,* an incorporated, tax-exempt 501(c)(4) organization called Citizens United challenged the electioneering communication provision. The group presented itself not as an interest group, as the organization was generally perceived, but as a media company that made documentary films. Citizens United contended that its film about then-presidential candidate Hillary Clinton (*Hillary: The Movie*) did not qualify as an electioneering communication and, therefore, that the group should not be required to form a PAC to air the film in theaters and through video-on-demand cable, as it planned to do ahead of the 2012 elections. The FEC disagreed and Citizens United sued.

After a district court sided with the FEC, Citizens United appealed to the Supreme Court, which heard initial oral arguments on the electioneering communication questions in March 2009. In an unusual move, instead of issuing a decision, the Court ordered the parties to file additional briefs and appear again for a second round of oral arguments. Among other questions, the Court asked whether, in order to rule on whether Citizens United's film qualified as an electioneering communication and, as such, had to be paid for with hard money (i.e., by a PAC rather than Citizens United itself), the Court should reconsider its 1990 opinion in *Austin v. Michigan Chamber of Commerce.* In *Austin,* the Court determined that political speech could be restricted based on the speaker's corporate status. *Austin* essentially confirmed that corporations could not spend funds to influence federal elections.

Once the Court broadened *Citizens United* to include not only the status of the electioneering communication provision, but also the broader question of corporate-funded independent expenditures, the case transformed from addressing the relatively narrow question of whether the electioneering communication provision applied to limited-distribution films, to considering the much broader question of corporate independent expenditures in general. The case, therefore, now had the potential to alter the decades-old ban on corporate spending in elections, in addition to, or maybe even regardless of, the electioneering communication issue. The legal and policy communities immediately took notice both because of the substantive questions involved and because the second round of oral arguments were scheduled for September 2009. Even if an expedited decision was issued as expected, most observers expected that the best-case scenario would be a ruling in the mid- or late fall of 2009—setting the stage for a potentially major change in campaign finance law and practice halfway through the 2010 election cycle.

The Decision: A Brief Overview

In fact, the *Citizens United* decision didn't arrive until January 21, 2010. When the Court issued its ruling, it spurred a policy and public debate over campaign finance issues perhaps never before seen in the United States. *Citizens United* and corporate political spending were suddenly the topic of sustained national news and cultural importance that continue to this day. As this chapter is being written almost three years after *Citizens United,* the case's implications are still unfolding—both in terms of campaign practice and public policy.

In *Citizens United,* the Court overruled its previous decisions in *McConnell* (finding for the constitutionality of the electioneering communication provision generally) and *Austin* (regarding the government's ability to restrict independent political speech based on the advertiser's corporate status), among other points. What does this mean for the more general discussion here of the case's implications for campaign finance policy and campaign practice? At least three issues in *Citizens United* are relevant for the policy and political issues discussed in this chapter. First, was *Hillary: The Movie* an electioneering communication (and, therefore, subject to the hard-money funding and reporting requirements in BCRA)? Second, what did the case mean for the FECA ban on corporate independent expenditures? Third, what were the implications for disclaimers and disclosure—both of which provide regulators and the public with information about funding surrounding expenditures?[16] All three issues are related, particularly those of the spending provisions raised in the first two questions.

On the first point, Citizens United contended that the film was a documentary and should be exempt from the electioneering communication provision.

The Court disagreed, finding the movie clearly took a position on Senator Clinton's fitness for office and qualified as an electioneering communication. As the Court explained (*Citizens United* 2010, 8):

> Under the standard stated in *McConnell* and further elaborated in *WRTL*, the film qualifies as the functional equivalent of express advocacy. . . . Citizens United argues that *Hillary* is just "a documentary film that examines certain historical events." We disagree. The movie's consistent emphasis is on the relevance of these events to Senator Clinton's candidacy for President. . . . There is no reasonable interpretation of *Hillary* other than as an appeal to vote against Senator Clinton.[17]

At first glance, this finding was good news for those who supported BCRA and the electioneering communication provision because the Court had rejected the contention that even though the format was not specifically addressed in BCRA (in addition to other technical issues not discussed here), it would not carve out an exception for documentary-style films. Thus, the electioneering communication provision in and of itself did not offer safe harbor for messages that criticized candidates during preelection periods just because the messages were transmitted via on-demand video. If the decision ended there, the integrity of the electioneering communication provision would, indeed, have stood. In the end, however, although the electioneering communication provision survived for disclosure purposes, its restrictions requiring that communications be paid for only with hard money collapsed. For those supporting additional campaign finance regulation, the fate of the electioneering communication provision would become a relatively minor concern in the universe of *Citizens United*.

In an opinion written by Justice Anthony Kennedy (a Republican appointee), the majority went on to say that, essentially, the case had to be decided on broader grounds than just the electioneering communication provision. The option to form a PAC, Justice Kennedy explained, also didn't provide a reasonable resolution because PACs still restricted political speech of the corporation itself (*Citizens United* 2010, 21):

> Section 441b [of FECA, the corporate expenditure prohibition] is a ban on corporate speech notwithstanding the fact that a PAC created by a corporation can still speak. A PAC is a separate association from the corporation. So the PAC exemption from §441b's expenditure ban, §441b(b)(2), does not allow corporations to speak. Even if a PAC could

somehow allow a corporation to speak—and it does not—the option to form PACs does not alleviate the First Amendment problems with §441b. PACs are burdensome alternatives; they are expensive to administer and subject to extensive regulations.

Here we come to the second point noted at the beginning of this section—the question of what *Citizens United* meant for FECA's ban on corporate independent expenditures. In short, *Citizens United* struck down the ban, and in so doing marked the most fundamental change in federal campaign finance law since at least *Buckley*.[18] As a result, corporations were permitted to use their treasury funds—rather than having to form a PAC—to make independent expenditures calling for election or defeat of political candidates. Although the case did not address the ban on union treasury expenditures, it was widely understood also to permit unions to use their treasuries to encourage votes for or against candidates.

The presumption of independence was essential because although the government had long ago established a reasonable risk of quid pro quo corruption arising from *contributions*, the same logic did not apply to independent ads. Although contributions entail the candidate receiving money and potentially being "bought," independent expenditures, by definition, involve no financial exchange with the candidate. As Justice Kennedy explained (*Citizens United* 2010, 45):

> If elected officials succumb to improper influences from independent expenditures; if they surrender their best judgment; and if they put expediency before principle, then surely there is cause for concern. We must give weight to attempts by Congress to seek to dispel either the appearance or the reality of these influences. The remedies enacted by law, however, must comply with the First Amendment; and, it is our law and our tradition that more speech, not less, is the governing rule. An outright ban on corporate political speech during the critical pre-election period is not a permissible remedy. Here Congress has created categorical bans on speech that are asymmetrical to preventing quid pro quo corruption.

The third key issue concerns disclosure. In *Citizens United*, although the Court found that elements of the electioneering communication provision and ban on independent expenditures were unconstitutional, requiring disclaimers and disclosure was permissible. Although these requirements placed some burden on political speech, they provided important information about who was responsible for political spending and did not prevent speech itself. According to the majority opinion, "Disclaimer and disclosure requirements may burden the ability to speak, but they "impose no ceiling on campaign related activities," [quoting *Buckley*] and "do not prevent anyone from speaking" [quoting *McConnell*] (*Citizens United* 2010, 51–53). The Court continued, "[Citizens United] contends that the governmental interest in providing information to the electorate does not justify requiring disclaimers for any commercial advertisements, including the ones at issue here. We disagree. . . . At the very least, the disclaimers avoid confusion by making clear that the ads are not funded by a candidate or political party."[19]

The *Citizens United* opinion generated substantial controversy, including within the Court. There were a variety of dueling arguments among the several concurring and dissenting opinions filed by the justices. Justice John Paul Stevens, a Republican appointee generally viewed as being sympathetic to campaign finance regulation, served as the lead dissenter. Justice Stevens's objection to the majority opinion was clear from the outset. He rejected both the scope of the ruling and the implications for corporate campaign spending. In the opening paragraphs of his dissent, Stevens protested (*Citizens United* 2010, Stevens dissent, 1–2):

> All that the parties [in the case] dispute is whether Citizens United had a right to use the funds in its general treasury to pay for broadcasts during the [electioneering communication period]. The notion that the First Amendment dictates an affirmative answer to that question is, in my judgment, profoundly misguided. Even more misguided is the notion that the Court must rewrite the law relating to campaign expenditures by *for profit* corporations and unions to decide this case. The basic premise underlying the Court's ruling is its iteration, and constant reiteration, of the proposition that the First Amendment bars regulatory distinctions based on a speaker's identity, including its "identity" as a corporation. While that glittering generality has rhetorical appeal, it is not a correct statement of the law.[20]

Debate over the legal, policy, and political significance of the ruling continues to this day. The basic facts, however, were clear. The ruling represented a major change in federal campaign finance law. To summarize, the Court determined that the spending restrictions in the electioneering communication provision impermissibly violated First Amendment speech protections, as did the FECA ban on corporate independent expenditures. Disclosure and disclaimer provisions, on the other hand, were reasonable accommodations to ensure transparency about who was speaking and where their funds came from and how they were spent. Importantly, the Court's ruling did not affect the FECA ban on corporate or union treasury-fund contributions. That is, the decision did not grant corporations or unions permission to contribute to candidates or parties. The decision also did not affect an individual's ability to spend unlimited amounts on independent expenditures—a practice that the Supreme Court permitted in *Buckley*.

SpeechNow and the Rise of Super PACs

One of the most notable legal and policy developments surrounding the 2010 and 2012 election cycles—the rise of Super PACs—is often included in explanations of *Citizens United*. The impetus behind Super PACs is related to *Citizens United*, but they are not a product of the case per se. In fact, Super PACs arose from a second case that was decided by the US Court of Appeals for the District of Columbia (the "DC Circuit"). *SpeechNow.org v. Federal Election Commission* was already making its way through the federal courts when *Citizens United* was decided.[21]

In *SpeechNow*, relying on the *Citizens United* precedent, the DC Circuit held in March 2010 that unlimited contributions to PACs that make only independent expenditures were constitutionally protected. The connection between *Citizens United* and *SpeechNow* might be thought of informally as follows: where *Citizens United* permitted corporations (and labor unions) to use their treasuries to fund unlimited independent expenditures, *SpeechNow* permitted corporations and unions to use their treasuries to give funds to other entities to make unlimited independent expenditures. The FEC and some practitioners began informally referring to these new entities as "independent expenditure-only committees" (IEOCs). The media and other observers called them simply "Super PACs." Like traditional PACs, Super PACs are political committees and, therefore, are regulated under FECA. Among other requirements, this means that Super PACs must report their receipts and expenditures to the FEC. However, they may not make contributions and their activities must be independent from campaigns. They can spend as much as they like advocating for or against candidates.

Super PACs and Other Groups
in the Policy and Political Environments

Super PACs are significant in federal elections because they provide a new mechanism for people and groups to aggregate unlimited funds calling for election or defeat of federal candidates. But where do they fit in the policy and campaign environments? What can they do that other groups cannot, or vice versa? The answer is important because how a group is regulated determines what it can do—and where policymakers are typically engaged in debate over whether the activities of people or groups should be condoned as protected political speech or regulated as a perceived loophole that could facilitate corruption.

The name "Super PAC" suggests that these groups are both similar to and different from traditional PACs. Traditional PACs (e.g., those that have been on the scene since the 1970s) also allow their donors to pool resources to support or oppose candidates and, like Super PACs, are primarily regulated by the FEC. Super PACs are unique, however, because of their ability to amass unlimited contributions. Traditional PACs and Super PACs also differ in their ability to make contributions: traditional PACs can do so; Super PACs cannot.

Perhaps most importantly, Super PACs and traditional PACs are both political committees. As noted earlier in this chapter, being a political committee means the entity is regulated primarily by FECA. Among other important points, political committees must regularly file financial reports with the FEC and can make only limited contributions. Super PACs, however, essentially are a different kind of political committee, because although they report to the FEC they can accept unlimited funds but cannot make contributions.

Understanding Super PACs also raises the important distinction between political committees and other entities this chapter calls "politically active organizations." While political committees are party committees, candidate committees, and PACs, and are regulated primarily by FECA and the FEC, politically active organizations are regulated primary by the Internal Revenue Code (IRC, i.e., federal tax law) and the Internal Revenue Service (IRS). Politically active organizations include two major kinds of entities designated by their placement in the IRC—527s and 501(c)s. Sometimes colloquially referred to as "nonprofits," both kinds of groups are tax-exempt entities.

Best known for the relatively brief period in the early 2000s—particularly the 2004 presidential election—two prominent 527 groups, Swift Boat Veterans for Truth on the Republican side and the Democratic group America

Coming Together, battled over Democrat John Kerry's presidential campaign. Although all political committees are 527s for tax purposes (e.g., reporting investment income to the IRS), not all 527s are political committees. The small subset of groups claiming to be 527s, but not political committees, generated controversy before and after the 2004 election cycle. The FEC eventually levied substantial fines on some 527s for failing to register as political committees.[22] In some ways, Super PACs appear to have assumed the role that 527 organizations played in previous elections. Like Super PACs, 527s, too, can accept unlimited funds and may make unlimited expenditures, but the extent to which the groups should be regulated by FECA and the FEC has been hotly debated. Because Super PACs are widely understood to be political committees—in this case, with clear permission to accept unlimited contributions and make unlimited independent expenditures—they appear to offer more regulatory certainty than the case-by-case assessment employed with 527s.

Three kinds of 501(c) organizations—501(c)(4) social welfare groups, 501(c)(5) unions, and 501(c)(6) trade associations—were particularly important in 2010 and 2012, both independently and when interacting with Super PACs.[23] These entities engaged in political activities before *Citizens United*, but some observers viewed the decision as giving (c)(4)–(5), and (6) organizations more freedom to engage in independent expenditures because typically the groups are incorporated (and, hence, can use corporate treasuries to make independent expenditures). The degree to which these 501(c)s can engage in independent expenditures versus other activities (e.g., conducting more general "social welfare") while maintaining their tax-exempt status remains open to debate.[24] Nonetheless, particularly in 2010 and 2012, many 501(c)(4) s, (5)s, and (6)s made substantial independent expenditures on their own and funneled funds to Super PACs.

Using these 501(c) entities to route funds to Super PACs has important implications for transparency. Unlike political committees, some politically active organizations—including 501(c)s—do not typically report their donors to the FEC. Although any entity making an independent expenditure or electioneering communication must report that activity to the FEC, donors are only identified if they contributed specially for the "purpose of furthering" independent expenditures or electioneering communications.[25] Therefore, routing contributions through 501(c) organizations permitted Super PACs— at least in 2010 and 2012—to avoid disclosing the original source of funds used for independent expenditures as long as those funds were given to the 501(c) for general purposes and not specifically for independent expenditures.

Policy and Politics: The Aftermath of 2010

The monumental changes in campaign finance law in 2010 did not necessarily spur public policy changes. In fact, as of this writing, Congress has not amended campaign finance law to respond to *Citizens United,* the development of Super PACs, or the other post-2010 topics discussed above. Dozens of bills—mostly sponsored by Democrats—proposed various options, ranging from disclosure to constitutional amendments—but none became law. During the 111th Congress (2009–2011), the House narrowly passed the DISCLOSE Act (H.R. 5175), a bill that would have required additional reporting about the original sources of contributions and additional documentation throughout political transactions. Amid criticisms about the bill's applicability and proposed spending restrictions, however, the measure died in the Senate.

The FEC also has not issued new regulations on the topic—partially due to a partisan split among the agency's six commissioners. The agency did issue advisory opinions providing guidance to campaigns and other players in some circumstances. The first wave of AO activity occurred in the summer of 2010, when the FEC approved two related AOs in response to questions from the Club for Growth[26] and Commonsense Ten.[27] In these instances, the commission determined that the organizations could solicit unlimited contributions for use in independent expenditures.[28] In both AOs, the FEC also advised that, while post–*Citizens United* rules were being drafted to amend agency reporting forms, would-be Super PACs could file letters with the commission indicating their status. Hence, the FEC had recognized—albeit not through regulation—the concept of Super PACs. AOs also permitted federal candidates and party officials to solicit contributions for Super PACs. The commission advised, however, that contributions solicited by federal candidates and national party officials must be within the PAC contribution limits established in FECA (for example, $5,000 annually for individual contributions).

Given the monumental changes in campaign finance law post-2010, it might seem surprising that more than a full election cycle later so few concrete policy changes have occurred. Indeed, proregulatory campaign finance groups sharply criticized President Obama, Congress, and the FEC for not responding to limit the decision's effects—just as others have cheered *Citizens United* as a restoration of corporate and union speech that requires no response. As this chapter has shown, finding policy options that are constitutionally viable, that would have the desired effect, and that are politically viable is easier said than done.

This chapter has introduced the rules of campaign finance and tried to demystify how various contribution limits and reporting requirements apply to various people and groups. As the discussion has shown, 2010 ushered in substantial changes in permissible campaign spending. In the next chapter, Anthony Corrado explores how that spending affected campaigns. Even as monumental as the changes in 2010 and beyond were, however, the history reviewed here serves as an important reminder that *Citizens United* did not occur in a vacuum. The decision was the culmination of decades of debate about who should be permitted to participate in campaigns and how. That debate shows no signs of subsiding in the future.

Notes

1. The $1.3 billion figure comes from the Federal Election Commission website, accessed December 12, 2012, http://www.fec.gov/disclosurep/pnational .do?cf=phome.

2. 34 Stat. 864.

3. See 57 Stat. 167 (1943) and 61 Stat. 136 (1947).

4. FECA is 2 U.S.C. § 431 et seq.

5. Because the discussion here is intended to be general, it does not address the specific contents of one set of FECA amendments versus another. For additional detail, see the original public laws at P.L. 92-225 (1971), P.L. 93-443 (1974), P.L. 94-283 (1976), and P.L. 96-187 (1979). For an overview, see Mutch (1988) and Corrado (2005).

6. The requirement that Senate committees report to the secretary of the Senate rather than directly to the FEC is statutory and has historically been viewed as an institutional prerogative. The House and Senate generally defer to each other's preferences regarding institutional matters affecting only one chamber. In recent Congresses, some senators have proposed legislation that would change the place of filing to the FEC and require electronic filing of campaign finance reports now filed on paper. In the 112th Congress (2011–2013), see S. 219, sponsored by Sen. Jon Tester (D-MT).

7. *Buckley* is 424 U.S. 1. For additional discussion of legal issues, see, for example, Whitaker (2010) and Ortiz (2005).

8. The Court upheld spending limits for publicly financed presidential campaigns on the grounds that participating candidates chose to voluntarily accept public funds and could be required to meet reasonable conditions on receiving those funds.

9. There is substantial debate over whether ads characterized as "negative" and "attacks" are illegitimate criticisms or whether they raise legitimate contrasts that inform voters. Of course, that determination depends on individual context. For additional discussion, see, for example, Pfau and Kenski (1990).

10. This information comes from comments by Elizabeth Wilner, vice president, Kantar Media Intelligence/Campaign Media Analysis Group (CMAG) at a December 3, 2012, panel discussion for the "PAC Balance: How the Balance Has Shifted Post *Citizens United*," session at the Women in Government Relations, PACS, Politics, and Grassroots Conference, Washington, DC.

11. For additional discussion, see Mutch (1988).

12. "Soft money" is a term of art referring to unlimited funds that were often given to parties pre-BCRA. It stands in contrast to "hard money," referring to funds subject to FECA contribution limits.

13. These include terms such as "vote for," "vote against," "elect," and "defeat." See note 52 in *Buckley,* 424 U.S. 1 (1976).

14. BCRA amended FECA and is, therefore, codified with FECA at 2 U.S.C. § 431 et seq. On BCRA itself, see P.L. 107-155.

15. In addition to the case itself, several amicus curiae ("friend of the court") briefs were filed and are available on the FEC website at http://www.fec.gov/law/litigation_related.shtml#cu_sc08. See also, for example, Lowenstein, Hasen, and Tokaji (2012) and Youn (2011).

16. In general in campaign finance policy, "disclosure" refers to financial reports filed with the FEC. "Disclaimers" refers to identifying information contained in an advertisement, usually a statement naming the individual or group responsible for the ad.

17. Internal citations omitted. Pagination cited in this chapter is based on the slip opinion.

18. There is debate about whether *Citizens United* was a departure from precedent or a return to it. See the majority and dissenting opinions in *Citizens United* for additional discussion.

19. Internal citations omitted. Pagination cited in this chapter is based on the slip opinion.

20. Internal citations omitted. Pagination cited in this chapter is based on the slip opinion. Emphasis in original.

21. *SpeechNow.org v. FEC,* 599 F.3d 686 (D.C. Cir. 2010).

22. For historical background, see, for example, Garrett, Lunder, and Whitaker (2008). Joseph E. Cantor served as an original coauthor of earlier versions of the report.

23. Importantly, the 501(c)s discussed here do *not* include 501(c)(3)s. These public charity organizations (e.g., schools and houses of worship) only may engage in limited political activity.

24. On tax issues, which are beyond the scope of this chapter, see, for example, Lunder and Whitaker (2011).

25. This distinction takes root in litigation surrounding FEC disclosure regulations and FECA reporting requirements. For additional discussion, see Garrett (2012b).

26. AO 2010-09.

27. AO 2010-11.
28. Ibid.

References

Austin v. Michigan Chamber of Commerce. 1990. 494 U.S. 652.

Biersack, Robert, Paul S. Herrnson, and Clyde Wilcox, eds. 1994. *Risky Business? PAC Decisionmaking in Congressional Elections.* Armonk, NY: M. E. Sharpe.

Buckley v. Valeo. 1976. 424 U.S. 1.

Burton, John Michael, and Daniel M Shea. 2003. *Campaign Mode: Strategic Vision in Congressional Elections.* Lanham, MD: Rowman & Littlefield.

Citizens United v. Federal Election Commission. 2010. 130 S. Ct. (slip opinion).

Corrado, Anthony. 2005. "Money and Politics: A History of Federal Campaign Finance Law." In Anthony Corrado, Thomas E. Mann, Daniel R. Ortiz, and Trevor Potter, *The New Campaign Finance Sourcebook,* 7–47. Washington: Brookings Institution Press.

Dulio, David A. 2004. *For Better or Worse? How Political Consultants Are Changing Elections in the United States.* Albany: SUNY Press.

Garrett, R. Sam. 2010. *Campaign Crises: Detours on the Road to Congress.* Boulder, CO: Lynne Rienner Publishers.

———. 2012a. "Seriously Funny: Understanding Campaign Finance Policy Through the Colbert Super PAC." *Saint Louis University Law Journal* 56 (3): 711–723.

———. 2012b. "The State of Campaign Finance Policy: Recent Developments and Issues for Congress." Congressional Research Service report.

———. 2012c. "Super PACs in Federal Elections: Overview and Issues for Congress." Congressional Research Service report.

Garrett, R. Sam, Paul S. Herrnson, and James A. Thurber. 2006. "Perspectives on Campaign Ethics." In *The Electoral Challenge: Theory Meets Practice,* edited by Stephen C. Craig, 203–224. Washington: CQ Press.

Garrett, R. Sam, Erika Lunder, and L. Paige Whitaker. 2008. "Section 527 Political Organizations: Background and Issues for Federal Election and Tax Laws." Congressional Research Service report.

Hohnenstein, Kurt. 2007. *Coining Corruption: The Making of the American Campaign Finance System.* DeKalb, IL: Northern Illinois University Press.

La Raja, Raymond J. 2008. *Small Change: Money, Political Parties, and Campaign Finance Reform.* Ann Arbor: University of Michigan Press.

Lowenstein, Daniel Hays, Richard L. Hasen, and Daniel P. Tokaji. 2012. *Election Law: Cases and Materials,* 5th ed. Durham, NC: Carolina Academic Press.

Lunder, Erika, and L. Paige Whitaker. 2011. "501(c)(4) Organizations and Campaign Activity: Analysis Under Tax and Campaign Finance Laws." Congressional Research Service report.

McConnell v. Federal Election Commission. 2003. 540 U.S. 93.

Medvic, Stephen K. 2001. *Political Consultants in U.S. Congressional Elections.* Columbus: Ohio State University Press.

Mutch, Robert E. 1988. *Campaigns, Congress, and the Courts: The Making of Federal Campaign Finance Law.* New York: Praeger.

Nelson, Candice J., Stephen K. Medvic, and David A. Dulio, eds. 2002. *Shades of Gray: Perspectives on Campaign Ethics.* Washington: Brookings Institution Press.

Ortiz, Daniel R. 2005. "The First Amendment and the Limits of Campaign Finance Reform." In Anthony Corrado, et al. *The New Campaign Finance Sourcebook,* 91–122. Washington: Brookings Institution Press.

Pfau, Michael, and Henry Kenski. 1990. *Attack Politics: Strategy and Defense.* New York: Praeger.

SpeechNow.org v. FEC. 2010. 599 F.3d 686 (D.C. Cir.).

Thurber, James A., and Candice J. Nelson, eds. 2000. *Campaign Warriors: Political Consultants in Elections.* Washington: Brookings Institution Press.

Whitaker, L. Paige. 2010. "The Constitutionality of Campaign Finance Regulation: *Buckley v. Valeo* and Its Supreme Court Progeny." Congressional Research Service report.

Wisconsin Right to Life v. FEC (WRTL II). 2007. 551 U.S. 449.

Youn, Monica, ed. 2011. *Money, Politics, and the Constitution: Beyond Citizens United.* New York: The Century Foundation Press.

5

Fundraising Strategies in the 2012 Presidential Campaign

ANTHONY CORRADO

The 2012 race for the White House featured a battle for financial supremacy that lasted until Election Day and drove campaign fundraising to unexpected heights. Candidates, parties, and organized groups engaged in a frenetic chase for political contributions, turning the contest into a race to the top of a rising mountain of campaign cash. In the final two weeks of the election alone, candidates and their principal partisan allies reported spending more than $500 million, a sum comparable to the total spending in support of presidential candidates reported in the entire 2004 general election campaign.[1] What's more, this total did not include the monies spent by dozens of groups active in the presidential race or the monies spent by tax-exempt organizations that are not required to disclose most of their expenditures under federal law. The expenditures of these groups added to the deluge of money in the final days, which capped an election year marked by extraordinary levels of spending.

In all, more than $2 billion was spent in the presidential contest. Yet what distinguished campaign finance in 2012 was the *source* of much of the funding, rather than the unprecedented amount that was spent. Hundreds of millions of dollars flowed into the race from an array of nonparty organizations, including Super PACs, nonprofit groups, and labor unions. Most of this money came from Super PACs, a new form of political committee that emerged out of the legal and regulatory decisions made after the 2008 election. Super PACs were permitted to use unlimited contributions from wealthy donors and sources prohibited for candidates and parties to pay for activities that directly advocated the election of a candidate, so long as they did not make direct contributions to candidates but only spent money independently in support of them. These committees received most of their funding from contributors who gave $1 million or more, which allowed them to amass sizable war chests and spend substantial sums in the presidential race. Consequently, million-aires and billionaires became a major source of campaign money, and Super PACs and their allies dwarfed the national parties as a source of presidential campaign spending.

This chapter examines the strategies and tactics employed by the candidates and their partisan allies, with a focus on the general election. It illustrates the ways in which the strategic context and regulatory environment influenced the flow of money and produced a steep rise in the amount of unlimited and often undisclosed funding in the race. It thus explains what made the financ-ing of the 2012 election unlike that of any other in the post-Watergate era.

The Strategic Environment

As the presidential race began to take shape in the year before the election, President Obama was in a vulnerable political position and his reelection was a matter of great uncertainty. A majority of the public expressed dissatis-faction with the president's performance in office, especially in regard to his handling of the economy, and polls consistently showed that less than half of the electorate supported his reelection to office. Moreover, many of those who supported the president in his historic first bid for office had lost their enthu-siasm, since the prospect of hope and change that energized his constituency had dissipated in the face of bipartisan political conflict and the reality of unfulfilled campaign promises. Most political observers therefore anticipated a very close race, with the president's chance of reelection basically judged to be a fifty-fifty proposition.

Nonetheless, most observers assumed that Obama would have a major fi-nancial advantage in the race, regardless of whom the Republicans chose to run against him. Some even speculated that he would be the first candidate to raise $1 billion.[2] In 2008, Obama became the first candidate since the adop-tion of the public funding program in 1974 to win the presidency without taking public funds in either the primary or general election campaign. He raised $745 million in his bid for office, surpassing all other contenders by far, and outspent his general election opponent, John McCain, by a substan-tial margin.[3] By the end of the campaign, Obama had recruited close to four million donors and built an e-mail list of thirteen million names.[4] Even with significant attrition in donor support from one election to the next taken into account, he would still begin his reelection campaign with the largest base of prospective donors ever recruited by a presidential candidate.

Furthermore, because the president would once again forgo public funding, he could raise contributions for the general election throughout the primary campaign. In 2012, individuals were allowed to contribute $2,500 per election to a presidential candidate, with the primary and general election considered separate elections for purposes of the limit. So the total amount an individual could give was $5,000. A PAC is allowed to give $5,000 per election, for a total of $10,000.[5] But a candidate does not have to wait until the general election, which formally begins after the nominating convention, to begin soliciting general election funds. Monies for both elections can be raised at the same time, so long as the general election donations are maintained separately and not used to pay primary expenses. A Republican primary contender would also be permitted to accept general election contributions for possible use in a fall campaign, but candidates in a primary contest focus their efforts on primary fundraising and do not want to appear presumptuous by raising general election funds before the primaries are decided. Obama was thus in a better position than a prospective opponent to begin raising general election money.

In addition to a significant head start on fundraising, Obama also had other strategic advantages. As an incumbent seeking the party nomination without serious opposition, he would not have to allocate substantial sums of money to a primary campaign. In 2008, Obama expended $251 million before he wrapped up the nomination in his hard-fought primary contest with Hillary Clinton.[6] In 2012, he would not need to spend anywhere near that amount to secure the nomination. He could devote most of his resources to activities related to the general election. He could use funds from the very start of the campaign to establish offices and build organizations in crucial battleground states, finance voter contact and registration programs, and pay for early advertising. In essence, he could conduct an eighteen-month general election campaign.

The president could also get an early start on joint fundraising activities with national and state party committees. Under federal campaign finance rules, candidates and party committees may form joint fundraising committees, which are allowed to solicit contributions for both the candidate and the party.[7] Such committees, which have been used regularly in both parties in recent presidential elections, typically sponsor events at which donors may make contributions to a candidate and the national party committee, as well as state party committees. They are designed to seek large contributions from individuals, usually for the maximum amount permitted by federal law.

So, for example, in the 2012 election cycle, an individual could give a maximum contribution at one of these events ranging from $35,800 ($2,500 to the candidate for the primary, $2,500 for the general election, and the annual maximum of $30,800 to a national party) to $75,800 (the $5,000 allowed to a candidate and $70,800 to party committees, which is the total amount a donor may give to parties in a two-year federal election cycle, with no more than $30,800 per year allocated to a national party and the remainder divided among state parties, which are each allowed to receive $10,000 per year from a donor).

A joint fundraising committee is an efficient structure for presidential campaign fundraising, since even the monies received by party committees are subsequently used to support the presidential nominee in the general election. Joint fundraising operations, however, typically begin once a prospective nominee has emerged from the primaries, since at that point the party has a nominee with whom it can join forces. Because Obama was certain to be the party standard-bearer, the Democratic National Committee (DNC) did not have to wait for the primaries to initiate joint activity. In fact, the Democrats wasted little time in getting started. Their joint committee, named the Obama Victory Fund, was registered with the Federal Election Commission (FEC) in April 2011 at about the same time that Obama for America, the president's formal reelection campaign committee, was established.[8]

The strategic context of the 2012 fundraising race was thus very similar to that of the 2004 race. Indeed, in many ways it mirrored the 2004 election. In 2004, President George W. Bush faced no serious opposition from within his own party, but he was a vulnerable incumbent with relatively low public approval ratings due to deep opposition to the wars in Iraq and Afghanistan. The general election was expected to be a close contest, particularly given his narrow, controversial victory in 2000.

Bush began his bid for reelection amid expectations that he would have a significant fundraising advantage over any challenger who would emerge from the Democratic primaries. In 2000, Bush had become the first presidential contender since the adoption of public funding to win a party nomination without public funds. Bush raised $95 million in the primaries, or almost twice the sum that would have been permitted had he accepted public funding and its accompanying expenditure limits, before taking the public grant in the general election.[9] In 2004, he was expected to forgo public funding again and was likely to raise more money than he had in 2000 now that he was the incumbent. In addition, the Republican National Committee (RNC) was likely to raise significantly more money than the DNC, since 2004 was the first presidential election following the ban on party soft money, and the RNC had raised substantially more hard money (i.e., money raised in accordance with federal contribution limits) than the DNC in prior elections.[10] Bush was thus expected to have a significant financial advantage in the race.

Facing this prospect, Democratic partisans sought ways to level the playing field. They began to form independent political committees, known as Section 527 organizations, or 527s (for the section of the Internal Revenue Code under which they were established), to raise funds that were not subject to federal contribution limits for use on election-related activities. Eventually, Republicans followed this strategy and established committees of their own.

These 527s, fueled with multimillion-dollar contributions from wealthy donors, spent tens of millions of dollars in 2004. Committees aligned with the Democrats outspent those supporting Bush by a substantial margin, thereby countering any advantage held by Bush and his party over the Democrats and their nominee, John Kerry. Most 527 expenditures took the form of issue advertising or nonpartisan voter identification and mobilization programs, since any independent expenditures that directly advocated the election of a candidate had to be financed with monies subject to federal contribution limits, and any committee that spent $1,000 or more in this way was required by law to register with the FEC and thus become subject to the contribution limits imposed on PACs. These committees could, however, sponsor election-eering communications, which are broadcast advertisements that feature a federal candidate and are aired within thirty days of a primary or sixty days of a general election. But these communications could only be financed with individual contributions (the law prohibited the use of corporate or labor union contributions) and any spending in excess of $10,000 per year had to be disclosed, along with all contributors of $1,000 or more. Even with these restrictions, nonparty groups reported spending $55 million on electioneering communications in the general election.[11] But this sum did not compare to spending on other activities. For example, the two principal pro-Democratic 527s, America Coming Together, which focused on registering and turning out progressive voters, and the Media Fund, which financed mostly issue ads criticizing President Bush, spent a combined $130 million. The leading pro-Republican committee, Swift Boat Veterans and POWs for Truth, spent more than $22 million, primarily on advertisements attacking Kerry.[12] Much of the money raised by these groups came from wealthy individuals, particularly those who gave $1 million or more.[13]

In 2012, the Republicans were in a position similar to that of the Democrats in 2004: They faced the prospect of being substantially outspent in what was expected to be a close election. Republican partisans therefore had a strong incentive to pursue strategies that would help to level the financial playing field. The new rules governing independent political spending made it easy to develop such strategies.

What was different in 2012 as compared to 2004 was that the law permitted financial activity that was formerly restricted or outright prohibited. In 2004, 527s had pushed the boundaries of campaign finance regulations, and a number of these organizations were fined after the election for violating the rules.[14] In 2012, politically active nonparty organizations could act with greater certainty, since the law permitted the use of unlimited contributions, including funds from corporations and labor unions, to finance independent expenditures that directly advocated the election of a candidate (see Chapter 4). As a result of the court decisions in *Citizens United* and *SpeechNow* and the guidance offered by the FEC clarifying the impact of these decisions, political committees, nonprofit organizations (which are usually incorporated entities), labor unions, and business associations could now spend unlimited amounts on presidential campaign activity, so long as they acted independently of the candidates and their staffs and abided by any applicable Internal Revenue Service regulations regarding their tax-exempt status.[15] Most notably, the law now permitted "independent expenditure-only committees," Super PACs, which could accept unlimited contributions and spend unlimited amounts.

Super PACs emerged quickly once the FEC officially recognized this type of committee in July 2010.[16] By the time of the midterm election a few months later, eighty-four Super PACs had registered with the FEC and reported spending more than $65 million on independent expenditures supporting or opposing federal candidates.[17] The top spender was American Crossroads, a conservative Super PAC organized with the assistance of Republican strategist and former Bush White House chief of staff Karl Rove, which financed $21 million of independent expenditures. American Crossroads's associated 501(c)(4) nonprofit organization, Crossroads GPS, reported an additional $17 million in spending.[18]

In 2011, American Crossroads and Crossroads GPS began to focus on the presidential race, as well as congressional contests. In June, the two groups announced a fundraising goal of $120 million for the 2012 elections, a sum that was increased to $240 million in September when Mississippi governor and former RNC chairman Haley Barbour signed on to assist their fundraising efforts.[19] Dozens of other Super PACs were also established with an eye toward the presidential race. These included a new variant, the candidate-specific

Super PAC, which was a PAC established to support a particular candidate and essentially act as a parallel, albeit independent, campaign committee for that candidate. In most instances, these committees were established by a former staff member, political advisor, or associate of the candidate supported by the group. For example, Restore Our Future, a pro-Romney Super PAC, listed as treasurer Charles Spies, general counsel of the 2008 Romney campaign, and its board included Carl Forti, Romney's 2008 political director, and Larry McCarthy, a member of Romney's 2008 media team.[20] Similarly, only a few weeks after the Obama campaign committee was established in April, a pro-Obama Super PAC, Priorities USA Action, and an associated 501(c)(4) organization, Priorities USA Action Fund, were created. The Super PAC's leadership team included Bill Burton, who left his post as Obama's deputy White House press secretary in February; Sean Sweeney, who had served as a senior advisor to White House chief of staff Rahm Emanuel; and Paul Begala, a former Clinton political strategist.[21] By the end of the year, at least one candidate-specific Super PAC had been created for each of the major presidential contenders, and these committees played a significant role in the financing of the Republican nomination contest.

These developments in the preelection year made clear that the fundraising race would not simply be a match between competing candidates and party committees. Rather, it would be a contest between two teams, consisting of candidates, parties, and an array of allied organizations, with one team supporting Obama, the other supporting the Republican nominee.

An Overview of Campaign Funding

The participants in the financing of the presidential campaign operated under different regulatory frameworks. Candidates and party committees were subject to strict contribution limits, were not allowed to accept contributions from corporations or labor unions, and were required to disclose their contributions and expenditures of $200 or more to the FEC. Super PACs were allowed to receive unlimited contributions, including donations from corporations and labor unions, and were required to disclose all of their contributions and expenditures of $200 or more to the FEC.

Nonprofit groups and other groups that did not qualify as federal political committees operated under less stringent rules than those applied to Super PACs. Like Super PACs, they could accept unlimited contributions, but they were only required to disclose to the FEC the amounts they raised and spent on independent expenditures that advocated a candidate, or on electioneering communications that featured a candidate. However, prior to the 2012 election, the FEC had interpreted the electioneering communications disclosure rule to mean that an organization only had to report contributions designated to finance a specific communication.[22] Consequently, groups making electioneering communications could easily avoid disclosing their donors, so long as the donor did not specify how the money should be used. Since donors rarely give money with the intention of paying for a particular ad, nonprofits that reported electioneering communications expenses did not report the sources of funding.

Furthermore, nonprofit organizations could also offer their donors anonymity because any funds raised and spent on other activities, such as issue ads or voter registration drives, were not required to be publicly disclosed at all. Thus, untold millions in contributions received for presidential electioneering by these groups remained hidden from public view.

Given the limited scope of public disclosure, it is not possible to determine the total amount spent or the sources of all funding. Even so, the spending that was reported indicated that the financial activity in the 2012 race exceeded that of all previous elections and was dramatically higher than the sums expended in 2008.

Candidate Fundraising

The 2012 election was the first since the adoption of the public funding system in which public money was not a meaningful source of campaign funds. Both President Obama and his Republican challenger, Mitt Romney, refused the option of public funding in the primary and general elections. So did every serious candidate for the Republican nomination.[23] The election thus signaled the end of public funding as a resource of any concern, and candidates were free to spend as much as they could raise.

Presidential candidates raised a total of $1.4 billion, with more than half of this sum garnered by President Obama. According to FEC data, Obama took in $782 million, which exceeded his remarkable 2008 fundraising effort by $37 million. This total included the amount received by his campaign committee ($717 million) and the money attributed to his campaign by the Obama Victory Fund ($64 million), which represented the amount of money raised for the Obama campaign that was retained by the joint fundraising committee to pay the Obama campaign's share of the joint committee's expenses (see Table 5.1).

TABLE 5.1 Presidential Campaign Receipts and Expenditures, 2012 (in $ millions)

Candidate	Receipts	Expenditures
DEMOCRATS		
Obama	781.9	729.2
Subtotal	781.9	729.2
REPUBLICANS		
Romney	494.1	465.8
Paul	40.6	39.8
Gingrich	24.1	24.4
Santorum	22.6	23.0
Perry	20.0	20.2
Cain	16.7	16.9
Bachmann	9.4	9.3
Huntsman	8.9	8.9
Roemer	0.8	0.7
Subtotal	637.2	609.0
TOTAL	1,419.1	1,338.2

Source: Based on an analysis of FEC filings by the Campaign Finance Institute. Data reported as of November 26, 2012.

Romney raised $494 million, a sum that included $26 million retained by Romney Victory Inc., the Republican joint fundraising committee, to pay the Romney campaign's share of joint committee expenses. Romney took in about $143 million more than McCain did in 2008 ($351 million, including $84 million of general election public funds), but he still trailed far behind Obama. Romney did, however, significantly outpace all of his opponents in the nomination contest, raising $98 million by the end of April, which was more than twice the sum achieved by Ron Paul, who finished second in the Republican fundraising race, and more than the combined total of his top three competitors (Paul, Newt Gingrich, and Rick Santorum).

Small Donors

As in 2008, Obama's fundraising strength was largely due to his broad base of financial support and success in recruiting small donors. By the end of the campaign, the president had received contributions from 4.4 million donors, or 450,000 more than he recruited in 2008.[24] Most of these donors made their contributions through digital means, including e-mail, social media, text messages, and the campaign's website. The campaign reported that it received about $690 million through digital means in 2012, up from about $500 million in 2008.[25] This total included all contributions given electronically, including donations from large donors that were logged through the website. About $504 million of this total was initially solicited by the campaign through digital means, which represented about a 25 percent increase as compared to the $403 million that the campaign solicited online in 2008.[26]

A large share of the money contributed online was the result of the Obama campaign's sophisticated, metric-driven e-mail outreach program. The campaign continuously tested different fundraising appeals, with diverse subject lines, varying "senders" (e.g., President Obama, First Lady Michelle Obama, Vice President Biden, or campaign manager Jim Messina), and content specifically designed for targeted recipients. These messages typically asked for a small donation of three or five dollars as a way to prompt a contribution and get a donor into the system; thereafter the campaign would begin seeking additional donations from the supporter in a more targeted approach. One of the campaign's most successful messages was one distributed on June 26, 2012, in which the president, citing the "massive outside spending" by Super PACs and other groups, warned supporters that "I will be the first president in modern history to be outspent . . . if things continue as they have so far."[27] This one message brought in $2.5 million.[28]

Another technique that proved to be highly effective was an invitation to enter a contest or lottery to win an invitation to meet the president or attend a major campaign event. These invitations were offered throughout the campaign and typically asked recipients to give three dollars for a chance to win, even though entry did not require a donation, since federal law prohibits charging money to enter a contest.[29] The rewards offered in these lotteries included dinner with the president and first lady, free admission to a major fundraising event featuring a celebrity sponsor, and opportunities to attend a notable campaign event, such as the national convention or a presidential debate. The campaign even offered invitations to the president's birthday party.[30]

The most successful sweepstakes was the one that offered a trip to attend a fundraiser at the home of Hollywood star George Clooney. The campaign collected $15 million through this event, with most of the money coming from small donors hoping to win the trip, not the well-heeled donors who paid $40,000 to attend this joint committee fundraiser. Tens of thousands of donors entered the contest, giving an average contribution of twenty-three dollars.

These small gifts made up about two-thirds of the money received.[31] This example illustrates the way in which the Obama campaign used large-donor fundraisers to leverage small contributions. The success of the Clooney sweepstakes led the campaign to sponsor a series of similar events, including lotteries to attend an event sponsored by actress Sarah Jessica Parker and *Vogue* editor Anna Wintour, and a party hosted by music celebrities Jay-Z and Beyonce.[32]

The Obama campaign also encouraged small-dollar donations through its Quick Donate program, which allowed repeat giving online or via text message without requiring an individual to reenter credit card information. An internal analysis of this program conducted during the campaign revealed that these donors gave about four times as much as other small contributors. This finding led to an expansion of the program, including efforts to give first-time donors an incentive to join by offering a free bumper sticker or other gift to those who signed up. By the end of October, messages encouraging Quick Donate contributions had become an important part of the campaign's fundraising strategy.[33]

As a result of these and other fundraising tactics, Obama was again able to generate a substantial share of his campaign funding from small donors, individuals whose aggregate contributions amounted to $200 or less. According to an analysis conducted by the nonpartisan Campaign Finance Institute, Obama received $782 million from individual donors, with $216 million (28 percent) contributed by those who gave a total of $200 or less (see Table 5.2).[34] Obama thus raised more money from small donors than he did in 2008,[35] and $152 million more than Romney, who received $63.6 million from small contributors. Indeed, Obama raised twice as much from small donors as the entire Republican field. The president's substantial financial advantage over Romney was thus largely due to his ability to attract far larger numbers of small contributions.

In all, Romney received less than 14 percent of his total individual contributions from small donors, despite his use of some of the same tactics employed by Obama. The Romney campaign made extensive use of e-mail appeals, Facebook postings, digital advertising, and its website to solicit contributions. They held lotteries and contests for "Lunch with Mitt" and invitations to presidential debates and other campaign events. Yet, by the effective end of the primaries at the end of April, Romney had raised only 10 percent ($9.8 million) of his total individual receipts from those who gave small amounts.[36] Romney failed to develop a large small-donor base throughout the primaries, and even after he became the clear frontrunner, he did not experience a surge

TABLE 5.2 Source of Individual Contributions to Presidential Candidates, 2012 (in $ millions)

Aggregate Amount Contributed by Donor

Candidates	Total Individual Contributions	$200 or Less Dollar Amount	Percent of Total	$201–$999 Dollar Amount	Percent of Total	$1,000 or More Dollar Amount	Percent of Total
DEMOCRATS							
Obama	781.8	216.3	27.7	263.0	34	302.6	39
Subtotal	781.8	216.3	27.7	263.0	34	302.6	39
REPUBLICANS							
Romney	470.5	63.6	13.51	101.4	22	305.5	65
Paul	39.9	13.7	34	13.7	34	12.5	31
Gingrich	23.5	9.9	42	6.4	27	7.2	31
Santorum	21.9	9.9	45	6.3	29	5.7	26
Perry	19.7	1.0	5	1.1	6	17.5	89
Cain	15.9	8.3	52	3.8	24	3.9	24
Bachmann	7.3	4.3	59	1.9	26	1.1	15
Huntsman	3.7	0.5	13	0.5	14	2.7	73
Roemer	0.4	0.4	100	0.0	0	0.0	0
Subtotal	602.9	111.5	19	135.1	22	356.1	59
TOTAL	1,384.7	327.8	24	398.0	29	658.7	48

Source: Based on an analysis of FEC filings by the Campaign Finance Institute. Data reported as of November 26, 2012.

in fundraising similar to that experienced by Democrat John Kerry in 2004 or Republican John McCain in 2008.[37]

After Romney wrapped up the nomination and attention shifted to the general election, his small-donor fundraising improved, but he never developed robust small-donor support. From the beginning of May through to November, he raised $54 million from small contributors, which represented 85 percent of his small-donor total. However, during the same period, Obama received $128 million from small contributors. Romney's online fundraising did surge as the election neared, and his campaign reported $27 million in online contributions in the first two weeks of October, a sum that surpassed the total in any previous month of the election year.[38] How much of this total came from smaller gifts was not disclosed. By the end of the campaign, Romney had reached a million online donors and 2.2 million active e-mail addresses, but these metrics paled in comparison to those achieved by Obama.[39]

Large Donors

Romney did, however, raise substantial sums from large donors, particularly those who gave the maximum contribution. Romney's fundraising strategy can be best described as a large-donor strategy, since he emphasized the solicitation of large contributions, especially individual donations of the $2,500 maximum. Given his well-established business experience and deep ties in the financial community, this approach was well suited to his candidacy, particularly in light of the high levels of dissatisfaction expressed by business leaders with the Obama administration's policies. The Campaign Finance Institute analysis found that Romney received $305 million from individual donors who gave at least $1,000 or more, which constituted 65 percent of the total amount he received from individual contributions. This included $223 million, almost half (47 percent) of Romney's total, donated by individuals who gave $2,500 in either the primary or general election or both. In all, 19,495 individuals gave Romney the maximum of $5,000, which produced $97.5 million for the campaign.

Romney's success in attracting large contributions allowed him to raise significant sums of money from a relatively small cohort of supporters. The drawback to his approach was that it did not provide a foundation for a continuing stream of contributions, since donors could not give additional donations once they had given the maximum. To raise additional funds, Romney had to find more donors willing to give large sums.

Romney's emphasis on large contributors did not give him a relative advantage over Obama. Obama, too, concentrated on the solicitation of large donors and raised $303 million from donors who gave at least $1,000 or more, which represented 39 percent of his total individual receipts. He therefore raised only $3 million less than Romney from donors in this range. He did, however, trail Romney in the number of donors who gave the maximum amount. Obama raised $171 million, 22 percent of his total, from donors who gave $2,500. He had 16,505 individuals give the maximum $5,000 for a total of $83 million. In short, Romney led the president among donors who gave the maximum permissible amount, but the gap was not so great that Obama could not make up for it with his large number of donors who gave $1,000 or more (94,700 donors compared to 64,100 for Romney). Thus, the president kept pace with Romney at the top end of the donor spectrum and beat him significantly among donors who gave small sums or middling amounts.

Much of the money raised from donors at the top end of the contribution range was the result of the efforts of joint fundraising committees. As previously noted, the Obama Victory Fund was formed early in the campaign and began sponsoring major donor events in the late spring and early summer of 2011. By the time Romney had emerged as the prospective nominee, the Obama Victory Fund had already raised more than $160 million and transferred more than $50 million to the Obama campaign coffers. By the end of the general election, the committee had taken in a total of more than $454 million and transferred more than $176 million to the Obama campaign and about $155 million to the DNC and state party committees.[40]

The Republicans did not form their joint fundraising committee, Romney Victory Inc., until April of the election year and began fundraising in May. They thus began joint fundraising efforts almost a year after the Democrats. But the committee caught up quickly, relying on fundraisers with ticket prices of up to $75,800. In a span of less than seven months, Romney Victory Inc. raised a total of $492 million, surpassing the sum achieved by its Democratic counterpart. In all, Romney Victory Inc. transferred a total of more than $146 million to the Romney campaign and $197 million to the RNC and state party committees.[41] It thus provided the Romney campaign with a substantial influx of cash at a time when the campaign needed it most.

Super PACs and Nonparty Organizations

Although Obama achieved an impressive $287 million fundraising advantage over Romney, this gap was offset by the expenditures of pro-Romney Super PACs and other nonparty organizations, particularly nonprofit 501(c)(4) organizations. As a result, Obama and his partisan allies gained little advantage in the money race.

According to summaries of FEC data compiled by the nonpartisan Center for Responsive Politics, Super PACs and other nonparty organizations reported spending more than $568 million on independent expenditures and electioneering communications in the presidential race, including $442 million in the general election.[42] This sum dwarfed the $117 million the national parties spent on communications supporting their nominees, including both coordinated and independent expenditures. The RNC reported close to $95 million of expenditures in support of Romney, or four times the $23 million reported by the DNC. To put this party spending in perspective, American Crossroads and Crossroads GPS alone reported spending $113 million in the presidential race, a sum equivalent to the amount the national parties spent on communications directly supporting their candidates.

Super PAC and other nonparty organization expenditures heavily favored Romney. Of the $442 million spent in the general election, groups aligned with Romney reported spending $318 million on independent expenditures and electioneering communications, while those aligned with Obama reported spending slightly more than $107 million. Put another way, pro-Romney spending exceeded pro-Obama spending by a margin of 3 to 1. With the national party spending included, Romney supporters spent $413 million, Obama supporters $130 million. The difference between the two sides ($283 million) essentially made up for the financial gap created by Obama's commanding advantage over Romney.

Most of the money disbursed by Super PACs and other organizations was spent on advertising that criticized the candidate a group opposed. Of the $318 million spent by nonparty groups supporting Romney, $259 million was spent against Obama, with the remainder spent advocating Romney. Similarly, on the Democratic side, nonparty groups spent $87 million opposing Romney, as compared to $28 million advocating Obama. These group expenditures thus made a significant contribution to the overall negative tone of the advertising broadcast during the election.

Where this money came from is impossible to determine fully, since a number of the top spending groups were 501(c) organizations that reported their expenditures but did not disclose their sources of funding. Of the forty-eight nonparty groups reporting expenditures of $1 million or more in the presidential race, seventeen were 501(c) organizations. For example, Americans for Prosperity, a nonprofit organization supported by the billionaire Koch brothers, reported spending $33.5 million against Obama, while the conservative American Future Fund reported $19 million in expenditures, including more than $11 million in support of Romney and more than $7 million against Obama. Crossroads GPS reported $22 million in expenditures, including $15 million spent against Obama. None of these groups included in their reports a listing of donors who provided the funds for these expenditures. An analysis by the nonprofit policy advocacy group Demos estimated that $125 million in advertising expenditures came from sources that did not disclose their donors.[43]

Super PACs, however, were required to disclose their donors, and their reports revealed how they were able to amass such large war chests. These committees capitalized on the lack of constraints on their funding to raise megacontributions from wealthy individuals and sources that could not give to candidates or party committees. The top-spending Super PACs, which were responsible for the vast majority of Super PAC activity, primarily relied on contributions of $1 million or more to enable their efforts. Restore Our Future, the candidate-specific PAC that solely supported Romney, reported total receipts of $154 million. Of this amount, $65 million (about 42 percent of its total receipts) came from donors who gave $1 million or more. American Crossroads raised $117 million, with $77 million (66 percent) from such donors. Priorities USA Action, the PAC formed to solely support Obama, which became the top-spending Super PAC on the Democratic side, raised $79 million, with about $46 million (58 percent) coming from those who gave $1 million or more.[44]

These Super PACs particularly benefitted from the largesse of a very small number of donors. For example, Las Vegas casino mogul Sheldon Adelson and his wife gave $92.8 million in reported contributions in 2012, including $35 million to Restore Our Future and $23 million to American Crossroads. Texas home builder Bob Perry, who had helped finance Swift Boat Veterans and POWs for Truth in 2004, gave $10 million to Restore Our Future and $8.5 million to American Crossroads as part of his $26.8 million in total disclosed contributions. Dallas billionaire Harold Simmons, owner of Contran Corporation, gave $2.3 million to Restore our Future and $20.5 million to American Crossroads. On the Democratic side, Priorities USA Action received $5 million from hedge fund billionaire James Simons and his wife, and $4 million from Chicago media executive Fred Eychaner.

In some instances, a single donor was largely responsible for the funding of a Super PAC. For example, Ending Spending Fund was principally financed by Joe Ricketts, former CEO and chairman of TD Ameritrade. Ricketts contributed $12.6 million to this Super PAC, which reported spending $11.7 million in the presidential race, including $6.4 million against Obama and $5.3 million in support of Romney.

Super PACs also benefited from the new rules permitting the use of corporate and labor union contributions to finance independent expenditures. According to one analysis conducted before the final disclosure reports had been filed, Restore Our Future took in more than $26 million in business contributions, which represented about 20 percent of its total receipts at that time, while American Crossroads had taken in more than $13 million from corporations, which represented about 17 percent of its receipts at the time.[45] Priorities USA Action benefited from the support of labor unions, which might be expected of a group supporting the Democrats. The Super PAC received contributions of $1 million or more from seven different unions for a total of $9.3 million. These labor donations made up about 12 percent of the committee's receipts.[46]

Conclusion

The fundraising activity in the presidential race clarified the contours of the financial landscape in a post–public-funding, post–*Citizens United* world. While many of the practices and strategies employed in 2012 built upon those used in recent elections, new approaches also emerged, spurred by the more permissive rules on campaign funding established in advance of the election. These new approaches highlighted the sharp divergence that has taken place in the ways candidates and parties raise money, and the ways nonparty organizations do.

Although President Obama's fundraising once again demonstrated the valuable role that small donors may play in the financing of a presidential campaign, small-donor fundraising was not the defining characteristic of the financial strategies employed in 2012. Even within the limited sphere of campaign fundraising, the sphere in which candidates and parties operate under strict contribution limits, the solicitation of larger contributions was a priority. Both presidential contenders concentrated their fundraising time on events designed to raise large contributions, with much of their time in the summer and fall of the election year spent attending joint fundraising committee events, where attendees were asked to give the maximum contribution allowed by the law. As a result, joint fundraising committees played a much greater role in presidential fundraising than they had in the past. Consequently, more of the money raised by Obama and Romney came from the relatively small group of donors who gave $2,500 (a total of $394 million) than from the millions who made small contributions ($280 million). In addition, the national parties received a substantial amount of their funding from those who gave $30,000 or more.

Yet, even in pursuing contributions of larger amounts in an effort to keep pace with the fundraising of nonparty organizations, candidates and parties operated at a severe disadvantage. Nonparty organizations had an advantage prior to the 2012 election, since they operate in the unlimited sphere of campaign fundraising, without restrictions on the size of the contributions they receive. Changes in the law enhanced this advantage, sanctioning their role in financing election activity and allowing them to use their monies in ways that were previously prohibited. Nonparty organizations also have an advantage in that they can establish a variety of organizational structures to facilitate their fundraising—for example, a group can establish a Super PAC and a nonprofit entity—thereby offering prospective donors not only the option of making a substantial contribution that can have a meaningful impact, but also the option of making a disclosed contribution or an undisclosed one.

The strategic context of the 2012 election offered wealthy donors strong incentives to contribute to Super PACs and other organizations engaged in the battle to win the White House. These donors opened their checkbooks, and a relatively small group of contributors gave tens of millions of dollars. Donors who gave multimillion-dollar sums thus played a significant role in the financing of the 2012 election, and Super PACs demonstrated their efficacy as alternative vehicles for presidential fundraising. Their activities highlighted how the contribution limits applied to candidates have become functionally meaningless, since a donor who gives the $5,000 maximum to a candidate can simply augment their support by subsequently giving a hundred or a thousand times more to a Super PAC established to serve as a candidate's surrogate campaign organization.

The 2012 election thus offered a new approach to presidential fundraising, but whether multimillion-dollar donors will be willing to give so generously in the future remains to be seen. With an open race for the White House in 2016, it is likely that Super PACs and nonparty organizations will once again be active participants in campaign finance, and they may prove to be an even more important source of campaign funding. If so, the 2012 election may come to be viewed as the start of a new stage in the evolution of campaign finance, the time of the megadonor.

Acknowledgment

Andrew Pepper-Anderson of Colby College assisted in the research and preparation of this chapter.

Notes

1. The 2012 total includes the total amounts spent in the final two weeks reported by the Obama and Romney campaigns, Democratic and Republican National Committees, and the top-spending Super PACs, including Restore Our Future, American Crossroads, and Priorities USA Action. In 2004, the total reported spending in the presidential general election, including parties and independent groups, was $533 million. For 2004, see Anthony Corrado, "Financing the Presidential General

Election," in *Financing the 2004 Election,* edited by David B. Magleby et al. (Washington, DC: Brookings Institution Press, 2006), 143.

2. Chris Cilliza, "Obama's Reelection Campaign Could Hit Billion-Dollar Mark," *Washington Post,* December 12, 2010.

3. Anthony Corrado, "Financing the 2008 Presidential General Election," in *Financing the 2008 Election,* edited by David B. Magleby and Anthony Corrado (Washington, DC: Brookings Institution Press, 2011), 152–155.

4. Anthony Corrado, "Financing Presidential Nominations in the Post-Public Funding Era," in *The Making of the Presidential Candidates 2012,* edited by William G. Mayer and Jonathan Bernstein (Lanham, MD: Rowman & Littlefield, 2012), 48.

5. For a summary of federal contribution limits, see FEC, "FEC Announces 2011–2012 Campaign Cycle Contribution Limits," press release, February 3, 2011, http://www.fec.gov/press/20110203newlimits.shtml (accessed December 20, 2012).

6. John C. Green and Diana Kingsbury, "Financing the 2008 Nomination Campaigns," in *Financing the 2008 Election,* 93.

7. For a summary of the rules applicable to joint fundraising committees, see FEC, *Federal Election Campaign Guide: Political Party Committees,* Appendix B, June 2009, http://www.fec.gov/pdf/partygui.pdf.

8. Based on FEC filings.

9. Anthony Corrado and Heitor Gouvea, "Financing Presidential Nominations Under the BCRA," in *The Making of the Presidential Candidates 2004,* edited by William G. Mayer (Lanham, MD: Rowman & Littlefield, 2004), 53.

10. Ibid., 69–72.

11. Corrado, "Financing the 2008 Presidential General Election," 143.

12. Stephen R. Weissman and Ruth Hassan, "BCRA and 527 Groups," in *The Election After Reform,* edited by Michael J. Malbin (Lanham, MD: Rowman & Littlefield, 2006), 104–105.

13. Ibid., 92.

14. FEC, "FEC Collects $630,000 in Civil Penalties from Three 527 Organizations," press release, December 13, 2006, http://www.fec.gov/press/press2006/2006 1213murs.html, and "FEC to Collect $750,000 Civil Penalty from Progress for America Voter Fund," press release, February 28, 2007, http://www.fec.gov/press /press2007/20070228MUR.html.

15. *Citizens United v. Federal Election Commission,* 130 S. Ct. 876 (2010); *SpeechNow .org v. Federal Election Commission,* 599 F.3d 686 (D.C. Cir. 2010). For example, a nonprofit social welfare organization established under Section 501(c)(4) of the Internal Revenue Code may spend money on political activity, but influencing elections may not be the organization's "principal purpose." According to IRS regulations, any political spending on the part of the organization must be "insubstantial." While the IRS has not issued a clear standard as to how this is determined, it is generally interpreted to mean that political spending must constitute a minor share of an organization's total expenditures.

16. See FEC, Advisory Opinions 2010-09 and 2010-11.

17. Richard Briffault, "Super PACs," Columbia Law School Public Law & Legal Theory Working Paper Group, Paper Number 12-298, April 16, 2012, http://ssrn.com/abstract=2040941.

18. Based on data reported by the Center for Responsive Politics, http://www.opensecrets.org/outsidespending/summ.php?cycle=2010&chrt=V&disp=O&type=A.

19. Katy Steinmetz, "American Crossroads and the Ascendant Super PACs," Time, Swampland blog, June 24, 2011, http://swampland.time.com/2011/06/24/american-crossroads-and-the-ascendant-super-pacs/; and Shira Toeplitz, "Barbour Adds More Financial Heft to Crossroads Super PAC," Roll Call, September 8, 2011, http://www.rollcall.com/news/-208571-1.html.

20. Dan Eggen and Chris Cilliza, "Romney Backers Launch 'Super PAC' to Raise and Spend Unlimited Amounts," Washington Post, June 23, 2011.

21. Jeanne Cummings, "Exclusive: New Democratic Money Group to Take on Republicans," Politico.com, April 29, 2011, http://www.politico.com/news/stories/0411/53905.html.

22. FEC, "Electioneering Communication," Federal Register 72 (December 26, 2007), 72899, http://www.gpo.gov/fdsys/pkg/FR-2007-12-26/pdf/E7-24797.pdf.

23. Three minor candidates, Libertarian Party nominee Gary Johnson, Green Party nominee Jill Stein, and Republican Buddy Roemer, who ran on a campaign finance reform platform, qualified for public matching funds during the primary period. Johnson received $308,000 in public funds, Stein, $333,000, and Roemer, $352,000.

24. Michael Scherer, "Exclusive: Obama's 2012 Digital Fundraising Outperformed 2008," Time, Swampland blog, November 15, 2012, http://swampland.time.com/2012/11/15/exclusive-obamas-2012-digital-fundraising-outperformed-2008/.

25. Ibid.

26. Ibid.

27. See http://www.barackobama.com/news/entry/i-will-be-outspent/.

28. Paul Blumenthal, "Obama Campaign Fundraising Best in History," HuffingtonPost.com, December 7, 2012, http://www.huffingtonpost.com/2012/12/07/obama-fundraising-campaign_n_2257283.html?utm_hp_ref=obama-fundraising.

29. Jodi Kantor, "For the President, a Birthday Party with a Price Tag," New York Times, August 3, 2012.

30. Ibid.

31. Seema Mehta, "Los Angeles Event Brings in Nearly $15 Million for Obama Campaign," Los Angeles Times, May 10, 2012.

32. Michael Scherer, "Inside the Secret World of Quants and Data Crunchers Who Helped Obama Win," Time, Swampland blog, November 7, 2012, http://swampland.time.com/2012/11/07/inside-the-secret-world-of-quants-and-data-crunchers-who-helped-obama-win/.

33. Ibid.

34. The Campaign Finance Institute's postelection analysis is available at http://cfinst.org/Press/PReleases/13-01-11/Money_vs_Money-Plus_Post-Election_Reports_Reveal_Two_Different_Campaign_Strategies.aspx.

35. The Campaign Finance Institute's summary of presidential campaign fundraising in 2008 is available at http://www.cfinst.org/pdf/federal/president/2010_0106_Table1.pdf.

36. Campaign Finance Institute, "Obama's and Romney's Reports Each Point Up Vulnerabilities as the Campaigns Turn Toward the General Election," press release, May 23, 2012, http://cfinst.org/Press/Releases_tags/12-05-23/Obama's_and_Romney's_Reports_Each_Point_Up_Vulnerabilities_as_the_Campaigns_Turn_Toward_the_General_Election.aspx.

37. Ibid.

38. Kenneth P. Vogel and Dave Levinthal, "2012 Campaign Cash: $1 Billion vs. $1 Billion," Politico.com, October 21, 2012, http://www.politico.com/news/stories/1012/82671.html.

39. Kyle Trygstad, "In Private Meeting, RNC, GOP Digital Strategists Look to Improve," *Roll Call,* At the Races blog, December 6, 2012, http://atr.rollcall.com/in-private-meeting-rnc-gop-digital-strategists-look-to-improve/.

40. Based on FEC disclosure reports filed by the Obama Victory Fund.

41. Based on FEC disclosure reports filed by Romney Victory Inc.

42. Unless otherwise noted, the data in this paragraph is based on the amounts reported by the Center for Responsive Politics as of December 22, 2012. See http://www.opensecrets.org/outsidespending/index.php.

43. Adam Lioz and Blair Bowie, "Election Spending 2012: Post-Election Analysis of Federal Election Commission Data," November 7, 2012, http://www.demos.org/publication/election-spending-2012-postelection-analysis-federal-election-commission-data.

44. Based on an analysis of FEC filings conducted by Andrew Pepper-Anderson of Colby College and the author.

45. Lioz and Bowie, "Election Spending 2012."

46. Based on FEC reports as compiled by the Center for Responsive Politics.

6

Differences of Degree

Issue Agendas in a
Polarized Media Environment

DANNY HAYES

Barack Obama probably needed a Gatorade. Mitt Romney, too.

It was November 2, and the president and his Republican rival for the White House were in the last days of what had already been a bruising 2012 election campaign. The preceding months had been emotionally, mentally, and physically trying, as the two candidates had spent thousands of hours crisscrossing the country.

And now, four days before the election, they were making a final push. Obama, the Democrat trying to secure a second term, spent the day traipsing across the Midwest and West, from the battleground state of Wisconsin to the battleground state of Nevada to the (surprise!) battleground state of Colorado. Romney, for his part, was traveling hundreds of miles through the whole of Virginia, a state his campaign knew was critical to his chances of winning the presidency. Both gave speeches, rallied their supporters, and tried to win over that shrinking sliver of undecideds. Cold drinks were in order.

But for all their exhaustive and exhausting efforts, the news of the day wasn't on the campaign trail. Instead, it was emanating from a nondescript building on Constitution Avenue in Washington, DC, where the Department of Labor was releasing its monthly jobs report. That Friday's report indicated that the nation's employers had added 171,000 jobs in the month of October. Because more people had entered the job market, however, the unemployment rate ticked up one-tenth of a percentage point, to 7.9 percent. Good news, bad news.

But first and foremost, it was news. The report made the front pages across the country. *The Washington Post* noted that "the US jobs market in October sustained its slow trudge toward better times" in what was characterized as "the last major report card on the economy before the presidential election." A *Los Angeles Times* story said that the job growth foreshadowed a "smoother road" for whichever candidate became president. All the major media organizations, including the network news shows, followed suit.

It wasn't just the traditional media, however. The liberal blog Crooks and Liars devoted significant space to the story, one of three election-related dispatches it published that day. The jobs report also received prominent billing on the conservative blog Hot Air, in two separate posts. Not surprisingly, the sites had different takes on what the report meant. Crooks and Liars characterized the job growth as "more good news for President Obama." Hot Air, on the other hand, channeled a Tweet from conservative commentator James Pethokoukis: "Obama WH predicted unemployment rate would be 5.2% in October 2012, not 7.9%. Missed it by thismuch [*sic*]."

It is notable that news outlets across the political spectrum—from the mainstream media to the blogs of left and right—made identical judgments about what the big story of the day was. We have become accustomed to thinking of our media as irredeemably polarized, with different news audiences receiving wildly divergent portrayals of the political world. And to be sure, the tone of coverage of Obama and Romney was very different on Fox News and its conservative ilk than on MSNBC and its liberal media brethren.

But we know almost nothing about whether news organizations' campaign issue agendas—the collection of issues that receive the most attention—are as polarized as the tone or favorability of their coverage. Are consumers who get their news from mainstream, left-leaning, or right-leaning news sources encouraged to view the election as "about" wholly different political issues? Or do the shared news values and routines of journalistic organizations exert centripetal force that makes the issue agendas in campaign coverage more similar than the way those issues are covered?

In this chapter, I consider the extent to which the issue emphases of the Obama and Romney campaigns were reflected in different media outlets. I investigate whether left-wing news outlets were more likely to reflect the Obama campaign's portrayal of the campaign than were right-wing outlets, and whether the conservative outlets paid more attention than liberal ones to Romney's campaign messages. I also examine news judgments across the course of the election to determine whether outlets aligned with one party were more likely to react to campaign developments that benefited their favored candidate.

My findings show that these media outlets' issue agendas varied only slightly. Although the favorability of coverage toward Obama and Romney differed significantly among mainstream, left-wing, and right-wing media outlets, their emphasis on the campaign's major themes—the economy, budget deficits, Romney's tenure at Bain Capital, and Medicare—was very similar. In addition, as developments on the campaign trail led particular issues to become more or less prominent, news attention to those topics rose and fell in similar ways, regardless of whether the issue augured favorably for Obama or Romney. Ultimately, the data reveal that the media present a more homogenous portrayal of what elections are "about" than the oft-hyperbolic discourse about the current media environment would lead us to expect.

Agenda Setting, Priming, and Campaign Issue Emphases

A long line of research has shown that the media play a major role in shaping the public's perception of what political issues are important. Because citizens are inherently uncertain about what the most pressing political problems are, they look to media coverage for signals about which issues are most significant. As a result, there is a strong correlation between media coverage and public issue salience. When the media devote significant coverage to health care, for instance, more Americans are likely to say that health care is an important national problem. This is the agenda-setting effect, as the media establish the issue agenda that the public cares about.[1]

Agenda setting is particularly important during campaigns because salient issues are more likely to influence voting behavior than those that aren't on the public's radar. When the media devote sustained attention to an issue or candidate characteristic, such as integrity, that consideration becomes more cognitively accessible in voters' minds. As a result, evaluations of candidates are more likely to reflect assessments related to the particular consideration that has been "primed" by media attention (Druckman 2004; Iyengar and Kinder 1987; though see Lenz 2009). Priming can have electoral consequences if the criteria by which voters make their choices disproportionately put one candidate at an advantage.

For instance, George W. Bush during the 2004 campaign benefited from the fact that many Americans were concerned with the prospect of future domestic terrorism, just three years removed from the 9/11 attacks. In the exit poll, nearly one in five voters said terrorism was the most important issue to their vote.[2] Because surveys consistently showed that the public trusted Bush more than Kerry to handle terrorism—for example a *Time* poll in October gave him a 56 to 37 percent advantage—this was an issue that was advantageous to the president.[3] The more voters that cast ballots on the basis of terrorism as an issue, the better Bush was likely to do. Had fewer voters cared about terrorism, Kerry might have won more votes.

Candidates spend a lot of time trying to control a campaign's issue agenda for precisely this reason: They want voters to be thinking about things that give them an advantage and to ignore issues that put them at a disadvantage (e.g., Petrocik 1996). Bush certainly attempted to make his reelection bid a referendum on his handling of national security, emphasizing it in his speeches and television advertising. And in the 2008 election, Barack Obama spent much of his campaign emphasizing the struggling economy, knowing that the issue was a loser for Republican John McCain, whose party much of the public blamed for the deepening economic crisis. Obama did not, however, draw much attention to the two candidates' levels of experience, because this was an area that polling showed McCain had an advantage. In the end, Obama benefited from the fact that 63 percent of voters said in the exit poll that the economy was the issue most important to their vote (Holbrook 2009).

Through their campaign communications, candidates can try to place voters' focus on their preferred issue agenda. But they also need the news media to pass along their messages (Hayes 2008). Most voters never see a president give a speech, and many do their best to ignore political advertising when they can (click goes the remote).[4] Because the media are the public's primary source of political information, the issues that news organizations devote the most attention to are the ones most likely to influence voters' choices.

Issue Agendas in a Transformed Media Age

The proliferation of news outlets in the "post-broadcast" media environment (Prior 2007), however, has raised new questions about whether the agenda-setting process might play out differently in contemporary elections. For many decades, political coverage was largely homogenous—at any given time, what was news on one outlet was news on another, and there was relatively little variation in the issue content among media organizations (Graber 2009). In such an environment, discerning what voters would think was important was easy—all you had to do was look at the handful of issues being covered by the country's major newspapers and three broadcast networks. Those were the issues that would become salient to Americans.

But with the dizzying expansion of the media environment, this dynamic appears more complicated (Bennett and Iyengar 2008; Holbert, Garrett, and Gleason 2010). Major newspapers, network broadcasts, and local television news still command large audiences, but Americans can also turn to hundreds, if not thousands, of other sources. These include twenty-four-hour cable news channels and the ever-expanding menu of political news sites and blogs on the Internet.

As a result, the information environment is now less homogenous. Anyone who's watched even five minutes of Fox News and MSNBC's prime-time lineups can tell you that the two cable stations have starkly different takes on virtually any political issue. Fox's conservative hosts lionize Republicans and champion right-wing causes, while MSNBC's commentators do just the opposite, cheerleading for the Democrats and liberal solutions to policy problems. MSNBC's Chris Matthews once famously described "this thrill going up my leg" when he heard Obama speak.[5] The same is true throughout the blogosphere, where most political sites trade in an ideologically slanted take on the news.

But it is unclear whether the issue agendas of news outlets during an election season are equally diverse. On one hand, we might expect right- and left-leaning news outlets to cover campaigns in a way that is most beneficial to their favored party's candidates. In practice, this would mean that conservative outlets would devote a disproportionate amount of attention to the Republican candidate's preferred issue agenda. Likewise, liberal outlets would be expected to spend most of their time covering the talking points and messages of the Democratic candidate. If this is true, audiences for these outlets would presumably come away with very different interpretations of what the election was "about," which could complicate the winning candidate's attempts to persuade the public at large that their victory signaled an endorsement of particular campaign themes.

On the other hand, because even partisan media outlets are still news organizations, they might cover campaigns in a way that reflects a shared understanding of what the most newsworthy issues are. First, just like traditional media, left- and right-wing outlets have an incentive to cater to audience tastes. What their respective audiences want in terms of the tone or favorability of coverage will differ, but consumers still come to these organizations for commentary on and analysis of the news of the day. This means that news outlets have an incentive to cover the issues that they believe are most interesting and are at the center of political debate—lest viewers and readers turn elsewhere for information.

Second, similar news values may direct the attention of reporters, producers, and editors to the same kinds of stories. For instance, journalists seek novelty, because new developments draw in audiences far more than does the repetition of old information. That may lead media outlets to grow restless in their coverage (Bosso 1989) and seek new issues that emerge in the midst of campaigns, even if the resulting stories don't necessarily benefit their favored candidate. In addition, issues that highlight conflict between candidates are likely to draw the attention of reporters (Bruni 2003), regardless of which candidate appears to benefit from the exchange. In sum, these shared incentives and news values could produce more homogeneity in media issue agendas than we would see in the tone or favorability of coverage toward candidates.

Despite this emerging dynamic, there has been virtually no work examining the similarity or divergence in issue content in these new media outlets. Almost all of the election-related work on the new media has focused on the tone of coverage or favorability the candidates. But the 2012 campaign offers an opportunity to examine the convergence or divergence of issue agendas across different media outlets. The way that media outlets covered Obama's and Romney's preferred issues will shed light on how partisan news outlets cover campaigns and how candidate messages make their way to the public in the current media age.

The Romney and Obama Issue Agendas

In order to generate expectations for which messages might have been likely to appear in particular news outlets, we need to consider what the candidates' preferred issues in 2012 were. Let's start with Mitt Romney.

Since the financial crisis of 2008, the US economy had struggled to recover. As the presidential election formally began with the Republican primaries and caucuses early in 2012, Romney had already mapped out his strategy: He would make the campaign a referendum on Barack Obama's stewardship of the economy. Even before he had vanquished his Republican rivals, the former governor of Massachusetts was talking about the administration's economic shortcomings.

"This president has failed the people of Florida," Romney said during a January 23 Republican debate in Tampa. "We have to have a president who understands how to get an economy going again. He does not. He plays 90 rounds of golf when you have 25 million people out of work."

By the time the general election rolled around, Romney's message was unmistakable. In the second debate at Hofstra University, he mentioned six times the "twenty-three million" Americans—then down two million from January—who were unemployed or underemployed.[6] In drawing Americans' attention to the economy, Romney put himself in the role of the "clarifying candidate" (Vavreck 2009), encouraging voters to base their choices on economic conditions, which he believed were advantageous to him.

In reality, the economic conditions weren't as bad for Obama as Romney's campaign suggested. Given historical patterns, the economic growth rate was swift enough to give the president a reasonable chance to win reelection (Sides and Vavreck 2013). For instance, GDP growth in the first two quarters of 2012 was faster than in 1956, when Dwight D. Eisenhower won a second term easily. But the economic conditions were ambiguous enough that Romney's strategy seemed sensible, especially at the outset of 2012.

A second prong of Romney's strategy was focused on persistent budget deficits. Surveys showed that while Americans were primarily focused on the economy, they were also worried about rising levels of debt and the fiscal troubles of the United States. Romney made a point to link an economic recovery to the need to cut spending. This also was a reasonable strategy, as polling showed that Americans believed Romney would more effectively handle the issue than the president. A Pew Research Center poll in June found that 50 percent of Americans believed Romney would do a better job of reducing the federal deficit, while just 36 percent thought Obama would.

To be sure, Romney from time to time raised other matters on the campaign trail, including welfare spending and the attack on the US consulate and killing of the US ambassador in Benghazi, Libya. But for the most part, the economy and the deficit were his most prominent campaign messages.

Obama, meanwhile, took a different tack. The president did not ignore the economy, but unlike Romney, he argued that the economic recovery was under way and would continue to grow in the coming months. Unemployment was falling, he said. He also emphasized the success of the American auto manufacturers who had been propped up by the federal government in the wake of the 2008 financial crisis.

But with economic conditions not unequivocally in his favor, Obama also turned to messages that he hoped would portray him in a favorable light and cast a negative light on Romney. This is the imperative of the "insurgent candidate," in Vavreck's (2009) parlance, who needs to find an issue on which he is closer to voters than is his opponent, and make that salient to them.

Obama sought to exploit Romney's personal wealth and the fact that many voters didn't think the former Massachusetts governor understood their problems. The most clear and consistent attack focused on Bain Capital, the firm that Romney had run for many years. The Democrats attempted to use Bain to paint Romney as out of touch and unable to empathize with Americans who were struggling to get by. At certain points in the campaign, they attached Bain to the issue of outsourcing, something expected to play well with voters in swing states such as manufacturing-heavy Ohio.

At the Democratic National Convention (DNC) in Charlotte, North Carolina, in September, organizers brought to the stage Cindy Hewitt, who had worked at a Miami plant that had been acquired by Bain Capital. After describing how Bain had driven her plant into bankruptcy, Hewitt said Romney didn't understand the struggles of ordinary people. "So when Mitt Romney talks about his business experience, remember: It is not experience creating good-paying jobs," she said. "It is experience cutting jobs. It is experience shutting plants. It is experience making millions by making life tougher for hard-working Americans."

A second tactic followed Romney's August selection of House Budget Committee member Paul Ryan (R-WI) as his running mate. Ryan was the author of a controversial budget plan that included significant changes to Medicare, essentially turning it into a voucher program that would cap recipients' benefits. Ryan's nomination prompted Obama to focus heavy attention on the issue, especially late in the summer. Obama told voters that he would protect Medicare while the Republicans would threaten it.

At the DNC, former president Bill Clinton criticized Romney and Ryan for, as he put it, threatening the cherished program. If Romney was elected, Clinton said, "Medicare will now go broke in 2016. Think about that. That means, after all, we won't have to wait until their voucher program kicks in 2023 to see the end of Medicare as we know it. They're going to do it to us sooner than we thought."

Both campaigns hoped to enlist the media to disseminate these messages to voters. And the question is whether particular media outlets were more likely to disseminate the candidates' messages. Did conservative media pay more attention to the economy and deficits than other news organizations? And were liberal outlets disproportionately likely to pass along Obama's attacks on Romney over Bain and Medicare? Or did these partisan news outlets adhere to similar issue agendas, even as they tried to reframe those issues in ways that were favorable to their preferred candidate?

Tracking News Coverage of Campaign 2012

To gather data on media coverage of the 2012 campaign, I undertook a content analysis of news coverage from May—the first full month after Mitt

Romney had secured the GOP nomination—through November 5, the day before the election.[7] This allowed me to examine not only the topics to which media outlets devoted the most attention, but also how attention to various issues rose and fell over this six-month period.

I examined coverage in six news outlets. I chose two mainstream news organizations, ABC News and the *New York Times*. On ABC, I analyzed presidential campaign coverage on its thirty-minute nightly news broadcast *World News Tonight*. In the *Times,* I analyzed all campaign coverage from the print edition. I did not include material posted on the *Times*'s website that did not also appear in the paper itself. The coverage in these mainstream news organizations will provide a baseline to which I can compare coverage in left- and right-wing outlets.

On the left of the political news spectrum, I analyzed the liberal blogs Daily Kos and Crooks and Liars. On the right, I chose the blogs Hot Air and Red State. These are four of the most popular online news sites. As such, they are likely to produce a representative sample of the coverage that appeared on other partisan outlets with large audiences.

I first gathered the universe of stories that each outlet published about the election. To search ABC and the *Times,* I used the Lexis news database. For the four blogs, I employed the search functions on their websites to identify relevant articles.[8] For each outlet, I gathered all of the stories that mentioned both Barack Obama and Mitt Romney.[9]

The first evidence of similarity in the way these very different media outlets treated the election emerges in Figure 6.1. The graph displays the number of campaign stories in each news source for every month after Romney wrapped up the Republican nomination in April. For instance, the left-hand panel in the middle row shows that Daily Kos in May published 283 campaign dispatches. In October and the first five days of November, that number climbed to 565.

The pattern is virtually identical across the board. Mainstream, liberal, or conservative, every news source devoted more attention to the campaign as Election Day approached. The number of stories varied substantially (note that the scale for each graph is different), a reflection of difference in space and time constraints for each outlet (which exist for the traditional media, but not for the Internet outlets), as well as reporting resources.

While these patterns aren't especially surprising, the data demonstrate a commonality in how each of the outlets responded to the campaign, likely driven by news values and norms. Because people tend to be more interested in a campaign as its finish nears, all news organizations have an incentive to cater to that particular market demand. And from the perspective of news

FIGURE 6.1 2012 Presidential Campaign Coverage, by News Outlet

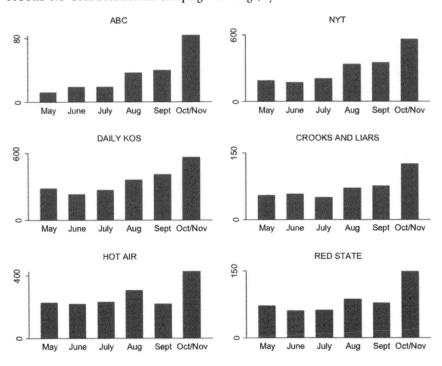

Source: Data come from a content analysis of campaign news coverage from May 1 through November 5, 2012.

Note: Chart shows the number of stories each month.

values, the election becomes more newsworthy as it gets closer. Just as a horse race is most interesting at the finish line—especially a close one—so the public and journalists view an election.

At the same time, the small differences that exist are illuminating. The increase in coverage tended to be steeper for mainstream outlets. For instance, there were seven times as many stories on ABC in October and November than in May, and about three times as many in the *Times.* In the liberal and conservative outlets, however, the corresponding increase was smaller, only about twofold.

This likely stems from the fact that ABC and the *Times* are general-purpose news organizations, covering not only politics and public affairs, but arts, entertainment, sports, and a host of other topics. As a result, the increasing salience of a presidential campaign—especially one whose outcome was uncertain even in its latter stages—likely made political events relatively more newsworthy and had a bigger effect on the amount of space allocated to campaign coverage in the mainstream outlets. Because the four blogs are interested in almost nothing but politics, their overall attention levels to the campaign were consistently high and less subject to a steep spike as Election Day neared.

One additional substantive difference is worth mentioning. From July onward, the amount of coverage in the mainstream and liberal outlets increased, consistent with an argument about the election becoming more newsworthy. But on the conservative blogs, coverage increased in August, declined slightly in September, and rose sharply the following month. A full investigation of this pattern is beyond the scope of this chapter, but one possibility is that coverage declined in the conservative media in the wake of the September 17 leaking of the Romney "47 percent" speech videotape. Unlike some other issues, such as the economy or Medicare, it might have proven more difficult for those outlets to frame coverage about the videotape in a way that was favorable to the GOP nominee.

Nonetheless, the homogeneity in media attention to the campaign is more apparent than any differences. All of the news outlets devoted more space to the campaign as it wore on, revealing similar news judgments. But what about the content of that coverage? How similar were the issue agendas across the various news sources?

Once Again, It's the Economy, Stupid

Figure 6.2 displays the amount of attention each news outlet devoted to the two "Romney" issues (the economy and the deficit) and the two "Obama" issues (Bain and Medicare). The bars represent the percentage of campaign stories that mentioned each issue. Multiple issues could appear in each story, and often did.

Because Romney and Obama both devoted significant time to the economy, we would expect the economy to receive top billing among all of the news outlets. But if the news organizations are principally devoted to promoting their own candidates' messages, we might expect the conservative outlets to spend relatively more time on the deficit than the liberal outlets, while the liberal outlets would devote relatively more attention to Bain and Medicare. Without partisan expectation for the mainstream news sources, we might expect their issue emphases to fall somewhere between those of the partisan media.

Even a quick glance at the profiles of the graphs reveals that the news out-lets made very similar judgments about the relative importance of the four issues. The economy, as expected, was the top for all. Just as news outlets across the political spectrum all devoted significant coverage to the November 2 jobs report in the closing days of the campaign, economic news dominated throughout the election year.

To be sure, there was variation in the percentage of campaign stories that mentioned the economy. For instance, 38 percent of *Times* stories talked about the economy, while just 26 percent of ABC reports did. On the left, 21 per-cent of Daily Kos and 26 percent of Crooks and Liars stories mentioned the economy, while the figures for the conservative Hot Air and Red State were 38 and 28 percent, respectively. In some ways, this suggests a bit of ideological divergence—Daily Kos came in with the lowest amount of attention to this "Romney" issue, while Hot Air was the highest. But the share of economic coverage in Hot Air was identical to that in the *Times*, a mainstream outlet whose coverage would not be expected to favor Romney. Furthermore, Red State's lower level of attention seems to undercut any argument that conser-vative outlets, generally speaking, spent more time on the economy because the issue would help Romney. And the fact that the economy was the number one issue for every news outlet, regardless of partisan stripe, reveals a largely shared news judgment about which issue was most important.

Not surprisingly, the substance and thrust of economic news was rather different in the partisan media. On September 27, for instance, Daniel Horo-witz of Red State reacted to the news that the nation's gross domestic product growth rate—a key economic indicator—had been revised downward in the second quarter from 1.7 to 1.3 percent. "Folks," he wrote, "this is not endemic of a recession. It's worse than that. This is a sickly recovery." By contrast, Jed Lewison at Daily Kos hardly saw an infirm patient when he considered the economic numbers just a week later. "Things are getting better," he wrote, "but all [Romney] wants to do is convince you that they're getting worse."

Because both Romney and Obama talked regularly about the economy, the issue may not offer the best test of a partisan issue agenda argument. The remaining three issues—the deficit, Bain, and Medicare—are more one-sided, which should allow for a "cleaner" test of the argument that partisan outlets prefer to cover issues perceived as advantageous to their favored candidate.

Even still, the data reveal only differences of degree, not kind. Consider the deficit, an issue that Romney sought to exploit but that Obama largely chose not to talk about. The conservative outlet Hot Air mentioned the deficit more often (15 percent) than either Daily Kos (8 percent) or Crooks and Liars (9

FIGURE 6.2 Attention to Issues in 2012 Presidential Campaign Coverage, by Outlet

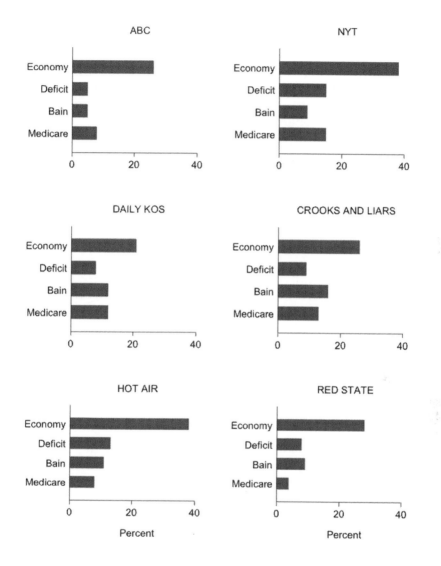

Source: Data come from a content analysis of campaign news coverage from May 1 through November 5, 2012.

Note: Chart shows the percentage of campaign stories that mentioned various issues.

percent). But Red State mentioned the deficit in only 8 percent of its stories, giving it the same amount of attention as the liberal media. And no outlet mentioned the deficit in its campaign coverage more than the *Times* (15 percent).

There is a bit more evidence of divergence along ideological lines for Bain and Medicare. Daily Kos (12 percent) and Crooks and Liars (16 percent) devoted more attention to Bain than the other outlets did. In the conservative media, Hot Air mentioned Bain in 11 percent of its stories, while Red State did in 9 percent. Bain appears to have been an issue that conservative outlets preferred to discuss less than their liberal counterparts, as might be expected for an issue that favored Obama. Likewise, Daily Kos and Crooks and Liars mentioned Medicare in 13 percent and 12 percent of campaign stories, respectively, while Hot Air and Red State covered the issue less frequently, at 8 percent and 4 percent.

But it is important not to make too much of these differences. The largest divergence in issue coverage between any two of the ideological outlets comes on Medicare, between the Daily Kos and Red State. But this nine-point gap is small in absolute terms. It is clearly not the case that conservative media were ignoring issues that were bad for Romney, while liberal outlets were doing the same for issues that did not advantage Obama. All of the news outlets agreed that the economy was the most important issue in the election, and they made similar, albeit not identical, determinations about how much attention various other topics should receive. The small differences are most likely driven by the particular tastes of reporters or editors at these outlets rather than a broader strategic plan to ignore certain issues because they were disadvantageous to a favored candidate.

All Together Now: The Dynamics of Issue Attention

Another way to determine whether outlets are responding to the campaign in a partisan way is to see whether they react similarly to events on the campaign trail—that is, to examine whether the changes in coverage over the course of the election differ across news sources. One way to do that is to look at monthly correlations between news outlets in the amount of coverage they devoted to a particular issue. For instance, we can examine whether the percentage of stories that mentioned Medicare rose and fell from month to month in a similar fashion for various media outlets. If the correlation between two outlets is positive and large, then that would indicate that their attention to Medicare moved in similar ways during the campaign. Negative or low correlations (those close to zero) would suggest little relationship in how

TABLE 6.1 Monthly Correlations for Issue Attention, by Issue

	ABC	NYT	Daily Kos	Crooks and Liars	Hot Air
ECONOMY					
NYT	0.52	--			
Daily Kos	0.89	0.62	--		
Crooks and Liars	0.47	0.98	0.66	--	
Hot Air	0.82	0.76	0.91	0.79	--
Red State	0.43	0.22	0.19	0.10	0.15
DEFICIT					
NYT	0.41	--			
Daily Kos	−0.07	0.63	--		
Crooks and Liars	0.29	−0.28	−0.04	--	
Hot Air	0.21	−0.52	−0.89	0.40	--
Red State	0.72	−0.11	−0.13	0.80	0.42
BAIN					
NYT	0.86	--			
Daily Kos	0.78	0.97	--		
Crooks and Liars	0.72	0.89	0.96	--	
Hot Air	0.38	0.78	0.87	0.86	--
Red State	0.54	0.88	0.87	0.77	0.89
MEDICARE					
NYT	0.63	--			
Daily Kos	0.78	0.97	--		
Crooks and Liars	0.75	0.75	0.82	--	
Hot Air	0.73	0.97	0.98	0.87	--
Red State	0.01	0.77	0.60	0.33	0.65

Source: Data come from a content analysis of campaign news coverage from May 1 through November 5, 2012.

Note: Table shows Pearson correlation coefficients for monthly attention to issues.

important Medicare was in two outlets from month to month. Correlations can range from −1 to +1.

Table 6.1 presents a correlation matrix for all six news outlets, split by issue. For instance, the top panel of the table presents the correlations among the six news outlets on the economy. The first column shows the correlations between

ABC and each of the other five outlets. The upper-left-most figure of 0.52 shows a fairly strong correlation in attention to the economy over the course of the campaign between ABC and the *New York Times*. As coverage of the economy in one month rose (or fell) on ABC, it also rose (or fell) in the *Times*. The second column shows correlations between the *Times* and all the other outlets (with the exception of ABC, which appeared in the first column). And so on.

What is important about the table is that almost all of the correlations are positive. In fact, for every issue but the deficit, every correlation is positive. With varying degrees of strength, the increases and decreases in coverage month to month were positively correlated across media outlets. For example, as coverage of Bain increased one month in Daily Kos, it also rose in Hot Air ($r = 0.87$). For Bain and Medicare especially—perhaps the two issues most obviously favorable to one side—the correlations are very strong.

Negative correlations, which indicate divergent patterns of attention between news outlets, appeared only on the deficit. For instance, there are several negative correlations between the *New York Times* and other news outlets, as well as between Daily Kos and other sources. Deficit stories appear not to be driven by the same political or campaign-trail developments across the various news outlets. This may be because deficit stories were not tied to events in the same way as were articles about the economy—such as those about the jobs report mentioned in the introduction of the chapter—or Bain and Medicare.

Of course, the correlations cannot tell us *when* attention to different issues increased or decreased during the campaign. To facilitate a longitudinal analysis, I grouped the outlets into their broad categories: mainstream, liberal, and conservative. I averaged together the amount of attention each outlet in the category gave to each issue for each month. These data are summarized in Figure 6.3. This presentation offers a way to see the patterns responsible for the correlations in Table 6.1.

Take the economy. In May, there were clear differences in the amount of economic news reported in mainstream and conservative outlets on one hand, and the liberal outlets on the other. On average, about 40 percent of stories in the mainstream and conservative media mentioned the economy, while the average was just 27 percent for liberal outlets. But although the economy drew somewhat less attention every month in Daily Kos and Crooks and Liars than it did in the other outlets, the general trend is very similar. As the campaign wore on, all the news outlets spent less time on economic issues.

One explanation for the downward trend is that as Election Day nears, news outlets typically devote less attention to the candidates' issue emphases

FIGURE 6.3 Attention to Issues in 2012 Presidential Campaign Coverage, by Month

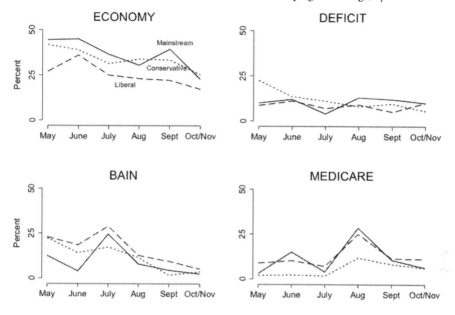

Source: Data come from a content analysis of campaign news coverage from May 1 through November 5, 2012.

Note: Chart shows the percentage of campaign stories that mentioned various issues. Mainstream outlets are ABC and the *New York Times,* liberal outlets are Daily Kos and Crooks and Liars, and conservative outlets are Hot Air and Red State.

(Hayes 2010). By the time October rolled around, Obama's and Romney's economic talking points had been reported so many times that they were probably stale for many journalists, regardless of their partisan orientation. Instead, as they often do, the media turned for news to the candidates' evolving campaign strategies and the horse race. Much of the October and early November coverage centered on Romney's late decision to put resources into Pennsylvania and the debate over the accuracy of the polls and forecasting models, such as that of statistician Nate Silver. This may have contributed to the downturn in the share of economic news. The trend suggests that the attention of all of the outlets was drawn to other topics in a similar fashion, indicating that the behavior of these news sources is borne of similar tendencies.

The trend lines for Bain and Medicare add a bit more to the story. It's important to note, first of all, that news coverage of Bain was actually relatively high early in the time series, with about 24 percent of coverage in both liberal and conservative outlets in May. Again, this seems to undermine the idea that conservative outlets might have ignored an issue because it was detrimental to the GOP nominee.

The Obama campaign's attacks on Romney's tenure at Bain Capital emerged in full force in July. It is easy to see the effect that had on media attention. Coverage of Bain spiked to 29 percent in liberal outlets and 25 percent in mainstream outlets in July. A Crooks and Liars story was representative of the way liberal outlets portrayed the issue. Correspondent Jon Perr wrote that Romney had "reaped whirlwind profits" at Bain even as companies the firm had acquired were shut down.

The conservative outlets were somewhat less responsive to the Obama attacks on average, but they did not ignore the issue. In July, 17 percent of conservative media stories mentioned Bain. But those outlets tried to reframe Bain as either a nonissue or an asset to Romney. For instance, Hot Air in August emphasized that Romney's "work in launching Staples," the office supply company, demonstrated that his time at Bain would actually help him turn the economy around as president. After July, coverage of the issue receded in a similar fashion in all outlets. Once the Bain attack had been launched, it was less newsworthy for all of the outlets and gave way to fresh issues.

One of those newer topics was Medicare, which peaked in coverage—in all three types of outlets—in August. This was largely due to the nomination to the GOP ticket of Ryan, the architect of a Republican budget plan that included significant alterations to Medicare. The bottom-right panel of Figure 6.3 shows that, not surprisingly, liberal and mainstream outlets responded most strongly to the Democratic attacks on the Medicare portion of Ryan's budget. Medicare was mentioned in 29 percent of August campaign stories in mainstream outlets and 25 percent of stories in liberal outlets. Just as with Bain, conservative outlets gave less attention to Medicare, consistent with a story of media seeking to protect the interests of their favored candidate. But as the attacks on the Ryan budget mounted, coverage of Medicare did increase in the conservative outlets—from 2 percent in July to 11 percent in August. Even on an issue that was not especially advantageous to their candidate, Hot Air and Red State could not completely ignore such a major part of the political debate.

The issue that produced several negative correlations in Table 6.1—the deficit—shows few clear patterns. The biggest divergence comes early in the campaign, when conservative outlets devoted significantly more attention (23 percent) to the deficit than the mainstream or liberal outlets did. The negative correlations in Table 6.1 likely stem from that, as well as from the fact that liberal coverage rose in September and then ticked up in October and early November, whereas the opposite was true for conservative outlets. There is no clear explanation for this pattern, but it's also the case that this was the issue that was clearly the least chronically salient for all of the news outlets.

In sum, there is clear evidence the ideologically slanted news outlets have not adopted a strategy of ignoring issues that are harmful to their side. Like more traditional news outlets, they respond to the campaign as it develops, covering whatever happens to be at the center of debate at a given moment. The coverage of these issues is framed very differently, of course, but audiences for these outlets are told a similar story of what the campaign is about through the issue agendas of these otherwise polarized news sources.

Conclusion

When Americans went to the polls on November 6, 2012, most of them had one thing on their minds. In the National Election Pool exit poll, 59 percent said the economy was the issue that mattered most to their vote, more important than foreign policy, health care, or the federal budget deficit. This wasn't just a response that reflected a pro-Romney or pro-Obama bias. Among voters who identified the economy as the top issue, 51 percent chose Romney and 47 percent cast ballots for Obama.[10]

That so many people on opposites sides of the political divide agreed about the election's central issue owes much to media coverage of the presidential campaign. News outlets across the political spectrum in 2012 spent more time covering the economy than any other issue, helping establish the public's agenda in the months before Election Day. Left, right, or mainstream, the media converged on the same message—the election was all about the economy.

In addition, news outlets devoted similar amounts of attention to other issues that were being emphasized by one campaign or the other. The federal budget deficit, an issue on which Romney hoped to focus voters' attention, received little sustained attention, even from right-leaning news outlets. And the amount of coverage devoted to Bain Capital and Medicare—both issues that the Obama campaign sought to play up—was nearly identical on both liberal and conservative blogs, as well as in the mainstream media. Furthermore, attention to the economy, Bain, and Medicare also rose and fell in nearly identical ways throughout the general election campaign, as both the partisan and mainstream outlets responded to political developments in a similar fashion.

The substance of coverage was very different, of course. Conservative outlets emphasized high unemployment and anemic growth, while liberal news sites focused on the slow but steady improvement in Americans' economic fortunes. The treatment of Bain and Medicare also reflected the news outlets' political loyalties.

But the similarity in the issue agendas of these highly partisan news outlets is striking. Partisan media certainly seek to promote their favored candidate's fortunes, but they do not do so by ignoring issues that appear to be disadvantageous to his campaign. Americans, regardless of where they turned for news in 2012, were likely to come away from campaign coverage with a similar sense about which issues were most important. Partisan news outlets are now a fact of life in American politics. But even the ideologically motivated media appear to possess a traditional definition of "news" that creates more homogeneity in the coverage of campaigns than one might expect.

Notes

1. The academic literature on agenda setting is vast, to put it mildly. For a review, see McCombs (2004).

2. CNN, "Election Results," 2004, accessed February 20, 2013, http://www.cnn.com /ELECTION/2004/pages/results/states/US/P/00/epolls.0.html.

3. "Time Poll: Bush Opens 5 Point Lead Against Kerry," *Time*, October 22, 2004, http://www.time.com/time/election2004/article/0,18471,733715,00.html.

4. Even changing channels is increasingly unnecessary. With the rise of digital video recorders, voters find it even easier to skip the barrage of ads that hit the battleground states every election year.

5. Huffington Post, "Christ Matthews: 'I Felt This Thrill Going up My Leg' as Obama Spoke," March 28, 2008, http://www.huffingtonpost.com/2008/02/13/chris -matthews-i-felt-thi_n_86449.html.

6. Romney often cast this as the number of people out of work. But it is more accurate to say that twenty-three million Americans were looking for work or held jobs that put them in the category of "underemployed." See Don Lee, "Fact Check: Romney Overstates the Number of Americans out of Work," October 3, 2012, http:// articles.latimes.com/2012/oct/03/news/la-pn-fact-check-debate-romney-unem ployment-20121003.

7. Romney's last serious challenger, Rick Santorum, dropped out of the GOP race in April, clearing the way for Romney's nomination.

8. For Daily Kos, I restricted the analysis to "frontpaged" diaries.

9. By restricting the search only to articles that mentioned both candidates, I am likely missing campaign-related articles that mention just one of the candidates. But I chose this strategy for two reasons. First, the search strategy prevents me from including articles that are not about the campaign—and this is especially true

for stories about Obama, which could be about his presidential responsibilities not connected to the election. Second, my strategy probably leaves me missing only a handful of articles. Rare is the campaign story that doesn't at least mention both candidates.

10. Fox News, "2012 Fox News Exit Polls," accessed February 20, 2013, http://www.foxnews.com/politics/elections/2012-exit-poll.

References

Bennett, W. Lance, and Shanto Iyengar. 2008. "A New Era of Minimal Effects? The Changing Foundations of Political Communication." *Journal of Communication* 58 (4): 707–731.

Bosso, Christopher. 1989. "Setting the Agenda: Mass Media and the Discovery of Famine in Ethiopia." In *Manipulating Public Opinion: Essays on Public Opinion as a Dependent Variable,* edited by Michael Margolis and Gary A. Mauser, 153–174. Pacific Grove, CA: Brooks/Cole Publishing.

Bruni, Frank. 2003. *Ambling into History: The Unlikely Odyssey of George W. Bush.* New York: Harper Perennial.

Druckman, James N. 2004. "Priming the Vote: Campaign Effects in a US Senate Election." *Political Psychology* 25 (4): 577–594.

Graber, Doris A. 2009. *Mass Media and American Politics,* 8th edition. Washington: CQ Press.

Hayes, Danny. 2008. "Does the Messenger Matter? Candidate-Media Agenda Convergence and Its Effects on Voter Issue Salience." *Political Research Quarterly* 61 (1): 134–146.

———. 2010. "The Dynamics of Agenda Convergence and the Paradox of Competitiveness in Presidential Campaigns." *Political Research Quarterly* 63 (3): 594–611.

Holbert, R. Lance, R. Kelly Garrett, and Laurel S. Gleason. 2010. "A New Era of Minimal Effects? A Response to Bennett and Iyengar." *Journal of Communication* 60 (1): 15–34.

Holbrook, Thomas M. 2009. "Economic Considerations and the 2008 Presidential Election." *PS: Political Science & Politics* 42 (3): 473–478.

Iyengar, Shanto, and Donald E. Kinder. 1987. *News That Matters: Television and American Opinion.* Chicago: University of Chicago Press.

Lenz, Gabriel S. 2009. "Learning and Opinion Change, Not Priming: Reconsidering the Priming Hypothesis." *American Journal of Political Science* 53 (4): 821–837.

McCombs, Maxwell E. 2004. *Setting the Agenda: The Media and Public Opinion.* Malden, MA: Blackwell.

Petrocik, John R. 1996. "Issue Ownership in Presidential Elections, with a 1980 Case Study." *American Journal of Political Science* 40 (3): 825–850.

Prior, Markus. 2007. *Post-broadcast Democracy: How Media Choice Increases Inequality in Political Involvement and Polarizes Elections.* New York: Cambridge University Press.

Sides, John, and Lynn Vavreck. 2013. *The Gamble: Choice and Chance in the 2012 Presidential Election.* Princeton, NJ: Princeton University Press.

Vavreck, Lynn. 2009. *The Message Matters: The Economy and Presidential Campaigns.* Princeton, NJ: Princeton University Press.

7

How the Media Covered the 2012 Election

The Role of Earned Media

DOTTY LYNCH

We aim to supply news.
—Ivy Ledbetter Lee, public relations maestro, 1906

"Earned media" is a public relations term that refers to positive news media coverage of an event, issue, or person that is initiated by a campaign. According to *Texas Politics*, an online textbook from the University of Texas, "one of the most efficient and cost-effective ways to reach a large audience is through earned media. Earned media is positive news coverage that you actively work to get. By creating newsworthy stories or events and offering the stories to news outlets in your area, you can generate effective media coverage that targets specific audiences with your specific message."[1]

In this chapter we will look at the history of earned media and its evolution in political communications theory. We will then examine the news environment of 2012, which formed the backdrop for presidential campaign communications. Finally, we will examine how attempts at earning positive media, controlling the message, and setting the news agenda were executed, how successful they were, and what lessons candidates and political professionals can learn for the future.

The History of Earned Media

The concept of communicating information to positively influence opinions and behavior has been a staple of public relations since antiquity. Examples can be seen as far back as 1800 BCE in Iraq, when farm bulletins were produced on how to sow crops. Art was designed to deify kings; the walls of Pompeii were inscribed with election appeals. Julius Caesar's *Commentaries,* the reports he sent back to Rome about his epic campaign, are considered great examples of propaganda. In the seventeenth century the Catholic Church created the Congregatio de Propaganda Fide to put out information to spread the faith.[2] Using "third party validators" is a common practice in public relations campaigns today.

In the United States in the 1790s, the drive to gain popular support occupied much of the fight between Alexander Hamilton and Thomas Jefferson. Around that time there were numerous examples of what we think of as modern public relations techniques designed to mold public opinion and frame debate. Symbols, slogans, and staged events like the Liberty Tree, "No Taxation Without Representation," and the Boston Tea Party helped establish an image to gain public approval. Getting your story out before anyone else does, a public relations commandment, is exemplified in the pamphlet about the Boston Massacre and the engraving of Paul Revere that rallied colonists to the cause.

Historian Allan Nevins has called the *Federalist Papers* "history's finest public relations job." Andrew Jackson's kitchen cabinet, headed by Amos Kendall, was filled with public relations geniuses (almost all of them former newspapermen who knew how to engage the press). Around the turn of the twentieth century, public relations and press agentry took hold in America in general and in political campaigns in particular. In the late 1800s, P. T. Barnum beat the drum and created a desire for the circus. In 1896 the William McKinley campaign created a publicity bureau, which disseminated press releases and cartoons to the news media and posters and pamphlets to voters. The Republicans spent $3.5 million on that campaign and at least $500,000 on publicity and press bureau activities.

The granddaddy of American public relations, Ivy Ledbetter Lee, changed the Rockefeller family image from mean corporate millionaires to philanthropic giants. He described his prime function as a publicist. "We aim to supply news," he proclaimed in connection with the anthracite coal strike. Henry Ford used "free media" successfully to build credibility for his cars. Ford viewed good publicity as a necessary complement to paid ads. He put Fords into racing events, formed clubs of Ford owners, and rocked the industry by announcing five-dollar pay for an eight-hour day as a way to build support for his cars. Paid advertisements came into their own in the1920s. Ford also used opinion surveys; in 1912 he asked Model T owners why they had bought the cars.

Survey research became an important part of public relations when George Gallup discovered sampling in the late 1920s. Gallup joined Young and Rubicon as the advertising industry's first marketing director in the 1930s, and he conducted polls to measure the opinions and behavior of the public and provide guidance on how campaigns were working. Gallup's methodology and success spawned a proliferation of survey and marketing research, which became a staple of strategic communication plans.

Franklin Roosevelt's mentor, Louis Howe, is credited with steering FDR to the use of radio to communicate directly with the public and sell his New Deal. Howe died in 1936, but New Dealers carried on his legacy in using communications media to build public support for economic programs, paving the way for the American entrance into World War II. The war produced a new understanding of public relations and propaganda techniques, which modern campaigns have built on steadily as technology has developed. The advent of television in the 1950s and the Internet in the 1990s has created new channels for communications and an escalation of costs and new techniques.

Earned or Free?

In political circles, the term "earned media" didn't receive currency until the late 1980s. Campaign communications (other than paid advertising) intended to generate good publicity for the candidate in the news media were known as free media and included press releases, relationships with reporters, news advisories, press conferences, conference calls, books, speeches, endorsements, interviews, debates, visuals, op-ed pieces, and even stunts. Having up-to-date press lists, knowing which reporters are covering a story, identifying coverage decision makers, and cultivating relationships with reporters and editors are part of the communications professional's toolbox.[3]

Toward the end of the 1980s, campaign consultants, who prided themselves as maestros of media manipulation, insisted that this task was not free. Like Ronald Reagan proclaiming, "I paid for this microphone," political media consultants wanted the world to know it was their good work that was responsible for good press and that there was nothing free about it! (Campaigns, of course, were well aware of this since they paid the consultants' bills.)

The term "earned media" applied to campaigns in news coverage seems to have appeared in a *Newsweek* article about sound bites in 1988. "Satellite hookups and cable TV, which furnish saturation coverage of the campaigns, have made the search for the perfect line a near obsession. Campaigns spend—and often waste—thousands of dollars boiling down all of the issues into broad themes that can be used in both 'paid media' (political TV ads) and 'earned media' (which recently replaced 'free media' as the favored euphemism for news)."[4]

Positive news coverage is crucial to successful campaigns, since the news media have more credibility than paid advertising, even amid skepticism toward the press and the use of direct online communication. One of the first hurdles campaigns face is letting voters know who their candidates are and getting an audience to pay attention to their messages. It is mainly the news media who will carry that information to voters in either a positive or a negative light. Getting the candidate covered and conveying the message you want to transmit takes great skill and some luck.

A memo from the Kansas Democratic Party to local campaigns in 2004 is a good example of the calculation behind earned media strategies and the attitude of campaigns toward the press: "Realistically, how much of your campaign will the press be interested in? . . . There is a reason this is called earned media and not free media. You do not pay for the media to cover your campaign but you will have to earn it. You cannot expect the press to cover your campaign just because you are running for office. That is why you have to have a plan for how you will earn media coverage."[5]

These strategists thought that the word "earned" made campaign coverage more acceptable to reporters and editors than the word "free," although many reporters bristle at both terms, since they believe they are more than just a conveyor belt for campaign publicity.

Framing and Delivering the Message

There are three basic components to earned media: the messenger, the message, and the conveyor of the message through the news media to the public. Campaigns spend time and money on public opinion research to determine which messages will move voters. A multitude of facts must be transmitted to the public about a candidate, and strategies are devised on how to get the most salient messages to the voter through multiple channels, including the news media.

The concepts of framing the argument and setting the agenda are dominant among modern campaign media consultants. University of California linguistics professor George Lakoff, who translated framing theory into political applications, has been a guru of former Democratic National Committee chair and presidential candidate Howard Dean. Lakoff has participated in numerous Democratic Party strategy sessions during the past five years. His book *Don't Think of an Elephant* was studied religiously by Democrats on

Capitol Hill who were desperate to come up with a winning message after years of Republican dominance in the House of Representatives. Some of his work was in reaction to that of Frank Luntz, a Republican campaign consultant who gained great currency with his memos on the power of using certain words in political dialogue. Luntz's idea of "fourteen words never to use" was instrumental in selling Newt Gingrich's Contract with America. (The words *government, privatization,* and *outsourcing* were to be replaced by *Washington, personalization,* and *overregulation.*) Lakoff suggested that Democrats needed to choose better language if they were to compete with Republicans and choose issues that had positive cultural connotations.[6]

Both Lakoff and Luntz draw on anthropologist Erving Goffman, who in the 1970s did groundbreaking work on how individuals make sense of events by organizing and filtering them through their predispositions. Effective communicators are those who are able to shape judgments by using existing cultural meanings to describe events.[7]

Lakoff and Luntz have their detractors among campaign professionals, but the concepts of framing the message, using and avoiding specific value-laden words, and setting the agenda are staples among practitioners of "earned media."

Creating Narratives

Candidates use stories to make their biographies coherent and maybe a tad more interesting than their resumes might suggest. Certain qualities are emphasized and others are played down to craft an image that will appeal to the widest cross section of voters. Until the 2012 convention, Mitt Romney rarely mentioned all the good works he did as a Mormon bishop but highlighted his success as a business man, and Barack Obama deemphasized his days at Occidental College while emphasizing his decision to leave a big law firm and become a community organizer. Reporters also use narratives to explain and characterize these campaigns. An analysis by the Project for Excellence in Journalism in 2004 reported:

> To a large degree, journalists and political scientists have noted that presidential campaigns are dominated by a handful of themes, usually those that revolve around the character of the candidates. These might be called the "master narratives" of the campaign and they can raise or sink a candidacy. In a way, these master or metanarratives are the modern equivalent of pack journalism. While the reporters are no longer all

standing together in a group, literally looking over each others shoulder as they write, they tend to synthesize and react to each other's coverage to such an extent that it can be difficult for candidates to escape the impression created by these narratives or to project a different one. In 2000, a study by the Project found that Vice President Gore was dogged by the notion that he was tainted by scandal. Then-Governor Bush was portrayed primarily as a different kind of Republican but he was also tagged with the idea that he was dim.

Pew has done an extensive study called "Master Narrative of the 2012 Campaign," which we will discuss later in the chapter.

The News Media

The news media spend a lot of time trying to get access to political operatives, listening to and reading their spin, and begging to be "fed" while at the same time resenting attempts at manipulation. There is a dance that goes on between the media and political operatives, and the 2012 campaign was no different. If anything there was more dancing, more attempts at "earning" and controlling media, and greater use of new technologies to get it and to report on it. And there were more reporters checking more facts and begging, resisting, and decrying at the same time.

News Values

In their landmark book, *The Interplay of Influence,* Kathleen Hall Jamieson and Karlyn Kohrs Campbell detail the relationships among news, politics, advertising, and the Internet and emphasize the two-way communication between the media and society. Not only does the media influence and persuade the public but individuals, groups, institutions, and politicians influence the media. They also describe the elements of hard news that the media use to determine what gets covered: drama; conflict; violence; personal stories (over process); actions or events; things that are novel, deviant, or extraordinary; or issues and events linked to other issues that are already in the media. It is against this set of news values that political communications are assessed, and successful campaign practitioners know them instinctively. Good news, celebrity news, and exclusives will also get coverage if news executives and reporters believe they are important or will boost audience ratings.[8]

News norms are changing, and in 2012 campaigns had to adjust to a different media landscape. Opinion journalism flourished on cable and online, stories and their shelf lives became shorter, and the 24/7 news cycle and the widespread use and speed of the Internet meant a constantly changing and sensationalist news environment. Twitter became a standard part of news gathering and dissemination, and analysis via 140 characters was SOP. Media sound bites from Herman Cain's 999 plan to Rick Perry's "oops" and Joe Biden's "unchained" gaffe screeched around the cables for a few days and then gave way to the next hot item.

The 2012 Campaign

No political story gets more media attention than presidential campaigns, and in 2012 there were more reporters (professionals and citizens) and more venues than ever before. In addition, over $2.6 billion was spent on paid advertising on TV ($1,235,000 in the general election and the rest during the primaries), which added to the amount of time people were exposed to information about the presidential campaign.[9] Campaigns created narratives and produced events and ads to tell their story and deliver messages received by audiences of political elites and voters.

Announcements, debates, and conventions are three types of opportunities for candidates to get media coverage, and each campaign had strategies to maximize these opportunities. The 2012 campaign was significant for the dominance of debates in the coverage and for their impact. We will evaluate at the three major phases of the campaign—the Republican primaries, the conventions, and the general election debates—on the success or failure of the earned media strategies, and we will also examine what happens when media coverage is negative.

First Phase: The Republican Primaries

Coverage of the 2012 campaign began in earnest with the first GOP debate in South Carolina in May 2011, although not all the candidates participated. In June, front-runner Mitt Romney and conservatives Newt Gingrich and Michele Bachman joined the pack at Saint Anselm College in New Hampshire. By August, Jon Huntsman began participating at Iowa State University, and other than the much-hyped straw poll at that Iowa event, debates became the central organizing principle of campaign coverage. There were twenty Republican debates and seven forums, which were viewed by 97,491,000—more than twice the number who watched in 2008 (see Table 7.1).[10] The final debate was a Huckabee Forum on March 3, after which Mitt Romney decided to call it quits since he was doing better in the primaries than in many debates.

TABLE 7.1 Republican Primary Debate Viewership, 2008 and 2012

Election Year	Number of Republican Debates	Total Viewership
2008	21	42,918,000
2012	20	97,491,000

Source: The Nielsen Company.

Debates overshadowed many other attempts of candidates to make news and attract public attention. In January 2012 in New Hampshire, there were actually two national debates held back to back on Saturday night and Sunday morning. NBC's Meet the Press anchor began the Sunday morning debate: "I just want to say on behalf of all Americans that I thank you for being willing to debate each other every 10 hours, whether you feel you need it or not."[11] The candidates seemed a lot more chipper than many reporters who trekked up to Concord before sunrise on January 8. With a field of eight or more candidates, debates are a cost-effective way of covering campaigns, since a reporter can catch a variety of candidates at one location and assess their interactions with each other.

Beyond the debates themselves there are four types of events that occur early in the campaign and will get highlighted by the media: scandals, wins, announcements, and gaffes (SWAG). Individual announcements typically get covered, or at least acknowledged, and wins, gaffes, and scandals are the other individual candidate events that are the most likely to get significant coverage.

Wins

Since there are few elections in the off year, the straw poll conducted at the Iowa State Fair has become the one place a candidate can score a "win," and many candidates spend huge amounts of money to claim that prize and the media celebrity that comes with it. The "poll" is a fundraiser for the Iowa Republican primary at which "voters," who are party activists, support candidates by paying thirty dollars to cast a ballot.[12] In 2012 Michele Bachman, an unlikely presidential contender who had never even run statewide in her home state of Minnesota, had the backing of the conservative Tea Party and spent a considerable amount of money to win the straw poll. Bachman hired a number of veteran organizers and managed to come in ahead of her fellow Minnesotan,

FIGURE 7.1 2012 Presidential Election Coverage over Time

Percentage of Weekly Newshole

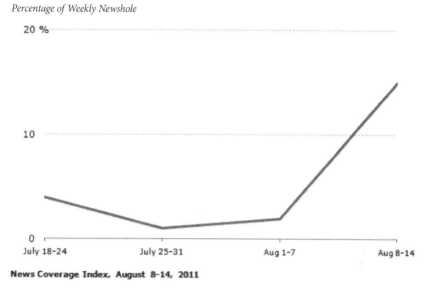

News Coverage Index, August 8-14, 2011

Source: Pew Research Center, "Economy Coverage Down But Still Top Story," August 14, 2012, http://www.journalism.org/index_report/pej_news_coverage_index_august_814_2011.

former governor Tim Pawlenty. The straw poll in early August 2011 brought presidential politics back into the news, which had been dominated for weeks by the fight in Washington over raising the debt ceiling (see Figure 7.1).

Bachman became the third top newsmaker that week, just behind President Obama and Rick Perry, but her win was marred by a controversial answer in the Iowa debate on marriage and cervical cancer[13] and she was upstaged by the entry of Texas governor Rick Perry into the race. Perry, who was described as the Texas miracle, skipped the straw poll but arrived in Iowa for the debate, and made it into 55 percent of all news stories tracked by Pew (Mitt Romney was in 8 percent that week). Perry's statement that Federal Reserve chair Ben Bernanke's printing money was potentially treacherous earned him a lot of media attention, but not all of it was positive.

Announcements

Mitt Romney, the sort-of front-runner for the GOP nomination, announced his candidacy on June 2, 2011, in New Hampshire, complete with a web video and a tour that included a satellite speech to a Faith and Freedom Forum in DC. But his event was upstaged in New Hampshire by a visit from Sarah Palin on her bus tour. The New Hampshire *Union Leader* covered Palin with a major story and a big picture and relegated Romney to a reference with a small picture.

The candidate who got the most positive coverage on his announcement was Rick Perry, who announced his candidacy on the heels of the Iowa straw poll at a conservative Red State meeting in South Carolina. "Rick Perry tossed his cowboy hat into the ring Saturday, shaking up the GOP race as he puts his undefeated political record on the line in his first presidential rodeo," according to Fox News.[14]

Perry's campaign team was ecstatic. They said at a postelection conference at Harvard that this was the best publicity they could remember for an announcement, and it catapulted him to the top of the national polls.[15] They raised a huge amount of money quickly, which also enhanced the impression that he would be a formidable contender and guaranteed even more press coverage. Rick Santorum, who became the "last man standing" in the primaries, received very little coverage on his announcement when it occurred a few days after Romney's; Santorum was mainly covered in an interview on *Good Morning America*.

A portent of problems to come in a party where conservatives dominated, Jon Huntsman chose the much-despised Council on Foreign Relations to signal that he was going to run for president, although his official announcement was Reaganesque in the use of classic American symbols at Liberty State Park in New Jersey. He received glowing coverage by the mainstream press but was the target of much criticism from the right. His work as ambassador to China in the Obama administration was viewed as an act of disloyalty.

Red State's Erick Erickson wrote in May 2011, "The reason I will never, ever support Jon Huntsman is simple: While serving as the United States Ambassador to China, our greatest strategic adversary, Jon Huntsman began plotting to run against the President of the United States. This calls into question his loyalty not just to the President of the United States, but also his loyalty to his country over his own naked ambition."[16]

Books, which are often part of the preannouncement or the introduction of the candidate, or are folded into the announcement tour itself, are another tool in the earned media toolbox, and the 2012 Republican candidates had their share:

Herman Cain: *This is Herman Cain! My Journey to the White House* (October 2011)
Michele Bachmann: *Core of Conviction: My Story* (November 2011)

Ron Paul: *Liberty Defined: 50 Essential Issues That Affect Our Freedom* (April 2011)

Mitt Romney: *No Apology: The Case for American Greatness* (March 2008); coauthor of *Turnaround: Crisis, Leadership, and the Olympic Games* (June 2007)

Newt Gingrich: *A Nation Like No Other: Why American Exceptionalism Matters* (June 2011)

Tim Pawlenty: *Courage to Stand: An American Story* (January 2011)

Rick Perry (with Newt Gingrich): *Fed Up! Our Fight to Save America from Washington* (November 2010)

Rick Santorum: *It Takes a Family: Conservatism and the Common Good* (April 2006); *Rick Santorum* (June 2005); coauthor of *American Patriots: Answering the Call to Freedom* (October 2012)

Sometimes campaigns were built around book tours. Both Gingrich and Cain were accused of being more interested in selling books than in running for president, but book tours can be an important source of earned media. They give candidates a forum for sending a message and allow them to put out their life stories on their own terms. Barack Obama enjoyed great success in 2008 with his autobiography, which included many details of his life (including "doing a little blow") that could be cast as "old news" during the campaign. On the other hand, Rick Perry ran into a little trouble because of some of the things he wrote in *Fed Up* about the overreach of the federal government.

Most of these books were not best sellers and were bought heavily by campaigns to give away to supporters and the media.

Gaffes

If Perry is the king of the announcements, he also won the gold for gaffes. Perry's gaffes were covered heavily, and most of them came during debates. Perry's hugely positive media coverage was based mainly on his resume. But his propensity to make very public mistakes in the debates called into question his qualifications for office. The most publicized was his famous "oops" moment at the CNBC debate in November 2011, when he couldn't recall the third agency he would cut if he were president.[17] In August Perry catapulted in the polls from 31 percent to 4 percent, and he was never a serious player once the primary election campaign started for real in January.[18]

Perry's advisors blame his poor performance on his lack of preparation, since he had decided to get into the campaign late, and also on his constant back pain, which was a huge distraction for him. The media adage "We make them and we break them" fits Perry to a T.[19]

Scandals

Herman Cain (a.k.a. the Pizza Guy) won the award for scandal coverage in the 2012 primary campaign season. Cain, a novice to politics, started to gain some traction with his showmanship in debates and his simple, catchy 999 plan for solving economic problems. He gained so much traction that he led the Gallup Poll the week of November 2 to 6, 2011.[20] With his increased publicity came charges of sexual harassment. Cain's notoriety increased even more and he was the Pew's top newsmaker the week of November 7 to 13, beating out Penn State coach Joe Paterno, who had his own share of sexual allegations. Cain's media attention for the scandals and lack of information about major foreign policy issues led to his withdrawal from the race on December 3.

Newt Gingrich also had his share of scandal coverage when his ex-wife came forward and claimed he had asked for an open marriage while he was having an affair with his current wife Callista. Gingrich made a short-term gain out of the scandal by blaming the press, in particular attacking CNN moderator John King at the beginning of the debate on the eve of the South Carolina primary.

King began the debate, which was seen by 5,022,000 viewers, with "Your ex-wife gave an interview to *ABC News* and another interview with the *Washington Post,* and this story has now gone viral on the Internet. In it she says you came to her in 1999, at a time when you were having an affair. She says you asked her [for] an open marriage. Would you like to take some time to respond to that?"

"No—but I will," Gingrich said. "I think the destructive, vicious, negative nature of much of the news media makes it harder to govern this country, harder to attract decent people to run for public office. And I am appalled you would begin a presidential debate on a topic like that."

The hall erupted in cheers for Gingrich and the conservative South Carolina Republican primary voters responded favorably enough to give him his one primary victory, outside of the one in his home state of Georgia two days later.

Mitt Romney finally called a halt to his own participation in the debates because they were becoming a platform for the other candidates who didn't have the financial resources he had, and they were exposing the public to a number of positions that would come back to bite Romney in the general election. In a talk to his top donors after the election he said, "We had 20 Republican debates, that was absolutely nuts, it opened us up to gaffes and to material that could be used against us in the general, and we were fighting these debates for a year, and the incumbent president just sat back and laughed." Romney suggested fewer debates in 2016 and only friendlier venues (read: Fox News). The Republican Party should "agree that we're gonna do, you know, I don't know, eight debates, and we're gonna, we're gonna do one a month, and we're gonna pick stations that are reasonable. It's not all gonna be done by CNN and NBC, all right. I mean we're gonna try and guide this process so that it's designed to showcase the best of our people as opposed to showcasing liberals beating the heck out of us."[21]

Romney had a bit of a rocky road immediately following the debate cessation, especially on February 7, losing the primaries and caucuses in Colorado, Minnesota, and Missouri to Rick Santorum, but he rebounded in Michigan, and his coverage became more and more positive with that win. According to Pew, Romney's coverage was 33 percent positive to 37 percent negative before the Michigan primary, and it was 47 percent positive to 25 percent negative following it.[22]

The Pew study quantified the candidate coverage in the GOP primaries over time: In the first phase, which they call the "media primary" (from May 2 to October 9, 2011), Texas governor Rick Perry received the most coverage and also the best. (See Figure 7.2.)

During the second phase, from January 2 to April 15 when the Republican primaries and caucuses took place, the "tone" of coverage tended to follow the wins. Newt Gingrich, who rarely had a good week in press coverage, got substantially more positive than negative coverage only once—the week he blasted CNN debate moderator John King and went on to win the South Carolina primary.[23]

Coverage Impact

One interesting aspect of the primary coverage and the importance of debate wins and gaffes was the impact they had on the national polls. With the Republican race very fluid, the ability of a candidate to emerge on top of the national polls and plummet equally quickly was fascinating. Candidates' movement in the polls was in synch with the positive media coverage they received, mostly from the wins in the debate performances, or the negative coverage from gaffes in debates or scandals. Looking at the Gallup Polls among registered Republican voters at various times in 2011 and 2012, Rick Santorum, Rick Perry, Herman Cain, and Newt Gingrich all led the pack, though with less than 36 percent of the vote. The chicken and egg of good media and

FIGURE 7.2 Amount of News Coverage of GOP Candidates

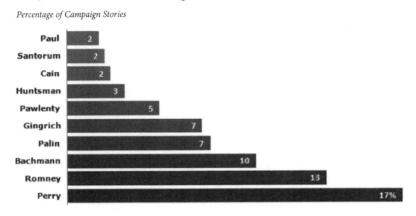

Percentage of Campaign Stories

Date Range: May 2–October 9, 2011, for all candidates but Tim Pawlenty. His data reflect May–August 14.

Note: This data is derived from the News Coverage Index which examines 52 news outlets. A political figure must be in at least 50% of the story to register as a primary newsmaker.

Source: Pew Research Center's Project for Excellence in Journalism, "The Media Primary," October 17, 2012, http://www.journalism.org/analysis_report/media_primary.

good polls is hard to tease out, but clearly the relationship is there. For example, Herman Cain, a novice on the national political stage, zoomed into the lead only to plummet in the next few weeks, eventually dropping out of the race less than a month after he was leading in the polls.[24]

Second Phase of Campaign 2012: The Conventions

Much to the annoyance of the media, the political parties now view their conventions not as decision-making bodies but as ways to get their strongest messages out in the most positive ways. While the old gavel-to-gavel coverage is out even on most cable stations, there is still saturation coverage, media attention, and interest from the public in these extravaganzas.

In 2012, fifteen thousand members of the media received credentials to cover the conventions.[25] TV viewership was high, although down from 2008 (see Tables 7.2 and 7.3), but Internet and multiplatform coverage increased significantly, with both conventions offering live YouTube channels. Each convention broke records on Twitter, with the RNC drawing roughly five million tweets over the course of the convention and the DNC having 9.5 million tweets related to the events.[26]

One of the interesting findings from the Pew Research study is how different the tone of convention coverage was between traditional and social

TABLE 7.2   TV Viewership of Republican National Convention, 2008 and 2012

	Rating 2008	Number of Viewers 2008	Rating 2012	Number of Viewers 2012
Day 1		No common coverage due to Hurricane Gustav		No common coverage due to Hurricane Isaac
Day 2	7.3	21,528,000	7.7	22,301,000
Day 3	12.9	37,244,000	7.7	21,942,000
Day 4	13.4	38,933,000	10.5	30,251,000

Source: Nielson Wire, "Final Night of Republican National Convention Draws 30.3 Million Viewers," August 31, 2012, http://blog.nielsen.com/nielsenwire/politics/final-night-of-republican -national-convention-draws-30-million-viewers/#redirect?thread=826060066&forum=[object %20Object]&zone=internal_discovery&variant=metadata&imp=1347932291650263506 &source_thread_id=835074363.

Note: 2008 networks included: Day 2—ABC, CBS, NBC, CNN, FOX News, MSNBC; Day 3—ABC, CBS, NBC, CNN, FOX News, MSNBC; Day 4—ABC, CBS, NBC, CNN, FOX News, MSNBC, Univision, and Telemundo. 2012 networks included: Day 2—ABC, CBS, CNBC, CNN, FOXNC, CRNT, MSNBC, NBC, and PBS; Day 3—ABC, CBS, CNBC, CNN, FOXNC, CRNT, MSNBC, NBC, and PBS; Day 4—ABC, CBS, CNBC, CNN, FOXNC, CRNT, MSNBC, MUN2, NBC, PBS, and UNI.

TABLE 7.3   TV Viewership of Democratic National Convention, 2008 and 2012

	Rating 2008	Number of Viewers 2008	Rating 2012	Number of Viewers 2012
Day 1	7.8	22,297,000	9.1	26,245,000
Day 2	9.0	25,974,000	8.8	25,121,000
Day 3	8.4	24,029,000	12.3	35,716,000
Day 4	13.4	38,379,000		Convention only scheduled for 3 days

Source: NielsenWire, "Closing Night of Democratic National Convention Draws 35.7 Million Viewers," September 7, 2012, http://www.nielsen.com/us/en/newswire/2012/closing-night -of-democratic-national-convention-draws-35-7-million-viewers.html.

Note: 2008 networks included: Days 1, 2, 3—ABC, CBS, NBC, CNN, FOX News, MSNBC, BET, and TV One; Day 4—ABC, CBS, NBC, CNN, FOX News, MSNBC, BET, TV One, Univision, and Telemundo. 2012 networks included: Day 1—ABC, CBS, NBC, BET, CNN, Current TV, FOX News, MSNBC, and PBS; Day 2—ABC, CBS, CNN, Current TV, FOX News, MSNBC, and PBS; Day 3—ABC, CBS, NBC, BET, CNN, CNBC, Current TV, FOX News, MSNBC, MUN2, PBS, TV One, and Univision.

TABLE 7.4 Tone About Candidates and Conventions in Social Media, 2012

Candidates Get No Convention Bounce in Social Media
Percentage of assertions and stories

	Week of RNC Convention	Week of DNC Convention
TONE ABOUT ROMNEY		
Twitter		
Positive	17%	19%
Negative	59	59
Facebook		
Positive	24	22
Negative	67	65
Mainstream Media		
Positive	36	7
Negative	15	44
TONE ABOUT OBAMA		
Twitter		
Positive	25	31
Negative	44	42
Facebook		
Positive	17	20
Negative	66	62
Mainstream Media		
Positive	4	32
Negative	57	22

Note: Coverage deemed "neutral" is not shown. Positive, negative, and neutral coverage total 100 percent. PEJ analysis using Crimson Hexagon technology.

Source: Pew Research Center's Project for Excellence in Journalism, "How Social and Traditional Media Differ in Treatment of the Conventions and Beyond," September 28, 2012, http:// www.journalism.org/commentary_backgrounder/how_social_and_traditional_media_differ _their_treatment_conventions_and_beyo.

media. Traditional media typically run long set pieces on nominees and their families and give the political parties blocks of unfiltered airtime to present their case. In 2012 Romney's coverage was 36 percent positive to 15 percent negative the week of the GOP convention, and Obama's was 32 percent positive to 22 percent negative the week of his convention. But on Facebook, over 60 percent of related posts were negative about both candidates during their respective conventions. Twitter was more negative on Romney than Obama, but Obama's was a net negative as well. (See Table 7.4.)

The Advantage of Going Second

According to the Pew Research Center studies, positive reactions to the Democratic National Convention, especially to the speech by former president Clinton, helped Obama increase his small lead in national polls. However, according to Pew:

TABLE 7.5 Tone of Candidate Campaign Coverage over Time

Percentage of stories with tone

	Republican Convention *Aug. 27– Sept. 2*	Democratic Convention *Sept. 3–9*	Post-Conventions *Sept. 10–Oct. 3*	Post-1st Presidential Debate *Oct. 4–16*	Post-2nd Presidential Debate *Oct. 17–21*
OBAMA					
Positive	3 %	35 %	20 %	12 %	17 %
Mixed	39	45	56	51	49
Negative	58	21	24	37	34
ROMNEY					
Positive	36	9	4	23	14
Mixed	49	45	45	54	41
Negative	15	47	52	23	45

Date Range: August 27–October 21, 2012.

Source: Pew Research Center's Project for Excellence in Journalism, "The Conventions to the Debates: Set Piece Moments Still Matter," November 2, 2012, http://www.journalism.org /analysis_report/conventions_debates_set_piece_moments_still_matter.

> The real bounce in coverage for Obama came not the week of his convention, but afterwards, and not from a rise in his coverage, but in spreading skepticism about Romney's chances as journalists tracked the trajectory of opinion polls. Indeed, from September 10, after the Democratic convention, until the first debate in Denver on October 3, 52% of the stories about Romney were clearly unfavorable in tone while just 4% were positive—a differential of 13-to-1. Obama's coverage during this period, by contrast, was noticeably better, with 24% unfavorable stories compared to 20% favorable, and 56% mixed or neutral.[27]

Whether it was the contrast in the conventions or a series of Romney campaign blunders—especially the "47 percent" video—the Obama bounce happened in the weeks after the convention, not during or immediately following the event itself. (See Table 7.5.)

Third Phase: The General Election Debates

The third phase of the general election campaign in 2012 was marked by four more debates—three presidential and one vice-presidential—which dominated coverage in the month of October. These debates were carried on all network and cable news networks, and viewership for the presidential debates was higher than in 2008, although the VP debate viewership was down from

TABLE 7.6   TV Viewership of General Election Debates, 2008 and 2012

	2008	2012
First Debate	52.4 million	67.1 million
Second Debate	63.3 million	65.6 million
Third Debate	56.5 million	59.2 million
Vice Presidential Debate	69.9 million	51.4 million

Sources: Nielsen Wire, "Final Presidential Debate Draws 59.2 Million Viewers," October 23, 2012, http://blog.nielsen.com/nielsenwire/politics/final-presidential-debate-draws-59-2-million-viewers/; Jack Mirkinson, "Vice Presidential Debate Ratings: 51.4 Million Viewers Tune In," HuffPost Media, October 12, 2012, http://www.huffingtonpost.com/2012/10/12/vice-presidential-debate-ratings_n_1962145.html.

the Biden-Palin 2008 debate. (See Table 7.6.) In addition, 14 percent of all viewers and 32 percent of those under forty watched the first debate on the Internet or on double screens, TV and Internet simultaneously.[28]

The first debate was assessed as a huge loss for President Obama (by 67 to 25 percent, viewers picked Romney as the winner in the instant poll conducted by CNN).[29] The Pew data documents Obama's decline in positive coverage and an even greater drop in Romney's negative coverage, going from 52 percent before the debate to 23 percent in the weeks following.

According to Pew, "Romney's narrative in the press changed instantly. In the days just before the debate, October 1–3, the number of negative stories about Romney (37 percent) outstripped positive (6 percent) by 6-to-1. In the days immediately following the Denver encounter (October 4–7), the positive narrative soared to 32 percent while negative shrank to 23 percent."[30]

Viewership was not quite as high for the remaining debates but Obama was able to stop the flow of bad coverage, and the instant surveys found that viewers rated those debates a tie or a win for Obama. The debate phase of the campaign ended with the polls almost the same as they were before the debates began.

The Final Weeks of the General Election

The final two weeks of the campaign were marked by an uptick in President Obama's news coverage and a surge of positive reviews in the final week as Hurricane Sandy started to dominate the news. According to Pew, "During this final week, from October 29 to November 5, positive stories about Obama (29%) outnumbered negative ones (19%) by 10 points. A week earlier, negative coverage of Obama had exceeded positive by 13 points. The final week of the campaign marked only the second time in which positive stories about Obama outnumbered negative dating back to late August."[31]

Some of the positive coverage also stemmed from Obama's improvement in the polls, Pew contends. In fact, the main impact of the storm may have been the lack of attention to Mitt Romney in that final crucial week. "We saw ourselves positioned where we could win," said Stuart Stevens, Romney's media consultant. "The impact of the storm was we lost control of the race. . . . We went from large sweeping rallies to sitting in our hotel room watching TV." Obama strategist, David Axelrod, agreed and said that the hurricane was "certainly helpful in that it froze the race."[32]

Obama received more attention than Romney, and the attention that Romney got was 2-to-1 negative in the mainstream media. Pew also found that in the final week Fox's coverage was even more pro-Romney and MSNBC's more for Obama. In social media Romney actually picked up on Twitter, while Facebook remained relatively constant for both candidates.[33]

In the end, that last week of good press gave Obama's overall coverage from the convention to the election a boost, although both candidates' general election coverage was a net negative in the mainstream media. For Obama, 20 percent of stories were favorable and 29 percent unfavorable, while Romney's were 15 percent favorable and 37 percent unfavorable. Pew found that in 2012 there was less horse-race coverage than in recent years and more stories about personal qualities, policy, and election administration. During the 2012 general election, 39 percent of stories were about the horse race, down from 50 percent in 2008, 21 percent were about policy, 8 percent on voting laws, and 10 percent about public record or personal qualities of candidates.[34]

Campaign Narratives and Frames

One of the major tugs-of-war in campaigns is to be the major force in framing issues and creating campaign narratives. Each campaign and the news media create narratives, and the one that "sticks" is often the one that moves public opinion. The Obama campaign and their Super PAC, Priorities USA, spent millions of dollars "defining" Mitt Romney as a wealthy businessman who cared only about the bottom line and who was out of touch with average Americans. On the earned media side they did everything from stunts (sending former Bain Capital employees to large media events to tell their story)

TABLE 7.7 Negative Tone of Candidate Narratives, 2000–2012

Percentage of personal assertions

	Positive	Negative
Mitt Romney	29%	71%
Barack Obama	28	72
John McCain	43	57
Barack Obama	69	31
George W. Bush	25	75
John Kerry	30	70
George W. Bush	48	52
Al Gore	20	80

Source: Pew Research Center's Project for Excellence in Journalism, "The Master Character Narratives in Campaign 2012," August 23, 2012, http://www.journalism.org/node/30588.

to tweeting quickly any Romney gaffe (saying Anne Romney was driving a couple of Cadillacs, making $10,000 bets in debates, recalling selling stock as a student to pay the bills, etc.) to reinforce this narrative in the news media. Barack Obama's acceptance speech at the Democratic Convention included a not-so-subtle contrast between his upbringing and Romney's.

The Romney campaign was busy trying to portray Obama as a well-meaning but failed president and leapt on any opportunity to reinforce that idea—from a misguided tweet about the killings in Benghazi to pounding away at reports showing weak job numbers. According to the Pew study, the "master negative narratives" about Obama, which were reflected in over 70 percent of news stories, were that he had not done enough for the economy and was a supporter of American exceptionalism and capitalism. The Romney negative narratives were dominated by mentions of his wealth and uncaring character and the fact that he had a poorly run campaign. Like Obama, Romney's coverage was over 70 percent negative. (See Table 7.7.) This was in marked contrast to 2008, when Obama's coverage was 69 percent positive and McCain's 43 percent positive, but is similar to 2004.

With all this negative coverage, then, how did Barack Obama get high ratings on personal likeability and other character traits, and how did Mitt Romney get an image as more competent to deal with the economy?

Tom Rosenstiel, former director of the Project for Excellence in Journalism at Pew, offered the following explanation: "I think anything the press says about Obama has less impact because the public already has so much information about him. The inverse is true for Romney. The analogy I use is the blackboard. Any new writing on the Obama blackboard for people means less, because there is already so much else written. For Romney, the media messages mean more because people know less about him. If the only thing written on the blackboard is a few phrases, they make more of an impression." He also offered an explanation of why debates and conventions, the two big opportunities for positive earned media, continue to have such impact.

> Debates, and conventions, and even leaked videos, also probably leave a deeper impression than any single story or even set of media stories. One reason for that, I believe, is that people are seeing that event for themselves. The other is that some campaign events are more important than others. Debates are key moments in campaigns because they are the only ones in which people see the candidates in a comparative setting interacting. They in that sense are learning something different, or seeing a new facet of the candidates they haven't seen before. And as a result, people are more inclined to take in new information during those moments and even perhaps change their opinions. The same used to be true of conventions, and may still be. They are the first time for a non-incumbent that many voters will hear them give an extended speech. The prolonged primary debate season may be having an effect on that somewhat.[35]

Another explanation for the higher positive ratings for Obama despite the negative tone of coverage is the visual side of media coverage. The Pew study analysis is only of *words*, the traditional venue of content analysis. The University of Maryland did a study of the *pictures* of the candidate that appeared in the final weeks of the campaign on Pinterest, from the mainstream press, and found the positive pictures of Obama dominated.

Campaigns spend a lot of time orchestrating pictures, and visuals can have a powerful impact. However, scandals, gaffes, and sensational moments were a sure way to get the attention of the media, and campaigns resorted more than ever to paid advertising, late night comedy shows, and social media to control messages and leave a positive impression.

Where People Got Their Campaign Information

Pew has been asking Americans where they regularly get their campaign news since 2000. The Internet has continued to rise as a source (from 9 percent in

TABLE 7.8 Where People Turn for Campaign News

Percentage of US adults who regularly turn to each source

	January 2012	October 2012
TV		
Cable News	36 %	41 %
Local News	32	38
Network News	26	31
Cable News Talk Shows	15	18
Late Night Comedy Shows	9	12
Internet	25	36
Print		
Local Newspapers	20	23
National Newspapers	8	13
Radio		
NPR	12	12
Talk Radio Shows	16	16
Social Media		
Facebook	6	12
Twitter	2	4
YouTube	3	7

Date Range: January 4–8, 2012, and October 18–21, 2012.

Note: Figures do not add up to 100 percent because respondents could answer "regularly" to more than one item.

Source: Pew Research Center's Project for Excellence in Journalism, "Internet Gains Most as Campaign News Source but Cable TV Still Leads," October 25, 2012, http://www.journalism.org /commentary_backgrounder/social_media_doubles_remains_limited.

2000 to 36 percent in 2012), but TV remains the dominant source. Cable TV news is the number one source named, with 41 percent citing it, another 38 percent citing local TV news, and 31 percent citing network news. Another 12 percent of Americans cited late night comedy shows as a place they checked on campaign news. (See Table 7.8.)

Social media became a very important campaign vehicle in 2012, and the Obama campaign used it heavily to mobilize their base groups. At the Harvard conference in November 2012, Obama field and digital media directors, Jeremy Bird and Teddy Goff, outlined their use of Facebook to build relationships. "In 2008 Facebook was one-tenth of what it is now," said Goff. "Twitter hardly existed and the iPhone wasn't invented until 2007." He estimated that the 33 million people who "liked" Obama on Facebook had circles of Facebook friends that included 98 percent of all Facebook users. Their strategy was to get their supporters to reach out to others and build grassroots organizations though social media and build "communities of trust."[36] Unlike

FIGURE 7.3 The Role of the Internet in Campaign News

Percentage of online adults who regularly or sometimes get campaign news from these sources

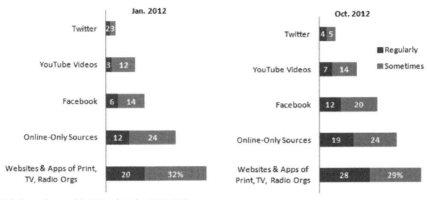

Date Range: January 4-8, 2012, and October 18-21, 2012
Source: Pew Research Center

Source: Pew Research Center's Project for Excellence in Journalism, "Internet Gains Most as Campaign News Source but Cable TV Still Leads," October 25, 2012, http://www.journalism .org/commentary_backgrounder/social_media_doubles_remains_limited.

TV advertising, which was heavily negative, they found that positive posts on Facebook were particularly effective in motivating supporters to organize.

However, social media was just starting to emerge as a regular source of campaign news for all Americans in 2012. One in five told Pew they regularly used Facebook, 14 percent used YouTube, and 5 percent regularly used Twitter. These were new sources that grew over the course of 2012. In January, 20 percent said they turned to Facebook regularly or sometimes, and by October this had increased to 32 percent. (See Figure 7.3.)

Obama also relied heavily on an e-mail list that his campaign had developed since 2007 for recruiting volunteers, raising money, and getting messages out to motivate their base supporters.

LESSONS LEARNED BY POLITICAL PROFESSIONALS ON USING EARNED MEDIA AND DEALING WITH THE PRESS:

1. *Nothing is off the record in the age of cell phones and video cameras.* In 2008 Barack Obama was caught on audiotape telling people at a San Francisco fundraiser that he was struggling with blue collar voters in Pennsylvania who "cling to religion and guns," and he never quite recovered the trust of these voters. But the damage to Obama was very small compared to the impact the "47 percent" video had on Mitt Romney in

2012. The video of Romney's remarks at a "closed" Florida fundraiser in May was discovered by the grandson of former president Jimmy Carter, an opposition researcher, and given to *Mother Jones* magazine. It provided fodder for the Obama campaign and the media for over a week and did significant damage to Romney. Candidates' remarks at fundraisers and when they otherwise think microphones are off have often gotten them into trouble when they get wider distribution, but the "47 percent" video may finally convince them that everything is now on the record.

2. *Turn lemons into lemonade.* It is impossible to overestimate the importance the Obama campaign placed on energizing the base. Digital media and niche advertising both on TV and online made it easier to target messages to specific groups to maximize their impact and to minimize any damage these issues might do to a wider segment of the electorate. According to Jeremy Bird at the Harvard conference, Obama's loss in the first debate energized his supporters who were becoming complacent.[37] Similarly Romney's selection of Paul Ryan, whom many Democrats feared would make Wisconsin a competitive state, was a wake-up call to the Obama organization in the state, which had been quite active in 2008 but was not excited about the 2012 election. The blow-up with the Catholic hierarchy over contraceptives being mandated by the Affordable Care Act served to activate many young and disaffected women voters, and voter suppression stories may have motivated African Americans and Latinos who were angry about the prospect. All of these issues were hammered home via the media, e-mail, and social media and rarely made it into big national TV buys.

3. *What you say early may come back to haunt you.* Romney's campaign manager Matt Rhodes says he regrets Romney's strategy of trying to outflank Rick Perry on the right on immigration and his advocacy of "self-deportation" as a solution during a primary debate. Romney was never able to regain the trust of Latino and other immigrant voters despite a significant amount of paid advertising targeted toward Latinos in the general election. The idea of the "etch-a-sketch" campaign, in which the primary slate can be wiped clean for the general election, didn't pan out.[38]

4. *Earned media trumps paid ads at the end.* There was a lot of discussion of the Obama campaign and their Super PACs' decision to spend money early on paid ads. The Romney campaign, which spent about the same amount as Obama during the general election, believed in holding down

spending until the final month (holding $20 million for a late October blitz) and even went completely off the air during the Democratic convention. Obama media strategist, David Axelrod, said their decision to go early was because there is so much media coverage of the presidential race in October (and so many other candidates' ads at the end) that the paid ads do not have the impact that they had in the late spring and summer.[39] The Obama PAC's decision to blitz ads about Romney's role at Bain Capital, including laying-off workers, provided a backdrop for the "47 percent" video, which reinforced the message of an uncaring wealthy candidate in September.

5. *TV still matters.* Despite the growth of online media the presidential campaigns and their "allies" spent almost three billion dollars on TV advertising. In addition, TV news interviews generate a significant amount of coverage, although not all of it is positive. Both campaigns went on CBS's *60 Minutes* and fared well. Obama also made heavy use of late night and cable comedy shows to appeal to young voters. Romney avoided many interview shows and networks other than Fox News, and he even avoided Fox for the final two weeks of the campaign. Romney struggled in these interviews, and his campaign decided it was best to try to control their message through other vehicles, but he dropped out of the news and lost some visibility because of that decision.

6. *Use digital media to target positive messages and energize your base voters.* Data mining and microtargeting were used by both campaigns, but the success the Obama campaign had using it to energize and turn out their voters is a model that will be copied by campaigns for years to come.

7. *Conventions still matter.* Don't let an eighty-two-year-old actor dominate prime time convention coverage unscripted. This should be a no brainer, but in an attempt to put some excitement in their convention, Romney himself invited Clint Eastwood to speak, and it turned out to be a PR nightmare. The Romney campaign had many powerful speeches in the non–prime time hours leading up to Eastwood, but they were overwhelmed in viewership and press coverage (aided by Democrats' social media) by Eastwood and his empty chair.

8. *If you decide to debate, debate.* President Obama's disastrous performance in the first debate was based on a deliberate "nonengagement strategy." The campaign wanted to avoid a "vituperative exchange" that would turn off undecided women voters. "We made him phobic about engaging," Obama advisor David Axelrod said after the election.[40] Mitt

Romney also found that when he stayed "above the fray" he lost the debates. He made a huge comeback during the Florida primary when he became more aggressive. In the fall Romney did sixteen mock debates to get ready for the debates with President Obama, and his preparation showed.

9. *Focus earned media on the battlegrounds too.* The Obama campaign never did a national poll, but in the fall they did eight to nine thousand interviews a night in the battleground states. Looking at the exit polls, it is clear that targeting those states and their base voters with social media paid off in turnout and vote support. Obama actually increased his vote support among young people in Florida, Ohio, Nevada, and New Hampshire from the 2008 level, although it was down a bit nationally.

10. *Hurricanes matter, especially when competing for earned media.* There may have been nothing the Romney campaign could do about Hurricane Sandy, but Hurricanes Gustav and Isaac stole the first nights of the Republican conventions in 2008 and 2012. The wisdom of late conventions and the potential complication of hurricanes may force some rethinking in 2016—especially locating conventions in vulnerable states.

What's Next?

Looking ahead to 2016, it is clear that the Internet will be dominant, although TV is holding its own. Data mining and microtargeting are likely to be even more sophisticated, and campaigns at all levels will be devising strategies for niche audiences. Reporters will be using more technology as well, and YouTube (or the next generation of YouTube) is likely to grow even more.

The future of multiple primary debates is something that is being discussed, but the same forces that drove them in 2008 and 2012 are likely at work again—each major news organization, state party, and interest group wants to "own" one, and lesser known candidates use them as opportunities to "break out" and will force the top candidate to show up.

The much maligned status of Iowa and New Hampshire as "first in the nation" will continue (potential candidates for 2016 started visiting those states weeks after the 2012 election), and the local media there will be important. The Republican Iowa straw poll may not survive, but candidates will think up something to try to get publicity in 2015 and make it into the top tier. News organizations will happily cooperate—and then regret it later.

And some candidate will say something he or she regrets at a closed fund-raiser, which will be recorded and get more coverage than ten major speeches combined!

Acknowledgment

Thanks to the Pew Foundation and the Project for Excellence in Journalism, in particular Tom Rosensteil and Amy Mitchell, for the data included in this chapter. Special thanks to American University graduate student Becky Moylan for her research and editing.

Notes

1. *Texas Politics,* "Talking Politics: Free Media Versus Earned Media," Voting, Campaigns & Elections (2006), http://www.laits.utexas.edu/txp_media/html/vce/features/0903_01/freemedia.html (accessed March 15, 2013).

2. Scott M. Cutlip and Allen H. Center, *Effective Public Relations* (Englewood Cliffs, NJ: Prentice-Hall, 1978). See chapter 4. Much of the history of public relations is from this book, one of the bibles of the PR industry.

3. Jason Salzman, *Making the News* (Boulder, CO: Westview Press, 2003). See chapters 5 and 13.

4. Jonathan Alter and Howard Fineman, "The Search for the Perfect Sound-Bite," *Newsweek,* January 18, 1988, 22.

5. Kansas Democratic Party, "Your Campaign Plan: Earned Media," KSDP.org, as sited in http://www.laits.utexas.edu/txp_media/html/vce/features/0903_01/freemedia.html (accessed February 4, 2009).

6. Matt Bai, "The Framing Wars," *New York Times,* July 17, 2005, 38.

7. Matthew C. Nisbet, "Communicating Climate Change: Why Frames Matter for Public Engagement," *Environment* (March–April 2009), http://www.environmentmagazine.org/Archives/Back%20Issues/March-April%202009/Nisbet-full.html (accessed March 15, 2013).

8. Kathleen Hall Jamieson and Karlyn Kohrs Campbell, *The Interplay of Influence: News, Advertising, Politics, and the Mass Media* (Belmont, CA: Wadsworth Publishing, 2006).

9. Mike Ludwig, "Big Money Breakdown: Why 2012 Is the Most Expensive Election Ever," Truthout.org, November 6, 2012, http://truth-out.org/news/item/12561-big-money-breakdown-why-2012-is-the-most-expensive-election-ever.

10. Chris Ariens, "Final 2012 GOP Primary Debate Ranker: ABC, NBC on Top; Fox News #1 on Cable," TVNewser, WebMediaBrands, February 23, 2012, http://www.mediabistro.com/tvnewser/final-2012-gop-primary-debate-ranker-abc-nbc-on-top-fox-news-1-on-cable_b113360.

11. "Meet the Press Transcript for January 8, 2012," NBC News, http://www.msnbc
.msn.com/id/45917518/ns/meet_the_press-transcripts/t/meet-press-transcript
-jan/#.UMIXnkITvu0.

12. Scott Conroy, "Branstad Opens Gates for Iowa Straw Poll Criticism," Real Clear
Politics, November 22, 2012, http://www.realclearpolitics.com/articles/2012/11/22
/branstad_opens_gates_for_iowa_straw_poll_criticism_116225.html.

13. Carrie Gann, "Michele Bachmann's HPV Vaccine Safety and 'Retardation'
Comments Misleading, Doctors Say," ABC News, September 14, 2011, http://abc
news.go.com/Health/Wellness/michele-bachmanns-hpv-vaccine-safety-retardation
-comments-misleading/story?id=14516625.

14. "Perry Makes It Official: He's Running for President," Fox News.com, August 13, 2011, http://www.foxnews.com/politics/2011/08/13/perry-to-announce
-candidacy-for-gop-presidential-nomination/.

15. Harvard University Institute of Politics, 2012 Campaign Decision Makers
Conference, November 29, 2012.

16. Erick Erickson, "Why I Will Not Support Jon Huntsman. Ever," RedState.
com, Eagle Publishing, May 9, 2011, http://www.redstate.com/erick/2011/05/09/why
-i-will-not-support-jon-huntsman/.

17. Elyse Siegel, "Rick Perry: 'Oops' (VIDEO)," Huffington Post, November 10,
2011, http://www.huffingtonpost.com/2011/11/10/rick-perry-oops-video_n_108
5336.html.

18. Susan Page, "Poll: Perry, Romney Draw Support from Distinct Groups," USA
Today.com, September 20, 2011, http://usatoday30.usatoday.com/news/politics/
story/2011-09-19/republican-poll-gop-perry-romney/50467944/1; Mark Murray,
"GOP Support for Perry Plummets after Debate Flub," NBCNews.com, November
13, 2011, http://firstread.nbcnews.com/_news/2011/11/13/8782807-gop-support
-for-perry-plummets-after-debate-flub?utm_source=dlvr.it.

19. Harvard University Institute of Politics, 2012 Campaign Decision Makers
Conference.

20. Frank Newport, "Cain Ties Romney Atop GOP Field," Gallup.com, November
7, 2011, http://www.gallup.com/poll/150617/cain-ties-romney-atop-gop-field.aspx.

21. Michael Falcone, "Republicans Return Romney's Parting Gift (The Note),"
ABC News, November 15, 2012, http://abcnews.go.com/blogs/politics/2012/11
/republicans-return-romneys-parting-gift-the-note/.

22. Pew Research Center's Project for Excellence in Journalism, "How the Media
Covered the 2012 Primary Campaign," April 23, 2012, http://www.journalism.org
/analysis_report/romney_report.

23. Pew Research Center's Project for Excellence in Journalism, Topline, http://
www.journalism.org/sites/journalism.org/files/PrimaryCampaignTopline.pdf (accessed December 4, 2012).

24. Newport, "Cain Ties Romney."

25. William Browning, "15,000 Media Credentials and Other Convention Numbers
in Tampa," Yahoo!, August 27, 2012, http://news.yahoo.com/15-000-media-credentials
-other-convention-numbers-tampa-170800307.html.

26. Beth Fouhy, "For Conventions, TV Viewing Down, Social Media Up," Associated Press, September 3, 2012, http://bigstory.ap.org/article/conventions-tv-viewing-down-social-media-0.

27. Pew Research Center's Project for Excellence in Journalism, "The Conventions to the Debates: Set Piece Moments Still Matter," November 2, 2012, http://www.journalism.org/analysis_report/conventions_debates_set_piece_moments_still_matter.

28. Pew Research Center for the People & the Press, "One-in-Ten 'Dual-Screened' the Presidential Debate," October 11, 2012, http://www.people-press.org/2012/10/11/one-in-ten-dual-screened-the-presidential-debate/.

29. CNN Politics, "CNN Poll: Most Watchers Say Romney Debate Winner," October 3, 2012, http://politicalticker.blogs.cnn.com/2012/10/03/cnn-poll-romney-wins-debate-by-big-margin/.

30. Pew Research Center's Project for Excellence in Journalism, "The First Debate: How Much It Changed the Narrative," November 2, 2012, http://www.journalism.org/analysis_report/first_debate_how_much_it_changed_narrative.

31. Pew Research Center's Project for Excellence in Journalism, "Obama Enjoys Surge in Positive Coverage the Last Week of the Race; Attention to Romney Drops," November 19, 2012, http://www.journalism.org/node/31621.

32. Harvard University Institute of Politics, 2012 Campaign Decision Makers Conference.

33. Ibid.

34. Pew Research Center's Project for Excellence in Journalism, "The Final Days of the Media Campaign 2012," November 19, 2012, http://www.journalism.org/sites/journalism.org/files/Topline_6.pdf.

35. Tom Rosenstiel, e-mail interview, October 8, 2012.

36. Harvard University Institute of Politics, 2012 Campaign Decision Makers Conference.

37. Ibid.

38. Ibid.

39. Ibid.

40. Ibid.

8

Dimensions of Campaigns in the Age of Digital Networks

ALAN ROSENBLATT

While the fundamental goals for electoral campaigns remain the same—get your message out, make sure voters know your candidate, turn out your supporters to vote, and get more votes than your opponent—how campaigns do this is undergoing some fundamental changes. As the use of e-mail and websites join tried and true offline tactics as commonplace in campaigns, the rise of social media, nanotargeted online advertising, and the integration of online behavior data with general voter and opinion data are dramatically changing the electoral landscape.

Social Media

Social media is steadily transforming the electorate and, as a result, how campaigns are engaging the electorate. On a macro level, 39 percent of Americans are using social media to engage in civic and political life, learning about issues and candidates; engaging in political and policy conversations; and influencing their personal networks on how to vote.[1]

Throughout the 2012 presidential campaign, voters were able to redirect the focus of the national conversation away from the campaigns. During the Republican National Convention, despite the fact that the Romney campaign purchased promoted hashtags (#RomneyRyan2012 and #BelieveInAmerica) on Twitter, their efforts were quickly overshadowed by a spontaneous eruption on Twitter and other social networking sites of talk about Clint Eastwood's "invisible Obama" in an apparently empty chair. Overnight, @InvisibleObama on Twitter collected over 30,000 followers and the Romney campaign lost control of the narrative. A couple weeks later, *Mother Jones* released its secretly recorded video of Mitt Romney telling a roomful of big donors that his job was not to worry about the "47 percent" of Americans who pay no federal income tax and, as a result, see themselves as victims who are entitled to government handouts. The #47Percent hashtag quickly overtook the paid-for Romney campaign hashtags, capturing the national narrative then, and still.

Throughout the general election campaign, the Romney narrative was interrupted by memes popping out of the debates. #BigBird, #BindersFullOf-Women, and #HorsesAndBayonets dominated the public reaction to the three debates on social media. Even before the general election, Romney's debate gaffes in the primaries spurred similar results; his awkward $10,000 bet offer to Governor Rick Perry spurred a Twitter meme #WhatWould10KBuy, which repeatedly highlighted Romney's apparent disconnection from ordinary Americans.

In congressional races, politically foolish comments revealing positions on rape and abortion from Todd Akin in Missouri and Richard Mourdock in Indiana derailed two Senate campaigns the Republicans had high hopes of winning. Social media allowed citizens to participate and drive a national outcry that forced the media to cover these gaffes and the underlying issues throughout the election campaign. The feedback loop, generated by their comments being broadcasted on C-SPAN, reported in the news, and continually tweeted and posted on Facebook, allowed the Obama campaign and Democratic congressional candidates around the country to leverage the "war on women" issue at a time when all previous expectations would have predicted that nothing would displace the economy in the minds of the voters.

I have often joked that when politicians say they feel the pulse of the voters, that they are usually using their thumbs to feel that pulse (in other words, they feel their own pulse from their thumb). In many ways, social media exposes the inaccuracies of politicians' assessment of voters' opinions.

Sorting out the meaning of social buzz vis-à-vis public opinion polls is an interesting challenge for political analysts. In the 2008 New Hampshire Democratic primary, the last poll, which was completed the Sunday before the Tuesday vote, had Obama in the lead over Clinton. When Clinton won, it surprised most people, but not the election team at Yahoo! They were monitoring searches on Yahoo.com for Clinton and Obama, observing a significant uptick on Clinton searches (even after eliminating searches for her crying at the diner) and a flattening of searches for Obama. In this spirit, Twitter teamed up with Topsy and *USA Today* to create the Twitter Election Meter, which not only measured how many tweets mentioned each of the two presidential candidates, but roughly assessed the sentiment of those tweets. The meter not only presented the national data, but also broke out the swing states by using the location data, which is turned on by about 10 percent of Twitter users. In 2012 the meter showed Obama steadily pulling away nationally, increasing the gap for positive tweets about him versus Romney, leading into November 7 and neck and neck in the swing states.[2]

Contrasting the Obama and Romney campaigns' use of social media, one key difference stands out. While the Romney campaign ran its social media outreach primarily through its top-level national campaign social media channels, the Obama campaign created a network of state-level social media channels, especially on Twitter, in parallel to its field operation. So while Obama volunteers were canvassing neighborhoods and setting up tables at local events, @OFA_VA, @OFA_NV, and a slew of other state-specific social media channels were engaging voters in each state with state-specific messages. These state-level channels were created in 2008 by Obama for America, then transformed into Organizing for America channels until they were converted back to Obama for America channels for the 2012 election.

By maintaining the 2008 state channels and growing their audiences in between the elections, the Obama campaign was able to "hit the (virtual) ground running" when the 2012 campaign launched. They had tens of thousands of followers already in place in each state. They did not have to start from scratch, as so many congressional campaigns historically have done. This virtual implementation of the perpetual campaign concept pioneered by Bill Clinton played a big supporting role in the Obama 2012 ground game.

Nanotargeted Online Advertising

In 2010, Senator Harry Reid narrowly defeated Sharron Angle in his bid for reelection. Much of the success of this campaign can be attributed to a late, highly targeted online negative ad campaign that effectively discouraged enough Republican voters from going to vote. These ads were "nanotargeted," especially using Facebook and Google to deliver the ads to exactly the right Nevadans.[3] An analysis of this ad campaign found that by diverting 20 percent of the campaign's TV ad budget to online ads, they doubled the effectiveness.[4] More recently, ads on Comcast Cable stations have claimed that a 20 percent diversion yields an 80 percent improvement. In other words, the return on investment for using TV and online ads in conjunction is well established and significantly impactful.

Nanotargeting ads, especially on Facebook, provides tremendous opportunities for campaigns. While it is inadvisable in the Internet age to pander to the point of promising contradictory things to different audiences—the likelihood of getting caught is tremendous—tailoring messages for specific audiences and using the targeting features of Facebook and other online ads allow campaigns to emphasize the best message to each segment of the electorate.

Additionally, instead of sinking all your ad budget into an ad campaign you think will work (in the *Mad Men* style), campaigns are able to test a range of ads, targeted to a range of audiences, and then choose based on performance which ads to run with for each audience segment. This replaces much of the art of advertising of bygone days with marketing science. And with the use of marketing science, ad budgets are spent more efficiently and the ads run are more effective.

Data Integration

In 2008, up until about a month before the election, the Obama campaign had not integrated its mobile phone database with its general campaign database. As a result, they did not know who the people mobilized via phone messages were. But once they integrated the data, they were able to have a more complete picture of their supporters, and to know with more accuracy which supporters were their biggest champions.

In 2012, data integration has truly transformed how campaigns can work. In addition to the traditional voter file, which includes name, address, party registration, and voter turnout history, there is much more data we can append to create a more complete picture of each voter. E-mail addresses can be appended to the voter file. With an e-mail address, we can find and append Twitter names and Facebook profile addresses. This allows us to append Klout scores and other measures of social media influence. Appending LinkedIn data allows campaigns to incorporate full resumes into their database of supporters and voter. And using advertising with cookies allows campaigns to know what websites people visit and to use that information to place ads with the perfect message to target each voter.

While very few campaigns have yet to use the full power of this data integration opportunity, reports suggest that the Obama campaign used it quite extensively. As a result, according to reporting by Candy Crowley on CNN the day after the election, while the Romney campaign felt they were going to win, the Obama campaign knew they were going to win and had the data to back it up.

Why Digitally Networked Campaigns Are Different

Just a few cycles ago people were asking when the Internet would win a presidential election. When the 2008 campaigns began in 2007, the iPhone did not exist. Now the iPhone and its many copycats have transformed the way voters, campaigns, and the press connect with each other. Today we recognize that no one can win the presidency without an Internet strategy, for certain, and probably none can win without a social or mobile strategy. Indeed, it no longer makes sense to talk about Internet and social media strategy in isolation. Digital network strategy is integral to every part of a campaign, from field organizing to fundraising, from branding and messaging to press relations, and from registering people to vote to getting people out to vote.

Campaigns always come down to message and organization, regardless of the technology used. But digitally networked technology, specifically Internet, social, and mobile, offers more ways to package and deliver messages, and more ways to connect and organize volunteers, supporters, and voters than ever before. Touching on every aspect of a campaign, digital networks create economies of scale and the ability to overcome time and distance, both representing significant advances in campaign capacity.

Network technologies are distinguished from earlier campaign tools in several ways.

- *They are ubiquitous.* The widespread market penetration of mobile social tools puts the ability to produce and distribute original content, as well as the ability to redistribute existing content, into the hands of voters everywhere. And the voters are often better at using these tools than the campaigns, especially when it comes to congressional campaigns, which typically have smaller budgets and too often trim the social media expenses.
- *They are unfiltered.* With thousands of people attending the party nominating conventions, each equipped with a smartphone, a tablet, or a notebook, the ability for the campaigns to control the message coming out of the conventions is severely eroded. Where the campaign may want to focus on an economic message, events on the convention floor or out on the campaign trail may shift the message to racism or abortion

(as experienced by the Romney campaign during the 2012 Republican convention). In congressional races, the probability of an unflattering video or photo of the candidate spreading on Twitter and Facebook grows daily. Just ask George Allen or Anthony Weiner.

- *They are powerful.* Mobile devices have more computing power than the room-sized mainframes of the 1980s or the desktop computers of the 1990s and early 2000s. And the applications these mobile devices run can produce rich multimedia content and share it with hundreds of millions of people.

- *They are social.* The true power of mobile social technology is that it is social. Each time someone shares a photo, video, or text message, it gets passed along from friend to friend, from trusted messenger to trusted messenger. And as Duncan Watts has demonstrated, anyone can reach the most influential person on any issue within just six degrees of separation.[5] And for congressional races, the social nature of online networks quickly amplifies offline rumors circulating in the district.

The Dimensions of Digitally Networked Campaigns

Online campaigns can be envisioned in three dimensions. At the core, the dimensions are about the directional flow of communication (see Table 8.1). One-dimensional (1-D) strategies are about broadcasting a one-way campaign message, with tight language control, to voters. Two-dimensional (2-D) strategies are about building a transactional or two-way relationship with voters—getting them to register to vote, for example. And 3-D strategies unleash the social masses, with communication flowing to and from the campaign, as well as in any direction between and among voters. And in reality, 3-D campaigns are three-plus dimensions because digital networks allow for time shifting and overcome distance obstacles in addition to facilitating omnidirectional messaging and organizing. While many campaigns assume that being social is all about their 2-D strategy, the truth is that social strategy lives predominantly in the 3-D space. Taking advantage of how your audience talks to each other and to their audiences, as well as the ripple effect throughout the social graph, is the key to being social.

Campaigns that effectively tap into the power of the Internet, social, and mobile networks, fully integrating these new dynamics into overall campaign strategy, will have a decided edge on opponents who do not. And just as online strategies integrate into rather than replace offline strategies, these dimensional strategies also integrate together. Campaigns should have one-, two-, and three-plus-dimensional strategies.

TABLE 8.1 Strategic Dimensions of a Digital Network Strategy for Campaigns

	Level of Measurement	Direction of Communication	Activity	Message Control
1-D Strategy	Information	One-way	Broadcasting	Tight
2-D Strategy	Action	Two-way	Transacting	Tight or relaxed
3-D+ Strategy	Community	Three-way+	Networking	Chaotic

The ability of voters to take campaigns into their own hands is the big game changer for politics. Because voters can talk to each other, produce and share their own media content, and create local and national countercampaigns (even from within a candidate's own Facebook page), they can take the campaign in directions of their own making. By enabling voters to create mass messages, process large numbers of transactions, and build large social networks, social networking tools make voters' impacts on the political process on a level once reserved to well-funded countercampaigns or the occasional mass ground protest.

Examples of Voter-Generated Chaos

George Allen's "Macaca" Video. In 2006, Senator George Allen was coasting towards reelection as a prelude to a highly anticipated 2008 presidential bid. But his campaign was derailed by a Jim Webb campaign staffer, S. R. Sidarth, who was shadowing the senator with a camera. At one campaign event, Senator Allen decided to point out the cameraman and make an example of him.

Staring straight into his camera, Allen bullied him, welcoming him to the "real" Virginia and calling him "Macaca."[6] Macaca, it turns out, is a French racial slur. The video, after being turned down by the *Washington Post* for not being newsworthy, was posted on YouTube and shared with several bloggers. It spread like wildfire and played a big hand in sinking both Allen's reelection bid and his presidential aspirations.

That was 2006. Today, every new phone has the ability to take video. And most new phones are able to post that video immediately to the web and share it over Twitter, Facebook, e-mail, and other social media channels. In other words, anyone in a candidate's audience could be the next S. R. Sidarth. Candidate beware (*caveat candidātus*).

ParkRidge47's "Think Different." The 2008 Obama campaign faced two moments of voter-generated chaos early on. The first occurred when an anonymous video producer, ParkRidge47, produced and posted a video "mash-up" commercial for Obama on YouTube.com.[7] The video took the 1984 Apple Macintosh commercial featuring Big Brother on a video screen while a blue-lit audience of citizens watches mesmerized and superimposed a video of Senator Hillary Clinton giving a speech on Big Brother's image and her voice replacing his on the soundtrack. Then a runner enters the room wearing an Obama T-shirt and hurls a hammer at the screen, smashing Clinton's face into a million pieces.

The video made waves through the early Obama campaign, first because it was such a compelling voter-generated commercial, and second because its creator turned out to be Phillip de Vellis, an employee at the Obama campaign's Internet consulting firm Blue State Digital. De Vellis created the video at home on a Sunday afternoon because he said, "I wanted to express my feelings about the Democratic primary, and because I wanted to show that an individual citizen can affect the process."[8]

The controversy set off by de Vellis cost him his job. But the impact he made hit home, and he quickly landed a senior position at a top Democratic media firm. But the impact of this video went deeper. True, de Vellis was a professional with high-end video editing software, but the "Think Different" video could have just as easily been made with a ninety-nine-dollar piece of software.[9]

In the months that followed, the campaign saw many videos pop up on YouTube that captured the attention of the media and the voters. From the scantily clad Obama girl singing her Barack a love song to the more rotund McCain Girls singing out of tune and with gusto, lots of videos helped shape the public perception of the candidates.[10] Indeed, within the Obama campaign, a decision was made to work with volunteers to help them make videos, in addition to the campaign-produced clips.

Joe Anthony's MySpace Page. When Barack Obama was elected senator, Joe Anthony launched a MySpace page in support of the new senator. Anthony made his first foray into political activism after being "blown away" by Obama's 2004 speech at the Democratic National Convention. Anthony had built his MySpace.com/barackobama friend list up to about 30,000 by the time Obama announced his candidacy. With the announcement, the number of friends on the MySpace page grew fast, reaching more than 160,000 friends in short order. Then a power struggle emerged between Anthony and the campaign over control of the page. The campaign offered Anthony a job in Chicago to come run the group from campaign headquarters. Anthony declined the offer and asked for a buyout instead.[11]

Leaving aside the specifics of the negotiating, in the end the Obama campaign wrestled control of the URL from Anthony by appealing to MySpace directly. But Anthony was allowed to keep his community list for his own MySpace page. In the span of a day, Obama's MySpace page went from number one among candidates with 160,000 friends to last, with zero.[12] Despite this setback and the controversy around it regarding the takeover of the page, Obama was able to rebuild his friend list and overtake all opponents within a few weeks. As of the writing of this chapter, Obama's MySpace friends list is still climbing and exceeds a million people.

While neither of these events derailed or guaranteed a win for any campaign, they did create a "must deal with" issue for the campaigns to manage. And while there are always things popping up during campaigns that must be dealt with, these examples illustrate a whole new capacity for individual citizens to make a substantial impact on a large audience.

1-D Strategy

Optimists would say these new tools will transform E. E. Schattschneider's underrepresented masses into an organized (even if in a swarm fashion) political force. Observers of the Tea Party and Occupy Wall Street movements in the United States and the Arab Spring in Egypt and elsewhere across the Middle East would say it already has. Already, the multiplication of online communications channels is creating a voter-driven challenge to campaigns seeking to distribute its message. One-way broadcasting is being supplemented, and at times replaced, by narrowcasting: distributing messages to nanotargeted audiences.[13] While many voters still rely on e-mail, many others are moving to other channels like Facebook, Twitter, Instagram, Pinterest, SMS text messaging, or instant messenger for their primary mode of online communication. Others are compartmentalizing their channels, preferring personal communication through some channels, work communication through others, and consumer and political communication through others.

Given this proliferation of online channels to reach people, campaigns are already finding new challenges when using network technology to deliver their message. In the early days of online campaigns (before 2000), setting up a website and building a modest e-mail list was the extent of online voter outreach. Websites were seen as informational storefronts and e-mail lists were focused on sending out campaign messages. Indeed, an e-mail list of 5,000 supporters in a congressional district is still incredibly valuable, especially for organizing volunteers. And a candidate's website is still an essential front office. But disseminating a message can no longer rely on centralized, limited channels if a campaign wants to reach the majority of voters. Respecting communication channel preferences is essential for campaigns seeking to develop deeper relationships with voters.

It is important to note that traffic volume is not the only, or even a necessary, metric of success for a campaign website. In some cases, it is less about how many people visit a campaign website and more about who visits the site. In 1998, for example, NetPolitics Group created a campaign website called MissedVotes.org for a Democrat running for an open seat in Ohio. The site simply provided a list of links to the Ohio state legislature's online roll call record to document the many votes the Republican candidate missed while serving in the statehouse. The site had very few visitors, perhaps only dozens. But among those few were most of the reporters covering the race. Whenever the Democratic candidate claimed the Republican candidate missed a particular vote, the reporters went to the site to verify it before writing up their stories. The website was a primary factor in shaping the earned media for the campaign despite its small immediate audience. The lesson here is that it is always important to know who your audience is and deliver content that matters to them.

More recently, many people found themselves impressed by Newt Gingrich's 1.4 million Twitter followers during the 2012 Republican presidential primaries. But a careful analysis of those followers revealed that half were inactive for more than a year, half lived in other countries, and less than 1 percent of those that lived in the United States lived in one of the early primary states. Given Gingrich's loss in the primaries, it is easy to see that "size isn't everything."[14]

The optimal 1-D campaign strategy uses all available channels, each targeted to the appropriate audience, to get the message out. In the early days of the Internet, there were relatively few channels and only a couple of dominant ones: websites and e-mail. Today there are many channels to track, though the field is not as far-flung as it was in 2008. In addition to websites and e-mail, people also communicate via social network sites like Facebook, Twitter, and, increasingly, Pinterest; social media sites like YouTube.com and Reddit.com; and instant messenger online and SMS text messaging over mobile phones. There will be new channels in time, and some of these existing channels may die off at some point.

Increasingly, the challenge is to rise above the noise to deliver campaign messages to voters in a respectful way, a way that will be received positively. Voters have preferences for how they wish to interact with campaigns. The receivers increasingly are choosing the channel for getting their messages, whether they are political or personal. If campaigns do not deliver to the right channel for each voter, that message may never be seen—or worse, may be seen as a sign of disrespect because the campaign is not sending it through the preferred channel.

2-D Strategy

An essential element of the online experience is the ability to couple transactional tools to the information being disseminated. Networked communication technology allows us to integrate action tools, like e-mailing Congress, donating money, registering to vote, or writing letters to editors, not to mention facilitating meaningful feedback, into any piece of content delivered to voters.

Delivering opportunities for online citizens to take action is not only desirable and necessary but is expected by the people. The people, to a large extent, are more adept at using the Internet and mobile networks than campaigns, more even than all public and private institutions. That creates great expectations of campaigns and a sophisticated level of scrutiny. This is especially true now that the Internet has overtaken television as the primary source of political news for eighteen- to twenty-nine-year-olds and of approximately equal use for thirty- to forty-nine-year-olds.[15]

There are several technology vendors specializing in building campaign websites, complete with 2-D action capabilities. Among them are Blue State Digital, which built President Obama's campaign website for 2008 and 2012; SalsaLabs, which builds dozens of progressive congressional candidate websites; Engage, which builds sites for Republican candidates; and many more.

These web developer services have much in common. All build basic candidate websites with essential features: e-mail list sign-up, donation processing, and content pages that present essential candidate- and issue-related information. The best of these ensure that the ability to join the campaign e-mail list, volunteer, or donate money are present on every page of the website. And, with the mainstream explosion of social media, the best integrate ways to follow the campaign on social networks and share the content of campaign websites to social media.

How campaigns use these websites and their social media channels is a set of strategic decisions that can vary across campaigns. Each page on the site presents information that should encourage voters to want to support the candidate, during the campaign and at the voting polls. Campaigns should use social media to reach wider audiences, engage supporters across the country, monitor what people are saying about their candidate, and share their views and policy plans.

The challenge of every campaign is to present the right combination of information about the candidate that encourages voters to look to the campaign website to stay informed and to follow or like the campaign's social media channels. Whereas in the pre-Internet days campaigns steered totally clear of giving any coverage to what the other candidate was saying, partly to avoid giving the opponent validation and partly because the bandwidth to deliver information to voters was limited (limited inches of news column space, limited pages of pamphlets and postcards, etc.), in the Internet age, scarce bandwidth is no longer a factor.

With increased bandwidth for presenting more thorough information, campaigns can now present their opponents' views fairly, but framed with their own context and response. The 2-D aspect of the Internet creates a new pressure to present both sides of arguments. In this case the dynamic is twisted a bit. If a campaign does not show both sides, voters can take action by opening up a search engine like Google or Yahoo! and find the opponent's website. Once voters leave one candidate's site for another, the ability for the first candidate to frame the information is lost. Preempting, or delaying this action by giving information about an opponent on a campaign website helps to ensure that voters process the opponent's campaign message with the first campaign's context.

The key to the second dimension of online campaign strategy is to make sure all campaign messages and content are in some way actionable and that the action is one click away.

3-D Strategy

The greatest source of chaos in the political environment is the enhanced ability granted by the Internet for people to connect with each other in any combination, across time constraints and geographic boundaries, and with the same array of tools available to campaigns. The potential for a Joe Anthony, a Phil de Vellis, or a Joe da Plumber to steal attention from the campaign is ever present. And while many claim to be able to create viral campaigns, the truth is we have little idea what causes one idea to go viral and another to fizzle. The same network strategy employed by two different candidates cannot yield the same result. And like chaos models, changing the starting point of a campaign strategy will change its results.

The 3-D nature of digital networks gives an individual the ability to set off movements, even if small, through the polity. Consider the efforts of Eli Pariser and David Pickering, two college students whose e-mail petition opposing a military response to 9/11 spread like wildfire as it gathered 500,000 signatures in less than one month.[16] Their success helped supercharge Move On.org when Pariser took his list and became its executive director. There are many more stories of students launching new advocacy groups from their dorm rooms and of a few friends getting together to start a group online that becomes a prominent voice in a campaign.[17]

In a world where the power of the people is enabled by digital and mobile networks, campaigns have to adjust how they view their supporters. Rather than viewing them as message receptacles and followers to organize, campaigns have to treat supporters as strategic partners.

Regardless of whether or not campaigns treat followers as strategic partners, many of them will implement some strategy to organize their own personal networks. It is important to remember that the 2004 Howard Dean campaign discovered 7,500 voters already organized into monthly meet-ups across the country on MeetUp.com. And like the Dean campaign, all campaigns must monitor these types of developments and develop a strategy for incorporating them into the campaign plan—whether or not they become a formal part of the campaign. And as the 2008 Obama campaign showed, enabling new individual efforts to emerge and flourish is now a permanent part of the campaign playbook.

The Tools of the Trade

Keeping up with the networking tools available to campaigns is a daunting task, to say the least. And the odds of a new one emerging by the time this chapter is published is high. That said, it remains helpful to understand the types of software available and some examples of each.

Grassroots Organizing Tools

The core of any campaign is organizing the voters, especially the most engaged and supportive of them. Many of the online tools available to political campaigns are variations of tool suites developed for the advocacy community in the mid-1990s.

One of the key features of grassroots organizing tools is the ability to match people to their political jurisdiction (state, district, and precinct) by their zip code or address. This allows campaigns to collect basic contact information from voters, information relatively easy to collect, and build a contact list that can be nanotargeted based on the political culture and configuration of each precinct.

Once voters are matched to their precinct, the campaign can send e-mail alerts with links to take action to anyone on the list. With zip-code matching it is possible to automate the process of sending contextualized messages to every voter; messages that refer to specific impacts of an issue or a policy to the area where the recipient lives. This increases the stickiness and persuasiveness of the campaign message. And it increases the likelihood that people will do what the e-mails asks them to do—give money, volunteer, register to vote, and so on.

The products in this category of software are available from SalsaLabs, Blue State Digital, CapWiz, BlackBaud-Convio, and NGP VAN. These tools have overlapping functions and serve a majority of the campaign market.

Constituent Relations Management

As campaigns build larger lists of supporters and constituents, they must be able to sort them based on a variety of factors, including demographics, issue opinions, level of influence, and behavior interacting with the campaign. But beyond being able to sort and target communications, it is crucial that campaigns develop meaningful relationships with voters, in terms of providing each side with value and respect.

A constituent relations management (CRM) system allows campaigns to track and cross-reference information about supporters, integrating everything from contact information to attendance at events, to donations, to what e-mails people open and what web pages they visit. With this information, some aspects of the relationship between the campaign and the constituent can be automated, such as delivering newsletters and web pages that reflect the interests of each person. The manual aspects of the relationship are enhanced, allowing for more meaningful personal communications, such as fundraising phone calls.

While there are many small open-source and proprietary CRM software platforms, the industry leader is Salesforce. Coupled with e-mail management systems like Eloqua, another industry leader, the e-mail relationship and the website relationship can be fully integrated with the back end Salesforce database. Likewise, fundraising systems also integrate in the back end with CRM.

The newest trend in CRM is social CRM. These technology platforms integrate social media into the CRM model. Among the new tools in this space are Attentive.ly, Thrive (by SmallAct.com), and Radian6 (owned by Salesforce).

E-mail

The partner to CRM is the blast e-mail service. Rather than try to use an end user e-mail client like Microsoft Outlook, or a web e-mail service like Gmail .com, campaigns must use an e-mail service that is designed for mass e-mails. The email services include keeping your e-mail blasts from being blacklisted as spam. If you try to use your office e-mail server to send mass messages, you may quickly find that you are unable to send e-mail to anyone.

Online services like Constant Contact are stand-alone and inexpensive options. Many content management systems (CMS) and constituent/customer relations management (CRM) systems have e-mail blasts built into their service. And there are many e-mail marketing vendors that can provide the e-mail services, as well as strategic advice.

But as with all use of technology, it is about delivering the right message over the right channel. From a strategic perspective, the disintermediation of communication channels has shifted control over the distribution channel from the producer of the message to the consumer of the message. But the tools are still not available to customize message delivery to accommodate sending messages to the communication channel of the voters' choice.

Social Networking

Social networking affected electoral campaigns for the first time in 2004, when MeetUp.com swept Governor Howard Dean into the front-runner position before the first caucus and primary. MeetUp let people register online to form offline groups that met monthly. By 2006, social networks had evolved to Facebook and MySpace, wildly popular online communities that allow people to create robust personal networks and share all forms of media within it. Indeed, these networks continued to provide offline organizing tools, like MeetUp, but so much more could be done online with them that the impact of the offline activities was boosted considerably, as evidenced by Obama's ability to turn out more than 100,000 volunteers for the Texas primaries and caucuses.[18]

With over 240 million Americans on Facebook, 100-plus million on Twitter, and 30 million on Pinterest, organizing online communities is as important as organizing individual states.

Despite popular perceptions, these communities are not just for kids. Facebook's demographics now look very much like America's, Twitter started out reaching an older audience, and Pinterest is mostly women over the age of forty-five.

To the extent that these social networks are where the voters are and to the extent voters prefer to be contacted via them, campaigns must have a strategy for organizing and distributing its message on them.

Social Media

The other side of the social web is social media. Sites like YouTube, Instagram, and Reddit let people share with the world all types of media they create or find interesting.

YouTube, Vimeo, Facebook, and other sites let people share videos. Given the experiences of Virginia senator George Allen and Montana senator Conrad Burns, getting caught on tape in an embarrassing moment can destroy a campaign, even if the mainstream media ignore the story. George Allen's famous "Macacca" video and Conrad Burns falling asleep at an agriculture committee hearing set to music helped derail both incumbents.

During the 2008 presidential campaign, user-generated videos like "Obama Girl" and "1984–Think Different" captured the news cycle and drew popular attention to the Obama campaign. And in 2012, the video recorded secretly of Mitt Romney disparaging 47 percent of the voters as slackers that he does not have to worry about can easily take a campaign off its message strategy. While the "Obama Girl" video was hardly a decisive factor in his win, it is entirely possible that the "47 percent" video was a factor in Romney's loss.

If the media to be shared are photos, then Instagram and Facebook are the tools. Facebook is also a great tool for promoting offline events before the event, and Foursquare is great for promotion during the event. And for all things media, Twitter and Reddit allow campaigns and people to promote media content they find online and take advantage of peer reactions to vote the content up or down in the rankings presented on those websites.

By posting content to these sites and then mobilizing supporters to view the content and vote it up, campaigns can better expose positive media coverage of the candidate (or negative coverage of opponents). And, of course, any voter can use these tools to the same effect.

Blogs

The rise of blogs in general and political blogs in particular has dramatically altered the media landscape. As much as any other development online, blogs represent the epitome of the 3-D characteristics of the web. Bloggers have large audiences of devoted readers, engage in cross-blog communication, and are capable of driving the political narrative.

As a result, campaign strategy must adapt. The agenda-setting power of the blogs, A-list blogs and others, means campaigns must implement a comprehensive strategy for monitoring, responding to, and engaging bloggers.[19]

Monitoring blogs using specialized search engines like Technorati.com, SocialMention.com, and Google's blog search (blogsearch.google.com) gives campaigns the ability to identify emerging issues. Other sites like Alexa.com, QuantCast.com, and Compete.com measure the size of a website's audience. Together, these tools allow campaigns to identify which bloggers will have the biggest impact on the race.

Once a campaign identifies blog posts and bloggers that need to be engaged, there are three basic ways to do so. First, a campaign can post comments on the blog in response to an article. It is important that these comments be authentic. If the commenter is a campaign representative, that should be disclosed, to avoid backlash for misrepresentation. If the commenters are volunteers mobilized to post responses by the campaign, those comments should be in the commenters' own words. Otherwise, the appearance of "canned" comments would create backlash from the bloggers.

Second, a campaign can reach out directly to bloggers to ask them to cover a story from the candidate's perspective. When doing this, it is important to remember that bloggers are publishers, editors, and reporters all rolled into one. Because they answer to no one, they must be treated with extra care. Before making contact—preferably one-on-one contact—be sure that the campaign representative is familiar with the blogger's writing. Ensuring positive, respectful exchanges with bloggers is essential to success.

Finally, while there is no quid pro quo, if a campaign is advertising on a blog, it is likely that the interactions on particular stories will go more smoothly. Advertising on blogs can be placed using a variety of services. Many blogs use Blogads.com to serve their ads. Others use the Common Sense Media ad network (csmads.com). And still others use Google ads.

Mobile Devices

Perhaps the most exciting tools available to campaigns are the least understood. Mobile devices, especially smart phones, are delivering a combination of voice, text, and Internet communication channels to individuals on the go. While much attention has been focused on the digital divide between rich and poor on the Internet, minority populations that are severely underrepresented on the Internet are overrepresented on mobile networks. According to the Pew Internet and American Life Project, by 2010, 71 percent of whites had a mobile phone, compared to 74 percent of African Americans and 84 percent of English-speaking Hispanics. Of those owning a mobile device, whites are 73 percent likely to send or receive data on them, while African Americans are 79 percent likely and English-speaking Hispanics are 90 percent likely.[20]

And while early use of basic SMS text messaging over cell phones has been effective at fundraising, volunteer coordination, demonstration mobilization, and message distribution, perhaps the most powerful applications are those that integrate the Internet with mobile networks. The leading application in this space is Twitter.

Twitter is essentially a microblogging platform that delivers posts via the web and SMS text messaging. Posts are limited to 140 characters; thus developing skills for conveying effective messaging in short bursts, often compared to the art of writing haikus or giving sound bites, is the key to success.

Twitter offers a few basic features that have enormous flexibility for organizing and driving public discourse. The key to using Twitter rests with its three built-in methods for creating hyperlinks. The first, and most basic, is the ability to distribute live web links.

Second is the ability to use the "@TwitterName" convention to send a public message to anyone on Twitter. This form of hyperlink not only identifies the conversation partner but also provides a direct link for any reader to explore the posts from that person and allows Twitter users to aggregate and read posts directed at them.

The third type of hyperlink, the hashtag, is perhaps the most powerful. By including in any post "#topicX," users are able to associate their comments to public conversation. Each conversation, by using a common hashtag, effectively creates a group, or community, on Twitter. Each hashtag becomes a hyperlink to search for all posts employing the tag (via http://search.twitter.com).

There are numerous examples of how mobile networks have been used to shape the outcome of elections. One is the flash mob demonstration of 900,000 people the day before the incumbent Spanish government lost the election following the al Qaeda train bombing. Another is the use of an audio recording of the president of the Philippines trying to fix the election with the head of the elections commission as a ringtone that spread across the country like wildfire.

With so many people keeping their mobile phones within arm's reach at all times, the ability to connect voters, supporters, and volunteers via mobile networks has become an important part of the campaign landscape. But, unlike advertising on other media, there are concerns that overusing mobile messaging could conceivably turn off the audience and create a political backlash.

Again, the key here is to be respectful of the audience. Since communication channels are becoming disintermediated, the blunt use of them, as we have used broadcast channels, is less effective.

Collaboration

In *The Wisdom of Crowds,* James Surowiecki explores the power of crowd sourcing—farming out labor to the masses.[21] As we know from generations of survey research and the central limits theorem, on average, the views of the aggregate are more likely to be accurate than an individual or small sample. Elisabeth Noelle-Neumann reported in *The Spiral of Silence* that aggregating who people think will win an upcoming election is a better predictor, especially months out from Election Day, than asking them how they plan to vote.[22]

Tapping into this collective brain trust is made much easier with digital networking technology. Collaboration tools like wikis—platforms that allow large groups of people to collaborate on editing a single document—make managing the process of integrating the ideas of thousands of contributors easy. And new variations of wikis that incorporate thumbs-up–thumbs-down voting tools make the process even more effective.

For campaigns looking to be responsive to constituents as delegates, in contrast to a trustee relationship, these collaboration tools help make that process manageable. For example, in 2006, when faced with a popular, well-funded incumbent opponent for the Senate, Utah Democratic candidate Pete Ashdown employed such a wiki in his bid to defeat Senator Orrin Hatch. Ashdown gave voters the ability to shape the details of his policy platform with a policy wiki on his campaign website. Such a tactic goes a long way toward deepening relations with voters.

Fundraising

While incorporating tools into campaign websites to collect donations is a pretty simple concept, the rise of peer-to-peer fundraising takes the process to a new level. Websites like ActBlue.com, which is set up for Democratic candidates only, allow anyone to create a fundraising page for any registered candidate. Once the candidate or candidates are selected, a URL is generated that can be distributed to personal networks to ask them to contribute funds.

Fundraising pages can be set up for slates of candidates, even candidates in other districts. Many campaigns choose to use this platform instead of paying for their own. ActBlue.com takes care of forwarding the donations to the candidate, checks to ensure donors have not exceeded their FEC limits, and provides reporting to the campaigns.

Volunteer Management

In addition to using the various social networks, social media sites, and collaboration tools to organize volunteers, there is software specifically designed to organize volunteers for canvassing and virtual phone-banking. These tools allow campaigns to upload contact databases with addresses and phone numbers and then download them to mobile devices and remote users. The systems can parse out in small batches address and phone lists for either canvassing or phone-banking. Canvassing lists are distributed with walking maps and phone lists are coupled with web forms to report the results of each call.

Conclusion

The range of digital networking tools and strategies for using them will continue to make a big impact on electoral campaigns. That these tools are in the hands of voters as well as campaigns creates a more chaotic environment for spreading campaign messages than in the past. They also provide new solutions to getting the message out and organizing voters and volunteers. To be effective, campaigns must continue to develop strategies that consider all of the strategic dimensions created by these new technologies. While message and organization remain paramount, digitally networked technology has altered the playing field, not just in scope and scale but in more fundamental ways.

Notes

1. Lee Rainie, Aaron Smith, Kay Lehman Schlozman, Henry Brady, and Sidney Verba, "Social Media and Political Engagement," Pew Internet & American Life Project, October 19, 2012, http://pewinternet.org/Reports/2012/Political-engagement /Summary-of-Findings.aspx.

2. See the *USA Today*/Twitter Election Meter at http://usatoday30.usatoday.com /news/politics/twitter-election-meter.

3. Jon-David Schlough, Josh Koster, Andy Barr, and Tyler Davis, "Persuasion Points Online: Helping Harry Reid, One Click at a Time," Campaigns & Elections,

May 17, 2011, http://www.campaignsandelections.com/case-studies/176152/per suasion-points-online-helping-harry-reid-one-click-at-a-time.thtml.

4. Josh Koster, "Long-Tail Nanotargeting: Al Franken's Online Ad Buys Earned an Unbelievable Return on Investment," Campaigns & Elections, February 1, 2009, http://www.campaignsandelections.com/case-studies/176102/longtail-nanotarget ing.thtml.

5. Duncan J. Watts, *Six Degrees of Separation: The Science of a Connected Age* (New York: W. W. Norton, 2003).

6. See the video on YouTube at http://bit.ly/georgeallen.

7. ParkRidge47 is the pseudonym for media political consultant Phillip de Vellis. His YouTube channel, where the Think Different video can be viewed, is www .youtube.com/user/ParkRidge47. Park Ridge, Illinois, is Hillary Rodham Clinton's hometown and 1947 is the year of her birth.

8. Phillip de Vellis, "I Made the 'Vote Different' Ad," HuffPost, March 21, 2007, www.huffingtonpost.com/phil-de-vellis-aka-parkridge/i-made-the-vote-differen _b_43989.html.

9. Justin Hamilton, who is not a professional videographer, "deconstructed" the "Think Different" video and recreated it with all but one small effect (keeping Clinton's face perfectly framed in the video screen as the camera angle changed) using FinalCut Basic, a ninety-nine-dollar piece of software.

10. Alan Rosenblatt, "Obamagirl Video as a Teaching Moment," TechPresident, June 14, 2007, http://techpresident.com/blog-entry/obamagirl-video-teaching-moment.

11. Micah Sifry, "The Battle to Control Obama's Myspace," TechPresident, May 1, 2007, http://techpresident.com/blog-entry/battle-control-obamas-myspace.

12. See http://techpresident.com/blog-entry/battle-control-obamas-myspace for a time-series chart of MySpace friends for the candidates.

13. Jon-David Schlough, Josh Koster, Andy Barr, and Tyler Davis, "Persuasion Points Online: Helping Harry Reid, One Click at a Time," Campaigns & Elections, May 17, 2011, www.campaignsandelections.com/case-studies/176152/persuasion -points-online-helping-harry-reid-one-click-at-a-time.thtml; and Koster, "Long-Tail Nanotargeting."

14. Alan Rosenblatt, "Turning Twitter Followers into Newts," BigThink.com, November 20, 2011, www.bigthink.com/digital-politics/turning-twitter-followers-into -newts.

15. Andrew Kohut, "The Internet Gains in Politics," Pew Internet and American Life Project, January 11, 2008, http://pewInternet.org/PPF/r/234/report_display .asp.

16. Wikipedia, http://en.wikipedia.org/wiki/Eli_Pariser.

17. Other examples include a crew of Swarthmore College students that launched the Genocide Intervention Network and the group of My.BarackObama.com members forming a group of 25,000 MyBO members opposing the candidate's vote on the Federal Intelligence Surveillance Act (FISA).

18. Tim Dickinson, "The Machinery of Hope: Inside the Grass-Roots Field Operation of Barack Obama, Who Is Transforming the Way Political Campaigns Are Run," *Rolling Stone*, March 20, 2008.

19. Kevin Wallsten, "Agenda Setting and the Blogosphere: An Analysis of the Relationship Between Mainstream Media and Political Blogs," *Review of Policy Research* 24, no. 6 (2007): 567–587.

20. John Horrigan, "Mobile Access to Data and Information," Pew Internet & American Life Project, March 5, 2008, www.pewInternet.org/PPF/r/244/report _display.asp.

21. James Surowiecki, *The Wisdom of Crowds* (New York: Doubleday, 2004).

22. Elisabeth Noelle-Neumann, *The Spiral of Silence* (Chicago: University of Chicago Press, 1993).

9

The Ground Game
Fieldwork in Political Campaigns

ALICIA KOLAR PREVOST

"It's all about the ground game," conclude countless reporters and pundits in the week leading up to Election Day, every election cycle. Inevitably, there is some point in every campaign when conventional wisdom coalesces around the conclusion that TV ads in battleground states have reached the point of diminishing returns. This is when "the ground war," a campaign's army of foot soldiers, becomes more important than the "air war," a campaign's arsenal of TV and radio ads. Of 222 mentions of "ground game" in newspaper articles about the 2012 presidential campaign, more than two-thirds were published after October 22, the date of the last presidential debate and the start of the final phase of the campaign.[1]

For the "ground game" to be effective, a campaign must start planning it many months before Election Day. As Jeremy Bird, Barack Obama's field director, said, field is not a "turnkey operation. You can't throw up some phone banks in late summer and call that organizing."[2] A successful field operation, be it for a presidential campaign, a congressional campaign, or a statewide ballot initiative, needs a specific and detailed plan for finding voters, communicating with them over the course of the campaign, and getting them out to vote on Election Day or during the early voting period.

In this chapter, I review the core functions of a field program: first, finding voters—by identifying supporters or potential supporters among already registered voters, or by registering new voters; second, communicating with voters—persuading those who could be supporters but aren't yet, and encouraging your strongest supporters to attend events and volunteer; and finally, getting voters to the polls by creating a precise plan for making sure each precinct will deliver the votes needed to win on Election Day.

The tradition of *Campaigns and Elections American Style* has been to offer the perspectives of academics who study campaigns along with the perspectives of staffers and consultants who work on campaigns. I offer both perspectives: as a campaign staffer and consultant for fifteen years, as a political scientist for the last five, and as an instructor at American University's Campaign Management Institute for the last two years. In that time, the work of campaign professionals and the political scientists who study them has increasingly overlapped. The emergence of randomized field experiments to determine the most effective methods for contacting voters has systematized and professionalized voter contact methods. Pioneered by Yale political scientists Don Green and Alan Gerber starting in 1998, the revolution in scientific testing of campaign tactics has become a mainstay of political campaigns and political science conferences alike. Gerber and Green's *Get Out the Vote: How to Increase Voter Turnout* (2008, 2nd edition) has become required reading for anyone working in campaigns.[3]

My experience working in field has spanned from walking door-to-door with a candidate for state representative in Michigan in 1996, where canvassing was our main campaign tactic—and where my primary job was to keep her from accepting too many offers of coming in for lemonade and a chat in the voter's living room ("Ma'am, we have twenty-three more doors to knock on today, we can't spend fifteen minutes at each one")—to hiring a professional canvassing firm to knock on half a million doors in three states for an environmental campaign in 2012. In between, I worked on a congressional campaign where a canvasser was stabbed, a gubernatorial campaign where I hired canvassers from a neighborhood homeless shelter, and a presidential campaign where we proudly recruited grassroots organizers in every one of Ohio's eighty-eight counties. Because field is the most labor-intensive department on any campaign, it provides many entry-level jobs for new campaign staffers. At the end of this chapter, I include resources for finding work as a field organizer and ideas for further reading about writing a detailed field and Get Out the Vote (GOTV) plan.

Field is where the most exciting innovation is happening in campaigns. The integration of new technologies for contacting voters, like mobile phone tools and social networking applications, combined with old-fashioned grassroots organizing, has revitalized an area of campaigns that has traditionally taken a backseat to TV ads, debates, rallies, and speeches. It is possible that field was the campaign division that was most in need of innovation—for decades, the work done by field directors was passed down from campaign to campaign and had little grounding in what actually worked. Journalist Sasha Issenberg reviews the revolution that has occurred in field and in voter contact in the last several election cycles, with the infusion of research from behavioral psychology and the use of randomized experiments. Issenberg's book, *The Victory Lab: The Secret Science of Winning Campaigns,* is the new required reading for campaign staffers for its comprehensive overview of the culture of testing that currently exists in campaigns.[4]

Field operations are major logistical endeavors: they require precise planning and more personnel and volunteers than any other area of the campaign. Field is one of the many areas of political campaign work that seems aptly compared to war preparations: there are vehicles, routes, personnel, fuel, food, lines of communication, and even reconnaissance (in the form of observers at polling places on Election Day, who report back to headquarters on turnout levels at predetermined "bellweather" precincts). On some campaigns, field is pretty much everything that happens involving "real people"—as in, outside of the campaign headquarters. This can include setting up tables at county fairs, recruiting volunteers to walk with a candidate in a Labor Day parade, building attendance for a massive rally or speech, and organizing voter registration drives. Regardless of a campaign's size, from a campaign for state representative to a presidential campaign spanning fifty-six states and territories, there are a few key functions that every field team should perform: identifying voters, contacting them, and turning them out to vote on Election Day.

What Does a Field Team Do?

The main task of a campaign's field team has not changed much since the election of 1840, when Abraham Lincoln instructed his precinct captains to "organize the whole state, so that every Whig can be brought to the polls." Marty Stone, a lecturer at American University's Campaign Management Institute and the founder of Stone's Phones, a communications and strategy firm, shares the timeless Lincoln quote with students each semester, just as the first field director I worked for shared it with me. Here is the full passage from the still-instructive Whig Party campaign literature:

> Our intention is to organize the whole State, so that every Whig can be brought to the polls in the coming presidential contest. We cannot do this, however, without your co-operation; and as we do our duty, so we shall expect you to do yours.

After due deliberation, the following is the plan of organization, and the duties required of each county committee.

1st. To divide their county into small districts, and to appoint in each a sub-committee, whose duty it shall be to make a perfect list of all the voters in their respective districts, and to ascertain with certainty for whom they will vote. If they meet with men who are doubtful as to the man they will support, such voters should be designated in separate lines, with the name of the man they will probably support.

2nd. It will be the duty of said sub-committee to keep a constant watch on the doubtful, and from time to time have them talked to by those in whom they have the most confidence, and also to place in their hands such documents as will enlighten and influence them.

3d. It will also be their duty to report to you, at least once a month, the progress they are making, and on election days see that every Whig is brought to the polls.

4th. The sub-committees should be appointed immediately; and by the last of April, at least, they should make their first report.

5th. On the first of each month hereafter, we shall expect to hear from you. After the first report of your sub-committees, unless there should be found a great many doubtful voters, you can tell pretty accurately the manner in which your county will vote. In each of your letters to us, you will state the number of certain votes, both for and against us, as well as the number of doubtful votes, with your opinion of the manner in which they will be cast.[5]

And there you have it—the primary functions of a field team, laid out very clearly by our (then future) sixteenth president:

1. "Make a perfect list of all the voters" and "ascertain with certainty for whom they will vote." This is your voter file and your ID program.

2. "If they meet with men who are doubtful as to the man they will support, such voters should be designated in separate lines, with the name of the man they will probably support." This is targeting, which can happen at the individual level or the precinct level.

3. "Keep a constant watch on the doubtful, and from time to time have them talked to by those in whom they have the most confidence, and also to place in their hands such documents as will enlighten and influence them." This is voter contact and persuasion, which is carried out through mail, phones, text, social media, or face to face. Lincoln

even has figured out who the best messenger is: someone the undecided voter already knows—such as a Facebook friend, fellow union member, or fellow church parishioner.

4. "Our intention is to organize the whole State, so that every Whig can be brought to the polls in the coming presidential contest." This is your GOTV program, turning out your supporters on election day.

Fieldwork can also include outreach to specific constituencies, such as youth, seniors, veterans, and ethnic groups. It can include coordinating campaign events and visibility at candidate appearances, depending on the size of the campaign—a presidential campaign would have an event staff, or an "advance team" that is separate from the field team. In 2004, I was working at the DNC and helped manage the field team in Ohio. We had a rule that no field staff were allowed to attend John Kerry rallies or other candidate visits to the state (and there were a lot of candidate visits to the state). Our rationale was that candidate rallies were too distracting and our field organizers should stay focused on "meeting their metrics," which means reporting to headquarters every night how many doors their teams knocked on and how many phone calls were made. (We made one exception, for a late October rally at Ohio State University featuring Bruce Springsteen.) In retrospect, just meeting metrics was not enough—instead of our laser focus on racking up our nightly voter contact numbers, we should have sent our organizers to the rallies to sign up volunteers and new supporters, as the Obama campaign did in 2008.

Another activity field teams can engage in is voter registration. This is part of "making the list" too, especially if the current list of registered voters doesn't include enough supporters or potential supporters to get your candidate to 50 percent.

Building the List and Identifying Voters

The main goal of any electoral campaign, be it a candidate campaign or an issue campaign, is to win the election. In a two-candidate race or a yes-no ballot initiative, this means acquiring just over 50 percent of the vote. The first thing a campaign manager should do is figure out how many votes she needs to get that 50 percent–plus, and who the voters are who will cast those ballots to get her candidate or issue to victory. In 1840, at the time of Lincoln's Whig Party circular, it was probably fairly easy to "make a perfect list of all the voters"—there weren't that many of them. Today, most campaigns use professionally vended voter files to organize their lists. A voter file is a database of registered voters that is publicly available in each state and includes basic personal information like address and date of birth, plus other useful information such as a record of whether or not the person participated in past elections. Although voter files can be purchased from state election officials for use by campaigns or academic researchers (but not for commercial use), they are usually provided to a campaign through a vendor such as Catalist or TargetSmart for Democratic candidates, and Data Trust for Republicans.

In my academic research, when I couldn't afford a Catalist subscription and didn't have access to resources that we take for granted on well-funded campaigns, I worked with a voter file purchased directly from the Michigan Secretary of State. With seven million individual records and dozens of data points for each record (including whether or not an individual voted in elections going back to 1988), it was extremely cumbersome to manipulate, append additional data to, or feed into data analysis software for running regressions and finding relationships in the data. On a campaign with a clear end date of Election Day (as opposed to an academic calendar without a clear sense of urgency, when research can be drawn out over many months or even multiple election cycles), it is impractical for field staff to create their own voter file. In addition to being able to provide immense data storage capacity, voter-file vendors add commercial data and census data to improve what campaigns know about each voter, and they "clean" the lists by performing tasks like updating phone numbers and checking against death certificates (so your campaign doesn't include someone who has recently died in its direct mail program). According to its website, Catalist has records for more than 265 million people, including 180 million registered voters and 85 million unregistered adults, with thousands of data points each.

Campaigns buy subscriptions to the vendors' databases, and even though a campaign's access would be limited to a certain subset of voters in the state or congressional district, the list is informed by the "data soup," as Catalist's Bob Blaemire, a longtime instructor at the Campaign Management Institute, calls the millions of data points that go into the algorithms or models that campaigns use to guess which voters are most likely to support them, which are most likely to contribute, which are most likely to vote or not vote, and in general how to best use campaign resources.

Once a campaign has access to a voter file (in the words of Lincoln, its "perfect list"), the next task is to identify its voters, or "ID" them, to see who they support. This will allow the campaign to allocate its scarce resources appropriately, so it's not spending money to persuade voters who aren't persuadable (because they are already staunch supporters of the opponent), or on voters who are already very likely to vote or very unlikely to vote.

An ID program can supplement whatever polling data the campaign has collected to gauge base-level support for their candidate, and it can serve to train volunteers and give them something to do in the early stages of a campaign. IDs can be done over the phone, by volunteers or with robocalls, or through door-to-door canvasses. A robocall is an automated call that prompts a voter to press, for example, 1 if you support John Kerry, 2 if you support George Bush, or 3 if you haven't made up your mind yet. These IDs, collected by volunteers or by automated robocalls, will be recorded on the voter file— the campaign's database of voters.

Once the ID is collected and the voter has been identified as supporting, opposing, leaning in either direction, or undecided, that information is recorded on the voter file. On many campaigns, the process of recording the ID is done instantaneously—either on the phone, or at the door with a volunteer using a PalmPilot or other portable digital device (yes, we still used PalmPilots in 2012—iPhones, iPads, and other devices can be used but they aren't as durable and they are more likely to disappear). That information is then used to inform the voter contact and GOTV phases of the campaign.

In most campaigns, it is impossible to individually ID every voter who will make up your 50 percent. The information that is collected from an ID program and added to the voter file can be used to infer information about voters who are similar to those you have identified. For example, a campaign might learn from its ID program that single moms in racially diverse neighborhoods are likely to be supporters. That information can be fed into one of the voter file models, a "support model," that is used to help identify other single moms in racially diverse neighborhoods. Similar models, which generate scores for voters from 1 to 100, can be created to estimate the likelihood of a voter turning out to vote or the likelihood of a voter being persuaded on a certain issue.

Targeting

After a campaign has built its list and segmented voters according to IDs and support or turnout models, the next step is targeting voters. Targeting is the process of deciding what kind of communication each voter will get from the campaign. The first thing we teach at the Campaign Management Institute is that every campaign has a limited amount of resources—time, money, and people are all available to a campaign in a limited supply. Even if the amount of money available is in the tens of millions, a campaign manager still must decide how best to spend it. Campaign managers know that they cannot talk to every voter, and even if they did, some voters just aren't going to vote for their candidate. Candidates sometimes think otherwise—such as Kathleen

Kennedy Townsend, who in her campaign for Congress in 1986 tried to knock on every door in her district and still lost. Mitt Romney's comment that 47 percent of Americans will never vote for him was a truly terrible thing for a candidate to say, but every campaign manager needs to know who the 47 percent of voters are in her district, and who her campaign should avoid wasting resources on.

Some voters won't need any communication—those who are your strongest supporters and who always turn out to vote (such as the candidate's mom), and those who are your opponent's strongest supporters. Even if you are a proponent of higher turnout overall because it is good for democracy, when you're working on a campaign, the main goal is to win; so, although no one should ever spread misinformation about when an election is occurring, when you are trying to get 50 percent of the vote, you shouldn't waste your limited campaign resources by reminding your opponent's mom to vote. The simplest targeting chart for any two-candidate race, to determine how to allocate limited campaign resources, could be conceptualized like Table 9.1.

According to this system of allocation, a campaign would focus all of its voter contact program resources on boxes B1, B2, and C2, with resources going to box C3 only if there is a voter registration or early vote program in the state. With limited campaign resources, it doesn't make sense to try to communicate with people who never vote—your campaign might not be able to find them anyway, since if they have no vote history on the voter file, they might not be registered to vote. It also doesn't make sense to send persuasion mail to a voter who already supports you—in fact, if your campaign sends a persuasion message to a strong supporter, this almost guarantees a call to the campaign office berating the volunteer who answers the phone. So it is important to keep your list as "perfect" as possible, and to know what voters are in what contact program.

At American University's Campaign Management Institute (CMI), we teach students the basics of two types of targeting: geographic targeting, which typically occurs at the precinct level, and individual-level targeting, of which microtargeting is a subset. The geographic targeting techniques that we teach were first developed for progressive campaigns by the National Committee for an Effective Congress, commonly known as NCEC. Geographic targeting, which is typically conducted at the precinct level and is based on publicly available past election results, is accessible to any campaign staffer regardless of the campaign's financial resources. Individual-level targeting, which is informed by consumer data, survey results, and predictive modeling, can be prohibitively expensive for smaller campaigns.

TABLE 9.1   Allocating Campaign Resources for Voter Contact Programs

	A. Opposes	B. Undecided	C. Supports
1. Always Votes	No contact from your campaign	Persuasion voter contact program	Recruit for volunteers and fundraising
2. Sometimes Votes	No contact from your campaign	Persuasion voter contact program	GOTV voter contact program
3. Never Votes	No contact from your campaign	No contact from your campaign	Possible registration or early vote program

Dividing voters into "separate lines" as Lincoln instructs, based on their candidate preference or uncertainty, can be done by inference based on where a voter lives and the past election outcomes in that neighborhood. Past election data at the precinct level can show campaigns where their most solid bases of support are located, and where their opponent's support is strongest. Based on voter turnout levels in similar previous elections, campaign staffers can predict what future turnout will be and what party support is likely to be precinct by precinct. Precincts can then be ranked and prioritized into "base precincts," which typically have more than 65 percent support for your party based on past support; "GOTV precincts," which have high past support and low expected turnout; and "persuasion precincts," which have shown a tendency to elect candidates from either party. These calculations will help determine a campaign's voter contact programs for persuasion and GOTV.

Voter Contact

The primary methods of voter contact are mail, phones, canvassing, text messages, campaign literature, e-mail, and social media. Voter contact encompasses all personalized communication with voters (except fundraising appeals). This is different from the contact that occurs when a voter sees a candidate's ad on TV—which is an indirect form of communication, since every TV viewer in the media market will see the same ad. Direct voter contact includes mail sent to an individual voter on specific policy issues, phone calls to gauge support during the persuasion phase of the campaign or to urge participation during the get-out-the-vote phase, and canvassing by knocking on a voter's door.[6]

In the purview of the field department, most forms of voter contact are targeted—that is, they are directed at an individual voter or a specific group of voters. With limited campaign resources, it usually doesn't make sense to blanket an entire neighborhood with literature or randomly canvass people on a street corner. Instead, the field team will use its voter file and targeting information to craft specific messages for particular audiences. For example, predictive modeling based on IDs that were collected and recorded on the voter file might indicate that undecided women with children in North Carolina's suburbs are particularly interested in health care reform, so a campaign could target those women with mail pieces and phone calls that explain the candidate's position on health care. The cost of voter contact tactics can range from close to free (for e-mail and social media) to up to several dollars per contact (for paid canvassing or paid phone calls).

Assessing the cost effectiveness of voter contact tactics has been one of the major contributions of the behavioral science revolution in campaigns. Beginning with the early Green and Gerber randomized experiments, campaigns learned that many tactics they relied on were not very effective at moving voters.[7] Several subsequent experiments, both partisan and nonpartisan, have confirmed that robocalls and paid phone banks are not as effective as volunteer phone banks.[8] Although these voter contact experiments have been primarily aimed at increasing voter turnout, not at persuasion, in terms of effectiveness of the messenger they are in line with what Lincoln indicated— that the best messenger for a persuasion appeal is someone "in whom they [the undecided voters] have the most confidence."

Voter contact rates have increased dramatically in recent years (see Figure 9.1). I love to share the numbers with my Campaign Management Institute students, because in addition to showing the increasing rate of campaign contact with voters, it also represents employment opportunities for campaign staffers, since voters aren't usually contacted for free. Even when there are armies of actual volunteers, those volunteers must be organized by commensurate armies of paid field staff.

GOTV

Since long before Lincoln's directive, every candidate for elected office has had the imperative to get his or her voters to the polls. Once a voter is identified as a supporter, a campaign should move him or her into a turnout program if they are identified as an infrequent or unreliable voter. A voter turnout program could include direct mail, a knock at the door, and phone calls before and on Election Day. This is the most labor-intensive and logistically driven part of the field operation. A statewide GOTV operation could include

FIGURE 9.1 Voters Contacted by Either Major Party, 1956–2006

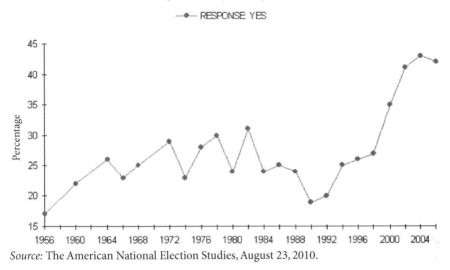

Source: The American National Election Studies, August 23, 2010.

thousands of volunteers, hundreds of staging areas, and round-the-clock activity in the days leading up to Election Day.

Increasing voter turnout has also been a primary concern of political scientists, as stated by Arend Lijphart in his presidential address to the American Political Science Association in 1996 when he said, "Low voter turnout means unequal and socioeconomically biased turnout."[9] E. E. Schattschneider argued that groups who do not turn out to vote will not have their interests represented in government.[10] Wolfinger and Rosenstone (1980) and Rosenstone and Hansen (1993) have similar findings.[11] For campaign staff, the memory of the 2000 election being decided by 537 votes is enough to motivate GOTV planning.

Today's voter turnout initiatives have the benefit of more than a decade of peer-reviewed academic research and evidenced-based scientific experiments to determine which methods are the most effective at increasing voter turnout. In the 2012 election, campaign organizers were able to draw on ten years of research to deploy the most effective turnout messages. Table 9.2 summarizes the research findings from several randomized experiments for a variety of field and voter mobilization tactics. One of the most effective turnout tactics identified by researchers is the "social pressure" tactic, which was first designed by Michigan political consultant Mark Grebner. Grebner's experiment, which he perfected after teaming up with political scientists Green and

Gerber, involved using the publicly available voting record for each voter to publicize who voted and who didn't in a particular neighborhood.[12] Although the social pressure tactic was found to increase the likelihood of turnout by a whopping 8.1 percentage points, it was not without controversy. Sasha Issenberg describes the negative backlash that came from the original mailing, with Grebner's phone voicemail system being overtaken by angry voters who didn't want him publicizing what they apparently thought was private information.[13]

Campaign managers who want to take advantage of the social pressure tactic will need to figure out how to do so in a way that doesn't anger their potential voters. One tactic that is similar to social pressure is the use of social media, including using Facebook to ask supporters to reach out to friends who aren't registered to vote. The Obama campaign used Facebook to reach voters it otherwise had no way of contacting. A *Rolling Stone* reporter who attended the Harvard Kennedy School's quadrennial campaign manager's conference in late November 2012 observed, "Social networks also gave the campaign a lifeline to contact sporadic voters." He continued:

> The campaign didn't have phone numbers for as many as 50 percent of its get-out-the-vote targets under age 30. But they could reach 85 percent of those voters through a Facebook connection of another supporter. This "targeted sharing"—friends lobbying friends on behalf of the campaign through Facebook—was a true revolution in digital campaigning, one the Obama team credits for nearly repeating the wave-election turnout of 2008.[14]

Another tactic that proved effective in randomized experiments and was deployed by progressive groups in 2012 is the "plan-making" script. It was devised by Todd Rogers, who was formerly executive director of the Analyst Institute, a progressive organization at the forefront of the behavioral science revolution in campaigns, and is now a Harvard professor. The plan-making tactic involves asking voters to visualize where they will be on Election Day, what time they plan to vote, and how they will get to the polls. This series of simple questions has been found to increase the likelihood of turning out to vote by 4.1 percentage points—earning itself a place in standard GOTV scripts, from now until the next best tactic is discovered.

In 2008, political scientist Seth Masket examined the location of field offices and the relationship to a candidate's local vote share. Masket analyzed counties in battlegrounds states to determine if the presence of an Obama campaign office in a county led to a disproportionately higher vote share for

TABLE 9.2 Results of Randomized Experiments to Measure Effectiveness of Voter Contact Methods

Voter Contact Tactic	% Point Change in Likelihood to Turn Out	Source
"Social Pressure" direct mail with appeal to public voting record, including record of neighbors who voted in past elections	+8.1	Gerber, Green, and Larimer 2007[i]
Phone script with plan-making" prompt	+4.1	Nickerson and Rogers 2010[ii]
Canvassing with knock on door and nonpartisan appeal	+6	Gerber and Green 2000[iii]
Script emphasizing high expected turnout	+3.5 (indication of intention to vote, among infrequent voters)	Gerber and Rogers 2009[iv]
Presence of field office in a county	+1	Masket 2009[v]
Phone bank with volunteer callers	+3.8	Nickerson 2006[vi]
Canvassing with partisan door hangers	+1.3	Nickerson, Friedrichs, and King 2006[vii]
GOTV robocalls	No effect	Ramirez 2005[viii] Green and Karlan 2006[ix]
GOTV e-mails	No effect	Nickerson 2006[x] Stollwerk 2006[xi]

Sources: (i) Alan S. Gerber, Donald P. Green, and Christopher W. Larimer, "Social Pressure and Voter Turnout: Evidence from a Large-Scale Field Experiment," *American Political Science Review* 102 (February 2008): 33-48; (ii) David W. Nickerson and Todd Rogers, "Do You Have a Voting Plan? Implementation Intentions, Voter Turnout, and Organic Plan Making," *Psychological Science* 21, no. 2 (February 2012): 194–199; (iii) Alan S. Gerber and Donald P. Green, "The Effects of Canvassing, Telephone Calls, and Direct Mail on Voter Turnout: A Field Experiment," *American Political Science Review* 94 (3): 653–663. (iv) Alan S. Gerber and Todd Rogers, "Descriptive Social Norms and Motivation to Vote: Everybody's Voting and So Should You," *The Journal of Politics* 71, no. 1 (January 2009): 178–191; (v) Seth E. Masket, "Did Obama's Ground Game Matter? The Influence of Local Field Offices During the 2008 Presidential Election," *Public Opinion Quarterly* 73 (5): 1023–1039; (vi) David W. Nickerson, "Volunteer Phone Calls Can Increase Turnout," *American Politics Research* 34 (3): 271–292; (vii) David W. Nickerson, Ryan D. Friedrichs, and David C. King, "Partisan Mobilization Campaigns in the Field: Results from a Statewide Turnout Experiment in Michigan," *Political Research Quarterly* 59 (1): 85–97; (viii) Ricardo Ramirez, "Giving Voice to Latino Voters: A Field Experiment on the Effectiveness of a National Nonpartisan Mobilization Effort," *The Science of Voter Mobilization*, edited by Donald P. Green and Alan S. Gerber, *The Annals of the American Academy of Political and Social Science* 601: 66–84; (ix) Donald P. Green and Dean Karlan, "Effects of Robotic Calls on Voter Mobilization," unpublished manuscript, Institution for Social and Policy Studies, Yale University, 2006; (x) David W. Nickerson, "Demobilized by e-Mobilization: Evidence from Thirteen Field Experiments," unpublished manuscript, Department of Political Science, University of Notre Dame, 2006; (xi) Alissa F. Stollwerk, "Does E-mail Affect Voter Turnout? An Experimental Study of the New York City 2005 Election," unpublished manuscript, Institution for Social and Policy Studies, Yale University, 2006.

Obama in that county. He finds that the presence of a field office does lead to increased vote share, and in three states (Indiana, Florida, and North Carolina) it could have made the difference in winning the state.[15]

The Partisan Divide in GOTV

Historically, the Democratic Party had been associated with massive voter turnout operations. According to Nelson Polsby and Aaron Wildavsky's classic political science text, *Presidential Elections* (10th edition, 2000):

> Most citizens who identify with [the Democrats] are found at the lower end of the socioeconomic scale and are less likely to turn out to vote than those with Republican leanings. So the Democrats put on mobilization drives and seek in every way to get as large a turnout as possible. If they are well organized, they scour the lower-income areas for voters, they provide babysitters, they arrange for cars to get the elderly and infirm to the polls, or make sure they have absentee ballots.[16]

But in 2004, the Republicans took the GOTV mantle from Democrats with the RNC's famed "72-hour project." I saw it firsthand in 2004, when I was stationed in Columbus, Ohio—our headquarters in the perennial battleground state. When I saw dozens of people carrying Bush signs arrive at my Holiday Inn Express approximately seventy-two hours before Election Day, I knew the Kerry campaign was in trouble. Following Kerry's defeat in 2004, Democrats regrouped in time for the 2006 midterm elections. By 2008 Democrats had a formidable GOTV operation in place. The mythical GOP "72-hour project" became the Democrats' impetus to invest heavily in creating a national voter database and sophisticated new targeting and modeling techniques, and the willingness to embrace the research-based culture of testing everything from voter contact methods to e-mail click-through rates to fundraising appeals.

By 2012, Democrats had clearly reclaimed to mantle of GOTV dominance. Several media reports document the Romney campaign's failure to successfully implement a complicated voter turnout system.[17] Reporters from The Daily Beast interviewed field-workers and campaign operatives about the Romney turnout system and found that they seemed to have invested the bulk of their resources on an Election Day system that was never fully tested:

> As campaign officials monitored central computers in Boston, instead of taking in the metrics of a proficient ground game, they saw

depressing evidence of a gang that couldn't shoot straight—anxious messages from operatives who were at the wrong polling place, couldn't work their smart phones, or were barred from a precinct because they lacked the proper credentials. "It was amateur hour," lamented one Romney official.[18]

The Obama campaign, on the other hand, had the good fortune of building on a field operation that it had started before the 2008 primaries—which in some states had been nearly continuously operating for almost five years. By the weekend before Election Day 2012, the Obama campaign had racked up some impressive GOTV statistics, as reported on its campaign website on November 3:

> This morning, as our volunteer Neighborhood Team Leaders opened 5,117 get-out-the-vote (GOTV) staging locations in the battleground states that will decide this election, they began to execute the final phase of a ground game unlike any American politics has ever seen. These staging locations are even more localized versions of our field offices—set up in supporters' homes, businesses, or any area that can serve as a central hub for a team's GOTV activities in the final days. . . . Volunteers have signed up for 698,799 shifts to get out the vote over the final four days of this campaign. The Neighborhood Team Leaders who are running our get-out-the-vote operation have been working in these neighborhoods for months, if not years.[19]

The Growth of Early and Absentee Voting

With more than one-third of voters nationwide casting ballots before Election Day, the reality for many campaigns is that Election Day can last more than a month. Depending on the state's absentee and early voting rules, campaigns can develop field and GOTV programs to take advantage of the longer voting period. Typical programs include adding absentee ballot applications into a direct mail plan, and designing a phone "chasing" program to follow the mailed absentee ballot with a phone call appeal to turn the ballot in. It is also important for field staff to develop relationships with county clerks and other election administrators, to stay on top of any changes to procedure (such as if there is a hurricane or other superstorm the week before Election Day, and early voting locations are changed or closed altogether), and so voters can be crossed off the list once they've returned their ballot.

Resources for Writing a Field Plan

The final project required by students in the Campaign Management Institute is to write a full campaign plan, which includes a detailed field and GOTV plan. Below is a sample ID script, which would be used to identify your campaign's supporters, your opponent's supporters, and those who are still making up their mind. Similar versions are available at the New Organizing Institute website, in addition to numerous other resources and materials, at http://new organizing.com. Plan writing and budgeting resources are also available at Wellstone Action, a field training program and organizing institute in honor of the late Senator Paul Wellstone. More information on Wellstone Action is available at http://www.wellstone.org.

Sample ID script

Hi, may I speak to [NAME OF VOTER ON LIST FROM VOTER FILE]?

Hello, my name is [CALLER'S FULL NAME]. I'm a volunteer with the [NAME OF CAMPAIGN], and I am talking with you and your neighbors about the important election in November.

First, [CANDIDATE'S NAME] wanted me to ask you what issue is the most important to you this election? Would it be:

1. the economy or jobs

2. health care

3. gas prices or energy

4. the environment, or

5. other

Great, thanks I'll pass that along to [CANDIDATE'S NAME].

Have you decided who you will be supporting for Congress this November?

[IF SUPPORTS] That's great! We'll need every vote to win. This is a grassroots campaign fueled by volunteers across the district. Would you like to join our campaign and volunteer for a few hours each week?

[IF OPPOSES] Thank you for your time today.

[IF UNDECIDED] Well, I'm supporting [CANDIDATE'S NAME] because we need leadership in Washington who will protect our families and get our economy moving again. [CANDIDATE'S NAME] has fought special interests and is a community leader who will focus on getting results. Take a look at his website at [CAMPAIGN WEBSITE ADDRESS].

Results key to be recorded on voter file

Candidate ID codes:

1—strong supporter
2—leaning supporter
3—undecided
4—leaning opponent
5—strong opponent
Issue ID codes:
1—the economy
2—health care
3—gas prices
4—the environment
5—other
Codes for other outcomes:
NH—not home
MV—moved
RF—refused
Vol—volunteer

Resources for Working on a Campaign

If you want to work on a campaign, field is the best gateway into campaign work. Because the field team is the most labor intensive, it offers the most opportunities for landing a paid staff position on a campaign. In the months before Election Day 2012, a progressive listserv, "JobsThatAreLeft," which was created by Democratic operatives after the 2004 campaign and boasts more than 50,000 members, featured job postings for paid field staff positions almost every day in cities across the battleground map. A typical e-mail, this one from September 10, 2012, advertised the following paid entry-level field jobs in Virginia:

OFA [Obama for America], Virginia is hiring Deputy Field Organizers! Deputy Field Organizers (DFOs) are the face of Organizing for America in communities across Virginia, working to advance President Obama's and the Democrats' agenda and grow the grassroots movement for electoral success in 2012.
Responsibilities
The primary responsibility of a DFO is to help Field Organizers recruit, manage, and train volunteers to organize their communities and neighborhoods into teams that register, persuade, and motivate voters through making phone calls, registering voters and canvassing. Their responsibilities include but are not limited to assisting Field Organizers

develop a plan to organize their turf based on its unique characteristics; identify and cultivate volunteer team leaders; plan and execute events and trainings; build relationships with community leaders; and ensure data integrity. DFOs report directly to their Field Organizer.

Requirements

- Organizing mindset and can-do attitude
- Ability to multi-task, meet deadlines, achieve goals, and creatively problem-solve
- Strong interpersonal skills and team player
- Attention to detail

This one was posted closer to Election Day, on October 14, 2012:

The Ohio Democratic Party is looking for dedicated, hardworking paid canvassers to work on the upcoming November elections. With a contested Congressional election, this will be a very exciting election season. Come be a part of this election season, help us elect Democrats to Congress and continue the trend of statewide Democratic Victories.

Canvassers will go door-to-door in Cuyahoga County to talk to voters about Democratic candidates, educate voters on the election, and encourage supporters to vote on November 6th.

No experience required. Must be able to work at least three (3) days a week, five (5) hours a day. Canvassers will be expected to work in the evenings, on weekends, and in inclement weather.

Must be able to start immediately and work through November 6th, 2012.

Access to a car and a cell phone is required.

Note that for both the Deputy Field Organizer job and the canvassing job, previous campaign experience is not a requirement. A Field Organizer or Deputy Field Organizer could expect to make $2,000 to $2,500 per month, and a paid canvasser could expect to make $10 to $13 per hour.

The best job bank for conservatives is the Leadership Institute, run by Morton Blackwell of Virginia, with posts at www.conservativejobs.com.

Fieldwork: The More Things Change, the More They Stay the Same?

The goals and objectives of a campaign's field team have remained the same over many cycles of presidential campaigns: identify supporters and persuadable voters, communicate with those voters using targeted and specific messages, and then mobilize those voters to cast a ballot on Election Day or before. But the tactics used to achieve those goals have changed remarkably in the last few cycles. The findings from carefully crafted randomized field experiments have allowed campaign managers to more effectively focus resources on proven voter contact methods for connecting with voters and mobilizing them.

Notes

1. LexisNexis search for "ground game" and "Obama" or "Romney" conducted on November 30, 2012.

2. Molly Ball, "Obama's Edge: The Ground Game That Could Put Him Over the Top," *The Atlantic,* October 24, 2012, http://www.theatlantic.com/politics/archive/2012/10/obamas-edge-the-ground-game-that-could-put-him-over-the-top/264031/.

3. Alan S. Gerber and Donald P. Green, *Get Out the Vote: How to Increase Voter Turnout,* 2nd edition (Washington, DC: The Brookings Institution, 2008).

4. Sasha Issenberg, *The Victory Lab: The Secret Science of Winning Campaigns* (New York: Crown Publishing, 2012).

5. Abraham Lincoln, *Collected Works of Abraham Lincoln,* vol. 1, 1809–1865. Available at http://quod.lib.umich.edu/l/lincoln/lincoln1/1:214.1?rgn=div2;view=fulltext.

6. Rasmus Kleis Nielsen, *Ground Wars: Personalized Communication in Political Campaigns* (Princeton, NJ: Princeton University Press, 2012).

7. Alan S. Gerber and Donald P. Green, "The Effects of Canvassing, Telephone Calls, and Direct Mail on Voter Turnout: A Field Experiment," *American Political Science Review* 94, no. 3 (2000): 653–663.

8. David W. Nickerson, Ryan D. Friedrichs, and David C. King, "Partisan Mobilization Campaigns in the Field: Results from a Statewide Turnout Experiment in Michigan," *Political Research Quarterly* 59, no. 1 (2006): 85–97.

9. Arend Lijphart, "Unequal Participation: Democracy's Unresolved Dilemma," *American Political Science Review* 91 (1997): 1–14.

10. E. E. Schattschneider, *The Semisovereign People: A Realist's View of Democracy in America* (New York: Holt, Rinehart, and Winston, 1960).

11. Raymond E. Wolfinger and Steven J. Rosenstone, *Who Votes?* (New Haven, CT: Yale University Press, 1980); Steven J. Rosenstone and John Mark Hansen, *Mobilization, Participation, and Democracy in America* (New York: Macmillan, 1993).

12. Alan S. Gerber, Mark Grebner, Donald P. Green, and Christopher Larimer, "Does Voter Turnout Increase When Neighbors' Voter Turnout Records Are Publicized?" paper prepared for presentation at the Annual Meeting of the Midwest Political Science Association, Chicago (Palmer House Hotel), April 20–23, 2006.

13. Issenberg, *The Victory Lab,* 198.

14. Harvard University Institute of Politics, 2012 Campaign Decision Makers Conference, November 29, 2012. Audio available at http://www.iop.harvard.edu/2012-campaign-decision-makers-conference.

15. Seth E. Masket, "Did Obama's Ground Game Matter? The Influence of Local Field Offices During the 2008 Presidential Election," *Public Opinion Quarterly* 73, no. 5 (2009): 1023–1039.

16. Nelson W. Polsby, and Aaron Wildavsky, *Presidential Elections: Strategies and Structures of American Politics,* 10th edition (New York: Chatham House Publishers, 2000).

17. Maggie Haberman and Alexander Burns, "Romney's Fail Whale: Orca the Vote-Tracker Team Left 'Flying Blind,'" Politico, November 8, 2012, http://www.politico.com/blogs/burns-haberman/2012/11/romneys-fail-whale-orca-the-vote tracker-149098.html.

18. Eli Lake, Daniel Klaidman, and Ben Jacobs, "The Romney Campaign's Ground Game Fiasco," The Daily Beast, November 9, 2012, http://www.thedaily beast.com/articles/2012/11/09/the-romney-campaign-s-ground-game-fiasco.html.

19. Mitch Stewart, Jeremy Bird, and Marlon Marshall, "Brick by Brick: Building a Ground Game for 270," Organizing for Action, November 3, 2012, http://www.barackobama.com/news/entry/brick-by-brick-building-a-ground-game-for-270?source=read-more.

10

The Evolution of Microtargeting

ROBERT BLAEMIRE

All political campaigns share the same goal: to win more votes than the opposition. And most candidates believe that if they could talk about their campaigns with each voter individually, they would win. Of course, in most electoral constituencies it isn't possible for candidates to talk personally with every voter even if they wanted to. So choices have to be made. In the time available and with the resources at its command, it is important for the campaign to identify those voters with whom it needs to communicate and those with whom it does not. It is crucial for campaigns to specifically target their potential supporters. They must, to use an old adage, "pick their cherries where the cherries are."

All campaigns have different resources for the tasks before them but only one is always shrinking: the calendar. Therefore, it is important for a campaign to be able to make intelligent decisions as to who its targets are, and to make sure they are of sufficient numbers to make a difference in the election. No time can be spent during a campaign on unproductive efforts. Once those targets are chosen, they must receive effective messages from the campaign. The only way messages can be effective is if they are relevant to the targeted voters. And the only way they have a chance to be relevant is if the campaign has enough information about those voters to be able to tailor the messages to the individuals.

When we meet someone on the street, there is very little we can talk about. We may have in common the location where we meet, or maybe we can talk about the weather. We can perceive the person's likely gender, likely age range, and likely race, all of which allow us to tailor our communication in the hope of being relevant. If we want to hold the person's attention and elicit a response to what we say, we need to talk about something the person may care about. While we won't necessarily know what that is, our assumptions are more likely to be accurate the more we know about the person. We might, for instance, assume that seniors care more about social security, that young people care more about college tuition, that males care more about sports, that minorities care more about civil rights and so on. Of course, assumptions based on broad categories like these will never be perfectly accurate, but the more we know about voters, the better we can communicate with them. If we are to have a hope of persuading enough voters to vote for our campaign, we must communicate with those who can be persuaded and use messaging that has the best chance of accomplishing that persuasion.

Targeting voters is not new. Early American candidates targeted voters by going to the places where they tended to gather—in the town square, at the saloon, or in the general store. Early targeted voters may have been only land-owning males. The franchise expanded throughout our history, broadening the field of potential targets but also making it more difficult to decide whom to target and what message to give them.

As the number of registered voters increased with the country's growth, the number of channels of communication for reaching the voters grew as well. As the US Postal Service matured, candidates began to use the mail to communicate with voters. Mailing materials to voters had become common by the nineteenth century. History tells us that Abraham Lincoln used the mail to send his campaign messages when running for the legislature and later for the US Senate.

The twentieth century brought in the phone as another mode of communication with voters, then e-mail late in the century, and the early twenty-first century has seen an explosion of communication channels such as texting, online advertising, Facebook, Twitter, and other social media. As the population grew, the costs of communicating with voters grew as well, and the growing costs made the necessity of targeting more pronounced. Campaigns could rely on the traditional methods of broadcast communication, through newspapers, magazines, television, and radio but these are broad-based communications that have been unable to communicate individualized messages to targeted voters while avoiding messages to those not targeted. These forms of communication are still critical in modern campaigns but can never fully replace the need to contact voters directly. As the American electorate grew more complex and dispersed, increasing expertise in more sophisticated methods of targeting became more important. Modern campaigners understand that all channels of targeting are important and that each must be done well.

Critical to the development of targeting techniques has been the rise of computer processing and, more recently, the proliferation of the personal computer. Computerizing databases of registered voters has accelerated the ability of campaigns to target more specific demographics, which helps the campaign avoid the waste of resources that occurs when communicating with voters who either cannot be won over or will not vote at all. Campaigns want to find the undecided voter who is also persuadable, and to use the data about that voter to have the best chance of persuading him or her to support the campaign and then to vote. As more and more information has become available on these computerized voter lists, the ability to target in a far more detailed fashion has become possible. Targeting at such a sophisticated level of precision is called microtargeting.

The Profession of Political Campaigning

The early history of political campaigns is marked by the existence of backroom politicians who were the architects of prominent successful politicians. William McKinley had Mark Hanna, Woodrow Wilson had Colonel House, and Franklin Roosevelt had Louis Howe. But few people spent their working lives on campaigns, in part because campaigns were relatively brief. For example, John Kennedy's 1960 presidential campaign did not commence until January of that year. And as recently as 1964, Robert Kennedy announced his campaign for the US Senate in New York a scant two and a half months before the election.

With the rise of primaries, the lengthening of the campaign season, and the advent of television campaigning, there arose a need for professional campaigners who could not only work in campaigns over a longer period of time but could also help the campaign allocate the larger budgets more effectively. The proliferation of presidential primary campaigning took the decision-making in the nomination process away from the backroom politicians and placed it squarely in the hands of campaign professionals. Also, the rise of television and radio made it easier for politicians to speak directly to the voters. The vacuum created by the weakening role of political parties has been filled by campaign professionals. Those who could help campaigns use modern communications to reach voters more effectively would be hired by the twentieth-century campaign.

Precinct Targeting

The era of the presidential candidate campaigning from his front porch ended with William McKinley at the conclusion of the nineteenth century. Personalities like Theodore Roosevelt made campaigning a much more publicly accessible event. The twentieth century moved campaigning toward greater democracy, not only in the way candidates became nominated but also in the way people became involved at all levels. Innovation that has contributed to the rise of professional campaigns came as the process opened up to involve other professions. Television marketers began producing the first campaign commercials, and computer programmers began to find ways to process political data to better inform the decisions each campaign must make.

One of these innovations was to compile precinct statistics to help make judgments about how each precinct performs in an election. As the smallest geographic unit in a candidate's political universe, a precinct has years of election results that can help determine how much it might swing from one party to another, what kind of turnout might be projected, or the level of consistent party loyalty. Organizations like the National Committee for an Effective Congress (NCEC), founded by Eleanor Roosevelt in 1948, began compiling precinct statistics to help Democratic and progressive candidates in just this manner. Predictions about how a precinct is likely to perform allowed campaigns to decide where to target. They could decide where persuasion was needed, where they might want to place their yard signs, or where they only needed to turn out the vote. Similarly, they could decide where their campaign time and resources would more than likely be wasted. A campaign could target its efforts toward precincts based on how they historically performed.

Data produced from organizations like NCEC defined the nature of direct-voter targeting well into the 1970s. With each election cycle, the predictability of precinct performance improved, and campaigns came to rely increasingly on sophisticated precinct targeting. Precinct targeting was part of a larger movement toward more individual-based targeting. This movement toward targeting individuals would continue to progress with the computerization of databases used for direct voter contact.

Geodemographic Targeting

The United States Census Bureau began using computers to compile national statistics during the twentieth century. Aggregate census statistics, compiled well before the advent of the computer, have also been computerized since. As the data became increasingly detailed and computer technology improved, the ability to process the data and learn from it improved as well. During the 1970s, firms like Claritas pioneered the development of clustering— grouping people according to shared demographic data and behavioral patterns—leading to geodemographic targeting in campaigns. All of the American populace could be categorized into one of forty clusters. The way the data was aggregated led to the categorization of every zip code into the same forty clusters. Claritas labeled those clusters in clear and understandable ways, allowing them to be used more easily in commercial marketing and later in political targeting.

A given cluster might, for instance, be labeled as "pools and patios," which denotes interests connected to upper-income, well-educated people who have more disposable income and live in comfortable surroundings. Another cluster, "shotguns and pickups," represents a demographic of lower-income, more rural, likely gun owners whose mode of transportation is more likely to be a pickup truck than an expensive sports car. The two groups may be targeted by the same campaign, but different methods and messages would be employed.

Claritas clusters were first used in a political campaign in 1978—a right-to-work referendum in Missouri, which was not an effort in favor of workers' rights but one designed to destroy the collective bargaining process and, in turn, organized labor. When that campaign began, polling showed that the measure would pass overwhelmingly. Organized labor understood that the only way the referendum could be defeated would be if their opposition never saw defeat as a possibility. Their overconfidence could be used against them. It called for a stealth campaign of person-to-person, door-to-door, and professional direct mail and telephone contact.

Claritas clusters were used to define the sampling for the initial polls and then to define the targets. The labor campaign saw that it could use Claritas clusters to define those voters who were receptive to the argument that the "right to work" would not help workers. This new form of targeting by clusters, with an intensive direct-voter-contact campaign, allowed the pro-labor forces to successfully defeat the referendum. The Democratic political community sat up and took notice.

Geodemographic targeting was another step toward more individual-based targeting, with the focus on reaching individuals within zip codes that fell into a particular cluster. This development conveniently intersected with my professional life and fully engaged me in the targeting business.

The Bayh Campaign

I grew up in Indiana, and like so many of my generation I was inspired by President Kennedy. In 1964, Indiana's senator Birch Bayh was in a plane crash with Senator Ted Kennedy and rescued him, creating a clear association between Bayh and the Kennedys in my mind. When I arrived in Washington, DC, in 1967 as a freshman at George Washington University, I traveled to Capitol Hill on the first day after my parents dropped me off to try and meet Senator Bayh. I was able to meet him, volunteered to work in his office, and was asked to do so a few weeks later. This changed my life and the course of my career.

While I was in DC as a student, my focus was the Bayh office. After a few months as a volunteer I worked my way into a paying job. One of the first projects I worked on was transcribing vote totals onto computer forms for a targeting project that would be a part of Bayh's 1968 reelection campaign. Once on the payroll, my responsibilities evolved, and I began working in the office almost every day between classes. From opening the mail in a small vestibule at the top of the stairs near the Senate attic to running errands for the office manager, I began to learn my way around the Senate. As I navigated around the various Senate services, I learned in the Computer Services Department that the Bayh office had a list of 13,000 names that received a mailing once a year at Christmastime. This Christmas list was largely made up of Bayh's friends, elected officials, donors, and political leaders throughout Indiana. It was at this point that I began my effort to build a mailing list so the office could have a more aggressive newsletter program. By the time Bayh left office twelve years later, we had a mailing list of 2.8 million Hoosiers with over 250 identification codes on it, and it had been the Senate's largest mailer for three years in a row.

I took every opportunity to develop the list. If we had a meeting with an interest group, I'd ask for a copy of their mailing list. As I worked more with federal agencies, I'd pursue lists of constituents that they might have. I acquired from the Veterans Administration a list of Indiana veterans to add to our database and a list of business owners from the Small Business Administration. Adding in teachers, union members, farmers, and a number of other groups grew our list to the size it eventually became. And I continually worked at cleaning up the list, taking home the green-bar printouts so I could scour them for updates, additions, deletions of the deceased, changes of address, and the like. This eyeball method of updating a list seems more than a bit antiquated today, but it was all we had at the time.

I also developed a variety of uses for the mailing list. When the senator decided to have a town meeting, I'd blanket all of the zip codes surrounding the meeting site with invitations. At the first of these meetings, we had far more people arriving than the room would hold—something all politicians love. And many of the people at the event had their invitations with them, proving to us that this targeting process and this form of communication worked.

When there were accomplishments in the Senate that impacted members of a given interest group or a specific geographic area of the state, the list provided the ability to send out informative mailings about those accomplishments in a targeted manner. When a government grant was extended, we sent mailings to make sure those who might be interested in the grant were made aware of it, thereby establishing a positive connection with the senator at the same time.

During that period, the strict firewalls between official and political business—restrictions that are fully appropriate—did not exist, and it was common for campaign staff to store paraphernalia in the Senate attic. In preparation for Bayh's 1974 reelection campaign, I went to the attic and began rummaging around in large cartons of index cards. These cards had voter names, addresses, and phone numbers on them, and each had code letters and numbers written on them—likely information gathered by phone banks. I never learned what the codes meant, but the cards were a glaring example of the data waste that took place before it could be maintained on a computer in a database. Data that costs a campaign thousands of dollars to acquire was often discarded after an election. This insight gained in the Senate attic provided a valuable lesson that I would put to use later in my professional work with voter data.

The 1974 campaign was successful. Bayh held off the challenge by Indianapolis mayor Richard Lugar, who would later serve in the US Senate even longer than Bayh did. It was clear that my advancement in the office during the ensuing years would place me in a key campaign role, and I was determined to learn as much as I could about campaigning. After the 1978 election season, I read an article about the right-to-work campaign in Missouri in which organized labor had defeated a referendum with the help of Claritas clusters. The effort had been directed by one of the pioneers in political consulting, Matt Reese. The article fascinated me, and I arranged to meet with Reese as well as the founder of Claritas, Jonathan Robbins. These proved to be very beneficial meetings, resulting in our campaign using Claritas for targeting and hiring Matt Reese to employ the technology in an aggressive (and expensive) voter-contact campaign.

No candidate had ever used this system before; clusters had been used up to that point only on issue campaigns. In preparation for Bayh's 1980 reelection campaign, we polled by cluster, bought television spots by cluster, ran phone banks and sent direct mail by cluster. We in the upper echelons of the campaign believed in the effectiveness of this sophisticated manner of segmenting voters and the capacity for messaging that came with it.

Back then we had to reach voters by mail and phone using lists of residents purchased on the commercial market. Even though we had this sophisticated method of targeting voters, we didn't know whether they were registered to vote or not. There were no such things as registered voter lists in a computerized form. We realized that we might be contacting people who were not even eligible to vote, but we had little choice.

That political year brought not only the end of Birch Bayh's Senate career, but the loss of enough Democratic incumbent senators to give the Republicans control of the Senate for the first time since the 1950s. California governor Ronald Reagan's election to the presidency was a landslide. In Indiana, Carter lost by over 400,000 votes out of two million cast. Our gubernatorial candidate lost by over 300,000 votes. Our campaign lost by just over 160,000 votes, almost a quarter million ahead of the ticket but clearly not enough.

I learned valuable lessons about targeting voters during this experience. I'll never forget Matt Reese's admonition that voters care more about their bowling scores than who is running in an election. It is an important lesson for us to remember: we are fighting a battle for the voter's attention. As we began to poll for that campaign, not only to get a temperature reading on how we were looking but also to be able to define our campaign targets, we did something unique.

Early in 1980, long before J. Danforth Quayle had earned substantial name recognition but after it became clear he would be our opponent, we conducted a statewide poll. First we asked who voters would support in a race between Democratic Senator Birch Bayh and Republican Congressman Dan Quayle. We won that match-up 72 to 10. Then we asked what we later called the "Jesus Christ question." If the election was today, and the Democrat was Birch Bayh and the Republican was a young conservative who agreed with you on the major issues of the day, how would you vote?" In other words, the question framed Quayle as the perfect candidate—something we knew he would never become—which helped us establish our worst-case scenario. We lost that one 46 to 40.

Our goal was to define Quayle in a way that would place him far from perfection. We also could quantify our task. There was a 32-percent portion of the electorate that would vote for Bayh against an unknown but would vote against him in a race opposed by an ideal image of Quayle. Our campaign was largely focused on that universe of voters—those with us when running against an unknown Quayle and those opposed to us when running against the ideal Quayle would like to become—as well as on the undecided voters. As the months rolled on it became clear that the atmosphere in the nation, as well as in Indiana, was leaning heavily against reelecting incumbent Democrats.

As already mentioned, we lost that campaign, but I was able to take lessons with me about targeting that have been valuable to this day. Our tracking polls showed us throughout the campaign that our targeting was accurate but we were failing to secure support from those voters we had to win. This was also a reminder that finding the right targets is only part of the battle. Message is critical, to be sure, but more important are the larger trends going on in the electorate. In 1980, America was suffering through double-digit inflation, double-digit unemployment, gas lines, the Soviet Union's invasion of Afghanistan, and hostages held captive in Iran for the entire year, with a very unpopular incumbent president running for reelection. Sometimes it doesn't matter how well you target or how effectively you deliver your message—sometimes you just can't win.

Post–1980 Election

Throughout that political year, people would constantly tell me not to worry—that even if Bayh lost I'd have no trouble getting a job I wanted. But not only did I not know what I wanted, there were 10,000 Democrats thrown out of work in DC. It was a dismal period for Democrats and a real challenge for me. I didn't know what I wanted to do, and offers were not forthcoming.

Not long after Bayh left office, Ken Melley, political director of the National Education Association (NEA), called me to see if I was interested in working with them on a project. He had heard that I ran the most sophisticated targeting system anyone had ever seen and thought that, despite the election loss, my experience might be useful to NEA. As a result, I began a contract with the NEA that had me assess the state of the organization's computer capabilities and recommend ways their political operations could be better served by their computer services division. It was a natural progression for me in the process of learning more about how to marry data processing with politics.

I spent 1981 on the NEA project and on launching a political action committee (PAC) to fight what I considered the destructive influences of the New Right on our politics. Organizations like Moral Majority and the National

Conservative Political Action Committee (NCPAC) had been active in the 1978 and 1980 elections in opposition to liberal Democratic senators, one of whom had been Birch Bayh. The level of name calling and vitriol that erupted as a result of their efforts motivated me to find effective ways to fight back, to lessen their influence where possible. Unfortunately, other organizations with similar goals were created around the same time and the competition in fundraising was intense.

The goals of our PAC—the Committee for American Principles (CFAP)—proved attractive to a direct-mail entrepreneur on the progressive side, Richard Parker. Direct-mail fundraising using modern computer technology had become something in which I was gaining expertise, and we had been very effective in using it to raise money for the Bayh campaign. Parker's firm decided that they would front the costs of a direct-mail prospecting campaign for CFAP. I was once again intensely engaged in computers and direct mail, coming to understand more than ever what worked and what did not.

Also during 1981, Matt Reese contacted me about helping him with some client problems. He had produced computer-generated direct mail using the Claritas cluster system for the franking programs of a few members of Congress, and they were unhappy with the large amount of returned mail they were receiving. No one wants their money wasted on bad lists. I became engaged with those offices as well as with the Reese direct-mail processes, using whatever political skills I had to offer and learning more about these computer-generated processes.

Working in the Voter File World

Early in 1982 I was offered an opportunity to join the political computer firm Datatron. The task the firm gave me was to acquire voter lists to match against the AFL-CIO membership in order to let them know whether members were registered to vote or not. This required an investigation on my part to learn where computerized voter lists existed, something we had not had in Indiana only two years earlier. Datatron would purchase these voter databases and the rights to market them to candidates. Datatron needed someone from the campaign world who might understand these databases and be able to sell them to campaigns.

Working for Datatron put me in a good position to become well educated about the state of voter file computerization in the country and to develop strategies for selling them. States were just beginning to computerize registered voter files, but virtually no candidates were using them. I would have used them in 1980 had they been available, and because I knew how valuable they were I was able to sell this voter data to campaigns.

The following year I left Datatron and soon accepted a job creating the Washington office of a Los Angeles firm, Below, Tobe & Associates, that provided political computer services. Below, Tobe & Associates had a contract with the Democratic National Committee (DNC) to acquire voter files where possible for the DNC's direct-mail fundraising program. The Reagan administration was perceived by the Democratic community as being against social security, and the DNC felt it could raise money from voters on that issue using direct mail. To do that, we needed to find computerized voter files that included party registration information and dates of birth. The target was Democratic households with people at least fifty-five years old. The number of people in that demographic category would be so large that, should the prospecting mail be successful, the potential to roll out to a large group of people would exist. They needed me to manage that project and to sell the files we acquired to campaigns across the country. This was similar to what I was doing at Datatron, but my role was much larger.

Looking back, I now know that I was doing this virtually alone, that the business of providing political computer services was not well known and had hardly penetrated the political community at all. I found myself able to sell these services to campaigns and to generate lists and labels for phones and mail based on targeted criteria. And once a voter file is built and enhanced with information like telephone numbers, that data can be useful for many other campaigns within the same geographic area. Below, Tobe & Associates worked only with Democrats, which fit my political orientation, and we began building databases all over the country—wherever we found campaigns that were willing to pay the necessary costs to use them.

Early in my second year at Below, Tobe & Associates, I was hired by the Al Gore for Senate campaign in Tennessee. The task there was to build a voter file statewide, which had never been done in Tennessee. Many of the county voter lists were available only on paper, requiring us to have them keypunched into a computer form. Those that were computerized were provided in a myriad of formats—nine-track tapes, eight-track cartridges, and floppy disks of several sizes. While the file was being built, I persuaded the Gore campaign to get the state Democratic Party to take over the project. Through them, we would be able to make this data available to candidates at all levels throughout the state, usually for the first time. This was wildly successful. Not only were these services available to campaigns, but the party had gained a role in elections that it had not had for many years. And as a vendor we would be able to touch campaigns that would otherwise be very difficult to reach without our connection to the state Democratic Party.

This concept of a state Democratic Party voter file project made enormous sense to me and fueled an energy and enthusiasm for my job that I had not previously felt. I took the concept to the Indiana Democratic Party, where I knew the leadership as well as the party's nominee for governor in 1984, Wayne Townsend. They soon agreed that this kind of project made sense for them, and we began building the first Indiana voter file with many of the same processes used in Tennessee.

After our success in 1984 for the Democratic Party in these states, I was compelled to take the state Democratic Party voter file project on the road. By 1986 I had added four more states, doubling that number by 1988. Two years later, the DNC got into the act by helping fund state party voter file projects, and we added more state parties to our client list.

In 1991, I left Below, Tobe & Associates and started my own company, Blaemire Communications. For the next seventeen years, the central part of our work was with Democratic state parties, and in 2007, the last year of my company, we had twenty-six state party clients.

With my own firm, I was far better able to experiment—to take on tasks that didn't necessarily make money but held out hopes of developing new processes or new projects, or of improving the way we worked. There was a simple adage that applied to our business: The more you know about voters, the better you can communicate with them. We did everything we could to help our clients know more about their voters so they could have better tools for targeting those they needed to communicate with and better knowledge of how they needed to communicate with them.

NCEC precinct data, matched to voter files, meant we could target voters based on two levels of information: the personal-level data and the precinct aggregated–level data. Adding census data meant another level of information, also aggregated at the census geography level, giving us sociodemographic information very much like the Claritas clusters I had used in 1980. We found that the clustering systems used in the marketplace didn't work as well in politics, due to high costs and slow turnaround. Claritas worked mostly with corporations that had less trouble spending money than campaigns did and that would tolerate longer turnaround times. The task was to create the same kind of databases for voter targeting but with information obtained by other means and with a final product specifically useful to campaigns.

Ideally, a voter list would provide the names and addresses of registered voters with an indication of status (active, inactive, canceled, suspended, or some other designation). In thirty states we could also acquire lists with political party registration as part of the data. In most states we would also get dates of birth and registration, and almost everywhere we would also have the necessary political geography on the file, such as county, precinct, or state legislative and congressional districts. In southern states still governed by the Voting Rights Act as well as in a few states outside the South, the data would include race. As database operations in the states developed, we would more commonly receive vote history data telling us which elections a person voted in, partisan primary votes cast, or even whether they voted early or absentee. We used surname dictionaries to encode likely ethnicity and went to commercial sources to append telephone numbers.

During the 1990s, the ability to track voters who moved and deceased voters became easier. We could acquire a database of deceased persons from the Social Security Administration, allowing us to regularly match that data and remove or encode those who were no longer with us. And the US Postal Service introduced the National Change of Address (NCOA), a process that allowed us to change the addresses of people who have moved. Both of these resources added complexity to our work but were enormously helpful in our efforts to improve voter databases.

Over time, candidates and consultants became far more familiar with computer-generated processes, and it became easier to sell our services. Consistency, retaining data from previous campaigns and future applicability of the data were of the utmost importance. Professional campaign consultants became early advocates of preserving the personal level of information—for instance, a voter responding to a phone call might provide his or her party, candidate, or issue preferences—as that information would be critical for targeting efforts in future election cycles. The high cost of the professional processes employed by campaigns for mail, phone, and field operations underscored even more the importance of preserving the information that could be used in future campaigns.

As we moved toward the end of the twentieth century, campaigns could increasingly rely on vendors for individual-level information from voter files, such as party, age, race, and vote history, as well as telephone matches, census data, NCEC precinct targeting data, and IDs from previous voter contact efforts by campaigns at all levels.

The evolution of targeting seemed to be moving fast, but it was really piecemeal. Because of the inconsistency of data from one state to the next—and often within a given state—the way you could target in one place might be very different than in some other place. A state in which some county voter files provided vote history and others did not, for instance, would mean you had to target differently based on the level of data coverage. As those of us in the industry kept tweaking the process to make it better, we came to understand that the use of data to target voters and to develop relevant messaging involved making judgments about voters' likely future behavior. We decide who to target because we predict that these people will be more easily convinced to support us or may be supporters who need motivation to go to the polls. We target messages because we predict that they will be more effective than others. We use precinct targeting with past performance in order to predict future performance. Without a crystal ball to aid in our predictions, we needed to rely on other tools at our disposal.

This need to predict voter behavior more accurately experienced a sea change in its growth and development with the introduction of modeling. Just as pollsters draw a sample of people to poll and employ techniques to extrapolate what they learn to the larger community, modeling uses enhanced computer techniques to score voters on their likelihood to fit into a particular profile. These models, done right, are enormously predictive. They can reveal the likelihood of a voter to be a Democrat or to care about the environment, or a voter's likelihood of taking certain actions, such as voting or contacting their representatives or senators in support of health care reform.

Models are becoming more and more powerful. Models now exist that predict the likelihood that a person goes to church at least once a week, is a gun owner or hunter, is conservative or liberal, or is for or against President Obama. For targeting, the implications are tremendous. Now we can select voters based on their predictive behavior and communicate with them on the issues that matter to them in a far more precise manner than ever before.

While early targeting was a more shotgun approach, applying more generally to geography and broad categories of voters, enhanced targeting, also known as microtargeting, is a more rifle-shot approach. The age-old effort to "pick your cherries where the cherries are" in the world of campaigns means to devote resources where they have the greatest chance of having the desired impact. It is said that half of all campaign money is wasted, but we just don't know which half. With microtargeting that uses sophisticated modeling, we have greater confidence that we are not wasting money by communicating with the wrong people with the wrong messages. There is a far greater chance that we can get this right.

The Age of the Internet

My own company created one of the early websites used for processing voter file data. Our system, known as Leverage, put the role previously reserved for programmers into the hands of the remote campaigner. Other systems were created around the same period of time, between 2002 and 2007. The most popular and widely used system on the Democratic side is Voter Activation Network (VAN). Because of the advent of these systems and the manner in which they have been embraced, there are now thousands of people around the country who access political data and voter files through web applications.

In 2007 I merged my company with Catalist, a company created to serve the data needs of the progressive community. Our efforts at Catalist have broadened the use of online tools among Democratic campaigns and progressive organizations. One such tool is the Q-tool, the Catalist online tool to query its massive database. Organizations subscribing to Catalist use the online Q-tool to access data for a variety of personalized organizing and political or civic contacts. But Catalist also provides clients a tool to match their own information to the Catalist database, whether it is membership information or campaign IDs. While solving the need to preserve this expensively obtained political intelligence for subsequent campaigns, this accumulation of data has also served the cause of creating predictive models. The advent of these online tools in politics has also led to applications developed to expand on the volunteer-to-voter experience.

The most effective form of communication obviously is between two persons who know one another. Politics has had to battle the limitations of that reality, and new technologies have helped overcome those limitations. When I worked with Senator Bayh in the 1970s, we had a program called Note Day, which was a simple, non-technological version of online social networking. Here's how it worked: As I traveled with Bayh, whenever someone asked how they could help the campaign they were handed a Note Day packet, which consisted of ten sheets of paper, ten envelopes, a sample letter, a postage-paid return envelope, and an instruction sheet. The job of the new volunteer was to write letters to ten friends explaining why he or she was going to vote for Birch Bayh (using the sample letter as a model, if needed), to address and stamp the letters appropriately, and to return them in the postage-paid envelope to our headquarters. The campaign would then mail them all at once in the final week before the election. If my memory is accurate, I believe we mailed more than a quarter million Note Day letters in each of the last two Bayh campaigns.

Early in the twenty-first century there was an explosion of activity in the online world. The broad public enthusiasm for the Internet has led to an amazing proliferation of websites, making virtually all knowledge reachable from our desktops. The current generation of eighteen- to thirty-five-year-olds hardly knows what it's like not to have online access. And as the culture has changed, political behavior has changed as well.

As entrepreneurs began creating websites that could put the voter files in the hands of the online user, software applications have sprung up that allow individuals to reach out through these apps to the people they know. The Internet has presented political campaigns with enormous opportunity. Modern campaigns can now make it possible for volunteers to carry their messages to their own acquaintances in a managed fashion. This sort of communication is effective and is bringing yet another transformation to campaign microtargeting.

Online apps exist that allow a volunteer to match his or her address book to voter files, communicate with those friends who are registered, and tell those who are not what they need to do to get on the rolls. This friend-to-friend communication is an effective way to take advantage of those who want to help. This intensive involvement by so many people, often individuals totally new to politics, has in many ways democratized the American political process. But it also presents risks to a campaign, which loses some control over the message and the targets. In many ways, these friend-to-friend programs trade targeting accuracy for communication efficacy. They can augment, but not replace, the more controlled system of microtargeted voter contact that is part of a campaign's strategy.

The Future

The evolution of targeting can be seen as an unbroken trend toward more precision and improved ability to zero in on the right people with the right messages, and it stands to reason that new technology will only speed up this trend, not inhibit it. The ability to find the right people and accurately predict how they will behave in the political marketplace has been enhanced by the accumulation of data by companies like Catalist. Because of this massive amount of individual-level data, the ability to accurately model voters has improved enormously.

And modeling can predict other kinds of political behavior besides voting. A donor model scores people on their likelihood to give money. A mail readership model scores people on the likelihood that they will open and read their mail. Activist models predict the likelihood that people will take actions on a range of issues or political necessities. A volatility model can tell a campaign which voters are likely to change their minds during a campaign, which helps a campaign use its resources more efficiently, since an election campaign should not leave a supporter alone if that supporter has a high likelihood of changing his or her mind. We also have models predicting what kind of media consumption a voter will engage in.

Channel-oriented modeling adds to the trend toward more individual-level precision by increasing our ability to know what the best channels are for political communication. We can know with a great deal of accuracy which voters are better reached by phone, mail, or e-mail. Whether households get political information through cable TV or broadcast television, the kind of viewing that reaches them, and even the time of day or length of time prior to the election to get the message to them are also questions that can be answered by channel modeling.

Other forms of political communication are also moving in the direction of personalization. Online advertising is moving toward greater individualization and more pinpoint targeting with the use of "cookie pools," data that tells us which websites a person visits. Similarly, in the world of online polling, campaigns are using survey responses of online panels—which serve as virtual focus groups—to target registered voters who may not be reachable by more traditional means. This practice has also led to a more efficient and less costly way to test ads and direct mail. Rather than convening focus groups for that purpose, the same things can be accomplished with online panels.

It also makes sense that eventually political targeting information will be used to change the way cable television broadcasts ads. In the future, it will be possible for campaigns to advertise to cable in the same precise way they now send mail and make phone calls, with different voters receiving different ads during the same show. There are technical challenges, to be sure, but there will likely be a time when completely variable advertising will be transmitted through our familiar cable boxes. New applications are being developed all the time for political campaigns that, by using voter data, allow for greater levels of targeting and individualized messaging.

One of the great challenges of politics in this first quarter of the twenty-first century in the midst of these tremendous technological innovations is reaching the young voter. A great many voters under thirty-five cannot be reached through commercial television or radio, do not read newspapers or magazines, do not have landlines, and do not read their mail. You would be hard-pressed even to find them door-to-door. The youngest voting demographic—growing at such a rate that they will soon overtake older voters in influence and numbers—cannot be reached by traditional campaign communication channels. Campaigns must turn to the new media, these emerging technologies, if they are to have any chance of influencing younger voters.

It is a greater expense and challenge to use voter data to target with these new methods, but it is more critical than it has ever been. It still wastes money and time for campaigns to employ communication tactics that end up contacting voters who will not support them or will not vote, but now the cost of sending too general a message to too broad an audience is unacceptably high. It still makes sense to use data to vary messages, but younger voters are used to a high level of personalization and have no patience for messages that are not relevant to their lives. The need for targeting and using data appropriately will not change, but the need for more complex and sophisticated microtargeting will continue to grow.

I feel I have been fortunate to have a front row seat to watch this trend toward greater targeting precision and to play a small part. The evolution of targeting can be summarized as follows:

Simple demographics. Early targeting was aimed at white males who lived in the states or districts in which the campaigns were being conducted. As the country matured, the franchise expanded to include former slaves and free African Americans, women, and those at least eighteen years old. The expansion of the franchise created a much larger voting universe and made it necessary to avoid contacting everyone.

Multiplying channels. The rise of television advertising had its initial focus on broad demographics, with ads placed on television shows that were being watched by the type of people the campaign needed to reach. As broadcast television became more of a staple in American life, the ability to narrow-cast toward smaller and smaller demographics developed rapidly. As the number of television channels available to Americans expanded drastically with the advent of cable, the challenges to reach a targeted audience over the airwaves multiplied.

Rising costs. As the country's population grew and campaigns became more expensive, largely due to the development of political television ads, it became increasingly important for campaigns to select their targets accurately and find ways to spend their precious funds communicating only with those they needed to. Wasting money on those who should not be targeted meant fewer available funds to contact those who should be.

Precinct targeting. The precinct is the smallest political geographic area. As computer technology developed that allowed a precinct's electoral history to be categorized, campaigners were able to target voters based on the kinds of precincts in which they lived—whether, for instance, they may be precincts that perform solidly Democratic or with large numbers of persuadable voters.

Geodemographic targeting. As computer processing developed further, it became possible for data processors to place all voters into a relatively small number of demographic composites, or clusters, allowing campaigns to choose which clusters to target according to which issues were important to voters within those clusters. The ability to poll by cluster was followed by the ability to send messages by cluster.

Computerized voter files. Once lists of registered voters became available in computerized form, campaigns could take advantage of the individual data items available on those lists to slice and dice the electorate as never before. They could target voters within the proper geography, and they could use precinct targeting to augment their choice and geodemographic targeting to overlay issue intelligence with the political intelligence. Computerization became democratized with the rise of the personal computer, a tool that was necessary for campaigns to utilize but not only by those who would call themselves campaign professionals. Methods of contacting voters in person or through direct mail or telephones became far more professionalized with the creation of a large number of campaign mail and phone firms. The need to target grew as quickly as the ability to target effectively with the computer. And smart campaigns could use precinct targeting, geodemographic targeting, and highly individualized voter targeting in combination.

Preservation of data. Campaigns contact voters to see how they feel about their candidates and the issues of the day. Campaigns now save that information in a form suitable for future use rather than reinventing the wheel with each campaign, and they build upon previous efforts with new information about voters. This has led to better voter targeting and messaging and less waste.

Microtargeting. All of these changes have led to the ability to fine-tune targeting in a way that allows the campaign to predict voter behavior. By massing this tremendous amount of political information with commercial data, census data, specialty data, and individual responses, modelers have been able to create predictive models on very esoteric yet critical political behavior.

Changing technologies and improvements in data compilation will continue the trend toward greater individualization and precision in campaign targeting and message delivery. While some things coming down the pike seem easy to predict, it is impossible to know what campaigning will look like in the second quarter of this century or beyond. But we can be sure that campaigners will only get better at zeroing in on the right voter and successfully motivating that voter with a message that makes sense and is entirely relevant. It is the challenge of modern campaigns and I have no doubt it is one that will be met.

11

Voter Turnout in the 2012 Election

PAMELA BACHILLA, JAN LEIGHLEY,
AND JONATHAN NAGLER

Within a week of President Barack Obama's election to his second term in office in 2012, the news media and political pundits found their narrative: the conservative wing of the Republican Party had dominated the primaries as well as the general campaign of Mitt Romney, whose campaign advisors and party strategists were simply out of touch with the demographics of the country and the political preferences of voters. Yet only one month prior to the election, the media and politicos were telling a different story: the election would be close, and the outcome would be especially dependent on voter turnout. If Obama was able to turn out his supporters (especially in battle-ground states) as he did in 2008, the race would tilt his way; if Romney was able to motivate his supporters, then it could tilt his way.

If journalists and politicos believed that turnout was key to the election outcome, one might expect that they would report on it after the election. Not so. Reporters and pundits earn a living by reporting and creating new stories, not evaluating their past claims. The latter task usually falls to academics and—as is typical in most scholarly research—usually requires more than a few weeks to be done. Moreover, reporting on the outcome of presidential elections is much easier, and more immediately newsworthy, than is reporting on who showed up at the polls on Election Day or what the turnout numbers were for various groups of voters. Although details about turnout on November 6, 2012, are still being gathered, one thing that we do know is that a sufficient number of voters—whoever they were—chose to reelect Barack Obama as president rather than elect Mitt Romney, and that this choice is likely to have important consequences across a wide range of policies.

The gap between campaign narratives and evidence is illustrated nicely by Philpot, Shaw, and McGowan's (2009) analysis of the 2008 election. Philpot, Shaw, and McGowan describe the narrative surrounding the 2008 election as emphasizing the importance of Barack Obama being the first African American president. A key part of his success, it was argued, was that this symbolic value increased the political interest, efficacy, and engagement of blacks, who turned out in especially high numbers and delivered most of their votes to Obama. The authors, however, raise another possibility: that blacks turned out in higher numbers in 2008 not because Obama was black, but because the Obama campaign targeted the African American community and spent a substantial amount of money to do so. Their evidence, while not definitive, nonetheless suggests that it was campaign mobilization, rather than African American political orientations, that helped deliver an Obama victory.

Our goal in this chapter is to evaluate early claims about the importance of turnout to the 2012 election outcome. We would like to know whether, as in 2008, higher levels of turnout among African Americans might help to account for Obama's victory, and whether the turnout of other demographic groups who also favor Obama matched that of 2008. We admit from the start, however, that because we are writing shortly after the election we do not have the sort of data that we would need to answer these questions fully. Others will do so years from now. What we offer in this chapter are some tentative answers, based on historical turnout data, the aggregate turnout data for 2008 and 2012, and exit poll data from 2008 and 2012. These data sources will be evaluated in the context of theories of voter turnout in order to strengthen our substantive inferences regarding turnout in the 2012 presidential election.

Turnout in US Presidential Elections:
A Note on the Historical Record

Usually discussions of contemporary voter turnout in the United States focus on the post-1972 period, reporting turnout levels ranging from around 50 to 60 percent and lamenting that so few citizens exercise their right to cast a ballot. Less than universal turnout is sometimes attributed to citizens' lack of interest in politics or limited political knowledge. Others explain nonvoting at least in part by characteristics of the American electoral system—such as the two-party versus multiparty system, a lack of competitiveness, or voter registration systems that place the responsibility (and therefore costs) of voting on the individual rather than the state (as is the case in Western European democracies).

We begin with a discussion of turnout levels in the United States from a pre-twentieth-century perspective because it highlights two important points. First, just because turnout in US presidential elections has hovered around 50 to 60 percent over the past fifty years does not mean that there is anything inevitable about this level of turnout, for other historical periods have evidenced much higher levels of voting. And, second, one of the distinguishing features of these historical eras is how the party system and election laws (i.e., voter eligibility and registration requirements) vary in significant ways. These variations underscore the importance of how the "rules" of the electoral system influence who votes. This is not to say that individual characteristics or attitudes do not matter in terms of why people vote; it is just a reminder that the turnout patterns we are typically interested in likely reflect, in part, the rules that govern voter registration and turnout.

That these rules are critical to understanding voter turnout is underscored by the fact that the right to vote, and the political battles associated with the election laws that determine who is eligible to vote, have been common points of contention for centuries. Systemic evidence during the early decades of the country is quite limited—and even what we do have is likely to be unreliable. Most estimates suggest that turnout rates in the period from 1789 to about 1824 were the lowest in US history (Keyssar 2000; McDonald 2010; Stanley and Niemi 2006). State eligibility laws prohibited most people from voting, typically limiting the franchise to white men who owned property. For those who were eligible, the practical costs of voting were substantial. Rural voters, for example, often had to travel long distances to reach designated polling places (Keyssar 2000).

The era of machine party politics, from about 1828 to 1896, gave rise to fierce political competition and efforts by the parties to mobilize the growing electorate through campaign propaganda and patronage systems that rewarded reliable party voters (Burnham 1965; Keyssar 2000; McDonald 2010). Turnout among eligible voters for presidential races in this period rose to a historic high of about 80 percent (Stanley and Niemi 2006). The adoption of the Fifteenth Amendment in 1870 also expanded the electorate to include all men of color and former male slaves, although disenfranchising techniques employed by local white officials often depressed turnout among these groups (Keyssar 2000; Kousser 1999). Southern states maneuvered around universal

FIGURE 11.1 Voter Turnout in US Presidential Elections, 1972–2008

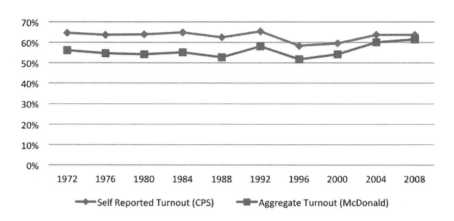

Sources: Data taken from Leighley and Nagler (forthcoming), table 2.1. Original source for CPS data: US Census Current Population Survey, November Supplement, various years, self-reported household turnout; original source for McDonald data: Michael McDonald's website, "United States Election Project," www.elections.gmu.edu/voter_turnout.htm.

male suffrage by adopting "Jim Crow" laws that used registration and voting requirements to intimidate African Americans from participating in elections. Informally, threats and physical violence were common tactics adopted to keep African Americans from the polls in the South (Key 1949; Keyssar 2000; Kousser 1999).

Women were enfranchised by the adoption of the Nineteenth Amendment in 1920, but this expansion of voting rights followed an era of Progressive reforms that ultimately depressed turnout. Although the new laws were primarily intended to root out fraud and machine party corruption, they also increased the individual costs of voting. The secret ballot, adopted by most states prior to World War I, eliminated party ticket ballots and other visual cues that assisted illiterate voters. Literacy tests were a more overt mechanism by which many immigrants and former slaves were prevented from voting. Onerous registration laws in many states required voters to reregister prior to each election or opened the rolls for new registrants only a few days at a time (Keyssar 2000; Kousser 1999). Recent immigrants and the poor—the constituents of "big boss" political parties—were the least equipped to bear the burdens of the new laws. Turnout among eligible voters declined in the Progressive era and did not recover throughout the first half of the twentieth century (Burnham 1980; McDonald 2010).

The second half of the twentieth century witnessed federal government intervention to tear down many of the barriers to voting adopted by states and establish national uniformity in election laws. The 1965 Voting Rights Act enforced the provisions of the Fifteenth Amendment nearly a century after its ratification. Section 5 of the Voting Rights Act allows the federal government to monitor elections and registration laws in states with a history of voter discrimination. Suffrage was extended to citizens eighteen and older by the Twenty-Sixth Amendment in 1971. The National Voter Registration Act of 1993 mandated that voter registration forms be available at driver's license and other public assistance offices. In 2002, the Help America Vote Act provided funding for states to upgrade old and failing voting equipment (for a discussion of the NVRA and HAVA and their effects on turnout, see Hanmer 2009).

Despite federal interventions intended to decrease barriers to voting, scholars and journalists alike reported a significant decline in turnout from the 1960s through the 1990s (see, for example, Abramson and Aldrich 1982; Cassel and Luskin 1988; Teixeira 1992), and this decline in voter turnout continues to be noted in contemporary election coverage. However, McDonald and Popkin (2001) demonstrated rather persuasively that the apparent decline of turnout was largely the result of bad data. Turnout appeared to decline, they argue, because the "official" turnout figures—which result from dividing the number of ballots cast by the size of the voting age population in the states—failed to recognize that the voting age population includes individuals who were not eligible to vote (e.g., felons and immigrants, legal and illegal). According to McDonald and Popkin, once these corrections are made to the data, the decline in turnout is nearly eliminated.

This revision to the standard approach to computing and reporting turnout is incredibly important. To underscore this contribution, we note that there is no "official" single turnout statistic created or reported for presidential elections. What journalists typically report as "official" turnout is based on the number of ballots reported by state election officers in each state. They must wait to include provisional ballots, mail-in ballots, and other types of ballots that may take months to count. In many states, election officials do not release the certified vote count until December or early January. Once all these numbers are in, scholars and election experts must determine the size of the eligible population for each state, another number that requires some care in estimating.

We present data on aggregate turnout in US presidential elections between 1972 and 2008 in Figure 11.1. The line with square markers represents McDonald's estimates of aggregate turnout, using the ballot numbers reported by state election officials divided by the size of the voting eligible population in each state. This corrected population number reduces the voting age population reported by the US Census for the number of ineligible adults in the state, including convicted felons, institutionalized individuals, and undocumented immigrants.[1] The line with diamond markers represents Leighley and Nagler's estimate of overall turnout based on individuals' self-reports about voting in the presidential election, taken from the US Census Current Population Survey (CPS), November Supplement.

As shown in Figure 11.1, neither measure of voter turnout suggests that turnout declined during the 1970s. Instead, rather than systematically trending downward, turnout in presidential elections increases or decreases by very small amounts from 1972 to 1992, then decreases a bit more in 1996. Using the CPS citizen voting age population measure, turnout ranges from 62.4 percent up to 65.5 percent over this period, and McDonald's voting eligible population turnout measure ranges from 52.8 to 58.1.

In 1996, turnout using either measure decreases more substantially, making this year the lowest level of turnout over the period. Turnout rebounds in 2000, 2004, and 2008. Although turnout in the last two elections is higher using McDonald's voting eligible population measure, it is also on the high end of the series for the self-reported measure in the last two elections. Using McDonald's measure, 2008 witnessed the highest level of turnout in contemporary elections (61.6), while using the CPS self-report, 2008 turnout was as high as, or higher than, that of most elections between 1972 and 2008. Thus, whichever measure one considers, the reality is that there is a great deal of election-specific variability in how many people vote.

The best estimate we have for turnout in the 2012 presidential election is provided by Michael McDonald, who reports the total number of ballots certified by state election officials. Because most national-level surveys of voter turnout are yet to be released, self-reported measures of voter turnout are not available, and McDonald's statewide turnout levels provide the best way to assess the overall level of turnout in 2012. By combining verified ballot counts for each state, McDonald estimates that national aggregate turnout among all eligible voters for the presidential race fell from 61.6 percent in 2008 to 58.2 percent in 2012 (McDonald 2013).

This aggregate measure of turnout, of course, tells us how many citizens voted, but does not indicate who among citizens voted. If each citizen was equally likely to vote, then we could think of "voters" as a random sample of the eligible voting population, and might imagine that this small group, comprising only about 60 percent of the eligible population, was representative—at least demographically, and perhaps in terms of their policy preferences or partisanship. But if some types of citizens are more likely to vote than others, it means that the set of individuals who cast ballots—and elect presidents—are not representative of all eligible voters (i.e., the electorate).

So who votes, in addition to how many vote, is a very important question. We turn to that question now, beginning with a review of demographic trends in turnout since 1972. We then use data from exit polls in 2008 and 2012 to assess the extent to which the turnout decisions of these demographic groups may have changed between 2008 and 2012.

Characteristics of Turnout: Demographic Subgroups, 1972–2008

In a classic study of voter turnout in the 1972 presidential election, Wolfinger and Rosenstone reported that highly educated voters, wealthier individuals, older individuals, men, married individuals and whites are more likely to show up at the polls (Wolfinger and Rosenstone 1980). Many, but certainly not all, of these findings were still true in 2008, as Leighley and Nagler's (forthcoming) new study shows.

Education and income, the two most important determinants of turnout in Wolfinger and Rosenstone's study, continue to have a strong influence on who votes. Turnout is higher among voters with higher levels of education as well as those who are wealthier. For example, in the 2008 presidential election, about 80 percent of individuals in the highest income quintile (i.e., the wealthiest 20 percent of the population) voted, while only about 54 percent of the poorest quintile voted. About 78 percent of individuals in the highest third of the education distribution reported voting, compared to about 50 percent of individuals in the lowest third of the education distribution. These large differences in turnout between the more educated and the less educated, and the wealthy and the poor, are about the same as they were in 1972 (see Leighley and Nagler forthcoming, chapter 2).

In contrast to the stability of turnout patterns for education and income, patterns of voter turnout by gender, age, and race are changing. Since 1980, women have turned out to vote at higher percentages than men. In 2008, the turnout gap between eligible women and men had grown to four percentage points: unlike voter turnout in 1972, we now see that women vote more than men in 2008 (Leighley and Nagler forthcoming).

Turnout has also increased among older voters since 1972. Turnout among the oldest voters (those age 76 to 84) has increased most dramatically, from 60 percent in 1972 to nearly 75 percent in 2008 (Leighley and Nagler forthcoming). Since 1980, turnout among voters aged 61 to 75 has remained the highest of any age group. Turnout in the youngest age group (18- to 24-year-olds) has remained the lowest of any age group since 1972, hovering between about 36 to 51 percent of eligible voters (Leighley and Nagler forthcoming). It is important to note that in 2008, turnout among the youngest voters was 51 percent, a high matched only in 1992 and exceeded slightly in 1972 (Hoban Kirby and Kawashima-Ginsberg 2009; Leighley and Nagler forthcoming).

Turnout has increased substantially among black voters since 1972, although in 2008 it still remains below levels of turnout for whites. Note that controlling for the effect of other factors that influence turnout and differ for whites and blacks, such as income, education, and age, the effect of being black is actually positive in 2008: African Americans are more likely to vote than are whites, if you compare individuals at the same education and income levels (Leighley and Nagler forthcoming). This is an important difference regarding race and turnout when comparing who votes in 1972 with who votes in 2008 or 2012.

The evidence for Hispanics suggests a slight increase in turnout since 1972. But in 2008, Hispanic turnout remains far below the levels for black and white voters: while about 68 percent of both whites and blacks reported voting in the 2008 presidential election, only about 50 percent of Hispanics reported voting (see Leighley and Nagler, forthcoming, chapter 2, figures 2.3 and 2.4). Accounting for the effect of other factors that influence turnout demonstrates, too, that Hispanics are substantially less likely to vote than are whites. In 2008, as well as previous election campaigns, the lower level of self-reported voting by Hispanics compared to whites cannot be accounted for by the distinctive demographic characteristics of Hispanics, such as lower education, income, and age.

These general patterns reported by Leighley and Nagler (forthcoming) are also reflected in the self-reports of respondents in the 2008 American National Election Study (see Table 11.1). The substantial differences in turnout reported by individuals with high levels of education compared to those with low levels of education, and by wealthy individuals compared to poorer individuals, is striking. Over 90 percent of individuals with a college degree report voting, compared to only 50 percent of individuals with a grade-school education. The wealthiest income group reports voting at 89 percent compared to only 64 percent of those in the lowest income group.[2]

This large difference in turnout across education and income categories has been referred to in previous research as class bias, or income bias (see, for

TABLE 11.1   Turnout by Demographic Groups, 2008

Education	
Grade School/Some High School	51%
High School Graduate	66%
Some College	82%
College Degree/Postgraduate	92%
Income	
Lowest Income Percentile (0–16%)	65%
17–33%	73%
34–67%	78%
68–95%	85%
Highest Income Percentile (96–100%)	89%
Race	
Whites	79%
Blacks	79%
Gender	
Males	74%
Females	80%

Source: "Voter Turnout 1948–2008," American National Election Studies, Cumulative File, The ANES Guide to Public Opinion and Electoral Behavior, accessed February 18, 2013, http://www.electionstudies.org/nesguide/2ndtable/t6a_2_2.htm.

example, Leighley and Nagler 1992, forthcoming). This overrepresentation of the wealthy among voters is a distinctive feature of turnout in the United States. It has also been relatively stable since 1972. That is, the overrepresentation of the wealthy compared to the poor has stayed about the same since 1972—it has not lessened, nor has it increased.

Whites reported voting at the same rate as blacks in 2008—79 percent— while women reported voting at a much higher rate than men, 80 percent compared to 74 percent. These data confirm that in 2008 more highly educated individuals (compared to less educated individuals), wealthier individuals (compared to poorer individuals), and women (compared to men) were likely to vote. Although levels of turnout based on American National Election Studies (ANES) self-reports are substantially higher than levels of turnout based on CPS self-reports, this data affirms that the well-established patterns observed in studies of electoral behavior since 1972 were clearly evident in 2008.[3]

Characteristics and Consequences of Turnout:
What Did Voters Look Like in 2012?

New approaches to campaign mobilization distinguished 2008 from previous election years and had a significant influence on voter turnout (Masket 2009; McDonald 2009; Panagopoulos and Francia 2009; Philpot, Shaw, and McGowan 2009). The Obama campaign established an unprecedented seven hundred field offices across the country, and these local hubs were successful at increasing Democratic turnout in the battleground states where most of the offices were located (Masket 2009; McDonald 2009). Mobilization efforts on the part of the Obama campaign also contributed to increased turnout among African American voters (Philpot, Shaw, and McGowan 2009). Similar efforts on the part of both political parties mobilized voters in communities where funds were spent on local outreach (McDonald 2009; Panagopoulos and Francia 2009).

Some political observers questioned whether these efforts would or could be replicated in 2012. If the Obama campaign did not mobilize voters as it had in the previous election, then turnout in 2012 might not resemble patterns from 2008. Obama's victory indicates that the campaign did something right, and that they may have replicated their successful strategy in 2012. While we cannot address that question directly due to data limitations, we can consider one related question: do the demographic characteristics of voters in 2012 differ from those of voters in 2008, or are they the same in 2012 as they were in 2008?

What we gain from this comparison is learning whether the demographic composition of exit poll voters is the same in 2012 as it was in 2008. Comparing the demographic makeup of those who vote from election to election can be a useful descriptive tool, but has clear limits and cannot be used as evidence regarding the predictors of turnout within specific demographic groups. Unfortunately, the only data we have available at this point is from exit polls. We must caution that inferences regarding the turnout of different demographic groups from exit polls are highly problematic. Since the exit polls are by definition polls of only *voters,* several assumptions are needed to infer the turnout rate of groups in the electorate based on what we see in exit polls.

One must assume that the poll samples each group in their proportion to the actual set of voters, or correctly weights their sample to match this unknown quantity. To do this requires that the sampling design of the exit poll accurately match the demographics of the voters, which can go awry if the precincts chosen for sampling have too few or too many voters from a particular demographic group. The exit polls also depend heavily on a supplemental telephone sample to account for persons voting early or by absentee ballot. Although these individuals do not come to the polls on Election Day, they should be included in any description of voters. However, with these caveats, one can compare the demographic makeup of the set of voters in the 2008 and 2012 exit poll and look to see if there are substantial changes.

Sampling issues aside, our expectations here are conservative with respect to observing substantial differences across elections. Campaign mobilization efforts or other factors that influence turnout within specific demographic groups would likely have to change dramatically from election to election, and have immense effects, to be evidenced in a post hoc comparison of the composition of who voted on Election Day. Moreover, these comparisons of whether demographic groups comprised the same proportion of voters in 2012 as they did in 2008 can mask, at the group level, the specific influences of numerous factors that affect turnout at the individual level. With our limited data, we cannot identify or sort out the importance of these many factors, which may include the individual and demographic characteristics of voters, the rules under which elections take place, and the unique dynamics of a specific election, such as national economic conditions and campaign mobilization efforts. Our observation that specific demographic groups comprised a similar proportion of who voted in 2008 and 2012 (or an observation that they did not), then, offers no additional insight as to why these groups voted at the same (or different) level in the two elections.

Because it is still too early to have individual-level data on turnout, we rely on data from exit polls in the 2008 and 2012 election. Most postelection stories relying on systematic data use exit polls, which are questions asked of samples of voters as they leave the polls on Election Day. These exit polls are used predominantly to assess the demographic patterns of vote choice—that is, whether various demographic subgroups differed in their choice of presidential candidates. Because the sample consists of voters, this data provides an efficient, fairly reliable way of estimating patterns of support for the major candidates, and often drives discussions of the campaign narrative, who the winning candidate's supporters were, and what policy positions they tend to support.

These data can also provide some basic insight into voter turnout—though of course without any nonvoters included in the exit poll sample, inferences regarding the demographic influences on individuals' decisions to vote (or not) are impossible. What we can do is evaluate how the composition of the exit poll samples varied between 2008 and 2012. To the extent that these patterns differ, we can compare patterns of turnout across these demographic subgroups between the two elections. The reasons for those differences, of course, or their precise magnitude, will still be unknown. But we can at least begin to assess whether the same demographic patterns that have emerged from studies of voter turnout over the past several decades seem to hold from the perspective of exit polls.

In Table 11.2 we present exit poll data for 2008 and 2012, as reported by CNN and *The Washington Post*. In many ways, the composition of voters in 2012 is the same as the composition of voters in 2008. Individuals at different education levels voted at about the same rate in 2012 as they did in 2008. Individuals at different levels of income, however, were represented differently between 2008 and 2012: individuals with less than $50,000 in income increased their proportion of voters by three percentage points, while those in the middle income group earning $50,000 and $99,000 represented a smaller proportion of voters in 2012 than in 2008 (decreasing from 36 percent to 31 percent). Women were equally represented as voters in 2008 and 2012, at 53 percent, reflecting their higher probability of voting compared to men. For age and race, there are few differences in the composition of voters between 2008 and 2012.

Of note is that blacks (who were mobilization targets of the Obama campaign in 2008, and likely so in 2012 as well) comprised 13 percent of the exit poll sample. This is a good example of the limits of the inferences we can draw from these data; although blacks comprised 13 percent of the sample, we do not know why. There might well have been differences in the mobilization strategies or effectiveness of the Obama campaign between 2008 and 2012. The similarity in black representation among voters does not demonstrate that the campaign was equally as effective in mobilizing blacks, for other factors might well have been at play in 2012 to motivate blacks to get to the polls. As we stated above, then, these numbers need to be interpreted cautiously.

While not conclusive, exit poll data also suggest that demographic trends in the composition of the electorate from 2008 were not undone in 2012. How much these patterns were sustained by similar mobilization efforts of the Obama campaign in 2008 and 2012 is unclear, requiring additional investigation. Concerns about whether young adults and blacks would stay home in 2012 rather than put the effort into supporting Obama on Election Day appear to have been unfounded.

The Costs and Benefits of Voting

Historical variations in turnout levels, as well as the fact that not all individuals vote, have led scholars to think about voter turnout as a rational decision, one in which individuals for whom the costs of voting are less than the

TABLE 11.2 Demographic Composition of Electorate, 2008 and 2012

	2008	2012
Education		
No High School Diploma	4%	3%
High School Graduate	20%	21%
Some College	31%	29%
College Graduate	28%	29%
Postgraduate Study	17%	18%
Income		
Under $50,000	38%	41%
$50,000–$99,000	36%	31%
$100,000 or More	26%	28%
Gender		
Male	47%	47%
Female	53%	53%
Age		
18–29	18%	19%
30–44	29%	27%
45–64	37%	38%
65 or Over	16%	16%
Race & Ethnicity		
White	74%	72%
Black	13%	13%
Hispanic/Latino	9%	10%
Asian	2%	3%
Other	3%	2%

Sources: 2008 numbers from CNN, Exit Polls, Election Center 2008, www.cnn.com /ELECTION/2008/results/polls/#USP00p1; 2012 numbers from Scott Clement, Jon Cohen, and Peyton McGill, "Exit Polls 2012: How the Vote Has Shifted," *The Washington Post,* November 6, 2012, http://www.washingtonpost.com/wp-srv/special /politics/2012-exit-polls/table.html.

benefits will choose to vote (Downs 1957; Aldrich 1993). The demographic characteristics of individuals we discussed above, such as income and education, are typically viewed as potential resources that can help individuals overcome the costs of voting. On the other hand, some features of the election context are viewed as influencing the costs of voting, either making voting easier (less costly), or making voting hard (more costly). The costs associated with voting include things like the time necessary to obtain a registration form, to register, and to vote by mail or in person. It also takes time and ability to learn about the choices presented in an election and to make an informed decision between two candidates.

Groups who traditionally have fewer resources, such as those with lower income or lower levels of education, are expected to be less able to bear the burden of voting costs (Leighley and Nagler 1992, forthcoming). Another example of the effects of the costs of voting is highlighted in the case of people who move. Because movers must reregister, the costs of voting are higher, and movers are less likely than nonmovers to vote. Because younger individuals are more likely to move, this helps to account for lower levels of turnout among youth compared to older groups (Highton 1997, 2000).

The costs of voting, however, are sometimes overcome by the efforts of parties, candidates, and groups to mobilize turnout (see, for example Rosenstone and Hansen 1993; Philpot, Shaw, and McGowan 2009). Mobilization refers to direct requests to vote, as well as the way in which individuals' social environments provide them relevant information or incentives. Access to others who are knowledgeable about elections may reduce the individual costs of learning about the rules for voting and the issues in a campaign (Highton 1997, 2000). Social group ties may also increase the value an individual recognizes in voting (Highton 1997, 2000).

Additionally, potential voters may be positively motivated by a candidate from their social group (Gay 2001; Philpot and Walton 2007; Lawless and Fox 2010). These factors might help to account for higher turnout in 2008 compared to 2004, with Hillary Clinton as the first woman to become a top contender in the Democratic primary, Sarah Palin as the first woman to run as a Republican vice presidential nominee, and Barack Obama as the first person of color to receive his party nomination and be elected president.

We briefly consider two potentially important and distinctive political features of the 2012 contest that may have influenced voter turnout by affecting the costs of voting. These features include changes in election laws governing voter registration and voting as well as changes in election laws governing independent campaign expenditures. Changes in these election laws have consequences for the costs of voting. For example, reforming voter registration and voting laws to make it easier to vote lowers the costs, while passing laws requiring photo identification to vote increases the costs of voting. Another example is that increasing advertising expenditures might lower the information costs imposed on voters in choosing between candidates.

We begin by speculating about the effects of campaign spending in the 2012 presidential election. The landscape of the 2012 election certainly changed after the Supreme Court decision in *Citizens United v. Federal Election Commission* (558 U.S. 310, 2010), which made contributing money to presidential campaigns much easier by prohibiting restrictions on independent campaign expenditures by unions and corporations. Greater campaign spending might be argued to either increase or decrease turnout. Scholars have argued that campaign advertising has the potential to mobilize or demobilize voters, whether the messages conveyed are positive or negative—though most attention has been paid to documenting the effects (both positive and negative) of negative advertising (see, for example, Clinton and Lapinski 2004; Goldstein and Freedman 2002; Stevens, Sullivan, Allen, and Alger 2008).

Most of the discussion around the *Citizens United* decision focused on how it would open the floodgates for very wealthy individuals and corporations to disproportionately influence the election through massive campaign contributions—that is, how it would give them the ability to "buy" an election. In thinking about voter turnout more specifically, an important question regarding this spending is whether the increased media visibility of the presidential election might mobilize more citizens to the polls, or whether spending devoted to extremely negative appeals might actually depress turnout, as some argue they are capable of doing.

As many scholars have observed, the relationship between spending and voter turnout is not a simple one. The 2012 presidential campaign witnessed higher levels of campaign spending than any election in history—and yet turnout overall was 2.7 percentage points lower in 2012 (58.9 percent) than it was in 2008 (61.6 percent). Clearly more money spent does not translate directly into more ballots cast.

Yet we also know that the record spending that occurred in the 2012 election was not distributed equally across the fifty states. Instead, presidential campaigns and outside groups spend their money strategically, where the additional dollars spent could swing the election one way or the other. Political commentators forecast that Obama could win the election if his campaign mobilized voters as impressively as it had in 2008.

State measures of aggregate turnout reveal that the story may have been more nuanced. Most states experienced a moderate decline in turnout of the voting-eligible population from 2008 to 2012 (see Table 11.3, where states are ordered by turnout level in 2008). Only two states and the District of Columbia experienced an increase in voter turnout, of less than 1 percentage point. In twenty-two states, aggregate turnout decreased by less than or equal to the national aggregate decrease of 2.6 percentage points. Turnout dropped between 2.6 and 5 percentage points in fifteen states and decreased by 5 percentage points or more in ten states. Although demographic groups favorable to Obama were represented among the electorate in proportions that are comparable to 2008, it appears that the Obama victory was not dependent on high levels of aggregate turnout in specific states.

What about turnout in the battleground states, where most campaign efforts were focused? Nine states (in boldface in Table 11.3) were commonly identified as battlegrounds in 2012: Colorado, Florida, Iowa, Nevada, New Hampshire, North Carolina, Ohio, Virginia, and Wisconsin. Of these nine states, five experienced a decrease in turnout from 2008 to 2012. The decrease in turnout ranged from 2.6 percentage points to 0.6 percentage points, while increases in voter turnout in the four remaining battleground states ranged from 0.1 percentage points to 0.9 percentage points. In comparison, changes in turnout in nonbattleground states ranged from a 9.1-percentage-point decline in Alaska to a 0.5-percentage-point drop in Massachusetts. Not a single nonbattleground state experienced an increase in turnout, although the District of Columbia experienced an increase in turnout of 0.40 percentage points.

In the days leading up to the election, media pundits also raised concerns about depressed turnout in northeastern states affected by Hurricane Sandy. Obama won in these states in 2008 and was predicted to win again if conditions were the same in 2012. Aggregate turnout in New York, New Jersey, Connecticut, and to a lesser extent Rhode Island, the four states with emergency areas declared by the Federal Emergency Management Agency, declined dramatically between 2008 and 2012. In New Jersey, New York, and Connecticut, turnout declined by more than 5 percent. In Rhode Island, turnout declined by 3.8 percent. Despite the decrease in turnout, Obama still won in each of the four states.

Comparing the turnout changes between 2008 and 2012 in battleground and nonbattleground states suggests that the extraordinary spending in 2012 likely translated into more votes, since the only increases in turnout in 2012 were in those battleground states. Of course, other factors operating within the battleground states might account more accurately for the modest increases in turnout they witnessed. Yet this data suggests that campaign spending is a strong, if not leading, contender for explanations of changes in voter turnout in 2012.

Changes in Election Laws and
Increased Costs in the Voting Calculus

Since 1972, many states have adopted a variety of laws intended to change who is eligible to vote, and the ways in which individuals who are eligible

TABLE 11.3 State Aggregate Turnout in Presidential Elections, 2008 and 2012

	2008 VE Population Highest Office Turnout Rate	2012 VE Population Highest Office Turnout Rate	Differences in Percentages from 2008 to 2012
United States	61.60%	58.90%	−2.70%
Minnesota	77.80%	75.70%	−2.10%
Wisconsin	72.40%	72.50%	0.10%
Colorado	71.70%	70.30%	−0.80%
New Hampshire	71.70%	70.10%	−1.60%
Iowa	69.40%	69.90%	0.50%
Maine	70.60%	68.10%	−2.50%
Virginia	67.00%	66.40%	−0.60%
Massachusetts	66.80%	66.30%	−0.50%
Maryland	67.00%	66.20%	−0.80%
Michigan	69.20%	64.70%	−4.50%
North Carolina	65.50%	64.60%	0.90%
Ohio	66.90%	64.60%	−2.30%
Washington	66.60%	64.10%	−2.50%
Florida	66.10%	63.50%	−2.60%
Oregon	67.70%	63.20%	−4.50%
Delaware	65.50%	62.70%	−2.80%
Montana	66.30%	62.60%	−3.70%
Missouri	67.60%	62.50%	−5.10%
District of Columbia	61.50%	61.90%	0.40%
New Jersey	67.00%	61.80%	−5.20%
Connecticut	66.60%	60.90%	−5.70%
North Dakota	62.70%	60.60%	−2.10%
Louisiana	61.20%	60.40%	−0.80%
Vermont	67.30%	60.40%	−6.90%
Nebraska	62.90%	60.10%	−2.80%
Mississippi	61.00%	59.70%	−1.30%
Idaho	63.60%	59.60%	−4.00%
South Dakota	64.70%	59.40%	−5.30%
Pennsylvania	63.60%	59.40%	−4.20%
Alaska	68.00%	58.90%	−9.10%
Illinois	63.60%	58.90%	−4.70%
Wyoming	62.80%	58.90%	−3.90%
Alabama	60.80%	58.80%	−3.90%
Georgia	62.50%	58.40%	−4.10%
Rhode Island	61.80%	58.00%	−3.80%
Nevada	57.00%	57.10%	0.10%
Kansas	62.00%	57.00%	−5.00%
South Carolina	58.00%	56.60%	−1.40%
Utah	56.00%	55.40%	−0.60%
Kentucky	57.90%	55.30%	−2.60%
California	60.90%	55.20%	−5.70%
Indiana	59.10%	55.10%	−4.00%
New Mexico	60.90%	54.70%	−6.20%
New York	59.00%	53.10%	−5.90%
Arizona	56.70%	52.90%	−3.80%
Tennessee	57.00%	52.20%	−4.80%
Arkansas	52.50%	50.50%	−2.00%
Texas	54.10%	49.70%	−4.40%
Oklahoma	55.80%	49.20%	−6.60%
West Virginia	49.90%	46.30%	−3.60%
Hawaii	48.80%	44.20%	−4.60%

Note: States are ordered by turnout rate (higher to lower) in 2008.

Source: Michael McDonald's website, "United States Election Project," www.elections.gmu.edu/voter_turnout.htm; difference calculations by author.

to vote may cast a ballot. In contrast to the successful efforts to make voting easier over the course of the mid- to late twentieth century, electoral reforms adopted by many states after 2008 focused largely on making voting more difficult. The most notable of these efforts included adoption of voter identification laws and limiting the time period available for early voting (National Conference of State Legislatures 2012).

We focus here on documenting these legal changes in the states rather than seeking to establish the magnitude of the effects of these legal reforms. But we do so in light of Leighley and Nagler's (forthcoming) findings that suggest that voting reforms adopted to make registration easier—including Election Day registration (EDR), absentee voting, and early voting—are estimated to have about a 2- to 3-percentage-point effect on voter turnout. Whether the post-2008 reforms making registration and balloting more difficult actually depressed turnout in the states that adopted these policies cannot be determined with the data that we have in hand.

EDR allows voters to register and cast a ballot at the same time on Election Day. Online registration eliminates the need to obtain a paper form and return it in the mail. In the 2012 election, ten states allowed EDR and twelve states had implemented online registration. Many states also have voter identification laws that make it harder to register or cast a ballot. Thirty states ultimately required voters to present identification at the polls in 2012. Among these states, eleven requested or required voters to present photo identification at the polls (National Conference of State Legislatures 2012).

Laws that require voters to show identification at the polls place the burden on voters to obtain the necessary identification documents. The burden is highest in the states that require photo identification. Voters with fewer resources, such as those with lower income and lower levels of education, are less able to meet this requirement. A report issued by the Brennan Center for Justice at the NYU School of Law found that 11 percent of voting-age American citizens do not have valid government-issued photo IDs (Brennan Center for Justice at NYU School of Law 2006). Of the eleven states that requested or required voters to provide photo ID at the polls in 2012, seven ranked among the bottom half of states in aggregate turnout in 2012 (National Conference of State Legislatures 2012). In the months leading up to the November election, many photo ID laws faced legal challenges that increased public uncertainty about what would be required of voters. At the time of the 2012 election, photo ID laws had been adopted but not implemented in six additional states, causing potential confusion among voters about what would be required of them at the polls (National Conference of State Legislatures 2012).

Laws requiring voters to present non-photo identification at the polls place a lower burden on voters. Among the nineteen states that required non-photo identification, a wide array of IDs were accepted on Election Day, including utility bills, medical insurance cards, voter registration cards, and many forms of photo ID (National Conference of State Legislatures 2012).

State voter ID laws can also be characterized as "strict" or "nonstrict." In states with strict ID laws, voters without identification are given a provisional ballot and must return to election officials to provide the required identification within a few days; if the voter does not return, the provisional ballot is not counted (National Conference of State Legislatures 2012). In states with nonstrict ID laws, voters who fail to provide identification are not required to return to election officials. They may be required to sign an affidavit confirming their identity or be vouched for by poll workers who know them personally before being given a nonprovisional ballot that will be included in election returns. Four states—Georgia, Indiana, Kansas, and Tennessee—implemented strict voter ID laws prior to the 2012 presidential election, and all four states ranked among the bottom half of states in total aggregate turnout.

Twelve states allowed voters to register online in 2012, eliminating the requirement to obtain a paper registration form and return it in the mail. By contrast, only two states allowed online registration prior to the 2008 election. Arizona was the first state to allow online registration, implementing this change in 2002. By 2012, 70 percent of Arizona voters registered online (National Conference of State Legislatures 2012). The preference of Arizona voters for online registration suggests that this method reduces the individual burden associated with registering to vote.

The number of states allowing EDR remained constant between 2008 and 2012. In both elections, ten states had policies in place to allow voters to go to the polls to register and cast a ballot on the same day. Two other states, California and Connecticut, adopted same-day-registration laws in this period that were not implemented prior to the 2012 election (National Conference of State Legislatures 2012). These provisions substantially reduce the individual burden of voting by eliminating separate steps for registering to vote and eliminating the requirement that eligible voters plan ahead to register.

EDR may also increase the stimulating effects of the election. As voter interest is aroused by media and campaign events and the immediacy of the pending election, potential voters who have not registered may make a last-minute decision to go to the polls (Gimpel, Dyck, and Shaw 2007). As Table 11.4 illustrates, seven states with EDR laws ranked among the top third of all states in aggregate turnout in 2012. The three remaining states with EDR were dispersed among the middle third of all states for aggregate turnout, and there were no states with EDR among the states that ranked among the lowest third in aggregate turnout.

Conclusion

In many ways, 2008 was a landmark election. Barack Obama rode to victory as the first African American president, and more women than ever were serious contenders throughout the primary and general races. This led some political pundits to question whether patterns of turnout in 2008 would be replicated in 2012. If voters were excited by the newness of 2008, the excitement could carry over to the subsequent election. On the other hand, the same candidates and similar political debates could become old hat by 2012. If voters were mobilized by successful campaign strategies in 2008, as Philpot, Shaw, and McGowan argue they were, then such efforts could be replicated to produce similar patterns of turnout in 2012. We do not yet have the necessary data to evaluate either claim about why voters were motivated to go to the polls in 2012, but we do know that the demographics of the electorate in 2012 were similar to those of 2008. Concerns that young voters and African Americans would comprise a substantially smaller percentage of the electorate in 2012 than 2008 were unsubstantiated.

Several other changes between the 2008 and 2012 elections also go into the "black box" of possible explanations for patterns of turnout. As a product of the Supreme Court's decision in *Citizens United v. Federal Election Commission,* campaign spending through independent expenditures in 2012 vastly exceeded spending in 2008. New voter identification laws increased the burden of voting in many states at the same time that new online registration laws and existing same-day-registration policies reduced the costs borne by voters. Even the weather distinguished 2012 from 2008 as election officials scrambled to maintain polling places in states affected by Hurricane Sandy in 2012.

Even if exit polls suggest that the demographic composition of the electorate in 2012 was similar to that of 2008, this data does not tell us if those who voted are representative of nonvoters. Better data from 2008 and previous years tell us that voters are not representative of the eligible voting population. Given the relative stability of demographic trends in voting from one election to the next, we have good reason to expect that those who actually voted in 2012 were similarly unrepresentative of all eligible voters. This expectation remains to be tested as we await more accurate data on turnout in 2012.

At the same time that demographic trends in the makeup of voters persisted in 2012, national turnout among all voters declined from 2008 to 2012,

TABLE 11.4 Turnout Change and Legal Reforms, 2008–2012

	2008 to 2012 Percentage Point Change	Election Day Registration (Year Adopted)	Online Registration (Year Adopted)	ID Required at Polls	Photo ID Required at Polls
Iowa	0.5 increase	2008			
Wisconsin	0.1 increase	1976			
Nevada	0.1 increase		2012		
Massachusetts	0.5 decline				
Utah	0.6 decline		2012	Nonstrict	
Virginia	0.6 decline			Strict	
Colorado	0.7 decline		2012	Nonstrict	
Louisiana	0.8 decline		2012		Nonstrict
Maryland	0.8 decline		2012		
North Carolina	0.9 decline	2008*			
Mississippi	1.3 decline				
South Carolina	1.4 decline		2012	Nonstrict	
New Hampshire	1.6 decline	1996			Nonstrict
Alabama	2 decline			Nonstrict	
Arkansas	2 decline			Nonstrict	
North Dakota	2 decline			Nonstrict	
Minnesota	2.3 decline	1976			
Ohio	2.3 decline	2008*		Strict	
Maine	2.5 decline	1976			
Washington	2.5 decline		2008	Nonstrict	
Florida	2.6 decline				Nonstrict
Kentucky	2.6 decline			Nonstrict	
Delaware	2.8 decline			Nonstrict	
Nebraska	2.8 decline				
West Virginia	3.6 decline				
Montana	3.7 decline	2008		Nonstrict	
Arizona	3.8 decline		2004	Strict	
Rhode Island	3.8 decline			Nonstrict	
Wyoming	3.9 decline	1996			
Idaho	4 decline	1996			Nonstrict
Indiana	4 decline		2012		Strict
Pennsylvania	4 decline				
Georgia	4.1 decline				Strict
Texas	4.4 decline			Nonstrict	
Michigan	4.5 decline				Nonstrict
Oregon	4.5 decline		2012		
Hawaii	4.6 decline				Nonstrict
Illinois	4.7 decline				
Tennessee	4.8 decline				Strict
Kansas	5 decline		2012		Strict
Missouri	5.1 decline			Nonstrict	
New Jersey	5.2 decline				
Connecticut	5.3 decline			Nonstrict	
South Dakota	5.3 decline				Nonstrict
California	5.7 decline		2012		
New York	5.9 decline				
New Mexico	6.2 decline				
Oklahoma	6.6 decline			Nonstrict	
Vermont	6.9 decline				
Alaska	9.1 decline			Nonstrict	

Sources: Change in turnout computed from data presented in Table 11.3. Data on adoption of legal reforms taken from National Conference of State Legislatures (2012).

* Ohio and North Carolina election laws do not allow individuals to register and vote on Election Day, but instead allow individuals to register and vote during an early voting period. It is more accurately described as "same day" registration during early voting. See "Same Day Voter Registration," National Conference of State Legislatures, accessed March 16, 2013, http://www.ncsl.org /legislatures-elections/elections/same-day-registration.aspx.

reversing a pattern of increasing aggregate turnout in presidential elections that had persisted since 2000. Decline in aggregate turnout also varied substantially by state, decreasing by as much as 9 percentage points in Alaska and increasing very slightly in only three states and the District of Columbia. This supports theories that overall turnout is election-specific. Efforts by candidates and political parties to mobilize turnout through targeting specific voters and choosing strategic campaign messages do affect the final national vote count. Exactly how the efforts of the Obama and Romney campaigns, as well as the many other factors that made 2012 unique, contributed to a decline in national aggregate turnout is a question that will be taken up as better data becomes available in the years following the election.

Notes

1. See McDonald's descriptions of how he computes estimates of the number of eligible citizens by state based on interpolations of US Census Bureau data, at http://elections.gmu.edu/FAQ.html.

2. These data are taken from the American National Election Studies Cumulative File, which categorizes individuals' income levels in each presidential election year by the percentile of the income distribution in which the individual's reported family income falls within each year so that the income measure is comparable over time. In this example, individuals in the lowest percentile are those who are in the lowest income percentile, 0 to 16, while the individuals in the highest income percentile are in the 96–100 percentile of income for 2008.

3. Self-reports of voter turnout typically result in higher estimates of turnout than with validated turnout data where researchers independently verify whether individuals have reported. But we have few sources of validated voting, and most studies of self-reported vs. validated voting suggest that the biases introduced by a reliance on self-reports are likely minimal (Berent, Krosnick, and Lupia 2011).

References

Abramson, Paul R., and John H. Aldrich. 1982. "The Decline of Electoral Participation in America." *American Political Science Review* 76 (3): 502–521.

Abramson, Paul R., John H. Aldrich, and David W. Rohde. 2008. *Change and Continuity in the 2008 Elections.* Washington, DC: CQ Press.

Aldrich, John H. 1993. "Rational Choice and Turnout." *American Journal of Political Science* 37 (1): 246–278.

Ansolabehere, Stephen, Nathaniel Persily, and Charles Stewart III. 2010. "Race, Region, and Vote Choice in the 2010 Election: Implications for the Future of the Voting Rights Act." *Harvard Law Review* 123 (4): 1385–1486.

Bafumi, Joseph, and Michael Herron. 2009. "Prejudice, Black Threat, and the Racist Voter in the 2008 Presidential Election." *Journal of Political Marketing* 8: 334–348.

Berent, Matthew K., Jon A. Krosnick, and Arthur Lupia. 2011. "The Quality of Government Records and Over-estimation of Registration and Turnout in Surveys: Lessons from the 2008 ANES Panel Study's Registration and Turnout Validation Exercises." ANES Technical Report Series No. nes012554, August 2011 version. Ann Arbor, MI, and Palo Alto, CA: American National Election Studies. http://www.electionstudies.org/resources/papers/nes012554.pdf.

Brennan Center for Justice at NYU School of Law. 2006. "Citizens Without Proof: A Survey of Americans' Possession of Documentary Proof of Citizenship and Photo Identification." Voting Rights and Elections Series (November). http://www.brennancenter.org/page/-/d/download_file_39242.pdf.

Burden, Barry C., David T. Canon, Kenneth R. Mayer, and Donald P. Moynihan. 2009. "The Effects and Costs of Early Voting, Election Day Registration, and Same Day Registration in the 2008 Elections." Report presented to the Pew Charitable Trusts (December 21).

Burnham, W. Dean. 1965. "The Changing Shape of the American Political Universe." *American Political Science Review* 93 (1): 99–114.

———. 1980. "The Appearance and Disappearance of the American Voter." In *Electoral Participation: A Comparative Analysis,* edited by Richard Rose. Thousand Oaks, CA: Sage.

Cassel, Carol A., and Robert C. Luskin. 1988. "Simple Explanations of Turnout Decline." *American Political Science Review* 82: 1321–1330.

The Center for Information and Learning on Civic Engagement. 2012. "Youth Turnout: At Least 49%, 22–23 Million Under-30 Voted" (November 7). Tufts University, Jonathan M. Tisch College of Citizenship and Public Service. http://www.civicyouth.org/youth-turnout-at-least-49-22-23-million-under-30-voted/.

Clinton, Joshua D., and John S. Lapinski. 2004. "'Targeted' Advertising and Voter Turnout: An Experimental Study of the 2000 Presidential Election." *The Journal of Politics* 65 (1): 69–96.

Downs, Anthony. 1957. *An Economic Theory of Democracy.* New York: Harper and Row.

Gay, Claudine. 2001. "The Effect of Black Congressional Representation on Political Participation." *American Political Science Review* 95 (3): 589–602.

Gimpel, James, Joshua J. Dyck, and Daron R. Shaw. 2007. "Election Year Stimuli and the Timing of Voter Registration." *Party Politics* 13 (3): 351–374.

Goldstein, Ken, and Paul Freedman. 2002. "Campaign Advertising and Voter Turnout: New Evidence for a Stimulation Effect." *The Journal of Politics* 64 (3): 721–740.

Hanmer, Michael J. 2009. *Discount Voting: Voter Registration Reforms and Their Effects.* New York: Cambridge University Press.

Highton, Benjamin. 1997. "Easy Registration and Voter Turnout." *The Journal of Politics* 59 (2): 565–575.

————. 2000. "Residential Mobility, Community Mobility, and Electoral Participation." *Political Behavior* 22 (2): 109–120.

Hoban Kirby, Emily, and Kei Kawashima-Ginsberg. 2009. "The Youth Vote in 2008." The Center for Information and Research on Civic Learning and Engagement. Tufts University.

Hugo Lopez, Mark, and Paul Taylor. 2009. "Dissecting the 2008 Electorate: Most Diverse in U.S. History." Pew Research Center and Pew Hispanic Center.

Key, V. O., Jr. 1949. *Southern Politics in State and Nation.* New York: A. A. Knopf.

Keyssar, Alexander. 2000. *The Right to Vote: The Contested History of Democracy in the United States.* New York: Basic Books.

Kousser, J. Morgan. 1984. "Race and Politics Since 1933." In *Encyclopedia of American Political History,* edited by J. P. Greene, 643–652. New York: Charles Scribner's Sons.

————. 1999. *Colorblind Injustice: Minority Voting Rights and the Undoing of the Second Reconstruction.* Chapel Hill: University of North Carolina Press.

Lawless, Jennifer, and Richard Fox. 2010. *It Still Takes a Candidate: Why Women Don't Run for Office.* New York: Cambridge University Press.

Leighley, Jan E., and Jonathan Nagler. 1992. "Socioeconomic Class Bias in Turnout, 1964–1988: The Voters Remain the Same." *American Political Science Review* 86 (3): 725–736.

————. Forthcoming. *Who Votes Now? Demographics, Issues, Inequality and Turnout in the United States.* Princeton, NJ: Princeton University Press.

Mas, Alexandre, and Enrico Moretti. 2009. "Racial Bias in the 2008 Presidential Election." *American Economic Review* 99 (2): 323–329.

Masket, Seth E. 2009. "Did Obama's Ground Game Matter? The Influence of Local Field Offices During the 2008 Presidential Election." *Public Opinion Quarterly* 73 (5): 1023–1039.

McDonald, Michael. 2002. "State Turnout Rates Among Those Eligible to Vote." *State Politics and Policy Quarterly* (2): 2.

————. 2003. "On the Over-Report Bias of the National Election Survey." *Political Analysis* 11 (2): 180–186.

————. 2007. "The True Electorate: A Cross-Validation of Voter File and Election Poll Demographics." *Public Opinion Quarterly* 71 (4): 588–602.

————. 2008. "Portable Voter Registration." *Political Behavior* 30 (4): 491–501.

————. 2009. "The Return of the Voter: Voter Turnout in the 2008 Presidential Election." *The Forum* 6 (4).

————. 2010. "American Voter Turnout in Historical Perspective." In *The Oxford Handbook of American Elections and Political Behavior,* edited by Jan Leighley. New York: Oxford University Press.

————. 2011. "Voter Turnout: Eligibility Has Its Benefits." In *Controversies in Voting Behavior,* 2nd edition, edited by Richard G. Niemi, Herbert F. Weisberg, and David Kimball. Washington, DC: CQ Press.

———. 2012. "2012 General Election Turnout Rates." *United States Elections Project.* (January 13).

———. 2013. "United States Elections Project: 2012 General Election Turnout Rates." George Mason University. http://elections.gmu.edu/Turnout_2012G.html.

McDonald, Michael P., and Samuel Popkin. 2001. "The Myth of the Vanishing Voter." *American Political Science Review* 95 (4): 963–974.

Michelson, Melissa R., Lisa Garcia Bedolla, and Margaret A. McConnell. 2009. "Heeding the Call: The Effect of Targeted Two-Round Phone Banks on Voter Turnout." *Journal of Politics* 71 (4): 1549–1563.

National Conference of State Legislatures. 2012. "Campaigns and Elections." Retrieved September 2012. http://www.ncsl.org/legislatures-elections.aspx?tabs= 1116,114,796.

Panagopoulos, Costas, and Peter L. Francia. 2009. "Grassroots Mobilization in the 2008 Presidential Election." *Journal of Political Marketing* 8 (4): 315–333.

Pasek, Josh, Alexander Tahk, Yphtach Lelkes, Jon A. Krosnick, B. Keith Payne, Omair Akhtar, and Trevor Tompson. 2009. "Determinants of Turn-out and Candidate Choice in the 2008 Election: Illuminating the Impact of Racial Prejudice and Other Considerations." *Public Opinion Quarterly* 73 (5): 943–994.

Philpot, Tasha S., Daron R. Shaw, and Ernest B. McGowan. 2009. "Winning the Race: Black Voter Turn-out in the Presidential Election." *Public Opinion Quarterly* 73 (5): 995–1022.

Philpot, Tasha S., and Hanes Walton. 2007. "One of Our Own: Black Female Candidates and the Voters Who Support Them." *American Journal of Political Science* 51 (1): 49–62.

Pitts, Michael, and Matthew D. Neumann. 2009. "Documenting Disenfranchisement: Voter Identification at Indiana's 2008 General Election." *Journal of Law and Politics* 25: 329–361.

Rosenstone, Steven, and John Mark Hansen. 1993. *Mobilization, Participation, and Democracy in America.* New York: Macmillan.

Smith, Aaron. 2009. *The Internet's Role in Campaign 2008.* Washington, DC: Pew Internet and American Life Project.

Stanley, H. W., and R. G. Niemi. 2006. *Vital Statistics on American Politics, 2005– 2006.* Washington, DC: Congressional Quarterly Press.

Stevens, Daniel, John Sullivan, Barbara Allen, and Dean Alger. 2008. "What's Good for the Goose Is Bad for the Gander: Negative Political Advertising, Partisanship and Turnout." *The Journal of Politics* 70 (2): 527–541.

Teixeira, R. A. 1992. *The Disappearing American Voter.* Washington, DC: Brookings Press.

Wolfinger, Raymond E., and Steven Rosenstone. 1980. *Who Votes?* New Haven, CT: Yale University Press.

12

Election Law Is the New Rock 'n' Roll

CHRIS SAUTTER

If Big Money ruled Campaign 2012, Election Day belonged to the lawyers. In the battleground state of Virginia, for example, between 4:30 and 5:00 a.m. on November 6, over 120 lawyers and law students filed into a large, unfinished, windowless ground-floor room located behind the elevators of a nondescript Falls Church suburban office building a block inside the Washington Beltway. It housed the state's Obama legal boiler room. The task for the day was to protect people's right to vote.

The Virginia Obama boiler room team took hundreds of calls from a swarm of lawyers and voter advocates who were stationed at polling places across the state. The issues the boiler room attorneys—experienced Election Day lawyers—would confront throughout a day that lasted well into the evening included complaints of malfunctioning voting equipment, polls opening late or closing early, insufficient paper ballots, voters who were denied access or turned away from the polls, disruptive or overly aggressive poll watchers bent on challenging legitimate voters, and questions about the application of Virginia's new voter ID law, among others. Each call was logged and tracked by a computer program. Problems that could not be resolved on location were addressed by contacting state election officials in Richmond. Litigation specialists were ready to take serious unresolved problems to court to seek injunctive relief, if need be. The status of any complaint could be instantly checked and cross-checked, as could the number of complaints in each category.

The Obama voter protection program in Virginia in 2012 was infinitely more sophisticated than the one Jack Young, Jay Myerson,[1] and I developed for 2001 Virginia gubernatorial candidate Mark Warner in the wake of the 2000 Florida electoral debacle. Then, the program consisted of three lawyers supported by five desk people taking calls from the field. The Warner boiler room was created because the three of us, veterans of the Gore recount legal team, believed the outcome of the 2000 presidential election would have been different had the Gore campaign responded quickly on Election Day to desperate complaints about the infamous butterfly ballot in Palm Beach County that resulted in nearly three thousand voters inadvertently voting for Pat Buchanan instead of Al Gore. (Even Buchanan conceded that the "Jews for Buchanan," as US Rep. Barney Frank called them, intended to vote for Gore.) Had the campaign responded to the complaints by directing Gore workers at the polls in Palm Beach to hand out warnings and directions, voters might have avoided confusion with the flawed butterfly ballot design. In other words, the Gore campaign could have spared itself and the country a controversial recount had the votes of those who intended to vote for Gore been preserved by a voter protection operation like the ones in place in 2012.

In 2012, both major parties dispatched large teams of lawyers nationwide to monitor Election Day activities. Obama's campaign placed boiler rooms similar to the Virginia operation in each of the 2012 battleground states as well as in several other states. The Obama campaign was especially concerned about the implementation of new voter ID laws across the country and the possibility of antifraud activists challenging legitimate voters. Republicans were focused on preventing fraud by making sure that noneligible people— noncitizens, felons, and the nonregistered—did not vote.

In spite of predictions of an electoral disaster, Election Day problems were mostly confined to extremely long lines, confusion about new voter ID laws, and inadequate staff and ballots. These are serious problems and demonstrate that very poor election administration remains the norm in too many states. But most issues appear to have been addressed on location or with the assistance of election officials rather than by Election Day litigation as was anticipated. Of course, lawsuits were flying back and forth in the weeks and months leading up to the election. But there was not a total breakdown that left the outcome of the presidential election in doubt.

The proliferation of combative legal activity around elections is a relatively new phenomenon. The enormous increase in interest and activity in political campaigns, the explosion in money raised to influence elections, and the increasing number of landmark cases, including several US Supreme Court cases, have all elevated election law in the public consciousness. A plethora of books on election law have recently been published on the subject. Election law is one of the more popular courses in law school now. Experienced election lawyers are in demand. Prominent election lawyers appear regularly on television news shows. In short, the world of election law is rocking. And, it rocked all the way through Election Day in 2012.

The exploding interest in election law is traceable directly to *Bush v. Gore,* the controversial US Supreme Court decision that handed the presidency to George W. Bush. Before *Bush v. Gore,* election law was a backwater specialty. One could almost count the number of prominent full-time election lawyers in each political party on one hand. Most were based in Washington, DC. The 2000 Florida presidential recount attracted thousands of lawyers from all over the country. Many returned to their home states, either exhilarated or angered by the outcome, to become election law specialists. Most of them—true believers to their respective causes—became a part of a national network of election lawyers for each of the political parties.

Florida's 2000 postelection dispute also opened the nation's eyes to the inherent flaws of America's election system. The first revelation was that voting technology is not only fallible, it can often systematically disenfranchise large numbers of voters—usually poor and elderly or both. Secondly, we learned that poll workers can act negligently, incompetently, and sometimes in a blatantly illegal manner. We learned that many election officials have partisan biases, and those biases sometime impact election outcomes. Finally, the 2000 Florida recount demonstrated that courts can and sometimes do act in a seemingly political way, tossing aside legal precedent and simple justice in the process. In short, not all elections in America produce a reliable result worthy of public confidence. The 2000 presidential election is one of those, in large part because of the Supreme Court's and the state of Florida's handling of the case.

Though bitter partisanship had been on the rise since the late 1970s, the Florida recount triggered an all-out partisan legal war between the two major political parties over who should be allowed to vote, when voters can vote, and whose votes are counted.[2] Since *Bush v. Gore,* lawyers, lawsuits, and postelection legal disputes have become a part of the "permanent campaign." Election litigation has more than doubled since the Florida recount. The political parties are in a never-ending battle over the laws and rules that govern elections. Recount preparation has become an integral part of campaigns and recounts themselves have become increasingly partisan and contentious. Many observers predicted that these partisan legal battles, along with defects in the system and a razor close election, would produce an electoral train wreck on November 6, 2012. America may have dodged a bullet in 2012 because of the unexpectedly wide margin in the presidential race.

Two contrary views that have existed for decades have become acutely po-larized since *Bush v. Gore* and lie at the core of legal disagreements between the two parties. Republicans believe that voter fraud permeates US elections tilting outcomes. Republicans want to use the political and legal process to curb voter fraud even if it means making voting more difficult and, in some instances, impossible for some voters.

On the other hand, Democrats believe that too many barriers to voting exist and want to eliminate all obstacles so that as many people who want to vote can vote, even if it means there might be some illegal votes cast. Demo-crats want to facilitate voting through reforms such as same-day registration, expanded early voting opportunities, and simpler procedures. Democrats also believe that Republicans are deliberately engaged for partisan gain in activities and promote laws that prevent legitimate voters from voting, while Repub-licans believe that Democrats facilitate voter fraud in order to win elections.

This fundamental disagreement in the way the two parties view how elec-tions are and should be conducted reached a peak during the 2012 election cycle. A newly elected crop of Republican governors and state legislators passed a series of restrictive election laws that Democrats claimed were the modern-day equivalent of poll taxes and literacy tests. Republicans countered that the new laws are necessary to confer legitimacy on the outcome of elec-tions, since fraud dilutes valid votes and undercuts legitimacy. Democrats went to federal and state courts to win judicial orders blocking implemen-tation of most of the new election laws, though the issues have hardly been settled.

Although the electoral meltdown that some predicted for 2012 failed to come to pass, serious election administration problems continue to plague many states. They include unacceptably long lines, ballot shortages, equip-ment glitches, poll location confusion, and misunderstanding over voter iden-tification requirements. It is impossible to determine how many voters may have been disenfranchised by the 2012 Election Day problems. Whatever the number, our system of election administration continues to be inefficient and irrational.

Many of the problems in the way America votes are rooted in the very nature of an election system that is highly decentralized and partisan-based. Other problems occur simply because of a lack of sufficient training of elec-tion officials and because so many who work on Election Day are volunteers rather than paid professionals. The partisan wrangling and legal battles add to the tension and confusion. And, the kind of comprehensive election re-form that is truly needed to cure this ailing system seems highly unlikely in Washington's current polarized political climate. For some reason, arguing over election rules and alleging fraud seems easier than fixing the systemic problems with elections.

Florida Changed Everything (So Why Are Things So Bad?)

It has become almost axiomatic that everything about elections and election law in America changed after the Florida presidential recount. Though the recount deepened partisan divisions, it also prompted efforts to improve voting procedures. Yet, the more things have changed in the election process, the more they seem just as dysfunctional as they were in 2000—worse in many respects.

More fundamentally, the Florida presidential recount changed how we perceive elections in America. What Watergate is today to cynicism about government institutions, the Florida recount is now to elections. Americans were shocked to learn that so much could go so wrong in tallying votes in a presidential election. Ever since 2000, voters have wondered whether and how their votes are being counted. The US Supreme Court's decision in *Bush v. Gore* is as inscrutable and controversial today as ever. The Supreme Court itself has yet to cite the case in a subsequent opinion, as if to concede that it was a flawed decision.[3]

In *Bush v. Gore*, the Supreme Court in its unsigned, logically tortured five-to-four opinion along ideological lines concluded that Florida's method of counting votes violated the Fourteenth Amendment's guarantee of equal protection of law because different counties allegedly employed different ways of counting the votes. In effect, the Court held that the process of counting ballots must occur under rules that are applied uniformly and fairly. But the majority declined to allow the recount to proceed under such uniform rules, thereby delivering the election to George W. Bush even though all the votes had not been counted. The majority opinion also famously contained the disclaimer that its ruling was "limited to the present circumstances." The opinion had a predetermined feel to it. Republicans praised the ruling (Justice Antonin Scalia advised critics to "just get over it"). Democrats reacted as if the presidential election had been stolen from Al Gore, winner of the popular vote. Indeed, Justice Stevens in his dissent stated, "Although we may never know with complete certainty the identity of the winner of this year's presidential election, the identity of the loser is perfectly clear. It is the nation's confidence in the judge as an impartial guardian of the rule of law."[4]

The chaos and irregularities surrounding the Florida presidential recount prompted Congress in 2002 to pass the Help America Vote Act (HAVA), legislation designed to raise election standards. HAVA was a compromise between congressional Democrats who want to increase voter access and Republicans who want to combat voter fraud. The legislation appropriated $4 billion to the states to upgrade voting equipment and established the Election Assistance Commission to help states modernize their voter registration systems, among other things. HAVA also required states to permit voters whose eligibility is in question to cast provisional ballots to be counted once eligibility is confirmed instead of simply being turned away. Finally, in a provision that would spawn future legal battles, Republicans insisted that HAVA require that voters who register by mail provide identification the first time they vote.

Though touted as a bipartisan solution to the country's electoral problems, HAVA created a whole new set of problems. The expensive new electronic voting machines that HAVA helped buy were built on still evolving technology. Most touch screen machines, for example, came without a system to verify results and were susceptible to tampering. Election officials who rushed to purchase the new voting machines were ill equipped themselves to operate them. Malfunctioning equipment became a regular occurrence on Election Day, and irregularities in vote tallies began undermining confidence in the results. The companies that manufactured the new equipment were often owned or managed by individuals with strong partisan ties, further undermining public confidence. Corporate lobbyists began to exert undue influence on what had always been a public undertaking—election administration.

HAVA's provisional ballot mandate also produced unintended consequences. The provisional ballot requirement was prompted by complaints that large numbers of voters in 2000 were improperly turned away from the polls because their names had been omitted from the voter rolls. But requiring that voters be allowed to vote by provisional ballot and having states actually count those ballots has proven to be two entirely different matters.

Because there are no clear and uniform standards for counting provisional ballots, the number of such ballots that are counted varies by state. For example, some states, such as California, count ballots cast in the wrong precinct, while others, like Ohio and Virginia, do not. Predictably, California counts a very high percentage—over 80 percent—of provisional ballots compared to a national average that is closer to 65 percent. The counting of provisional ballots is also subject to rules that are influenced by politics. Some election officials who exert influence over voting protocols are unabashed partisans who have made a concerted effort to limit the number of provisional ballots that should be counted.[5]

There is also evidence that people who should be voting by regular ballot are being steered by election officials to vote by provisional ballot.[6] In addition, new voter identification laws are forcing people who would normally cast regular ballots to vote by provisional ballot. Undoubtedly, that is one reason why there was a record surge in provisional ballot voting in 2012.[7] Another reason is that registration rolls are chronically inaccurate. The names of newly registered voters often do not appear on the precinct voter rolls though they are duly registered. Also, HAVA does not require state or local election officials to investigate possible administrative errors to determine whether provisional ballots should be counted. As a result, voters are dependent upon the sometimes flawed or biased judgment of local elections officials working often without the benefit of sufficient relevant information.

HAVA was supposed to help states modernize registration rolls, but many are still antiquated. One problem is that Congress failed to give the federal government authority to require the states to maintain up-to-date voter registration records. The Election Assistance Commission that HAVA established to assist the states in updating voter rolls has become dysfunctional as Congress has withheld funding and refused to fill vacancies on the commission. Voter registration processes are also sorely in need of national standardization.

Finally, HAVA failed to address the two most serious flaws in the way we run elections in America. The first problem is that politicians and political appointees are administering our elections. There are an insufficient number of trained professionals making key decisions. Partisanship increases the likelihood of conflicts of interest and manipulation of rules. Secondly, the extreme decentralization of elections ensures a lack of uniformity. *Bush v. Gore* held that like ballots should be treated in a like manner. But America's decentralized election system means like ballots are often not treated the same. Voting equipment, ballot design, quality of election officials, and interpretation of laws vary from state to state and often from county to county, ensuring a lack of uniformity in treatment of ballots. Meaningful change of serious problems that plague America's voting is impossible unless these two issues are addressed head-on.

The Battle Over Who Votes in America

One of the most obvious lessons from Florida is that it matters as much who votes in America as how the votes are counted. In the aftermath of the Florida recount, it became known that thousands of qualified voters—most of them African American and likely Democratic voters—had erroneously been labeled as "felons," and their names had been improperly purged from voter rolls. The scrubbing job was the handiwork of a private firm that had been hired by Florida secretary of state and Bush for President cochair Katherine Harris. Harris denied that her intent was anything other than to make sure noneligible people did not vote. However, she ignored repeated complaints by local election officials that the purge lists were riddled with errors. Democrats claimed the purge program was a deliberate effort not to combat voter fraud but to reduce the Democratic vote in 2000.[8]

Some maintain that the truly lasting lesson political operatives took away from the Florida recount was that election results can be manipulated and that even small changes in election laws can change the outcome.[9] Since 2000, there has been a battle raging nationwide between Republicans and their surrogate groups and Democrats and their surrogate groups over rules that govern how and when voters should be permitted to cast their ballots. Many observers have characterized the debates over voting lists, voter identification requirements, and early voting as being driven by Republicans who are attempting to reduce the number of Democratic votes by making it harder for otherwise eligible Democratic-leaning voters to vote.[10]

These debates are rooted in the Republican Party's infamous "Southern Strategy," designed by former Richard Nixon strategist Kevin Phillips for Nixon's successful 1968 presidential campaign. Beginning with passage of the Civil Rights Act of 1964 and the Voting Rights Act of 1965 (VRA), the major parties in effect traded positions on voting rights. Their respective positions have guided their approaches to elections ever since.

The Democratic Party—the party that tolerated and thrived under Jim Crow laws for almost a century—came to support expanded voting rights and universal access. Democrats not only began to take the lead on civil rights, but also pushed legislation designed to increase voter participation overall, including the National Voter Registration Act of 1993, popularly referred to as the "Motor Voter," which requires states to allow registration when residents apply for a driver's license.[11]

On the other hand, Republicans—the onetime party of Lincoln that expanded democracy and voting rights after the end of slavery—began to oppose most initiatives to increase voting rights and access. Beginning with adoption of the Fifteenth Amendment in 1870, which outlawed voting discrimination based on race, African Americans had voted overwhelmingly Republican until 1932, when Democrat Franklin Roosevelt carried 71 percent of the black vote. Yet, through the 1960 presidential election, Republicans actively sought and won an important share of the African American vote. For example, Richard M. Nixon garnered 32 percent of the black vote in his narrow loss to John F. Kennedy in 1960 while Dwight D. Eisenhower received over 40 percent in his two presidential races in 1952 and 1956. But after Lyndon Johnson pushed through the landmark Civil Rights Act of 1964 (outlawing segregation in public places, which his eventual Republican opponent Barry Goldwater opposed), Johnson captured 94 percent of the black vote, a record that held until Barack Obama won 96 percent in 2008.[12]

The Southern Strategy constituted both recognition of changing coalitions and a roadmap for maximizing the white vote by using wedge issues and coded language. The concept was to persuade whites—particularly southern whites who had historically voted Democratic—to vote Republican by talking about issues like forced busing and states rights in order to exploit racial fears without appearing to make overtly racist appeals.[13] Although he won a third of the black vote just eight years earlier, Nixon in effect wrote off the black vote in 1968 in order to win over white voters because of fear that George Wallace's third-party candidacy would siphon off enough votes in the South to throw the race to Democrat Hubert Humphrey. Nixon wound up carrying half the southern states, enough for a narrow win over Humphrey. In a larger sense, the Southern Strategy was also an attempt to permanently turn the South from Democrat to Republican, something Lyndon Johnson predicted when he signed the 1964 Civil Rights Act into law. In effect, Republicans were betting on white voters, particularly whites who were uncomfortable with aspects of racial progress, to carry them to victory for the indefinite future. The Southern Strategy worked for forty years as the only Democrats to win races to the White House from 1968 to 2008 were southerners Jimmy Carter and Bill Clinton. Obama's new coalition of minorities and younger voters turning out in record numbers broke up the Republican "electoral lock" in 2008.

Since 1968, Republicans have made little effort to compete for African American votes, instead continuing the use of racially coded communications in campaigns. Both Ronald Reagan and George H. W. Bush utilized racially tinged wedge issues in their campaigns for presidency. Most recently Mitt Romney aired TV ads falsely claiming that President Obama would end welfare work requirements, as a way to make deliberate appeals to racially resentful whites.

However, after Carter's election in 1976, the Republican Southern Strategy in general morphed into more sophisticated strategies national in scope that centered on efforts to limit turnout of minority voters through voter intimidation. Just as Democrats believe higher voter turnout is to their advantage, Republicans have concluded that lower turnout inures to their benefit. Paul

Weyrich, an architect of the New Right, told a conference of evangelical leaders in Dallas in 1980, "I don't want everybody to vote . . . our leverage in the elections quite candidly goes up as the voting populace goes down."[14]

During the 1980s and 1990s, the Republican Party initiated a series of "ballot security" and "voter integrity" campaigns that they claimed were aimed at reducing voter fraud but instead amounted to voter intimidation activities in minority communities. Some involved off-duty police officers hired to patrol polling places and post intimidating signs in targeted communities. Unfair challenges or "caging" practices were also utilized to great effect.[15] Several of these practices were successfully challenged in federal court, and Republican officials were forced to sign consent decrees agreeing to cease using them, though the practices have continued in alternate forms. In 1993, for example, Republican consultant Ed Rollins conceded he was involved in an effort to suppress black turnout in the New Jersey gubernatorial race.[16]

A Republican article of faith that goes hand-in-hand with Weyrich's view of voter turnout is the belief that Democrats, especially in urban areas, tend to be corrupt and routinely engage in voter fraud to win elections. This view is based on the political machine stereotype that city mayors pad voter rolls with the names of the deceased. Republicans believe to this day that Chicago mayor Richard J. Daley stole the 1960 election for John F. Kennedy. Many Republicans are convinced this kind of fraud thrives in urban areas where the poor and uneducated can be exploited. There is also a belief voiced by conservatives that illegal immigrants are voting in large enough numbers to change election outcomes.

Combating voter fraud is a legitimate goal, of course. But many conservatives and Republican activists have taken to using voter fraud as a kind of boogey man and a pretext to push legislation that would ostensibly prevent fraud, but have the effect of creating significant barriers to voting. The Bush administration's Department of Justice made prosecution of voter fraud a priority and even fired seven US attorneys who declined to proceed with flimsy cases. But in spite of its efforts, it found few cases to prosecute. In fact, there is scant evidence that voter fraud is a problem worthy of the effort undertaken by the Bush Justice Department.[17]

Meanwhile, a virtual cottage industry has sprung up based on the premise that voter fraud threatens our democracy. For years, Fox News has been pushing a narrative of voter fraud while former *Wall Street Journal* columnist John Fund and other conservatives have written books on the subject. The Republican spin machine has been beating the drum on voter fraud for so long that, according to a December 2012 Public Policy poll, 49 percent of Republicans believe Barack Obama won reelection because of voter fraud by ACORN, a group that ceased to exist in 2010.

The most common and controversial of laws pushed in recent years by Republicans under the guise that they will reduce fraud are voter identification laws. On its face, laws requiring photographic identification are reasonable. But voter identification laws have the effect of disenfranchising voters, mostly elderly, minority, and low-income people. The reason is that obtaining photo ID can be costly and burdensome. Even free state-provided IDs cost money, because obtaining a birth certificate is usually a requisite.[18]

Perhaps not coincidentally, there is virtually no evidence of the kind of voter fraud photo ID laws would prevent. A recent study by the Brennan Center for Justice at New York University School of Law concluded that an individual is more likely to be hit by lightning than to commit voter fraud.[19] That's because fraud by individuals impersonating other voters is both difficult and irrational. Why would anyone commit a felony that accounts for only one vote? In fact, most of what is said to be voter fraud is something else—either bureaucratic error or voter mistake. And, the kind of "fraud" that the controversial ACORN was engaged in before it folded was voter registration fraud, turning in registration forms in the names of people who do not exist or the names of celebrities. There is no evidence that any of these fictitious people actually ever voted. The reality is that the vast majority of fraud allegations are actually asserted to advance a political agenda rather than to clean up dirty elections.[20]

Laws requiring identification to vote have been around since the 1970s. However, passage of the Help America Vote Act in 2002 prompted new legislation tightening restrictions on voting in several states. Arizona, Georgia, and Indiana were among the first to enact ID laws following passage of HAVA. In 2008, the US Supreme Court considered a challenge to the constitutionality of the Indiana ID law. In the case, *Crawford v. Marion County Election Board,* the Supreme Court upheld the constitutional of a law requiring voters to provide photo ID, finding that requirement sufficiently related to Indiana's legitimate state interest in preventing voter fraud. Indiana provided no examples of voter fraud. Indeed, Indiana officials conceded that the rationale for passing the law was primarily political. But plaintiffs also failed to provide examples of voters being turned away from the polls for lack of ID. So the Court left the door open to future challenges depending upon circumstances. In other words, while voter ID laws are not unconstitutional per se, they may be struck down if there is evidence of related voter suppression or denial of the franchise sufficient to overcome the presumption of constitutionality.

The nature of Barack Obama's election in 2008 sent shock waves through conservative and Republican circles. Over a quarter of the votes that year were cast by minorities, the very voters that Republicans had been writing off for forty years. The rising percentage of Latinos, blacks, and young whites, especially in the states Obama carried, made clear that Republicans face a harsh demographic and political reality. But rather than trying to legitimately compete for minority and youth votes, Republicans decided to double down on their Southern Strategy.

With apparent Supreme Court approval, Republicans accelerated their efforts to make voting more difficult and reduce turnout after they won governorships and legislatures in 2010. According to the Brennan Center for Justice, eighteen states implemented voting restrictions that fall most heavily on "young, minority and low-income voters, as well as voters with disabilities."[21] Fifteen of those have Republican governors. Many of the states that passed stringent election laws were in the Deep South, but they also included the battleground states of Iowa, Florida, Ohio, Pennsylvania, Virginia, and Wisconsin.

Many observers have characterized Republican efforts to pass restrictive voting laws as no less than an organized and systematic plan to place serious obstacles in the way of qualified voters—mostly African Americans—who traditionally vote Democratic. Critics say the Republican effort has been orchestrated by the conservative American Legislative Exchange Council, funded by right-wing billionaires Charles and David Koch, and designed to prevent minorities from voting.[22] Pennsylvania State GOP House Leader Mike Turai bragged in what he thought was a private reception during the 2012 campaign that the purpose of his state's ID law was to elect Republicans. A post-2012 election report by the *Palm Beach Post* quoted several prominent Florida Republicans admitting that election law changes in their state were geared toward suppressing minority and Democratic votes.[23]

At one time, a voter's registration card, paycheck stub, or utility bill was considered sufficient proof of identity to vote in most jurisdictions. The newer laws tend to be more stringent, requiring voters to produce authorized photo identification cards, such as driver's licenses. Some of the laws seem to overtly target certain groups. In Texas, a hunting license is considered permissible identification while student ID is not. Urban voters seemed to be the target of the new Pennsylvania law in which only ID available from the state's department of transportation is acceptable to be permitted to vote. Many urban voters do not have driver's licenses.

Republicans pushed through other types of restrictive voting laws. Florida and Texas restricted voter registration drives of the kind the League of

Women Voters often sponsors. Kansas, Alabama, and Arizona passed laws requiring voters to provide proof of citizenship before registering. Florida, Ohio, Georgia, Tennessee, and West Virginia cut back dates for early voting. Florida and Iowa barred all ex-felons from voting, disenfranchising thousands of previously eligible voters. And, Maine repealed Election Day voter registration that had been on the books since 1973.

Democrats and progressive groups responded with legal challenges, and several courts blocked implementation of voter ID laws. The Wisconsin ID law was declared in violation of the state constitution's right-to-vote provision. In Pennsylvania, the state's supreme court blocked enforcement until after the 2012 election on the grounds that implementation would be too disruptive.

The Department of Justice (DOJ) also challenged several state ID laws under Section 5 of the Voting Rights Act. Section 5 requires jurisdictions that have a history of racial discrimination to clear new voting laws and rules before implementing them, a process called "preclearance." At the urging of the DOJ, federal courts blocked implementation of the South Carolina and Texas voting ID laws under Section 5.

The Republican strategy to counter a growing structural electoral disadvantage also included purging voter lists and reducing dates for early voting. Election officials in Iowa, Florida, and Colorado tried to purge suspected unqualified voters, but their lists proved to be flawed. In Florida, for example, officials targeted almost 200,000 voters, but in the end only 207 were not qualified to vote. Nearly 60 percent of those on the list had Hispanic surnames; another 14 percent were African Americans. One election official conceded that white voters were not likely to be purged.[24]

Many states expanded early voting prior to the 2008 election to accommodate the growing list of voters. But those states where Republicans took control in 2010 scaled back early voting for 2012. Ohio secretary of state Jon Husted was especially aggressive in attempting to reduce early voting. Husted proposed that voting hours in Ohio be extended only in white districts, but pulled back following public backlash. His effort to eliminate voting on the weekend before the election was blocked by a federal judge and eventually upheld by the US Supreme Court.

In Florida, election officials curtailed weekend and early voting, resulting in lines that stretched blocks and lasted as long as six hours. Republicans had pushed through a measure to cut early voting from fourteen days to eight days and cancel voting on the final Sunday before the election. The Florida Democratic Party and League of Women Voters asked Governor Rick Scott and state election officials to extend early voting when it became clear that the number of hours allotted was insufficient. But the governor and election officials denied the request, claiming expansion of hours was unnecessary. The result was a fiasco of unconscionably long lines.[25]

The legal fights over Republican attempts to limit voting remain largely unresolved and could wind up in the US Supreme Court, perhaps before the 2014 elections. In some instances, voter ID laws that were blocked for 2012—such as in Pennsylvania and South Carolina—could be ruled constitutional under the Supreme Court's 2008 decision in *Crawford* and implemented. On the other hand, as the enormity of the Republican systematic effort to limit the franchise becomes more evident, courts may be more willing to strike down such laws based on the fundamental relationship between voting and democracy. Nonetheless, the US Supreme Court has already agreed to take up a case challenging the constitutionality of Section 5 of the Voting Rights Act. While Section 5 may be unavailable in the future to challenge restrictive laws, overall the tide may have turned against efforts to depress voting.

Is the Era of Big Recounts Over?

Since Florida 2000 there has been at least one major recount in every election cycle. But the 2012 election proved to be the exception, as there were no recounts in federal races, in spite of predictions of a postelection crisis on the order of Florida 2000 or worse. The bombastic anticommunist crusader Allen West, a Tea Party favorite, refused to acknowledge for weeks that he had lost his reelection for Congress in spite being down some 2,400 votes. But eventually even the indomitable West had to recognize that the margin was too great to overcome in a recount. Aside from the West race and a handful of others where declaration of the winner was delayed by the counting of absentee and provisional ballots, the 2012 election season concluded almost anticlimactically.

Does this signal a trend away from contentious recounts? It's not likely.

Elections that are so close as to require a recount are a product of both real competition—the country is closely divided politically—and randomness. But the hyperpartisanship of the past thirty years means more people pay closer attention to election results because there is seemingly more at stake.

Close, hotly contested recounts did not begin with *Bush v. Gore.* And the closest US Senate race was not the 2008 Minnesota contest between Al Franken and Norm Coleman. The closest US Senate race in history was in 1974 in New Hampshire between John Durkin and Louis Wyman, when the Republican Wyman was declared the winner by a mere two votes after two statewide recounts. The US Senate took up the dispute and eventually ordered another election when senators could not agree on how to count a number of disputed ballots. Durkin easily won the special election.

In 1984 in Indiana's "Bloody 8th" the margin of the closest US House race ever was just four votes. In that race, Democrat Frank McCloskey was declared the winner over Republican Rick McIntrye after two full recounts. A little-known backbencher named Newt Gingrich claimed Democrats stole the election and led his party in staging a "walk-out" from the House floor. The 8th District recount contained many of the same issues that appeared in Florida sixteen years later—problems with punch card ballots, different counting rules, and an overly partisan secretary of state. Some observers point to the 8th District controversy as the beginning of an era of nasty partisan postelection disputes.

Major recounts continued throughout the 1980s and 1990s. In Indiana's 3rd Congressional District in 1988, a winner was declared by only 34 votes after a recount. In Connecticut's 2nd District in 1994, the ultimate margin was just 21 votes after a recount and review by the state's supreme court. Senator Harry Reid defeated challenger John Ensign in Nevada by 428 votes after a recount in 1998.

Nearly all recounts at the federal level, going back at least to the 1984–1985 Indiana House election dispute, have been hotly contested with partisan bickering. But Florida 2000 took it to an entirely new level, partly because the battle for the presidency played out with the entire nation glued to their television sets. Suddenly every recount began to reveal the broken nature of the electoral system and an ugly side of the legal process. In the 2004 Washington State gubernatorial race, it was the improper handling of provisional ballots. In the 2008 Franken-Coleman race, the problem was absentee ballots that had been wrongly rejected by officials on election night.

Lawyers took advantage of errors by election officials and loopholes in election laws long before the Florida recount. But partisanship escalated after 2000 as losers of close elections realized they might be able to generate political support for initiating a legal challenge to the results. Norm Coleman took what many legal experts considered to be a lost cause to the Minnesota Supreme Court because Republicans wanted to keep the Minnesota Senate seat vacant for as long as possible in order to deny US Senate Democrats their sixtieth vote. Franken was finally seated in July 2009, eight full months after the election.

A related point is that money is a major factor in determining whether to proceed with a recount. Most apparent losers of close elections throw in the towel because they cannot afford the expense of a legal challenge. Many recounts cost as much or more than the election campaign itself. But a candidate will carry on with an election recount or contest if his or her political party and funding sources put their weight and resources behind the challenge.

Most elections are genuinely not close enough to warrant a recount, even some that are within the margin that legally provides for one to be conducted at public expense. And the reality is that only an extremely small percentage of elections are reversed by a recount. But every so often an election is so close—a virtual tie—that it is impossible to determine the true winner without a careful and meticulous counting that a recount provides. It is those cases in which reasonable people can disagree on the outcome that a smoothly run recount is most critically needed.

Unfortunately, the chances of having a well-conducted recount have become less likely the narrower the margin, because of partisanship and because of the growing awareness of flaws in the election process. In Florida 2000, for example, Republicans adopted a strategy of delay because of the time deadline imposed by the Electoral College. Bush's team understood that if a recount were prevented, then regardless of how flawed the original results were, that count and its certificate of election would control.

The way to reduce the level of partisanship and the chances of a manipulated result is to adopt nationally accepted standards for counting and recounting votes. In addition, nonpartisan election officials and recount boards should be entrusted to make key decisions. Until the country adopts uniform ground rules for recounts, we can expect a continuation of divisive recounts that undermine public confidence in our elections process.

Conclusion

After his reelection, President Obama moved to address the nation's chronic Election Day deficiencies by announcing in his February 12, 2013, State of the Union message that he was establishing a bipartisan commission to recommend changes on how to improve America's troubled voting system. "When any Americans—no matter where they live or what their party—are denied that right simply because they can't afford to wait for five, six, seven hours just to cast their ballot, we are betraying our ideals," the president told Congress and the nation.

To underscore Obama's point, the White House invited as a guest to the State of the Union a hundred-and-two-year-old North Miami, Florida, woman who was informed she would face a six-hour wait if she wanted to cast her ballot last November. The woman, Desiline Victor, waited in line to vote for three hours on Election Day before it was arranged for her to return later to vote.

Obama appointed two election lawyers to lead the reform commission. Democrat Robert Bauer, who served as counsel to the Obama campaign, and Republican Benjamin Ginsberg, counsel to the Romney campaign, will try to reach an agreement on electoral reform proposals. Obama's announcement has generated both praise and criticism. Critics are dubious that such a commission can be either effective or nonpartisan given that it is being "co-chaired by two of the most partisan behind-the-scenes guys in the politics business." Some in the voting-rights community were particularly critical of the choice of Ginsberg, since he advised Republicans on many of the most controversial voting issues during the past presidential campaign.[26]

Other critics argue that President Obama is merely "kicking the can down the road," since the commission will not be recommending legislation. Further, a number of organizations identified the problems inherent in our voting system after the 2000 debacle in Florida. As recently as 2012, the Lawyers Committee for Civil Rights Under Law issued a 144-page report: "Our Broken Election System and How to Repair It." Meanwhile, many Republicans oppose any national approach to solving election problems on the grounds that elections should be left entirely to the states.

Nonetheless, the acknowledgment by a US president of the serious problems that beset America's voting and the need for reform is an important step. The reality is that the 2012 election brought another round of embarrassing incidents, though not the total meltdown some predicted. Voter confidence in the elections process has continued to decline since *Bush v. Gore*. The chronic problems of long lines, inaccurate poll lists, confusing new laws designed to restrict access, and voting-machine failures, among other issues, underscore the need for comprehensive reform and uniform national standards. It is the right time for a presidential commission, even if many of the issues are not satisfactorily resolved. The alternative is to allow the conduct of elections to continue to deteriorate with an accompanying loss of public confidence.

Notes

1. John "Jack" Hardin Young, a well-known Democratic election attorney and partner in the Washington, DC, firm of Sandler, Reiff, and Young, is coauthor of *The Recount Primer* (1994). Jay Meyerson is the former general counsel to the Virginia Democratic Party.

2. Richard L. Hasen, *The Voting Wars: From Florida 2000 to the Next Election Meltdown* (New Haven, CT: Yale University Press, 2012), 11–40.

3. Hasen, *The Voting Wars,* 8.

4. *Bush v. Gore,* 531 U.S. 98 (2000).

5. Hasen, *The Voting Wars,* 112. "Anyone who wants his or her vote to count should avoid casting a provisional ballot; you don't know how election officials will handle them." Also, see Andrew Cohen, "Think the 2000 Florida Recount Was Bad? Just Wait Until November 6," *The Atlantic,* October 22, 2012; and "Say Hello to the Ohio Official Who Might Pick the Next President," *The Atlantic,* October 29, 2012.

6. "Still Counting Votes 3 Week Later?" editorial, *USA Today,* November 26, 2012, www.usatoday.com/story/opinion/2012/11/26/counting-votes-voting-sytem /1728529.

7. 866ourvote.org, "Election Protection, Provisional Balloting," www.866ourvote .org/issues/provisional-balloting.

8. Gregory Palast, "Florida's Flawed Cleansing Program," Salon.com, December 4, 2000, www.salon.com/2000/12/04/voter_file/.

9. Hasen, *The Voting Wars,* 5. "Florida mainly taught political operatives the ben- efits of manipulating the rules, controlling election machinery, and litigating early and often. Election law has become part of a political strategy."

10. Elizabeth Drew, "Voting Wrongs," *New York Review of Books,* September 21, 2012. Drew writes that "Florida 2000 was the poisoned apple of our electoral sys- tems. Republicans saw that by manipulating the rules they could—when it comes down to it—steal an election."

11. Congress moved toward federalizing voting procedures for the first time with the "Motor Voter" law.

12. Brooks Jackson, "Blacks and the Democratic Party," FactCheck.org, April 18, 2008, www.factcheck.org/2008/04/blacks-and-the-democratic-party/; R. W. Apple, "G.O.P. Tries Hard to Win Black Votes, but Recent History Works Against It," *New York Times,* September 19, 1996.

13. See Jonathan Weiler, "Lee Atwater and the GOP's Race Problem," Huffing- ton Post, November 14, 2012, www.huffingtonpost.com/jonathan-weiler/legendary -gop-strategist-_b_2132029.html; Brian Gilmore, "GOP 'Southern Strategy' Is Not Working," *The Progressive,* November 28, 2012, www.progressive.org/gop-southern -strategy-not-working.

14. Republican operative Paul Weyrich: "I do not want everybody to vote." www .youtube.com/watch?v+QFIYS8xb-QY.

15. Chandler Davidson, Tanya Dunlap, Gale Kenny, and Benjamin Wise, "Repub- lican Ballot Security Programs: Vote Protection or Minority Vote Suppression—Or Both?" report to the Center for Voting Rights and Protection, September 2004.

16. Rachel E. Berry, "*Democratic National Committee v. Edward J. Rollins:* Politics as Usual or Unusual Politics?" *Race and Ethnic Ancestry Law Digest* 2, no. 1 (1996), http://scholarlycommons.law.wlu.edu/crsj/vol2/iss1/8.

17. Eric Lipton and Ian Urbina, "In 5-Year Effort, Scant Evidence of Voter Fraud," *New York Times,* April 12, 2007, http://www.nytimes.com/2007/04/12/washington/12fraud.html?_r=2&hp=&pagewanted=all&oref=slogin&.

18. "Policy Brief on Voter Identification," Brennan Center for Justice, New York School of Law, September 12, 2006, www.brennancenter.org/analysis/policy-brief-voter-identification.

19. "Policy Brief on the Truth About 'Voter Fraud,'" Brennan Center for Justice, New York School of Law, September 12, 2006, www.brennancenter.org/content/resource/policy_brief_on_the_truth_about_voter_fraud/.

20. Jane Mayer, "Who Created the Voter-Fraud Myth?" *The New Yorker,* October 29, 2012.

21. "Policy Brief on Voter Identification," Brennan Center for Justice.

22. Drew, "Voting Wrongs." See also Ari Berman, "The GOP War on Voting," *Rolling Stone,* August 30, 2011, http://www.rollingstone.com/politics/news/the-gop-war-on-voting-20110830.

23. Dara Kam and John Lantigua, "Former Florida GOP Leaders Say Voter Suppression Was Reason They Pushed New Election Law," *Palm Beach Post,* November 25, 2012, www.palmbeachpost.com/news/news/state-regional-govt-politics/early-voting-curbs-called-power-play/nTFDy/.

24. Rachel Weiner, "Florida's Voter Purge Explained," *Washington Post,* June 18, 2012; Lizette Alvarez, "After Mistakenly Purging Citizens, Florida Agrees to Let Them Vote," *New York Times,* September 12, 2012; Michael Peltier, "Federal Judge Approves Florida Voter Purge," *Reuters,* October 4, 2012.

25. Amanda Terkel, "Florida Early Voting Fiasco: Voters Wait for Hours at Polls as Rick Scott Refuses to Budge," Huffington Post, November 5, 2012, www.huffingtonpost.com/2012/11/04/florida-early-voting_n_2073119.html.

26. Meteor Blades, "Bauer-Ginsberg Election Commission Unlikely to Accomplish Much Despite Obvious Need," Daily Kos, February 15, 2013, http://www.dailykos.com/story/2013/02/15/1187382/--Bauer-Ginsberg-election-commission-unlikely-to-accomplish-much-despite-obvious-need.

13

Republican Strategies and Tactics in the 2012 Primary and General Elections

DAVID A. DULIO AND
JOHN S. KLEMANSKI

Introduction

The Republican Party and its candidates were well positioned for a successful challenge to President Barack Obama's reelection bid in 2012. The party was buoyed by the 2010 midterm election results that put Republicans in control of the US House of Representatives and found them just four seats short of gaining the majority of the US Senate. Going into 2012, Republicans were certainly looking for more electoral success.

The political context of the election cycle advantaged Republicans as several macropolitical indicators were trending in their favor. Key to the party's overall strategy throughout the election cycle was to exploit voter unhappiness at the president's perceived failure to improve the economy and lower unemployment. The economy had not improved despite massive federal spending in the 2009 stimulus package (the American Recovery and Reinvestment Act), bailouts of automakers General Motors and Chrysler, and other actions. As a consequence, President Obama's approval ratings stayed below 50 percent in the months before GOP candidates began to campaign in earnest.[1] Also by this time—mid-2011—about twice as many Americans said that the country was off on the wrong track than said it was headed in the right direction;[2] these figures were almost as high as the "wrong track" assessments late in George W. Bush's administration. Moreover, the US Supreme Court's narrow five-to-four decision to uphold the constitutionality of the Affordable Care Act (commonly known as "Obamacare"), gave further fuel for fundraising efforts and an additional attack on the president as a tax-and-spend liberal, whose solutions always involved more federal government involvement and regulation. This, as well as the overall dissatisfaction with the Obama presidency, gave Republicans a large advantage in the "enthusiasm gap" that indicates how excited voters of the two parties are to vote in the upcoming election.[3] Therefore, at the beginning of the campaign cycle in early 2011, it appeared as though the Republican Party's eventual nominee could employ a simple strategy to win the election—attack the president's record on the economy and argue that Republicans had better solutions to solving the nation's problems.

Before applying a general election strategy, however, the party needed to complete the process of selecting a challenger to President Obama. The primary nomination process has become a fairly extended one, beginning in earnest at least a year prior to the first state caucus (Iowa) and primary (New Hampshire), both held in the January before a November election. The "invisible primary," however, starts even earlier. This is the time when candidates raise money, build their organization, and begin to line up supporters, which can begin more than two years before Election Day. Different candidates adopt different strategies throughout this process, but they all must face difficult strategic choices as the primary season gets under way and the political terrain changes. Among other considerations, GOP candidates must often assess and respond to what can be termed the three "mo" factors of strategic choice—momentum, money, and the importance of morality voters (largely evangelical Christians) that are a large part of Republican primary electorate in many states.[4]

In this chapter, we outline some of the key strategic and tactical factors that led to Mitt Romney's nomination and general election run for the White House. First, we discuss the field of possible candidates, including those who ultimately decided *not* to run. Next, we analyze the primary debates and examine the role these played in helping to narrow the primary field. We follow with an exploration of the party's rules on primaries, including how delegates are apportioned and the scheduling of the primaries. Another important factor in any modern election is the role of money. In the aftermath of recent decisions made by the US Supreme Court, the emergence of so-called Super PACs and high levels of overall campaign spending became a distinguishing feature of the 2012 Republican primary campaign. We then take a brief look at the strategy of selecting Paul Ryan as the vice-presidential candidate. Finally, we review the dynamics of the general election. The general election campaign season normally is thought to begin in earnest after each party has held its nomination convention in late August or early September, but swing state voters saw many Obama- and Romney-focused TV ads from the candidates as well as their allies as early as May 2012, once Mitt Romney essentially had sewn up the Republican nomination.

Who's In, Who's Out

The strategy and tactics that played out during the GOP primary season were, in part, affected by decisions made many months prior to the start of the nominating season. The dynamics of the race were influenced by the field of candidates who declared their intention to run for president. In 2012, however, the candidates who did not run were perhaps an even bigger piece of this story.

The 2012 primary campaign began as many do: earlier than most voters would prefer. In April 2011, former New Mexico governor Gary Johnson declared his intention to seek the GOP nomination. While Johnson's declaration came roughly nineteen months before the presidential election, this was a late start to the process compared to earlier election cycles when some candidates had stated their intentions more than two years before the general election. Not long after Johnson stepped into the race, a flurry of candidates declared their intention to run, including former Minnesota governor Tim Pawlenty, former US House Speaker Newt Gingrich (GA), businessman Herman Cain, US Representative Ron Paul (TX), former US Senator Rick Santorum (PA), former Louisiana governor Buddy Roemer, US Representative Michele Bachmann (MN), former governor of Utah and former US ambassador to China John Huntsman, former Massachusetts governor Mitt Romney, and US Representative Thaddeus McCotter (MI). By the end of June 2011, the field of candidates was wide, if not deep. The relative weakness of the Republican field of candidates was even noted by conservatives such as talk-radio king Rush Limbaugh. More so, a *National Journal* poll of congressional insiders (members of Congress and political operatives) reported that 78 percent of Republicans who responded felt that the 2012 field of Republican candidates was "about average" or "weak."[5]

There were two striking and related facets to the race at this time. First, the list of candidates who had not entered the race but who were thought to be potentially strong contenders was rather long. It included former vice-presidential candidate and former Alaska governor Sarah Palin, Indiana governor Mitch Daniels, New Jersey governor Chris Christie, US Representative Paul Ryan (WI), and former Florida governor Jeb Bush, among others. It had been assumed by some observers that several of these individuals, with Palin leading the pack, would run for president, given some of their activities conducted during the year prior. Some in this group took trips to early primary and caucus states, including Iowa and New Hampshire. In particular, Palin's resignation as governor of Alaska in July 2009 was thought to be a signal that she would run in 2012.

A second striking aspect of the campaign was the GOP primary electorate's clear dissatisfaction with the field at the time. According to the Real Clear Politics national poll average, the presumed front-runner at the time, Mitt Romney, never polled above 25.5 percent before January 2012.[6] During the course of 2011, speculation about who might also get into the race was rampant. The results of a June 2011 poll showed Sarah Palin, who was not a declared candidate in the race, in a tie for second with Herman Cain at 15 percent, behind Mitt Romney at only 21 percent.[7] A July poll by Quinnipiac University found Palin at 12 percent, behind Romney and Michele Bachmann, with Texas governor Rick Perry registering 10 percent support.[8] Moreover, a Washington Post–ABC News poll that same month showed that given a choice of the current field plus Palin (but not Perry), Palin would receive 17 percent of the vote (behind only Romney). The same poll showed that with Perry in the field (but not Palin), Perry would also receive 17 percent of the vote. Both of these results put Palin and Perry behind only Romney.[9] The Post noted that Romney's support at the time was "tepid" and that Palin had "lingering power" and could "shake up the race" if she decided to run.[10]

But Sarah Palin never entered the race. The dissatisfaction with the field of announced candidates was palpable as many of the announced candidates were polling in the single digits at the time. The GOP electorate clearly wanted someone else to step into the race. The Republican base got their wish in early August 2011 when Governor Perry announced his candidacy. He immediately jumped to the lead in the polls.[11] It is interesting to note, however, that Perry was the only one of the rumored or expected candidates to enter the race. Even though others, such as Chris Christie, showed some serious strength in some polls,[12] the field was set after Perry's entrance in August.

The unsettled nature of the field had to be a distraction for the candidates who were actively running. Questions about who might also enter the race were asked on a daily basis. It is difficult enough for candidates to deliver their message to potential voters during a crowded primary campaign when the candidates are not all that different from one another on policy matters. It is even more difficult when the electorate and the press are focused on who is not in the race and who might get in. What is more, speculation of candidates entering the race continued into early 2012, even after several nominating contests had been conducted and delegates were awarded. Talk of a "brokered convention," where a candidate who had not competed in any primaries or caucuses would be drafted from the floor, started to take root.

The importance of how the field of candidates materialized may seem unremarkable. However, we believe that the choices before the GOP electorate helped shaped the strategy of the candidates in the race. Mitt Romney's strategy for facing a field that included Ron Paul, Rick Santorum, and others would likely appear much different than if that field had included Sarah Palin, Chris Christie, Jeb Bush, and Mitch Daniels.

One fascinating aspect of the 2012 nomination battle was how nearly all of Mitt Romney's opponents had their time atop the polls as the "anti-Romney" candidate.[13] Each time a candidate surged in front of Romney—first it was Perry, then Cain, then Gingrich, and finally Santorum—they fell almost as quickly as they rose. The GOP electorate was clearly looking for some alternative to the front-runner but failed to find it. We will never know how the presence of Palin, Christie, or Daniels would have affected the race, but the strong polling by candidates who never entered the race seems to indicate that their presence would have dramatically altered the strategic environment. In addition, and as we noted earlier, the candidates who were in the field had to fight through the distraction of having constant speculation about who might also join the race. In a way, they had to campaign against those who were not declared candidates as well as those who were. One arena where this was seen, and that proved to have a large impact in 2012, can be found in the many debates that took place during the primary campaign.

The Primary Debates

Televised candidate debates have become a central part of modern presidential campaigns. The debates provide the potential for millions of voters to see candidates discuss policy issues, to get a glimpse of candidates' character and personality, and to see how the candidates handle pressure. Frank Fahrenkopf Jr., a former chair of the Republican National Committee and a cofounder (with former Democratic National Committee chair Paul Kirk) of the Commission on Presidential Debates in the late 1980s, called the general election debates "the Super Bowl of politics."[14] If so, then the primary debates might be considered the divisional playoffs.

The sheer number of debates held during the 2012 primary season is note-worthy. There were at least twenty debates, with the first held on May 5, 2011, and the last on March 3, 2012. The large number of debates has become fairly common in modern presidential campaigns, especially in heavily contested primaries. The large number of debates during the 2012 primary provided a substantial amount of earned media coverage for the candidates. In addition, more than half of the debates were held prior to the Iowa caucus and the New Hampshire primary. This provided the candidates with a strategic opportu-nity to be more selective when spending their campaign's paid media budget. This can be especially helpful to lower-tier and lesser-known candidates, who might otherwise have dropped out of the race earlier because they could not raise enough money to sustain their campaigns. Having a large campaign war chest allows candidates to spend money on the paid ads that are used to in-crease their name recognition, convey their campaign message, and otherwise communicate to voters. This was especially crucial for a candidate like Rick Santorum, who ultimately became Mitt Romney's chief rival during the pri-maries, but whose candidacy did not really take off until later in the campaign. Given his relative lack of fundraising in calendar year 2011 (see Table 13.1), it is possible that Santorum would have dropped out of the race much earlier were there not so many earned media opportunities provided through the many debates held in 2011 and early 2012.

The large number of debates also affected the overall strategy of the Repub-lican Party message in 2012. In the beginning, virtually all candidates talked about the economy while criticizing President Obama. Former Speaker Gin-grich was considered to be a superior debater by a number of observers. His knowledge of history, his criticism of the media, and his early strategy (which was later abandoned) of staying positive about his primary opponents and focusing his criticisms on President Obama, gave him some initial impetus that included a victory in the South Carolina primary.

Early on, the candidates were largely united as they focused their attention on the president and avoided attacks on each other, for the most part. But as the campaign continued, the discussions began to change. While the economy continued to be a focus, a shift began to occur, with more attention being given to issues such as big- versus small-government philosophies (with Mitt Romney criticized as a big government conservative) and candidate positions on social issues. Some of Romney's opponents equated Romney's Massachu-setts health care program, which they called "Romneycare," with the federal Obamacare law. The social-issues discussion was driven mostly by Rick San-torum, who gained traction by adopting this strategy with primary voters who were social conservatives.

Despite the benefits that may come from the many earned-media opportunities, the debates also bring with them a large risk. This is because one mistake could mean the end of a candidate's run for president. Scholarly and journalistic treatment of presidential debates has tended to focus on general election debates,[15] but some of the same concerns regarding those debates exist with primary debates as well. For example, an ongoing question about debates has been who is invited to participate and who is not. Some have argued that the rules for general election debates established by the Commission on Presidential Debates have effectively limited the debates to major party nominees.[16] This generally has meant that third-party candidates are not invited (Ross Perot was a rare exception in 1992), but in 2012, primary debate rules (that typically require at least 4 percent support in national polls) excluded former governor Gary Johnson (NM) from participating in any but the first of the debates held throughout the 2012 primary campaign season. Others, such as former Louisiana governor Buddy Roemer, never were invited. Johnson later withdrew from the race and was nominated by the Libertarian Party as their presidential candidate.[17]

As with 2008, the 2012 Republican primary field was crowded, with ten candidates participating in at least one debate. Interestingly, although he was invited, Mitt Romney did not attend the first televised debate held in Greenville, South Carolina, on May 5, 2011. Michele Bachmann, Newt Gingrich, Jon Huntsman, and Rick Perry all had not officially declared their candidacy as of early May, so they did not participate in this first debate either. The South Carolina debate was followed by one in New Hampshire (June 13, 2011), and one in Iowa (August 11, 2011)—not a surprise, since these three states are the first three to hold caucuses or primary elections.

Unlike general election debates, one of the great challenges in the primary debates is contrasting one candidate against all of the others. After all, it is much more likely that candidates from the same party have at least similar views on questions regarding the military and foreign policy, the proper role of government, and how to fix the economy. Moreover, do voters who watch the debates care more about these policy position differences (sometimes small) or about other factors, such as candidate likeability, confidence, or demeanor? Whatever the criticisms leveled at debates regarding content, they do stand apart from virtually all other communications voters receive (e.g., paid ads, rehearsed talking points, stump speeches). Some scholars have set debates apart from other communications by noting that "in a televised world filled with pre-timed, candidate-packaged messages, a world surfeiting in speech writers, media masters, and press aides, the electorate is otherwise hard pressed to know what it sees is what it will get as president."[18]

One common debating strategy in a crowded primary field is for candidates to focus their toughest criticism on the front-runner. This serves two purposes if successful: it helps diminish the front-runner's lead, and it helps elevate lower-rung candidates who have not made much of an impression on voters. This strategy was used against Mitt Romney throughout a good portion of the primary campaign, and it was used against Herman Cain after he had taken a lead in the polls. Cain had been a lower-tier candidate who rose in the national polls and then handily won the Florida straw poll in late September. While his "9-9-9" tax plan (9 percent national sales tax, 9 percent flat income tax, and a 9 percent corporate tax) had a certain appeal because it was easy for voters to understand, it also came under criticism from many sources, including Newt Gingrich, who said, "As people look at 9-9-9 and disaggregate it, it gets to be a lot harder sale, I think."[19]

Despite the fact that each candidate has his or her own set of debate talking points, and despite the attempt to control the content and direction of the debates by each candidate, a certain amount of uncertainty and spontaneity exists in every debate. No overall strategy or plan can overcome the lack of candidate control over content and tone in a debate. This could emerge because of an unexpected question from a moderator, a comment from a debating opponent, or a mistake made by a candidate. During the 2012 election season, such a mistake came in a debate—this time made by Texas governor Rick Perry. As noted above, Perry had entered the race in August 2011, which was a bit later than most (so he had not suffered the negative attacks as much). A Gallup poll taken in mid-September 2011 showed him to be the front-runner among all of the Republican candidates,[20] although mediocre debate performances had seen his polling figures drop in October and early November.

At a debate held at Oakland University in Rochester, Michigan, on November 9, 2011, Perry was talking about which federal agencies he would eliminate if he were elected president. He started by saying, "It's three agencies of government when I get there that are gone—Commerce, Education and the um, what's the third one there? Let's see." While Perry struggled, Ron Paul offered that five agencies should be eliminated after which Perry continued, "Oh five—Commerce, Education and the um, um. . . ." Mitt Romney suggested that Perry intended to include the EPA. Perry initially agreed, but then backtracked, and when pressed by debate moderator John Harwood from CNBC, Perry tried again, "The third agency of government I would do away with— the education, the uh, the commerce and let's see. I can't. The third one, I can't. Sorry. Oops."[21]

This "oops" moment was devastating for Perry's candidacy. As one campaign expert tweeted shortly after Perry's slip, "To my memory, Perry's forgetfulness is the most devastating moment of any modern primary debate."[22] Two days before the January 21, 2012, South Carolina primary (and on the day a debate was scheduled in Charleston, South Carolina), Perry dropped out of the race and endorsed Newt Gingrich. Media speculation on the reasons noted his poor debate performances and predictions of a poor result for him in South Carolina.[23]

As we have described earlier, one aspect of the GOP primary debate dynamic was simply the large number of debates that were held. Because there were so many debates, even second- or third-tier candidates were able to stay in the race longer than has been typical in modern campaigns. In the past, a candidate that did not have much national polling support also found it difficult to raise campaign money. Without money to spend on advertising and on a campaign organization, presidential candidates cannot sustain a campaign for very long. However, with a large number of candidates (and where no one candidate was far ahead of the others in the polls), the earned-media opportunities for primary candidates allowed many to stay in the race for an extended time—they were less dependent on fundraising dollars that would flow into television ads as they could get their message out via the debates. Voters were able to see the large field of candidates in a number of debates. Even though Herman Cain, Michele Bachmann, and Tim Pawlenty were among the first candidates to drop out of the race, voters still had the opportunity to see Cain and Bachmann participate in twelve debates. As we approached the first caucuses and primaries, Jon Huntsman and Rick Perry also dropped out, although they had participated in eleven and thirteen debates, respectively.

One of the challenges in moderating debates is how—and whether—to give all participating candidates equal time. For the most part, debate sponsors and moderators have acknowledged that front-runners receive favoritism, with more questions asked of front-runners, and generally more time given to those with higher polling figures. When considering whether the 2012 debates showed any favoritism to front-runners, one conservative media watcher believed that "there is 'a tilt' at the networks toward 'front-runners.'" But he went on to note that in 2012, "The only thing that makes it less unfair is that the front-runners keep changing."[24]

The Rules Can Make a Difference

It took Mitt Romney much longer than it did John McCain four years earlier to accumulate the requisite number of delegates during the primaries and caucuses to secure the nomination; Romney did not have the magic number of delegates until the end of May compared to early March for McCain in

2008. During the 2012 GOP primary process there was a good deal of discussion about how Republicans had changed their delegate allocation rules to be more like the Democrats, requiring proportional distribution of delegates, and how this made the GOP process take longer than in prior years.[25] As one observer notes, however, the importance of this change in the rules was overstated by many in the press.[26]

Other rule changes did impact the length of time it took for Romney to secure the nomination and impacted the strategic decisions of the campaigns. One scenario that typically leads to a quick nomination process is when one candidate wins a string of early primaries and gains enough momentum to parlay into later successes, which almost forces his or her rivals into dropping out of the race (either because they see the writing on the wall or cannot raise enough money to continue). While Romney was the front-runner, he was not able to capitalize on that status and sew up the nomination early. This is seen in the surges of his opponents in the polls and more importantly the losses he suffered in the early contests.

In the first contest of the process—the Iowa caucuses—Romney was declared the winner on caucus night by eight votes over Rick Santorum—clearly not enough to claim a great deal of momentum going forward. Moreover, Santorum was declared the winner by the Iowa GOP almost two weeks later, after a final accounting of votes and paperwork.[27] Between the two confusing Iowa results—one on caucus night and one two weeks later—Romney, as expected, won the New Hampshire primary. Then, in South Carolina, Newt Gingrich beat Romney by twelve points. Romney then found some footing in Florida (more on this later) and Nevada (using some of the tactics Obama employed in that state four years earlier).[28] Santorum, however, went on to win the next three contests in Minnesota, Colorado, and Missouri. It was not until early March that Romney was able to take more control of the race.

The fact that Romney was not able to win all the early primaries delayed his ascension to the status of "presumptive nominee." This fact made the rules changes adopted by the national GOP matter more, later in the process. It was in the contests from March forward that the changes to the delegate allocation rules mattered more.[29] In addition, the calendar of nominating contests was not as "frontloaded" in 2012 as it had been in the past. Several factors led to the structuring of the calendar,[30] but the outcome is more important—that the process was going to take longer with contests more spread out than prior years.

When one candidate can grab front-runner status early and hang on to it with wins in early states, as noted above, they often can take control of the race. In those scenarios, a campaign strategy for later in the process is arguably less important (although the strategy that allowed the candidate to gain that position is likely critical). With the race uncertain after the candidates' performances in Iowa, New Hampshire, and South Carolina, the nomination was up for grabs. Which candidate would be able to strategically take control of the race? Even though Rick Santorum won some later primaries, the Florida contest remained an important and early step on the path to the nomination.

Florida is an important state in presidential contests for several reasons (during the general election its twenty-nine electoral votes are highly coveted). During the primary election, strategic choices need to be made because of the state's large geographic nature and its numerous media markets. Romney had the strategic advantage in Florida because he had the ability to air television ads in all the media markets while his rivals (and their allies) aired relatively few television ads.[31] Moreover, as the race stretched out into later months, the importance of strategically utilizing resources was even more important. In 2012, Romney had the advantage simply because he had the financial resources to have a strong presence across the nation while his opponents did not. These resources are what we turn to next.

Campaign Spending and Super PACs in the Primary

Presidential elections are easily the most expensive political campaigns, especially in years when there is an open field of candidates and the party nominations are competitive. This occurred in 2008 in both parties, and in 2012 a spirited Republican primary generated much interest and a considerable amount of campaign money. Other factors that influence the amount of money raised and spent in a presidential election include whether candidates opt to participate in the public financing system (John McCain did in 2008; only Gary Johnson and Buddy Roemer did in 2012), and the changing campaign finance laws and court interpretations of those laws. The modern era of campaign finance law (in place since the early 1970s) has seen the ebb and flow of both more and fewer limits and restrictions over the years.

Because of changes in the law, modern campaign spending is accomplished through several different types of organizations. First, there are candidate campaign committees, which are required by law to report contributions and expenditures and which also can accept only limited amounts of contributions by source. Party committees (those of both the national party and congressional campaign committees) also participate in raising and spending money, but the role of party committees in raising money for presidential candidates has declined since enactment of the Bipartisan Campaign Reform Act, which stopped the "soft money" stream of fundraising for campaigns. Traditional political action committees (PACs) continue to play a role in campaign finance, and their contributions, expenditures, and reporting are regulated as well, although they are now less important in presidential races. A set of groups that played an important issue advocacy role in the 2004 and 2008 presidential elections were the so-called 527 groups, which still exist but are now in relative decline because of the emergence of Super PACs. For example, the Center for Responsive Politics notes that federal expenditures by 527 groups in 2008 totaled over $253 million, but total 2012 expenditures were less than $126 million.[32]

A new force in campaign finance came with the creation of Super PACs. A Super PAC is considered an "independent expenditure-only" organization; that is, it does not make direct contributions to candidates. After court decisions in *Citizens United v. Federal Election Commission* and *SpeechNow.org v. Federal Election Commission,* a Super PAC is allowed to raise and spend unlimited amounts of money from any source (including corporations, labor unions, individuals, and other organizations).[33] In addition, these groups can expressly advocate for or against specific candidates. While reporting and disclosure requirements were upheld by the courts for these groups, some of these groups were formed as nonprofit 501(c)(4) organizations, and as such, are not required to report their sources of funding. Groups such as American Crossroads and Americans for Prosperity are Super PACs formed as nonprofit 501(c)(4) organizations. While a number of Super PACs have been created to support or oppose issues and multiple federal candidates, some of these Super PACs were created specifically to support a particular presidential candidate.

Campaign spending began to migrate toward these outside groups in 2012, especially in the primaries. For example, the Super PAC supporting Mitt Romney—Restore Our Future—spent more in the Iowa caucus race than the Romney campaign committee did, and the $5 million donated by Sheldon Adelson to Newt Gingrich's associated Super PAC, Winning Our Future, in advance of the South Carolina primary helped Gingrich to a win in that state's primary.[34] Moreover, Super PACs spent more in the key states of Ohio, Oklahoma, Georgia, and Tennessee prior to Super Tuesday than the candidate committees spent. One report found that the Romney, Santorum, and Gingrich candidate committees spent $2.4 million on TV ads in those key states in the two weeks prior to Super Tuesday, while the Super PACs spent $7.85 million on ads in those same states.[35] Because of this shift, candidates have more freedom to make strategic choices about where and when to spend their own committee's money. All of the major Republican candidates had Super PAC allies during the 2012 campaign, although the amount raised and spent by these groups varied widely. In addition to the Restore Our Future Super PAC formed by Mitt Romney supporters and the Newt Gingrich–related Winning Our Future Super PAC, Rick Santorum's supporters created the Red, White, and Blue Super PAC, and Rick Perry's supporters formed Make Us Great Again. As of July 21, 2012, there were 678 groups organized as Super PACs (supporting candidates and issues across the political spectrum) that reported total receipts of $281,530,578 and about $145,500,000 in expenditures. Among those supporting Republican presidential candidates, Restore Our Future (supporting Romney) spent $53,878,098; Winning Our Future (supporting Gingrich) spent $17,002,762; Red, White, and Blue (supporting Santorum) spent $7,529,554. Other conservative groups active in presidential and congressional campaigns included Club for Growth Action Super PAC, which spent $8,741,685, and American Crossroads, which spent $3,113,599 by July 21, 2012.[36]

Much of the focus on Super PAC spending has centered on the megadonors who gave hundreds of thousands or millions of dollars at a time to these groups. This has been true for both Priorities USA Action group, which supported President Obama, and Restore Our Future. Reports as of May 2012 showed that a very small percentage of donors to Restore Our Future were $250 or less. One journalist noted, "Restore Our Future has raised $55,628,000 from individuals and corporations so far this cycle. Of that, just $6,874 came in the form of contributions totaling $250 or less—just 0.012 percent of its total."[37] Smaller contributors did jump in once the US Supreme Court upheld the Affordable Care Act in late June 2012. Up to that point, almost 30,000 individuals had contributed small amounts to Restore Our Future. Shortly after the Court's decision, another 30,000 individual contributions poured into the Super PAC.

With billions of dollars raised and spent in the 2012 presidential election, it is interesting to speculate what effect this amount of spending has on the election process and outcome. First, money certainly matters in some elections—especially to primary election candidates who start the race with lower name recognition and polling numbers. Second, money can keep candidates in a race longer, especially if there are not enough earned media opportunities and the field is crowded. Third, money has brought a number of new groups who can purchase TV ads or other means of communication that either expressly advocate for a candidate or a particular issue. Because these communications cannot be coordinated with a candidate, such communications potentially could be "off message" and therefore not always entirely helpful to a candidate.

Early campaign fundraising and spending is crucial, so much so that some scholars have described the importance of raising money early in a presidential primary season. But success in raising early money helps purchase more than advertising. As Michael J. Goff has argued, "The pivotal importance of money in early presidential nomination politics is due in large part to the fact that it is a resource that can be used to purchase other campaign resources, namely professional staffing, campaign organization, and access to the media through advertising, all of which also are essential for a successful presidential bid."[38] Early fundraising is important enough for some scholars to make assessments about which candidates are "winners" and "losers" in what is called the "money primary." For the 2012 election cycle, the money primary would be the period from just after a candidate's announcement through the end of 2011, before the first primaries and caucuses are held. Table 13.1 summarizes the campaign money raised and spent by the major candidate committees, the most active of their related Super PACs,[39] and their highest and lowest public opinion polling results through December 31, 2011. As the table illustrates, Mitt Romney's candidate committee far outpaced any other candidate's committee, and the Super PAC supporting him also far outpaced any other Super PAC that supported one of his primary opponents.

As illustrated in Table 13.1, Mitt Romney's fundraising advantage through 2011 is clear. First, his campaign committee raised $30 million more than his closest opponent (Ron Paul), and because of that, Romney did not need to spend all of the money he raised in the "money primary." In fact, he spent $20 million less than he raised in 2011, which left him with a huge money advantage going into the primary season in 2012. Restore Our Future also raised and spent—by far—the most money of all candidate-centered Super PACs in 2011. In fact, Restore Our Future raised more money ($30 million) than any candidate committee (after Romney, the candidate committee to raise the most money was Ron Paul, at $25.9 million). Rick Perry's fundraising abilities were substantial also. He raised almost as much as Ron Paul, even though Perry had entered the race only in mid-August 2011, compared to most of the other candidates—including Ron Paul—who had officially declared their candidacy by May 2011. While Perry's flame burned brightly after he entered the race, it also burned out quickly, as he dropped out of the race in mid-January. One surprise is Rick Santorum's relative success in the primaries, despite his inability to raise early campaign money. Santorum and the Super PAC that supported him raised less than $3 million, a paltry sum compared

TABLE 13.1 Campaign Fundraising/Spending Summaries and Polling Data Through December 31, 2011

Candidate	Candidate Committee Funds Raised/ Spent[a]	Related Super PAC Funds Raised/ Spent[b]	Total	Highest/ Lowest Polling Results[c]
Michele Bachmann	$10,100,742/ $9,573,065	$13,162/ $13,015	$10,113,904/ $9,586,080	14.0%/ 3.3%
Herman Cain	$16,529,032/ $15,518,452	$617,620/ $414,093	$17,146,652/ $15,932,545	26.0%/ 2.0%
Newt Gingrich	$12,648,565/ $10,539,734	$2,087,171/ $910,688	$14,735,736/ $11,450,422	35.0%/ 4.4%
Jon Huntsman	$5,882,409/ $5,373,170	$2,680,560/ $2,553,973	$8,562,969/ $7,927,143	3.4%/ 1.0%
Ron Paul	$25,901,305/ $23,982,967	$1,000,000/ $415,721	$26,901,305/ $24,393,688	12.4%/ 6.0%
Rick Perry	$19,775,136/ $16,013,250	$5,485,885/ $4,881,413	$25,261,021/ $20,894,663	31.8%/ 5.3%
Mitt Romney	$56,073,108/ $36,157,457	$30,179,653/ $6,557,543	$86,257,761/ $42,715,000	25.4%/ 16.5%
Rick Santorum	$2,178,703/ $1,898,269	$729,935/ $651,821	$2,908,638/ $2,550,090	5.0%/ 1.5%

Sources: [a] Federal Election Commission, "Presidential Campaign Finance Summaries, Odd-Year Presidential Activity," December 31 year end reports, http://www.fec.gov/press /bkgnd/pres_cf/pres_cf_Odd.shtml; [b] FEC, "Independent Expenditure-Only Committees," 2011 year end, http://www.fec.gov/press/press2011/ieoc_alpha.shtml; [c] Real Clear Politics, "2012 Republican Presidential Nomination," RCP poll average, accessed February 24, 2013, http://www.realclearpolitics.com/epolls/2012/president/us/republican_presidential_ nomination-1452.html.

to the other candidates. However, his candidacy (and his fundraising success) improved substantially after the Iowa caucus and some victories in primaries in Minnesota, Missouri, Colorado, Mississippi, and Alabama.

Paul Ryan as a Strategic Pick for VP

Mitt Romney's selection of Wisconsin representative Paul Ryan as his vice-presidential running mate was one of the first important strategic choices that he made in the run-up to the party's national convention in Tampa.

Vice-presidential nominees typically are thought of as strategic selections by candidates of both parties. There are strategic advantages to choosing a candidate who can bolster the party's base, appeal to an important segment of the voting population, provide geographic, demographic, or ideological balance to the ticket, deliver needed Electoral College votes, or some combination of the above. Paul Ryan brought a number of strengths to the Romney campaign. As House Budget Committee chair, he became a symbol of the Republican Party's overall strategy to reduce government spending and the deficit, to shrink or eliminate government programs, to relax or eliminate regulations on business, and not to raise taxes. His knowledge of the federal budget was highly regarded, and he was thought, by some, to be an intellectual leader of fiscal conservatives in Washington. His budget strategy would mean hardships for many people, but this approach was at the heart of the party's success in the 2010 midterm elections, and it reflected a fiscal conservatism strongly supported by the Tea Party movement. To that point, Romney's selection of Ryan appears to be a similar strategy as employed by John McCain in 2008. In both 2008 and 2012, the Republican presidential nominee was thought to be a moderate within the party, which had disappointed elements of the party considered to be strong fiscal conservatives. According to one news report, the Tea Party movement had been disappointed in Romney, but at least some within the movement felt that it had "gotten one of its ideological heroes" with Ryan's selection,[40] despite Ryan's support of the TARP (the Troubled Assets Relief Program) and the automakers bailouts.

Ryan also was relatively young—forty-two during the campaign. His selection arguably could provide a continuity of Republican leadership for the next four presidential elections, since he could run twice as vice president and twice as president, if the tickets were successful. His home state of Wisconsin was a blue state in 2008 and in several cycles before, but it appeared to have turned more conservative recently with Scott Walker's election as governor, and the state was thought to be in play for the GOP with Ryan on the 2012 ticket.

Of course, there were other candidates that Mitt Romney could have selected. Many in the party wanted Florida senator Marco Rubio, and two well-known conservative pundits made a case for either Ryan or Rubio just prior to Ryan's selection.[41] Other possible candidates included former Minnesota governor Tim Pawlenty, Ohio senator Rob Portman, South Dakota Senator John Thune, Rick Santorum, former secretary of state Condoleezza Rice, former Florida governor Jeb Bush, Chris Christie, Rick Perry, and Virginia governor Bob McDonnell. Because the Republican ticket ultimately lost the election, there will be many who will criticize Ryan's selection, just as Sarah

Palin's selection was criticized after the 2008 Republican loss (including Dick Cheney's 2012 remark that her selection had been "a mistake").[42]

The General Election Debates

It is common for the media to focus most of its debate attention and analysis on "Who won?" Indeed, the fortunes of presidential candidates have risen or fallen because of their performance in the debates. In 2012, Mitt Romney was considered to have won the first debate rather handily, with 72 percent of those polled by Gallup feeling that an energetic Romney had done a better job in that debate than a passive and seemingly unenthusiastic President Obama. The second debate was a town hall format debate, in which undecided voters in the audience asked the candidates questions. Barack Obama apparently learned a lesson from the first debate and came out much more energized and confident during the second debate. According to Gallup, President Obama was thought to have done a better job during this debate than Mitt Romney, by a 51 percent to 38 percent margin. The president performed even better during the third debate, on foreign policy, with Gallup reporting a 56 percent to 33 percent advantage over Mitt Romney.[43] Even though Romney was thought to have lost the second and third debates, his enthusiastic performance in the first debate against a lackluster Barack Obama was viewed by over sixty-seven million people and gave his campaign new life at a time when it appeared he was faltering. After the first debate, Romney moved up 2 percentage points in the Gallup poll, so that he and President Obama were tied at 47 percent each.[44]

However, a candidate can achieve specific strategic objectives in a debate without necessarily being considered the overall winner. At the very least, candidates might be able to increase voter knowledge about their positions on issues, and for challengers, about their general suitability for office. Candidates that have defined themselves to voters prior to the debates often attempt to reassure their voter base by reinforcing their campaign message and offering their strongest talking points during a debate. Those candidates who have been defined negatively by their opponent will attempt to respond to those negatives by clarifying misconceptions, offering new information, or countering allegations previously made by their opponent. In the first debate, Mitt Romney successfully accomplished both by offering specific details on his plans to improve the economy, which he had not done very effectively prior to the debate. Candidates also can meet strategic objectives simply by exceeding voter expectations of their performance in a debate (in part due to low expectations, challengers were considered to have won the first presidential debates in 1976, 1980, 1984, 1992, and 2004).[45]

It is also quite common that viewers believe most challengers cannot "win" a foreign policy debate with an incumbent president. After all, incumbents can draw on their experience and speak in detail about the difficult choices they made while in office. In this regard, incumbents can appear more "presidential" in a foreign policy debate. But a challenger can show voters that he has leadership qualities appropriate for the presidency. In foreign and military policy, a challenger can demonstrate that he has the proper temperament to be commander-in-chief, even if he has not had the actual experience.

As such, Mitt Romney's strategy in the debate focused on foreign policy was to show voters that he could be a reasonable leader and commander-in-chief, and that he would provide continuity and stability to foreign policy-making even if voters chose to switch leaders. To that end, Romney spent a considerable amount of time agreeing with President Obama on foreign policy questions. In fact, while in the second debate he had criticized the president on the administration's response to the September attack in Benghazi, Libya, Romney did not pursue this criticism during the third debate. While some observers felt that Romney lost an opportunity to score debating points regarding Benghazi, it could be argued that he felt that it was more important to show his commander-in-chief qualities rather than snipe at the president.

In addition, Romney tried to exploit a strategy that both candidates engaged in during this debate, which turned the discussion away from foreign policy topics and put US foreign policy into a context of US domestic jobs and the economy. This strategy made some sense for Romney, because the prevailing wisdom was that the president was more vulnerable to challenges about his economic policies than foreign policy. On several occasions during this debate, Romney focused on how a strong economy at home could help promote principles of peace around the world, and how the national debt was one of our greatest national security threats. He also returned to a summary of his five-point plan for economic recovery and job creation. This strategy moved the discussion away from foreign and military policy issues and returned them to the economy, where he arguably had a competitive advantage over the president.

In the end, the presidential debates did help Mitt Romney in the polls, despite the fact that 2012 had a relatively small percentage of declared undecided voters in the two months prior to Election Day. In the Real Clear Politics national poll averages before and after the debates, Romney did pick up about two points and Obama lost about two points. On the day before the first debate, the polling average had President Obama at 49 percent and Romney at 45.7 percent. Romney's strong performance in the first debate was rewarded with a two-point increase, so that on the day before the second debate, he was just ahead of Obama 47.4 percent to 47.3 percent. Just before the third debate, Obama had regained a small lead of 47.1 percent to 46.9 percent. On October 23, the day after the third debate, the tracking poll averages had Romney ahead 48 percent to 47.1 percent.[46] These small differences were all within the margin of error of the individual polls that made up the average compiled by Real Clear Politics, but it did appear that Romney picked up some ground because of the debates—even though he was considered to have lost two out of the three debates. His decisive win in the first debate was key, in part because more people watched the first debate, and viewers saw a candidate who was better able to define himself and demonstrate his leadership qualities. In this regard, Romney achieved many of his strategic objectives even though he was thought to have lost two of the debates.

Money in the General Election

Simply put, modern presidential campaigns are expensive. In the 2008 election, Barack Obama's candidate committee raised over $700 million and John McCain's committee raised almost $400 million. The national Democratic and Republican parties raised almost $2 billion between them. Of course, the 2010 US Supreme Court decision in *Citizens United* opened the door for even more spending by "independent expenditure-only" Super PACs, which could raise and spend unlimited amounts of money from any source. Moreover, tax-exempt 501(c)(4) organizations are allowed to engage in lobbying and campaign activities, but are not required to report their sources of funding. This has been termed "dark money" by some advocacy groups. The result is that some big campaign spenders in 2012 were not required to report their funding sources.[47]

At first glance, it would appear that neither candidate had a huge money advantage in the general election, as each side raised and spent over $1 billion including candidate, party, and Super PAC activity combined. According to the Center for Responsive Politics, overall spending through late November by the "blue team" (Obama and his supporting groups) totaled $1,112,041,699, while overall spending by the "red team" (Romney and supporters) equaled $1,246,902,432.[48] However, upon closer examination, Romney was faced with more challenges regarding money than Obama. First, Romney's campaign committee spent only about two-thirds of what Obama's campaign committee spent. This meant that in terms of message development and controlling TV ad content, Romney was at a huge disadvantage. According to data compiled by the Wesleyan Media Project, the Obama campaign "out-advertised the Romney campaign by a 2.6 to 1 margin in both ads aired and estimated money spent" as of the week before Election Day.[49] During the last week of October, in the top twenty-five media markets, the Obama campaign aired more ads than the Romney campaign in every single market.[50] While outside groups' activity made up for some of this disparity (pro-Obama ads still outnumbered pro-Romney ads by about 50,000), the ability of Romney to control his message was substantially less than that of Obama.

In our earlier discussion of the role of money in the Republican primary, we argued that Romney had a substantial advantage over his opponents. In that discussion, we noted that several candidates were able to stay in the primary race longer because of the large number of debates and the role of Super PACs. This meant that Romney had to spend more money in the primary than he normally might, and so he was left with a relatively small campaign war chest once he became the presumptive Republican nominee. Romney's campaign was at another disadvantage compared to that of President Obama, because Obama had no primary opposition and was therefore able to raise money without needing to spend any in the first part of 2012.

Mitt Romney also suffered in the general election in part because he had become a major target of Super PAC negative advertising during the primary, notably by the Super PAC supporting Newt Gingrich, Winning Our Future. Many of the criticisms used against Romney in the general election were first heard and seen on TV ads sponsored by the Super PACs supporting his primary opponents. For example, Super PAC ads called Romney "greedy" and a "corporate raider" because of his time at Bain Capital. They claimed he cut worker benefits and sent jobs overseas. They showed Romney calling himself a "progressive" and a "moderate," in an effort to move conservative primary voters away from Romney. Some ads made comparisons between the Romney-led Massachusetts health care plan and Obamacare.

Despite the fact that Barack Obama's campaign committee held a substantial advantage over Romney's campaign committee, Restore Our Future's spending advantages were reversed in this election. Restore Our Future reported spending over $142 million, almost twice as much as Priorities USA Action, which spent over $65 million.[51] However, while the Super PAC supporting Romney spent much more than the one supporting the president, Restore Our Future's communications were not necessarily consistent with Romney's own campaign message. One of the main criticisms about Romney's

TABLE 13.2 Campaign Spending in the 2012 Presidential Election

Organization Type	Blue Team	Red Team	Total
Candidate Committee	$683,546,548 (Obama for America)	$433,281,516 (Romney for President, Inc.)	$1,116,828,064
National Party Organization	$292,264,802 (Democratic National Committee)	$386,180,565 (Republican National Committee)	$678,445,367
Outside Groups	$136,230,349	$427,440,351	$563,670,700
Total	$1,112,041,699	$1,246,902,432	$2,358,944,131

Source: Center for Responsive Politics, "2012 Presidential Race," accessed February 24, 2013, http://www.opensecrets.org/pres12/index.php.

Note: Spending by candidates and parties through November 26, 2012; spending by outside groups through February 24, 2013.

campaign was that voters did not know what he stood for, and this in part was due to the inconsistent messages being delivered by the Romney campaign and Restore Our Future. This was a particular problem for Romney, since Restore Our Future spent far more than his campaign did in the general election. Table 13.2 shows the amounts of money raised and spent by the candidate committees, their political party organizations, and the respective Super PACs supporting their candidacies (Restore Our Future for Romney, Priorities USA Action for Obama).

As Table 13.2 illustrates, the overall amount of money spent in 2012 was fairly evenly divided. However, the differences in what the candidates raised and spent—and where the candidates had the most control over content and message—was substantial. Mitt Romney was at a money disadvantage in the general election because his share of the overall amount spent on behalf of his campaign was relatively small. In addition, Romney (and Obama) had to spend a significant amount of time during the campaign just raising campaign money. This took him away from events with voters and from where he otherwise could have improved on his campaign message and made more contact with potential voters. In fact, the now-famous video of Romney making comments about "the 47 percent" of the population that he did not care about were made at a private $50,000 a plate fundraiser in Florida in May (with the video finally leaked in September). This comment hurt his election prospects and reinforced a belief among some voters that Romney was a member of the wealthy elite who did not care about average people.

Romney's Electoral College Strategy

Strategy in a presidential contest is somewhat different compared to a congressional race, in which a candidate needs to design a strategy to earn a plurality of votes cast. When it comes to winning the White House, designing a strategy to garner 270 electoral votes is the ultimate goal. For Mitt Romney and Paul Ryan, while the goal was clear in 2012, the path was not. They did have some things working in their favor, but other dynamics were not.

The 2012 election was the first presidential contest to fall under the electoral map created by the congressional reapportionment after the 2010 census. Had Romney won only the same states John McCain had in 2008, Romney would have won six more electoral votes simply because Republican states like Texas, Georgia, South Carolina, and others benefited from larger numbers of House members after reapportionment, and therefore more electoral votes in those states (not all Republican states gained votes, however, as Louisiana and Missouri each lost one vote in the Electoral College). This was clearly an advantage for Romney, but in the end it was not enough, as he still fell 64 electoral votes shy of 270.

In some ways, the 2012 presidential election was not that different from those of the recent past. Both candidates could count on the electoral votes from a set of states that make up their "base" and would need to battle over the remaining votes from the handful of "swing" or "toss-up" states. The consensus Democratic base states are:

- California (55 electoral votes)
- Connecticut (7)
- Delaware (3)
- Hawaii (4)
- Illinois (20)
- Maine (4)
- Maryland (10)
- Massachusetts (11)
- Minnesota (10)
- New Jersey (14)
- New Mexico (5)

- New York (29)
- Oregon (7)
- Rhode Island (4)
- Vermont (3)
- Washington (12)
- Washington, DC (3)

These states and the District of Columbia total 201 electoral votes. These are votes that Barack Obama could count on going into Election Day. The list of Republican base states Mitt Romney could rely on included:

- Alabama (9 electoral votes)
- Alaska (3)
- Arizona (11)
- Arkansas (6)
- Georgia (16)
- Idaho (4)
- Indiana (11) (even though President Obama won Indiana in 2008, it was not among the list of swing states in 2012)
- Kansas (6)
- Kentucky (8)
- Louisiana (8)
- Mississippi (6)
- Missouri (10)
- Montana (3)
- Nebraska (5)
- North Dakota (3)
- Oklahoma (7)
- South Carolina (9)
- South Dakota (3)
- Tennessee (11)
- Texas (38)
- Utah (6)
- West Virginia (5)
- Wyoming (2)

These states total 191 electoral votes. The 2012 presidential election, and the key to Romney's strategy, would be won in those eleven states that held the remaining 146 electoral votes:

- Colorado (9 electoral votes)
- Florida (29)
- Iowa (6)
- Michigan (16)
- North Carolina (15)
- Nevada (6)
- New Hampshire (4)
- Ohio (18)
- Pennsylvania (20)
- Virginia (13)
- Wisconsin (10)

As in many presidential elections, the list of battleground states is larger at the start of the campaign than at the end, and 2012 was no different. While Michigan, Pennsylvania, and Wisconsin were in the toss-up category, their political history and near-Election Day polling pointed to Obama victories in those states. Romney's choice of running mate, Wisconsin native son Paul Ryan, may have made Wisconsin more competitive, but that state has not voted for a GOP presidential candidate since 1984. Pennsylvania and Michigan have not voted for a Republican presidential candidate since 1988. While North Carolina voted for Obama in 2008, it has been a solid Republican state since 1976. Putting these states in each candidate's respective column puts their electoral vote totals at 247 for Obama and 206 for Romney.

This was the clear strategic problem for Romney and the GOP. Taking the states that could be counted for each candidate, the path to victory for Obama was simply much clearer than for Romney. To win, Romney needed nearly a clean sweep of the remaining battleground states, including Florida, Virginia, and Ohio, plus one additional state. If Romney were to have won only Colorado, Iowa, New Hampshire, and Nevada, he would still be 39 electoral votes shy of 270. While this seems like a daunting task, Romney was not in an impossible position. Many of the polls leading up to Election Day pointed to a possible Romney victory. In Florida Romney had a small lead (but within the margin of error) in five of the last ten polls taken in that state, along with two ties.[52] Virginia was a reliable Republican state dating back to 1972, until Obama won it in 2008; and Romney led or was tied in five of the last ten polls (again, all were within the margin of error). Ohio was always the trouble spot for the Romney campaign. While the reaction to Romney's comments on the auto bailout was hardest felt in his home state of Michigan, they had a profound effect in Ohio as well, which also has close ties to the auto industry. In part, this helped President Obama to a lead in eight of the final ten polls (two were ties) and a solid foundation for victory on November 6. Romney had a chance to win in Ohio, but it was a small one, and his campaign would need to turn its voters out. Again, even if Romney won these three states, he would need one additional state to reach 270 electoral votes.

Conclusion

There is a debate in political science about whether or not campaigns matter to election results. Some scholars argue that the campaigning undertaken by candidates and their campaigns have an important impact on voters in terms of their perceptions and behaviors and that these influence election outcomes. Others, however, argue that campaigns have little impact on election outcomes. Rather, they contend that outcomes lie with macropolitical and economic factors (presidential approval, unemployment, and Gross Domestic Product, for example).[53] We side with those who argue they do matter, and 2012 is a case in point. The election cycle was a series of ups and downs for Mitt Romney and the GOP. The macrolevel political indicators early in the election cycle—direction of the country, presidential approval, and economic performance—all pointed to a victory for the GOP nominee. If all that matters to an election outcome are these factors that are outside of campaigning, Romney would have won the election. But a difficult, expensive, and often bruising nomination battle left Mitt Romney in a difficult position heading into the general election, especially given some of the positions he had taken to secure the nomination. Comments on issues such as immigration, the aforementioned auto bailout, and some of Romney's background—like his time at Bain Capital—would provide President Obama the opportunity to define Romney for voters in a negative light early on in the general election phase of the campaign.

Romney got back within striking distance of Obama after the first presidential debate. His strong performance provided Romney with the opportunity to position himself for victory on Election Day. As we noted above, this would be a difficult task. In the end, Romney failed in his bid for the White House. His campaign's overall strategy was generally sound, but executing that strategy was arguably where the Romney campaign fell short. The electoral math was clear—he had to win a specific series of states to reach 270 electoral votes. However, the Obama campaign—having had developed voter contacts, organizational structure, and get-out-the-vote tactics in 2008—had a superior ground game compared to Romney's campaign.[54] Going into Election Day, as evidenced by the polls, Romney could have pulled out a victory. What the campaign needed was a better voter turnout effort. Tactically, the GOP and the Romney campaign stumbled when their new, high-tech voter identification and turnout effort—dubbed Orca, after the killer whale—did not perform as well as intended on Election Day.[55] Had this effort been better, it may have improved Romney's chances.

President Obama won a decisive victory in the Electoral College, winning 332 votes to 206 for Mitt Romney. In the popular vote, however, President Obama won a narrower victory, roughly 51 percent to 47 percent. Although the popular vote is less meaningful in determining the winner, it is instructive for students of the campaign. The reason for the large Electoral College victory but narrower popular-vote win for the president is simply that Obama won each of the battleground states (except North Carolina), albeit some by very small margins. For example, Obama won Florida by about 37,000 votes out of more than 8.4 million cast, Ohio by roughly 166,000 votes out of over 5.5 million cast, Virginia by less than 150,000 out of 3.8 million cast, and Colorado by about 138,000 out of 2.5 million votes cast.[56] Had Romney won these four states, he would have won the presidency. One thing that could have changed the outcome is a different electorate on Election Day. In other words, had Republicans made up a greater percentage of voters on Election Day, Romney may well have won.

In 2008, President Obama won a larger and more decisive victory in both the Electoral College and the popular vote than he did in 2012. In part, this was because of the makeup of the electorate on Election Day that year. Turnout was up generally in 2008, and groups such as African Americans and traditionally low-turnout groups such as younger voters went to the polls at higher levels that year. This helped to produce a 7-point Democratic turnout advantage.[57] In 2012, many outside the Obama campaign assumed that voter turnout would be much different compared to 2008. Given the large numbers of Americans who seemed dissatisfied with the direction of the country and the performance of the economy, the idea that turnout would be down—and down among groups key to Obama's coalition from 2008—did not seem far-fetched. For this reason, some pollsters, campaign experts, and Republican campaign consultants applied a voter turnout model based on 2004 election numbers rather than 2008. However, based on the 2012 election results, it appears that a Republican presidential candidate may no longer be able to rely on the party's base voters and still win a presidential election. The share of the electorate that is more likely to support a Democratic candidate (African Americans, Hispanics, and female voters) is becoming greater and will continue to climb.[58]

Indeed, voter turnout was down in 2012 compared to 2008 by more than 2 million voters. Nationwide, Democrats enjoyed a 6-point turnout advantage, as 38 percent of the electorate was self-described Democrats while only 32 percent identified as Republicans.[59] In some of the key battleground states, the Democratic turnout advantage was even higher. In Ohio, Democrats enjoyed an 8-point turnout advantage; that advantage was 7 points in Virginia. In Michigan 40 percent of voters were Democrats while only 30 percent were Republicans. Among the swing states, only in Florida and Iowa did Republican turnout come close to the Democrats. These figures helped produce another surprising result: Mitt Romney garnered less than one million more votes than John McCain did in 2008. Had Mitt Romney's campaign done a better job of getting their voters to the polls in a political context that favored the GOP, the result may have been different.

Notes

1. Gallup, "Gallup Daily: Obama Job Approval," accessed September 10, 2012, http://www.gallup.com/poll/113980/Gallup-Daily-Obama-Job-Approval.aspx.

2. Real Clear Politics, "Direction of the Country," polling average, accessed September 10, 2012, http://www.realclearpolitics.com/epolls/other/direction_of_country -902.html.

3. The difference between Democrats and Republicans on this measure, however, did fluctuate over the course of 2011 and 2012. Gallup, "GOP Slightly Ahead in Voting Enthusiasm," March 1, 2012, http://www.gallup.com/poll/153038/GOP-Slightly -Ahead-Voting-Enthusiasm.aspx.

4. Earlier research on presidential primaries has shown the importance of momentum, ideology, resource allocation to each primary, or some combination of these factors. See, for example, Larry M. Bartels, "Candidate Choice and the Dynamics of the Presidential Nominating Process," *American Journal of Political Science* 31, no. 1 (1987): 1–30; Steven J. Brams and Morton D. Davis, "Optimal Resource Allocation in Presidential Primaries," *Mathematical Social Sciences* 3 (1982): 373–388 (momentum and money); Bruce E. Cain, I. A. Lewis, and Douglas Rivers, "Strategy and Choice in the 1988 Primaries," *Electoral Studies* 8, no. 1 (1989): 23–48 (momentum and ideology); and Wayne P. Steger, "Forecasting the Presidential Primary Vote: Viability, Ideology, and Momentum," *International Journal of Forecasting* 24 (2008): 193–208.

5. Real Clear Politics, "What Makes the 2012 GOP Field So Weak?" May 20, 2011, http://www.realclearpolitics.com/articles/2011/05/20/what_makes_the_2012_gop _field_so_weak_109933.html.

6. Real Clear Politics, "2012 Republican Presidential Nomination," polling average, accessed July 31, 2012, http://www.realclearpolitics.com/epolls/2012/president /us/republican_presidential_nomination-1452.html.

7. Public Policy Polling, "Without Huckabee, Romney Leads in IA; Cain Tied for 2nd," accessed July 31, 2012, http://www.publicpolicypolling.com/pdf/PPP_Release _IA_0601513.pdf.

8. Real Clear Politics, "Bachmann Surges, But Romney Still Leads in National Poll," July 13, 2011, http://www.realclearpolitics.com/articles/2011/07/13/another _surge_for_bachmann_romney_still_leads_national_poll_110555.html.

9. Jon Cohen and Dan Balz, "Poll: Romney Still Ahead, but with Big Vulnerabilities in Quest for GOP Nod," *Washington Post,* July 21, 2011, accessed July 31, 2012, http://www.washingtonpost.com/politics/poll-romney-still-ahead-but-with -big-vulnerabilities-in-quest-for-gop-%20%20nod/2011/07/20/gIQAuqExQI_story .html?wpisrc=al_national.

10. Ibid.

11. Gallup, "Perry Zooms to Front of Pack for 2012 GOP Nomination," accessed July 31, 2012, http://www.gallup.com/poll/149180/Perry-Zooms-Front-Pack-2012 -GOP-Nomination.aspx.

12. The Hill, "Poll: Voters' Top GOP Picks Are Christie and Cain," May 10, 2011, http://thehill.com/blogs/blog-briefing-room/news/160339-poll-voters-top-gop -picks-are-christie-and-cain.

13. Real Clear Politics, "Republican Presidential Nomination," RCP poll average, accessed February 24, 2013, http://www.realclearpolitics.com/epolls/2012/president /us/republican_presidential_nomination-1452.html

14. Frank Fahrenkopf Jr., quoted in George Farah, *No Debate: How the Republican and Democratic Parties Secretly Control the Presidential Debates* (New York: Seven Stories Press, 2004), 1.

15. See, for example, Alan Schroeder, *Presidential Debates: Fifty Years of High-Risk TV* (New York: Columbia University Press, 2008); Kathleen Hall Jamieson and David S. Birdsell, *Presidential Debates: The Challenge of Creating an Informed Electorate* (Oxford: Oxford University Press, 1990); and Jim Lehrer, *Tension City: Inside the Presidential Debates, from Kennedy-Nixon to Obama-McCain* (New York: Random House, 2011).

16. Farah, *No Debate.*

17. Reid J. Epstein and Ginger Gibson, "Gary Johnson to Drop Out of GOP Primary to Run as Libertarian," December 20, 2011, http://www.politico.com/news /stories/1211/70727.html.

18. Jamieson and Birdsell, *Presidential Debates,* 4.

19. Seung Min Kim, "Gingrich No Fan of '9 9 9,'" October 16, 2011, http://www .politico.com/blogs/politicolive/1011/Gingrich_no_fan_of_999.html.

20. CNN, "CNN/ORC Poll," 6, accessed March 18, 2013, http://i2.cdn.turner.com /cnn/2011/images/09/26/rel16a-1a.pdf.

21. Arlette Saenz and Emily Friedman, "Rick Perry's Debate Lapse: 'Oops'—Can't Remember Department of Energy," November 9, 2011, http://abcnews.go.com/blogs /politics/2011/11/rick-perrys-debate-lapse-oops-cant-remember-department-of -energy/. See the full video clip at: http://www.youtube.com/watch?v=EZYQ9IYe OlU, accessed September 29, 2012.

22. From Twitter, @Larry Sabato, Professor Larry Sabato, University of Virginia, November 9, 2011.

23. Carl Cameron, "Perry Drops Out of Republican Presidential Race, Endorses Gingrich," January 19, 2012, http://www.foxnews.com/politics/2012/01/19/perry -to-drop-out-gop-presidential-race/.

24. David Bauder, "Networks Walk a Tightrope over Crowded Debates," November 22, 2012, http://www.realclearpolitics.com/news/ap/politics_topics/2011/Nov /22/networks_walk_a_tightrope_over_crowded_debates.html.

25. Traditionally, Republicans have tended to use more winner-take-all rules in primaries than proportional rules to allocate delegates.

26. See Josh Putnam's excellent discussion of primary rules in "Republican Delegate Allocation Rules: 2012 vs. 2008," FrontloadingHQ, December 24, 2011, http://frontloading.blogspot.com/2011/12/republican-delegate-allocation-rules .html.

27. David Fahrenthold and Debbi Wilogren, "Santorum Finished 34 Votes Ahead of Romney in New Iowa Tally; Votes from 8 Precincts Missing," *Washington Post,* January 19, 2012, http://www.washingtonpost.com/politics/report-santorum-finished -34-votes-ahead-of-romney-in-new-iowa-tally-votes-from-8-precincts-missing /2012/01/19/gIQAJGuRAQ_story.html.

28. See, for example, Anjeanette Damon, "How Romney Won Nevada Again," *Las Vegas Sun,* February 4, 2012, http://www.lasvegassun.com/news/2012/feb/04 /how-romney-won-nevada-again/.

29. See Putnam, "Republican Delegate Allocation Rules."

30. See Putnam's work on explaining this phenomenon in FrontloadingHQ, "Myth #2: Budgetary Constraints Have Driven 2012 Presidential Primary Movement," August 18, 2011, http://frontloading.blogspot.com/2011/08/myth-2-budgetary-con straints-have.html.

31. See the *Washington Post*'s resource on ad spending in 2012, "Mad Money: TV Ads in the 2012 Presidential Campaign," accessed August 2, 2012, http://www.wash ingtonpost.com/wp-srv/special/politics/track-presidential-campaign-ads-2012.

32. Center for Responsive Politics, "527s: Advocacy Group Spending," accessed November 11, 2012, http://www.opensecrets.org/527s/index.php.

33. Federal Election Commission Record 36, no. 5 (May 2010), http://www.fec .gov/pdf/record/2010/may10.pdf.

34. Editorial, *Los Angeles Times,* "Hunted by the 'Super PACs,'" January 14, 2012, http://articles.latimes.com/2012/jan/14/ opinion/la-ed-superpacs-20120114.

35. Brody Mullins and Alicia Mundy, "Super PACs Outspent Candidates in Run-Up to Tuesday," March 7, 2012, online.wsj.com/article/SB10001424052970203 961204577267822228233682.html.

36. Center for Responsive Politics, "Super PACs," accessed November 10, 2012, http://www.opensecrets.org/pacs/superpacs.php?cycle=2012.

37. Sam Stein and Amanda Turkel, "The Small Donors Behind Obama's and Romney's Wealth-Driven Super PACs," HuffPost Politics, May 22, 2012, http://www .huffingtonpost.com/2012/05/22/super-pac-small-donors_n_1537358.html.

38. Michael J. Goff, *The Money Primary: The New Politics of the Early Presidential Nomination Process* (Lanham, MD: Rowman & Littlefield, 2004), 3.

39. For Mitt Romney, Restore Our Future; for Newt Gingrich, Winning Our Future; for Rick Perry, Make Us Great Again; for Rick Santorum, Red, White and Blue Fund; for Michele Bachmann, Keep Conservatives United; for Jon Huntsman, Our Destiny PAC; for Ron Paul, Endorse Liberty; for Herman Cain, 9-9-9 Fund.

40. Washington Examiner, "Tea Party Gets Its Man in Ryan for Vice President," August 13, 2012, http://washingtonexaminer.com/tea-party-gets-its-man-in-ryan -for-vice-president/article/feed/2023610.

41. Stephen F. Hayes and William Kristol, "Go for the Gold, Mitt!" *The Weekly Standard,* August 13, 2012, http://www.weeklystandard.com/articles/go-gold-mitt _649299.html.

42. Jonathan Karl, "Dick Cheney: Picking Sarah Palin Was 'A Mistake,'" The Note, ABC News, July 29, 2012, http://abcnews.go.com/blogs/politics/2012/07/dick -cheney-picking-sarah-palin-for-vp-was-a-mistake/.

43. Frank Newport, "Viewers Deem Obama Winner of the Third Debate, 56% to 33%," October 25, 2012, http://www.gallup.com/poll/158393/viewers-deem-obama -winner-third-debate.aspx.

44. Jeffrey M. Jones, "Romney Narrows Vote Gap After Historic Debate Win," Gallup, October 8, 2012, http://www.gallup.com/poll/157907/ romney-narrows-vote -gap-historic-debate-win.aspx.

45. George Condon, "Why Incumbents Lose Presidential Debates," *National Journal,* September 27, 2012.

46. Real Clear Politics Poll Average, "General Election: Romney vs. Obama," accessed November 12, 2012, http://www.realclearpolitics.com/epolls/2012/president /us/general_election_romney_vs_obama-1171.html.

47. Brian C. Mooney, "Ruling Allows Major Donors to Hide Identities," *Boston Globe,* February 15, 2012, http://www.bostonglobe.com/news/nation/2012/02/15 /major-political-donors-can-hide-identities/JrQx1lLgLQNJ1Mfuz5LbjN/story .html?camp=pm.

48. Center for Responsive Politics, "2012 Presidential Race," accessed November 18, 2012, http://www.opensecrets.org/pres12/index.php.

49. Wesleyan Media Project, "Presidential Ad War Tops 1M Airings," accessed February 27, 2013, http://mediaproject.wesleyan.edu/2012/11/02/presidential -ad-war-tops-1m-airings/

50. Ibid.

51. Center for Responsive Politics, "Super PACs," accessed November 18, 2012, http://www.opensecrets.org/pacs/superpacs.php.

52. See the Real Clear Politics polling averages for all polling data in this paragraph, "Battle for White House," accessed November 20, 2012, http://www.real clearpolitics.com/epolls/2012/president/2012_elections_electoral_college_map .html#battlegrounds.

53. For an introduction to this debate, see Thomas M. Holbrook, *Do Campaigns Matter?* (Thousand Oaks, CA: Sage, 1996); Daron Shaw, "The Effect of TV Ads and Candidate Appearances on Statewide Presidential Votes, 1988–1996," *American Political Science Review* 93 (June 1999): 345–361; Daron Shaw, "A Study of Presidential Campaign Event Effects from 1952 to 1992," *Journal of Politics* 61 (May 1999): 387–422; and Andrew Gelman and Gary King, "Why Are American Presidential Election Campaign Polls So Variable When Votes Are So Predictable?" *British Journal of Political Science* 23 (October 1993): 409–451.

54. Rebecca Sinderbrand, "Analysis: Obama Won with a Better Ground Game," November 7, 2012, http://www.cnn.com/2012/11/07/politics/analysis-why-obama -won/index.html?iref=allsearch.

55. CNET News, "Why Romney's Orca Killer App Beached on Election Day," November 9, 2012, http://news.cnet.com/8301-13578_3-57547183-38/why-rom neys-orca-killer-app-beached-on-election-day/?part%3Drss%26subj%3Dnews %26tag%3DreadMore.

56. David Wasserman, "2012 National Popular Vote Tracker," accessed March 1, 2013, https://docs.google.com/spreadsheet/ccc?key=0AjYj9mXElO_QdHpla01o WE1jOFZRbnhJZkZpVFNKeVE#gid=19.

57. See 2008 exit poll data available at Election Center, CNNPolitics, accessed November 20, 2012, http://www.cnn.com/ELECTION/2008/results/polls/#USP00p1.

58. Nate Silver, "Base Turnout Strategy May Be Too Narrow for Romney," FiveThirtyEight, August 30, 2012, http://fivethirtyeight.blogs.nytimes.com/2012/08 /30/base-turnout-strategy-may-be-too-narrow-for-romney/.

59. See 2012 exit poll data available at Election Center, CNNPolitics, accessed November 20, 2012, http://www.cnn.com/election/2012/results/race/president #exit-polls.

14

Campaigns Matter

CANDICE J. NELSON

Political scientists look at the economy and presidential popularity as predictors of the outcomes of presidential elections, and certainly both of those were important in the 2012 elections. However, there were other election-related factors that were important as well. The 2012 election cycle saw changes to the way the presidential election was financed, new rules for how the elections were administered, the continued evolvement of the role of social media, and continuing changes in technology that impacted all aspects of campaigns. This chapter looks at both the predictors used by political scientists and the factors that influenced the campaigns to understand what mattered in the 2012 presidential and congressional elections.

Campaign Finance

The Federal Election Campaign Act (FECA) of 1972 provided for partial public funding of presidential nominating campaigns and full public funding of the general election. However, ever since George W. Bush decided to forgo partial public funding during his campaign for the Republican nomination in 2000, the continued viability of public funding of presidential elections came into question. The 2012 election was the first presidential election since the FECA was passed in which no major party candidate accepted public funding for both the nomination and the general election. As a result, candidates seeking the Republican nomination, and President Obama and Governor Romney in the general election, were free to raise and spend as much money as they could. The result, as Anthony Corrado points out in Chapter 5, was the most expensive presidential election in the history of the United States, with the

Obama and Romney campaigns and their affiliated groups each raising over a billion dollars. Not only was the amount raised and spent in federal elections the most in American history, but 2012 saw a continuation of the role of Super PACs that first arose during the 2010 congressional elections, as Sam Garrett describes in Chapter 4.

Having no limits on the amounts the campaigns could spend and no limits on the amounts Super PACs could spend on behalf of campaigns led to important strategic decisions on the part of the presidential campaigns, and those decisions had implications for the outcome of the election. As Tony Corrado points out in Chapter 5, the overall amount of money raised by the Obama and Romney campaigns, their respective party committees, and the Super PACs that supported them was approximately the same. However, the amount of money raised by the Obama campaign itself exceeded that raised by the Romney campaign by almost $270 million. This difference in the amount raised by the two campaigns had significance for how the two campaigns could spend their money. The campaigns had control over how the money they raised was spent; the campaigns had no control over how the money the Super PACs raised was spent. That meant, in practice, that the Obama campaign had more money to spend on tactics that it could use to influence the outcome of the election—hiring staff in key states, identifying and registering supporters and turning them out to vote, and putting out campaign messages in broadcast and social media outlets—while the Romney campaign was much more dependent on Super PACs intuiting how best to spend money to benefit the Romney campaign.

In an interview following the election, Karl Rove—the masterful campaign strategist behind President George W. Bush's successful campaigns and one of the creators of American Crossroads, a Republican-leaning Super PAC—pointed out the perils of relying on Super PACs to carry the campaign's message: "We can't talk to the campaigns," Rove said, "but we've got to understand what the candidate's message is by closely following their public statements and campaign activities, do a lot of research to understand what the weaknesses of their opponents are, and read the tea leaves." More specifically, Rove said, "In July, after Obama and his allies began pounding Romney's record at the private equity firm Bain Capital, Crossroads spent $9.3 million on ads in nine states, in which a female narrator asked: 'What happened to Barack Obama? The press and even Democrats say his attacks on Mitt Romney's business record are misleading, unfair, and untrue.' The response from the Romney campaign? Radio silence, which the Crossroads team read to mean the [Romney] strategists in Boston did not believe engaging on that issue was important. So Crossroads quit running the spots." When criticized after the election by some Republicans, even some inside the Romney campaign, for not giving Romney more cover on attacks on his business record, Rove replied that Crossroads's decision to stop running the spots "was the result of a missed signal."[1]

Because the Obama campaign controlled more of its own money than did the Romney campaign, the Obama campaign was able to take advantage of the lowest unit rate allowed to candidate campaigns for television ad purchases, and thus get more bang for its buck.[2] "The Obama guys put more lead on the target and were buying their bullets cheaper," said an attendee at a post election briefing comparing the Obama and Romney television advertising.[3]

Super PACs were not just major players in the presidential elections. In a number of congressional elections, spending by outside groups, including Super PACs, exceeded spending by candidate campaigns. For example, the Virginia senate race was the most expensive senate race in the 2012 election cycle, with candidates and outside groups collectively spending $80 million dollars. In that race the two candidates, Tim Kaine and George Allen, spent $30.1 million, while outside groups spent almost $50 million.[4] The implications for the campaigns are obvious. The more money spent by outside groups, which cannot coordinate their spending with the campaigns, the less control the campaigns themselves have over their messages.

Interestingly, the most expensive senate campaign in terms of just candidate spending—the Massachusetts senate race between incumbent Senator Scott Brown and consumer advocate Elizabeth Warren—saw much less spending by outside groups than was seen in other competitive senate races. Brown and Warren collectively spent $65.4 million dollars, yet outside groups, excluding party committees, spent just one tenth of that—$6.8 million dollars.[5] Early in the election both Brown and Warren decried outside spending and vowed that for every dollar spent by outside groups on radio, television, and Internet ads, their campaigns would donate 50 percent of the cost of the ad to a charity of his or her opponent's choice. Their pledge seemed to work, and could be a model for voluntarily limiting outside money in future elections.[6]

Strategy and Message

As in past presidential elections, the strategies each campaign employed and the messages the campaigns delivered influenced the outcome of the election. As discussed above, the ways the respective campaigns were financed influenced how much money they had to spend and what they could spend their money on. The campaigns also differed on their advertising strategies: the Obama campaign decided to emphasize spending on ads over the summer, while the Romney campaign chose to hold their heavy ad buys for the fall. At a postelection conference sponsored by the Institute of Politics at Harvard University, Romney campaign strategist Stuart Stevens and Obama campaign strategist David Axelrod described their respective strategies. "It was really a $20 to $40 million decision, and that we'd rather have $20 to $40 million to spend in October," said Stevens. In contrast, the Obama campaign "gambled, and we gambled on front-loading," said Axelrod.[7] Part of this strategy is exemplified by the Obama campaign's attacks on Romney's tenure at Bain Capital, which, as Danny Hayes describes in Chapter 6, were "in full force in July."

David Winston, Danny Hayes, and Dotty Lynch all point out in their respective chapters the role of issues in a campaign, and, perhaps even more importantly, how those issues are framed. An early ad buy enabled the Obama campaign to more effectively define the messages of the race. As David Winston points out in Chapter 2, the Romney campaign's message was that the 2012 presidential election was a referendum on the president, or what political scientists describe as retrospective voting. Danny Hayes also points this out in Chapter 6, noting that even before securing the nomination, Romney began talking about the economic failings of the Obama administration. In contrast, the Obama campaign's message was that the election was a choice between Obama's vision for the future and Romney's future agenda, or prospective voting. Because Obama spent more money earlier, he was able to define Romney, and define the election, on his terms, and thus neutralize the impact of the economy issue, which was a negative for the Obama campaign. In the end, as Glen Bolger points out in Chapter 3, voters "decided that they thought the direction the president is taking the country is generally the right one."

Election Laws

Beginning in the 1980s, more and more states began to experiment with changes in election laws to make registration and voting accessible to voters who found it difficult to cast a vote during the prescribed hours on the first Tuesday after the first Monday in November. By 2012 one-fifth of the states allowed some form of Election Day registration, allowing voters to register and vote on Election Day. States also began to allow various forms of "convenience voting"—no-excuse absentee voting, early voting, and voting by mail. In 2012 thirty states allowed no-excuse absentee voting, thirty-five states and the District of Columbia allowed early voting,[8] and two states, Washington and Oregon, had vote-by-mail elections, in which citizens could only vote by mail; there are no polling places in those states.

Following the 2010 elections, a number of Republican governors and Republican-controlled state legislatures began to roll back these convenient, more liberal voting procedures, arguing that they lead to the potential for voter fraud. Democrats argued that such changes, particularly eliminating early voting, in election laws weren't about voter fraud, but rather were efforts to make voting more difficult for those most inconvenienced by voting on Election Day—typically minorities and younger voters. African Americans, Latinos, and young people (eighteen- to twenty-nine-year-olds) contributed to President Obama's success in the 2008 election, and progressive organizations argued that making it more difficult to vote were efforts to reduce the influence of these demographic groups in the 2012 elections.

The days during which early voting could occur were curtailed in four states—Florida, Georgia, Tennessee, and West Virginia.[9] In Florida, the result of fewer days for early voting meant long lines on Election Day, with some voters waiting in line for as long as eight hours.[10] A postelection study by Ohio State professor Theodore Allen concluded that as many as 49,000 people did not vote in central Florida because of the long lines, and that many of those who did not vote were African American and Hispanic.[11]

However, the most controversial changes to voting laws were the provisions requiring voter identification to be presented before a citizen could vote. These laws took a variety of forms, as Chris Sautter describes in Chapter 12, but collectively they had the potential to depress the vote of minorities and young people. While the preliminary 2012 turnout figures suggest that these changes did not in fact affect turnout in any major way, the effect of these laws going forward remains to be seen, as new voter ID laws will take effect in some states, notably South Carolina and Pennsylvania, in 2013.

Changes in Technology

While strategy and message, issues, field, and fundraising have long been and continue to be important in elections, the role of technology has changed rapidly in the past decade, and has affected all of the above areas of a campaign.

The explosion in the use of cell phones over the past two election cycles has changed the way survey research is conducted. Cell phones, and the additional costs to surveys that their use requires, are now an accepted part of campaign public opinion research, and the use of cell phones in conducting surveys will only continue to increase, as Glen Bolger points out in Chapter 3.

The prevalence of mobile phones in the United States population affects not only survey research but other aspects of campaigns as well. No political event is "off the record," with the ability of attendees to record any statement on their cell phones. As a result, it has become increasingly difficult for campaigns to control their messages, as any inopportune comment can take the campaign off message (or reinforce an impression the campaign was trying to overcome). Perhaps the most obvious example of this in the 2012 election was Mitt Romney's reference to "the 47 percent" at a fundraiser in Florida in May, a comment that was recorded on a cell phone and made public during the fall campaign.[12] The comment reinforced the image that Romney cared only about people with wealth, and not the middle class—a message the Obama campaign was driving about Romney.

Technological advances have also enabled campaigns to more effectively target their resources. The Obama campaign did this more successfully than the McCain campaign in 2008. By using a combination of traditional field voter identification methods and voter modeling, the Obama campaign was able to predict the behavior of individual voters and use that information to turn them out to vote.[13] The campaign also used changes in technology to refine its media buying, as Sasha Issenberg decribes in *The Victory Lab*. The Obama campaign moved from "buying national ads to local ones in key markets, and then shifting from broadcast waves to cable television, where narrow audiences could be more easily pinpointed. Internet advertising, with its ability to track users' movements through cookies and their interests through search engines, was the latest breakthrough"(in 2008).[14]

In 2012 the Obama campaign again used technology to maximize its campaign goals. Building on the experiences of the 2008 campaign, the technological achievements of the 2012 campaign were particularly pronounced in three areas—fundraising, field, and media buying. As in 2008, the 2012 Obama campaign used tested metrics to encourage online fundraising. As Anthony Corrado points out in Chapter 5, the Obama campaign was able to use e-mail, text messages, and social media to increase electronic donations to the campaign by about 25 percent over 2008. One of the most successful programs was the campaign's Quick Donate program, which allowed previous donors to the campaign to contribute by just entering the amount of the donation online or by text message, without reentering credit card and other required information. The campaign found that Quick Donate donors gave four times as much as other small donors.

The Obama campaign also used sophisticated algorithms and social media to target potential voters, both for the "air war" and the "ground game." The campaign used Facebook, which barely existed in 2008, to "persuade more than 600,000 Obama supporters to reach out to 5 million swing states friends online with targeted messages in the days before the election."[15] During the fall campaign there was much discussion by political pundits about the ability of the Obama campaign to match its 2008 successes in turning out young people, African Americans, and Latinos; early accounts suggest the Obama campaign was just as successful in turning out these groups in 2012 as it had been in 2008.

The campaign was also effectively able to target its campaign ads. As Alan Rosenblatt points out in Chapter 8, the use of marketing science makes ad buys more efficient and more effective. The Obama campaign collected "vast quantities of information . . . to predict just which television shows various targets in certain cities were watching at just what time of day."[16] A study of the Obama and Romney campaigns' ad spending found that "Obama and his allies spent less on advertising than Romney and his allies but got far more— in the number of ads broadcast, in visibility in key markets and in targeting critical demographic groups, such as the working class and younger voters in swing states."[17]

Political Scientists' Election Predictions

For the past three decades political scientists who specialize in presidential election vote forecasts have predicted the outcome of the presidential election. Each model is different, but almost all models assume that the state of the economy and the popularity of the incumbent president will affect the outcome of the election. Moreover, these predictive models assume that there are certain factors that are known before the election is fully engaged, and these factors can correctly predict the outcome of the election irrespective of what happens during the election. In October 2012, *PS: Political Science & Politics* published thirteen articles predicting the outcome of the presidential election, and some articles also ventured to predict the outcomes of the House of Representatives elections. Of the thirteen articles, six predicted an Obama victory, four predicted a Romney victory, and three predicted a toss-up (with two of the three leaning toward Obama).[18] Of the two articles that predicted the outcome of the House elections, both predicted that the Republicans would retain control.[19] As David Dulio and John Klemanski point out in Chapter 13, predictions of a Romney victory made sense when looking at the macrolevel political indicators. Yet, because Obama was able to define the terms of the election first—a choice between Obama and Romney, not a referendum on the president—Obama ultimately succeeded. In short, the strategies and tactics of the two campaigns mattered.

Conclusion

Political scientists thought that the economy and President Obama's approval rating would be key factors in the election. Based on these factors, some predicted an Obama reelection, while others thought Governor Romney would prevail on November 6. The economy and the president's popularity were key factors in the election—particularly the economy, as the exit polls showed. However, messaging, organization, campaign finance, and election laws also were important to the outcome of the election. While the formulas used by political scientists have important predictive value in trying to understand presidential elections, the campaigns themselves still matter as well, as the chapters in this volume have shown.

Going forward, campaigns will continue to matter. Increasingly sophisticated modeling of individual voter behavior will enable campaigns to target potential voters based on specific interests, characteristics, and behavior. Experiential work in field turnout and persuasion techniques will give campaigns more precise ways to encourage potential voters to not only vote, but vote for particular candidates. As the Internet becomes not only a key tool for campaign organizing, but also for persuasion, campaigns will have more and more opportunities to reach voters.[20] Technological advances will continue to offer more and more ways to expand the 3-D strategy of campaigns described by Alan Rosenblatt in Chapter 8.

However, campaigns also face challenges. Both the rise of Super PACs (along with their messages that are supposedly uncoordinated with the campaigns) and the increased use of various types of social media may make it increasingly difficult for campaigns to control what messages are delivered to voters. As Dave Dulio and John Klemanski point out in Chapter 13, Restore our Future spent more money during the Iowa caucuses than did the Romney campaign. As we look forward to the congressional elections in 2014 and the presidential election in 2016, changes in technology, fundraising, and election laws suggest campaigns will matter, but how they are conducted will continue to evolve.

Notes

1. Karen Tumulty, "Rove Still Resolute in Face of Defeat," *Washington Post,* November 11, 2012, A30.

2. Candidates for federal office are eligible for the lowest unit rate charged commercial advertisers on a television or radio station. Political parties and political action committees are not eligible for the lowest unit rate.

3. Tom Hamburger, "In Election Postmortems, Romney's TV Advertising Strategy Comes Under Fire," *Washington Post,* December 12, 2012, A6.

4. Center for Responsive Politics, "2012 Overview: Most Expensive Races," OpenSecrets.org, December 2, 2012, http://www.opensecrets.org/outsidespending/summ.php?cycle=2012&disp=R&pty=N&type=A; http://www.opensecrets.org/races/election.php?state=VA&cycle=2012.

5. For Brown and Warren spending, see Center for Responsive Politics, "2012 Overview: Most Expensive Races," OpenSecrets.org, December 2, 2012, http://www.opensecrets.org/outsidespending/summ.php?cycle=2012&disp=R&pty=A&type=S; for outside group spending, see Center for Responsive Politics "2012 Overview: Most Expensive Races," OpenSecrets.org, December 2, 2012, http://www.opensecrets.org/overview/topraces.php?cycle=2012&display=currcands.

6. Shira Schoenberg, "Scott Brown–Elizabeth Warren 'People's Pledge' Could Become a National Model," masslive.com, November 16, 2012, http://www.masslive.com/politics/index.ssf/2012/11/scott_brown-elizabeth_warren_peoples_pledge_could_become_national_model.html.

7. Karen Tumulty, "Analyzing the Whys of Winning—and Losing," *Washington Post,* December 4, 2012, A5.

8. NPR, "Election 2012: Early and Absentee Voting by State," February 24, 2013, http://apps.npr.org/early-voting-2012/; United States Election Project, "2012 Early Voting Statistics," February 24, 2013, http://elections.gmu.edu/early_vote_2012.html.

9. Ohio also tried to restrict early voting, but that decision was overturned by a court just before the election. Brennan Center for Justice, "Election 2012: Voting Laws Roundup," October 11, 2012, http://www.brennancenter.org/content/resource/2012_summary_of_voting_law_changes/.

10. Amanda Terkel, "Florida's Long Lines on Election Day Discouraged 49,000 People from Voting: Report," huffingtonpost.com, December 31, 2012. http://www.huffingtonpost.com/2012/11/04/florida-early-voting-lawsuit_n_2072435.html.

11. David Damron and Scott Powers, "Researcher: Long Lines at Polls Caused 49,000 Not to Vote," orlandosentinel.com, February 24, 2013, http://articles.orlandosentinel.com/2012-12-29/news/os-discouraged-voters-20121229_1_long-lines-higher-turnout-election-day.

12. At a private fundraiser in May 2012 in Boca Raton, Florida, Romney said, "There are 47 percent of the people who will vote for the president no matter what . . . who are dependent upon government, who believe that they are victims. . . . These are people who pay no income tax . . . and so my job is not to worry about those people. I'll never convince them that they should take personal responsibility and care for their lives." The comment was posted online by *Mother Jones* magazine in September. John Christoffersen, "Mitt Romney 47 Percent Comment Chosen as

Yale Book of Quotations' Quote of the Year," huffingtonpost.com, January 1, 2013, http://www.huffingtonpost.com/2012/12/09/mitt-romney-47-percent_n_2267422 .html.

13. Sasha Issenberg, *The Victory Lab: The Secret Science of Winning Campaigns* (New York: Crown Publishers, 2012), 253.

14. Ibid., 275.

15. Michael Scherer, "Barack Obama," *Time,* December 31, 2012–January 7, 2013, 74.

16. Ibid.

17. Hamburger, "In Election Postmortems," A6.

18. *PS* Symposium, "Forecasting the 2012 American National Elections," *PS: Political Science & Politics* 45, no. 4 (October 2012): 614–674.

19. James E. Campbell, "Forecasting the Presidential and Congressional Elections of 2012: The Trial-Heat and the Seats-in-Trouble Models," *PS: Political Science & Politics* 45 (4): 630–634; Brad Lockerbie, "Economic Expectations and Election Outcomes: The Presidency and the House in 2012," *PS: Political Science & Politics* 45 (4): 644–647.

20. At a presentation at the Campaign Management Institute at American University on January 4, 2012, Mark Putnam, founder of Putnam Partners, a Democratic media consulting firm, said, "The Internet is becoming more and more a persuasion mechanism."

About the Contributors

Pamela Bachilla is a PhD student in political science in the Department of Government at American University. Her research interests include legislative politics, interest groups and political parties, mass behavior and representation, education politics and Latino politics. She has an extensive background as a legislative advocate and has represented many of California's largest urban education agencies in state and federal affairs.

Robert Blaemire has been an active participant in politics all of his adult life. Born and raised in Indiana, Robert's career began at the age of eighteen with Senator Birch Bayh (D-IN) during his freshman year at George Washington University and concluded with Bayh's unsuccessful reelection campaign in 1980. He began his career providing political computer services in 1982, working in the voter file business before there was any such business. During those early years, he created some of the very first Democratic state party voter file projects. In 1991, Bob created Blaemire Communications, a political computer services firm serving the Democratic and progressive political community. During that time, Blaemire Communications managed more Democratic state party voter file projects than any other vendor. In 2003, Blaemire Communications introduced Leverage, an online voter file management system that was used extensively across the country in Democratic campaigns. In late 2007, Blaemire Communications was acquired by Catalist, and Bob still serves there as Director of Business Development. Bob is married to Joanna Caplan and has two sons, Nick and Dan.

Glen Bolger is one of the Republican Party's leading political strategists and pollsters. He is a partner and cofounder of Public Opinion Strategies, a national political and public affairs survey research firm whose clients include leading political figures, Fortune 500 companies, and major associations. Public Opinion Strategies has as clients fifteen US senators, six governors, and more than seventy-five members of Congress. Glen is one of the few pollsters ever to twice receive the "Pollster of the Year" award from the American Association of Political Consultants, winning the prestigious award for his work in both 2002 and 2009. Prior to cofounding Public Opinion Strategies, Glen was the Director of Survey Research

& Analysis for the National Republican Congressional Committee, the political arm of the House Republican Conference. He is a graduate of American University in Washington, DC. Glen and his wife, Carol, have three daughters.

Anthony Corrado is professor of government at Colby College and a nonresident senior fellow of the Brookings Institution. He also serves as chair of the board of trustees of the Campaign Finance Institute, a nonpartisan research organization. He is the author or coauthor of numerous books and articles on campaign finance law, political finance, and presidential elections, including *Financing the 2008 Election* (2011), *Financing the 2004 Election* (2006), and *The New Campaign Finance Sourcebook* (2005).

David A. Dulio is professor and chair of the Political Science Department at Oakland University where he teaches courses on campaigns and elections, Congress, political parties, interest groups, and other areas of American politics. Dulio has published eight books, including *Cases in Congressional Campaigns: Riding the Wave* (2011), *Vital Signs: Perspectives on the Health of American Campaigning* (2005), and *For Better or Worse? How Professional Political Consultants Are Changing Elections in the United States* (2004). He has written dozens of articles and book chapters on subjects ranging from the role of professional consultants in US elections to campaign finance. Dulio is also a former American Political Science Congressional Fellow on Capitol Hill, where he worked in the US House of Representatives Republican Conference for former US Rep. J. C. Watts Jr. (R-OK).

R. Sam Garrett is adjunct professor of government at American University and holds a PhD in political science, an MPA, and a BA (summa cum laude), all from American University's School of Public Affairs. He serves as specialist in American National Government at the Congressional Research Service (CRS), Library of Congress. Sam was selected as a 2005 Presidential Management Fellow. He is also a research fellow at the Center for Congressional and Presidential Studies (CCPS). Prior to joining CRS, Sam served as a visiting instructor in AU's Department of Government and as assistant director for research at CCPS. He is author of *Campaign Crises: Detours on the Road to Congress* (2010). Sam and his wife, Karen, live in Washington, DC.

Danny Hayes is assistant professor of political science at George Washington University. His research focuses on political communication and political behavior. He is coauthor of *Influence from Abroad: Foreign Voices, the Media, and U.S. Public Opinion* (2013) and has published articles in the *American Journal of Political Science, Political Research Quarterly, Political Behavior,* and *Political Communication,* among other journals.

John S. Klemanski is professor of political science at Oakland University in Rochester, Michigan. His primary areas of research interest are campaigns and elections, and urban politics and policy. He is coauthor or coeditor of four books and has published over twenty-five articles and book chapters. His published research has appeared in *State Politics and Policy Quarterly, Judicature, Urban Affairs Quarterly, Journal of Urban Affairs, Economic Development Quarterly,* and *Policy Studies Journal.*

Jan E. Leighley is professor of political science in the Department of Government at American University. She has published in the *American Political Science Review,* the *American Journal of Political Science,* and *The Journal of Politics,* among other journals. Her two books are *Strength in Numbers? The Political Mobilization of Racial and Ethnic Minorities* (2001) and *Mass Media and Politics: A Social Science Perspective* (2003). She is currently serving as editor, with William Mishler (University of Arizona), of *The Journal of Politics.*

Dotty Lynch is an executive in residence in the School of Communication at American University, advisor to the MA program in political communication, and a political consultant for *CBS News.* The 2012 election was her twelfth presidential campaign as a professional journalist and pollster. She was the *CBS News* senior political editor (1985–2005) and is currently an on-air analyst for *CBS Radio* and a member of the *CBS News* Election Decision Desk. She began teaching at American University in 2006, and in 2008 and 2012 she team-taught a class on the presidential primaries that included a five-day field trip to New Hampshire. In the 1970s and 1980s she worked on polling for the presidential campaigns of George McGovern, Jimmy Carter, and Ted Kennedy, as well as dozens of US Senate and gubernatorial candidates. In addition, she developed the concept of the gender gap and is a leading expert on women in politics.

Jonathan Nagler is professor of politics in the Wilf Family Department of Politics at New York University. He has published articles on voter turnout, candidate choice, Latino politics, and political methodology in the *American Political Science Review, American Journal of Political Science, The Journal of Politics, Political Analysis,* and other journals. He is an inaugural fellow of the Society for Political Methodology and has served as an expert witness on several cases on election law as well as conducted polling for media organizations and national political candidates.

Candice J. Nelson is professor and chair of the Department of Government and academic director of the Campaign Management Institute at American University. She is author of *Grant Park: The Democratization of Presidential Elections, 1968–2008* (2011) and coauthor of *Vital Signs: Perspectives on the Health of American Campaigning* (2005), *The Money Chase: Congressional Campaign Finance Reform* (1990), *The Myth of the Independent Voter* (1992), and *Campaigns and Elections American Style* (2009), as well as numerous other books and articles.

Alicia Kolar Prevost is the Democratic program coordinator for the Campaign Management Institute at American University and a senior advisor to the Clean Air Defense Campaign, a coalition of environmental organizations. She has worked for the Democratic National Committee, the Michigan Coordinated Campaign, and John Dingell for Congress. She has an MPP from Harvard Kennedy School and is a PhD candidate at American University.

Alan Rosenblatt is a social media and online advocacy strategist, professor, and thought leader. He is executive director of the Internet Advocacy Center; Ombudsmen and cofounder at Take Action News; and adjunct professor at Johns Hopkins, American, Georgetown, and Gonzaga Universities, where he teaches courses on Internet politics. He was associate director for online advocacy at the Center for American Progress Action Fund from 2007 to 2013. Alan taught the world's first Internet politics course at George Mason University in 1995. He founded the Internet Advocacy Roundtable in 2005. He blogs at BigThink.com, DrDigipol.Tumblr.com, and HuffingtonPost.com, and he previously blogged at TechPresident.com. He serves on E-Democracy.org's board of directors and Social Media Today's advisory board; in 2008 he was a fellow at George Washington University's Institute for Politics, Democracy & the Internet, and he is a cofounder of MediaBureau.com. Alan has a PhD in political science from American University. Find him on Twitter @DrDigipol.

Chris Sautter is one of the most experienced recount lawyers in the country and coauthor of *The Recount Primer* (1994), the definitive guide to postelection disputes. He played key roles in the 2008 Minnesota US Senate election contest on behalf of Al Franken, the 2000 Florida presidential recount on behalf of Al Gore, and the controversial four-vote-margin recount in Indiana's "Bloody 8th"—the closest US House race in history. Sautter was also President Barack Obama's first media strategist and wrote and produced his first campaign commercials. As a documentary filmmaker, Chris Sautter directed and produced the award-winning *The King of Steeltown: Hardball Politics in the Heartland* (2001), about contemporary machine politics. Six public officials were sent to federal prison for actions documented in the film. Most recently, Sautter has been an adjunct professor at American University, where he teaches courses on election law.

James A. Thurber is distinguished professor of government and the founder (1979) and director of the Center for Congressional and Presidential Studies (american. edu/spa/ccps) at American University in Washington, DC. He is editor of the journal *Congress and the Presidency*. Dr. Thurber is the author, coauthor, and editor of numerous books, including *Obama in Office* (2011), *Rivals for Power: Presidential-Congressional Relations* (2013), *Improving How Washington Works* (2008), *Congress and the Internet* (2003), *The Battle for Congress: Candidates, Consultants and Voters* (2001), and *Campaign Warriors: Political Consultants in Elections* (2000). In addition, he has published numerous articles in academic journals including *Congress and the Presidency, Legislative Studies Quarterly, Policy Studies Journal, Political Research Quarterly, Presidential Studies Quarterly,* and *Public Administration Review.*

David Winston has served as a strategic advisor to Senate and House Republican leadership for the past ten years. He was formerly the director of planning for Speaker of the House Newt Gingrich, and he advises center-right political parties throughout Europe. Additionally, Winston was a senior fellow at the Heritage Foundation, where he did statistical policy analysis and econometric modeling. He has served in a senior staff role to four RNC chairmen. In the private sector, he has advised Fortune 100 companies on strategic planning and brand reputation. Winston has lectured widely, including at The Wharton School of Business, MIT, Harvard, and the National War College. He is credited for originating the concept of "security mom." Winston is an election analyst for *CBS News,* and frequently appears on cable and network news.

Index

Made in the USA
Middletown, DE
06 May 2017